The Innovation Journey of Wi-Fi

The Road to Global Success

Wi-Fi has become the preferred means for connecting to the Internet – at home, in the office, in hotels and at airports. Increasingly, Wi-Fi also provides internet access for remote communities, where it is deployed by volunteers in community-based networks, by operators in 'hotspots' and by municipalities in 'hotzones'. This book traces the global success of Wi-Fi to three key events: the landmark change in radio spectrum policy by the US Federal Communications Commission in 1985; the initiative by NCR Corporation to start the development of wireless local area networks; and the drive for an open standard IEEE 802.11, released in 1997. It also singles out and explains the significance of the initiative by Steve Jobs at Apple to include wireless LAN in the iBook, which moved the product from the early adopters to the mass market. The book explains these developments through first-hand accounts by industry practitioners, and concludes with reflections and consideration of the implications for government policy and firm strategy.

WOLTER LEMSTRA is Senior Research Fellow in the Department of Technology, Policy and Management at the Delft University of Technology and Senior Lecturer at the Strategy Academy, Rotterdam, the Netherlands. He has twenty-five years of experience in the telecommunications sector, at Philips, AT&T and Lucent Technologies.

VIC HAYES is Senior Research Fellow in the Department of Technology, Policy and Management at the Delft University of Technology. He is the recipient of eight awards, including *The Economist* Innovation Award 2004, the Dutch Vosko Trophy, the IEEE Hans Karlsson Award and the IEEE Steinmetz Award.

JOHN GROENEWEGEN is Professor of the Economics of Infrastructures at the Delft University of Technology. He is also a research fellow at the Tinbergen Institute in the Rotterdam School of Economics, Erasmus University Rotterdam.

The Innovation Journey of Wi-Fi

The Road to Global Success

Edited by

Wolter Lemstra, Vic Hayes and John Groenewegen

CAMBRIDGE
UNIVERSITY PRESS

University Printing House, Cambridge CB2 8BS, United Kingdom

Published in the United States of America by Cambridge University Press, New York

Cambridge University Press is part of the University of Cambridge.

It furthers the University's mission by disseminating knowledge in the pursuit of
education, learning and research at the highest international levels of excellence.

www.cambridge.org
Information on this title: www.cambridge.org/9781107645561

© Wolter Lemstra, Vic Hayes and John Groenewegen 2011

First published 2011
First paperback edition 2013

A catalogue record for this publication is available from the British Library

Library of Congress Cataloguing in Publication data
The innovation journey of Wi-Fi : the road to global success / edited by Wolter
Lemstra, Vic Hayes, and John Groenewegen.
p.   cm.
Includes index.
ISBN 978-0-521-19971-1 (hardback)
1. IEEE 802.11 (Standard)   2. Wireless LANs.   I. Lemstra, W. (Wolter)
II. Hayes, Vic.   III. Groenewegen, John, 1949–
TK5105.5668.I56   2011
004.6'8 – dc22   2010035494

ISBN 978-0-521-19971-1 Hardback
ISBN 978-1-107-64556-1 Paperback

Contents

Figures

Tables

Contributors

Editors/authors

JOHN GROENEWEGEN is Professor, Economics of Infrastructures, Department of Technology, Policy and Management, Delft University of Technology.

VIC HAYES was Chair IEEE 802.11 Working Group and is now Senior Research Fellow, Economics of Infrastructures, Department of Technology, Policy and Management, Delft University of Technology.

WOLTER LEMSTRA was Vice-president, Business Development and Marketing, Lucent Technologies, and is now Senior Research Fellow, Economics of Infrastructures, Department of Technology, Policy and Management, Delft University of Technology.

Authors

PETER ANKER is Senior Policy Adviser, Ministry of Economic Affairs, the Netherlands, and PhD researcher, Economics of Infrastructures, Department of Technology, Policy and Management, Delft University of Technology.

LEO VAN AUDENHOVE is Professor International Communication and Information Society, Vrije Universiteit, Brussels, and senior researcher at its Studies on Media, Information and Telecommunication research centre. He teaches a Jean Monnet module on the European information society at the University of Wisconsin – Milwaukee.

MATTHIAS FINGER is Professor, Management of Network Industries, and Director, Technology Policy Institute, Ecole Polytechnique Fédérale de Lausanne.

KAI JAKOBS is a member of the technical staff, Computer Science Department, RWTH Aachen University.

ELS VAN DE KAR is Assistant Professor, Department of Technology, Policy and Management, Delft University of Technology, and founder of EventsIT.

GERD-JAN DE LEEUW was MSc researcher, Economics of Infrastructures, Department of Technology, Policy and Management, Delft University of Technology, and is now at DELTA Netwerkbedrijf.

WILLIAM MELODY is Emeritus Director of LIRNE.NET, Emeritus Professor, Economics of Infrastructures, Department of Technology, Policy and Management, Delft University of Technology, and Visiting Professor, London School of Economics, University of Witwatersrand, South Africa, and Aalborg University, Denmark.

ELLEN VAN OOST is Associate Professor, Gender and Technology, Department of Science, Technology, Health and Policy Studies, and member of the Centre for Telematics and Information Technology, University of Twente, the Netherlands.

NELLY OUDSHOORN is Professor of Technology Dynamics and Health Care, Department of Science, Technology, Health and Policy Studies, University of Twente.

PIERRE ROSSEL is Maître d'enseignement et de recherche, Collège du Management de la Technologie, Ecole Polytechnique Fédérale de Lausanne.

MARIANNE VAN DER STEEN is Senior Research Fellow, Institute for Knowledge-intensive Entrepreneurship, University of Twente.

STEFAN VERHAEGH is PhD researcher, Department of Science, Technology, Health and Policy Studies, University of Twente.

Input providers

PIETRO BIGI was MSc researcher, Economics of Infrastructures, Department of Technology, Policy and Management, Delft University of Technology, and is now Network Design Engineer at Draka Communications.

LEO BRAND is Chief Executive Officer of Swisscom Hospitality Services.

RONALD BROCKMANN was co-founder and Chief Technology Officer of No Wires Needed and is now founder and Chief Executive Officer of Avinity.

YAHEL BEN-DAVID is co-founder of the Dharamsala Community Wireless Mesh Network.

JAAP HAARTSEN was PhD researcher, Department of Electrical Engineering, Delft University of Technology, and is now with Sony Ericsson.

ALBERT HEIJL was at Europe Container Terminals and is now at Agentschap Telecom, the Radiocommunications Agency Netherlands.

ALEX HILLS is Distinguished Services Professor, Carnegie Mellon University, Pittsburgh.

DONALD JOHNSON was Senior Consulting Engineer at NCR Corporation and is now retired.

DILLO LEHLOKOE was participant Executive Masters in eGovernance, Ecole Polytechnique Fédérale de Lausanne, and is now an information communications technology consultant for policy and development strategies.

CEES LINKS was Product Line Manager at NCR/AT&T/Lucent Technologies/ Agere Systems and is now founder and Chief Executive Officer of GreenPeak Technologies.

MICHAEL MARCUS was Chief, Technical Planning Staff, Office of Engineering and Technology, US Federal Communications Commission, and is now Director at Marcus Spectrum Solutions.

GERARD MOURITS was Manager Product Management at KPN and was a volunteer and adviser to the Board of the Wireless Leiden Foundation and is now freelancer and co-founder of the WifiSoft.org Foundation.

RICHARD VAN NEE was a member of the technical staff at Bell Labs/AT&T/Lucent Technologies and is now at Qualcomm.

BJARKE NIELSEN was founder of the Boevl- and the DjurslandS.net community, and is leader of the Djursland International Institute of Rural Wireless Broadband and chairman of the GrenaaS.net, the landscapenet in Djursland, Denmark.

ERMANNO PIETROSEMOLI is Professor of Electrical Communications, Universidad de los Andes, Mérida, Venezuela, and President of Fundación Escuela Latinoamericana de Redes.

MAHABIR PUN is founder of the Nepal Wireless Network Project.

HUUB SCHUURMANS was Scientific Attaché, Dutch Ministry of Economic Affairs, San Mateo, California (Silicon Valley), Senior Manager at Royal Dutch Shell and co-founder and board member of Wireless Leiden.

DOROTHY STANLEY was at Lucent Technologies/Agere Systems and is now at Aruba Networks.

BRUCE TUCH was Development Head of the Utrecht Systems Engineering Centre at NCR/AT&T/Lucent Technologies/Agere Systems and was with Motorola as Director Motorola Ventures Europe and Chief Technical Officer, Corporate Mergers and Acquisitions, and is now a consultant for the telecoms industry.

MARTEN VIJN was co-founder and Board member of Wireless Leiden and the WifiSoft.org Foundation, and is now Network and Unix System Administrator at the Netherlands Institute for Space Research and Leiden University, and an open source entrepreneur.

ALLERT VAN ZELST was PhD researcher, Eindhoven University of Technology, and is now with Qualcomm.

Preface

Preface to the paperback edition

Wi-Fi's global success story continues unabated. ABI Research, for instance, announced that Wi-Fi-enabled device shipments would exceed 1.5 billion in 2012, almost double the volume in 2010. The work on the IEEE 802.11ac standard operating in the 5 GHz band will provide for data rates up to 6.9 Gbit/s, 10-times the data rate provided by today's mainstream Wi-Fi products (see the updated version of Annex 3). Moreover, telecommunications operators announced the large-scale deployments of Wi–Fi to offload their mobile networks, as mobile data usage dramatically increases with the use of smartphones and tablets.

Delft, 2013

In 2003 the Dutch Ministry of Economic Affairs commissioned a study to assess the position of the Netherlands with respect to information communications technology (ICT) knowledge and ICT innovation. This project was awarded to a consortium led by Capgemini, in cooperation with the Strategy Academy and Zenc. As I was associated with the Strategy Academy, and in recognition of my experience in the telecommunication industry, I was invited to carry out a series of interviews with experts in the communications technology sector. A wide range of firms was being targeted, from start-ups to well-established companies, manufacturers and service providers, covering multiple technologies and applications. The list included Bruce Tuch, the director of technology strategy and standards at Agere Systems, leading the Wi-Fi efforts from the Utrecht Systems Engineering Centre, in the Netherlands.

At Lucent Technologies I had been involved with the WaveLAN product line to explore business opportunities in the public communications sector, but I was not aware of the genesis and development of Wi-Fi and the role NCR, AT&T and later Lucent Technologies had played, or, for that matter, the role of the Engineering Centre. The enthusiasm that Bruce Tuch conveyed in relaying the innovation story of Wi-Fi was captivating. I became convinced that this narrative had to be recorded and shared. When attending the 'Creative capital' conference in Amsterdam the following spring I observed that the TV series *Big Brother* was being presented by a government official as an important example of Dutch innovation. Clearly, Wi-Fi was not yet recognised as an applicable case example. Something had to be done. In the autumn I attended a seminar organised by the Royal Institute of Engineers featuring Vic Hayes on the topic of IEEE 802.11. For ten years Vic had been the chairperson of the working group responsible for the standardisation of wireless local area networks, to become commonly known as Wi-Fi. I learned that Vic was about to retire; this was the moment.

I persuaded Vic to join me as senior research fellow at the Delft University of Technology so that we could start a project together to document the 'innovation journey of Wi-Fi'. This book is the result of our efforts and those of many others, from the academic community and the communications industry. Vic, John and I have been in a very fortunate position in that our longitudinal case study could to a large extent be based on personal accounts of individuals who have been instrumental in the development of Wi-Fi. This includes Michael Marcus, who in 1980, while working at the US Institute for Defense Analyses, proposed the public use of spread-spectrum technology to the chief scientist of the US Federal Communications Commission; and, most importantly, Bruce Tuch and Cees Links at the Utrecht Systems Engineering Centre, which passed from NCR to AT&T, to Lucent Technologies and, finally, to Agere Systems. We would like to acknowledge the contribution of the many scholars and industry representatives who have made this project possible. Without their efforts, which included painstaking searches of archives in attics, this undertaking would not have been feasible. It has been their enthusiasm and willingness to share in the aim of this project that has made it a reality.

As authors and editors we would like to acknowledge the valuable feedback received during the many seminars in which early versions of the contents of the book were presented. A special 'thank you' is due to Frank van Iersel, Michael Marcus, John de Waal and Eric van Heesvelde, who took the trouble to review the typescript in full, and to Donald Loughry and Daniel Tijink, who reviewed particular chapters; they have all provided extremely valuable feedback. We would also like to thank the publishing team at Cambridge University Press: Paula Parish, Philip Good, Andy Woodfield, Sarah Roberts, Michelle Leblanc and Mike Richardson. In addition, we would like to acknowledge the funding provided by the Delft University of Technology for carrying out our Wi-Fi research project through its Senior Research Fellowship Programme.

Our aim has been to provide an accurate account of the innovation journey of Wi-Fi; where we have fallen short of this objective the responsibility is ours. The usual disclaimers also apply.

Delft, 2010   WOLTER LEMSTRA, WITH VIC HAYES
                                 AND JOHN GROENEWEGEN

Introduction

With the current popularity of Wi-Fi we expect that the account of its innovation journey will appeal to a broad audience: within business, academia and government, including strategists, policy makers and researchers in the fields of innovation, business management, standardisation and technology diffusion.

This book is divided into three parts. In Part 1 we capture the Wi-Fi journey from 1985 to 2008. We cover the early period, from invention, through innovation to mass-market success, characterised by broad diffusion and expanding applications. In so doing we recognise the shift in the application of Wi-Fi, from its original use as a wireless LAN within the enterprise to its current usage in the home and at 'hotspots' for internet access, whereby it has become instrumental in the hands of its users for the creation of Wi-Fi-based community networks in developed and developing countries.

In Part 2 we place the Wi-Fi journey in a broader context and pursue five different perspectives. First, we assess the role that Wi-Fi can play in providing universal access in remote areas that, hitherto, have been either underserved or not served at all. Second, we explore the Dutch connection, acknowledging the fact that most of the development of Wi-Fi (within NCR Corporation, AT&T, Lucent Technologies and Agere Systems) has taken place in the Netherlands, even though the products were originally developed for the US market and the activities were directed from US headquarters. Third, we explore the role of users in community-based innovation. In a fourth perspective we look at Wi-Fi in the context of radio spectrum management, recognising that Wi-Fi represents the first example of a global success story in the use of radio spectrum on a licence-exempt basis. Fifth, we explore possible future applications for Wi-Fi, bearing in mind that development efforts are ongoing, as reflected, for instance, in the issuance of new IEEE 802.11 standards on a regular basis. We conclude this part of the book with a reflection on our research findings, and from these derive implications for firm strategy formation and government policy making with respect to innovation and radio spectrum management.

Part 3 of the book consists of a series of annexes: a glossary, a timeline of major events in the development of Wi-Fi, an overview of the IEEE 802.11 standards and an impression of the Wi-Fi ecosystem.

Part 1 – Chapters 2 to 6 – collectively forms a longitudinal case study of the development of Wi-Fi. Each chapter thereby addresses a subsequent phase in the product life cycle of Wi-Fi. Each chapter is also topical, as they all deal with specific themes in the development of Wi-Fi, such as the creation of a wireless LAN standard, moving the business from early adopters to a mass market, the development of the 'hotspot' services business, and the emergence of community-based networks. Each chapter concludes with a summary and an interpretation of the case material in the context of related theory, provided by the editors. For these interpretations we use the theoretical perspectives on innovation as well as evolutionary and new institutional economics, which are introduced in Chapter 1. As common themes we use the innovation landscape metaphor, reflect on the role of the institutional environment and track the evolution of the industry.

This case study illustrates how the innovation process works in practice: with a close linkage to corporate strategy, and therefore to that extent planned, but with a high degree of emergence – that is, being shaped by individuals driving the course of events. The case study shows that innovation builds upon existing knowledge flows that combine, split and recombine. It also shows a change in the source of innovation, from the product manufacturers to the service providers and, finally, to the end users. Moreover, the case demonstrates that proactive radio spectrum regulation can foster innovation.

1   The case and the theoretical framework

Wolter Lemstra and John Groenewegen,
with contributions from Vic Hayes

1.1   Wi-Fi: an unexpected success story

In this book we explore and describe the genesis and development of Wi-Fi, which has become the preferred means for connecting to the Internet – without wires: at home, in the office, in hotels, restaurants and coffee shops, at airports and railway stations, at the university campus. Increasingly Wi-Fi provides access to the Internet for remote communities in developing countries, as in the Himalayas and in the Andes. Even in rural areas of developed countries, such as Denmark, where a community-based Wi-Fi initiative has emerged to provide wireless internet access, as the incumbent operator failed to extend the broadband infrastructure to less profitable areas in a sufficiently timely manner.

This is a remarkable result, considering that wireless local area networking was not even on the radar screen of the US Federal Communications Commission (FCC) in 1979 when it initiated the market assessment project that would lead to its landmark decision in 1985. In that year the FCC decided to open up three radio frequency bands designated for industrial, scientific and medical (ISM) applications for use by radio communication systems, on the condition that spread-spectrum techniques be used.

With hindsight, this outcome is a surprise. The Ethernet, which would become the standard for wired local area networks, had been demonstrated on an experimental basis in 1973, and in 1980 it was still the subject of a major standardisation battle within the Institute of Electrical and Electronic Engineers (IEEE). At that time business computing was *grosso modo* based on the use of mainframes. The increasing use of minicomputers had become the main market driver for the development of local area networks (LANs), first in universities and research centres, and then followed by corporations. It is worth recalling, moreover, that the personal computer (PC) had been invented only in 1974 and that the Apple II was launched in 1977, while the IBM PC was not introduced until 1981. The development of mobile computing equipment such as laptops and notebooks still lay in the future.

The current success of Wi-Fi is remarkable in many more ways. Previously, the most significant developments in radio frequency (RF) technology – radio

3

relay systems, radio and television broadcasting – had emerged under a licensed regime, whereby a government agency provided exclusive rights to the use of a specific part of the RF spectrum, thus giving the application protection from harmful interference by other radio frequency applications and users. The success of Wi-Fi was achieved under a licence-exempt regime, however, which meant that it had to contend with many other applications and users in the same RF band, including microwave ovens. As a result, the ISM bands were often referred to in the jargon of some professionals as the 'garbage bands'.

Following the assignment of the spectrum by the FCC, its principal use initially was indoor and corporate applications. The success of Wi-Fi resulted from at least two important changes in application, however. First, there was a shift in emphasis from corporate networking to private networking. In many homes Wi-Fi is the preferred solution over wired LAN alternatives for connecting computers to each other, to share printers and to connect to the Internet. Second, there was a move from the private to the public domain, as telecom operators now compete to provide internet access at 'hotspots' based on Wi-Fi. In this shift, Wi-Fi has moved from being a free service within corporations and homes to a fee-based service provided by hotspot operators. As a result, Wi-Fi has moved from indoor to outdoor applications and from stationary to nomadic use.

In the process Wi-Fi has progressed from a functionality that was added to a PC or laptop by way of an external plug-in to a functionality that is built into every laptop, based on an integrated chipset. Moreover, the example set by the FCC in the assignment of radio frequency bands for use by radio LANs has been followed by assignments by national regulatory agencies in the countries of Europe and Asia, including Japan, South Korea, India and China, thereby creating a global market for Wi-Fi products.[1] Meanwhile, the Wi-Fi logo introduced by the organisation that promotes the compatibility of products that adhere to the IEEE 802.11 standard, the Wi-Fi Alliance, has become synonymous with a globally recognised brand.

As indicated, it was not obvious at the outset that Wi-Fi would become a global success. The allocation of licence-exempt spectrum for radio communication by the FCC was not perceived favourably by all incumbents, And it resulted in an organisational reshuffle within the FCC. For the manufacturers it was not clear whether spread-spectrum technology, which had been developed in the military domain, could be produced at cost levels that would be commercially viable in the public domain. Nonetheless, the wireless alternative to wired infrastructure had a great deal of appeal. For NCR Corporation, the FCC's decision provided an opportunity to pursue solutions that would connect cash registers and point-of-sale terminals in a much more flexible manner at the customer's premises. It set in train a process that would involve a major change in corporate strategy, moving the corporation from industry follower

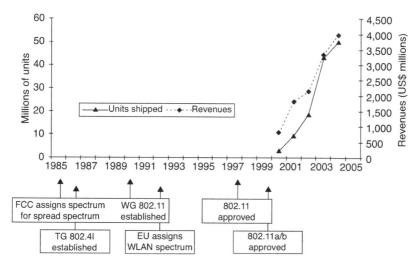

Figure 1.1 Wi-Fi product life cycle, 1985–2005
Source: This figure appears in 'Network modernization in the telecom sector', in *The Governance of Network Industries* (ed. Künneke, Groenewegen and Auger); copyright © 2009, Edward Elgar Publishing; reprinted by permission of the publisher.

to industry leader in this industry segment. It would require the tenacity of a small group of very dedicated engineers and marketers in pursuing an open standard, necessitating a commitment lasting for more than ten years, before global product success could be demonstrated. Figure 1.1 depicts the major milestones in the standardisation process next to the units of Wi-Fi shipped by the companies involved, and the corresponding revenues generated.[2]

The story of Wi-Fi is a good example of how the innovation process works in practice, and can be treated as a case history. It shows the linkage to corporate strategy, and it also shows the role of individuals in various parts of the organisation in driving the course of events. It shows the importance of teamwork, of personal commitment and of dedication. Moreover, it shows the importance of institutions in technology and product development. For example, the FCC plays a key role as a national regulatory agency in providing the governance of the radio spectrum; the IEEE provides the ICT industry with a platform to develop standards; and the ITU provides a platform for international coordination of the use of the RF spectrum.

The story illustrates that the development of Wi-Fi was not incidental – a one-off event; it shows clearly how knowledge that is accumulated and embodied in individuals migrates, combines and recombines as a result of people moving from one job or function to another and cooperating as part of a network of professionals. This has led to a continuous process of entrepreneurial activity that can be traced back to the radio expertise of the Netherlands-based Philips Electronics Corporation and the LAN expertise of the United-States-based NCR Corporation coming together in the Engineering Centre in Utrecht, the Netherlands. The story also demonstrates that the locus of innovation is not necessarily the locus of manufacturing or the locus where most value is ultimately appropriated.

1.2   The theoretical framework

In this book, we explore and describe the development dynamics of Wi-Fi. Because we are interested in understanding the developments over a significant period of time, and because we are interested in the developments of one particular technology, we apply a longitudinal case study approach (Yin, 1989). As a meaningful starting point for our case we take the 1985 decision of the FCC on the civil use of spread-spectrum techniques. The period from 1985 to the present is divided in line with the phases that are typically distinguished in the diffusion of new technologies and the related adoption of new products: (1) introduction, which includes invention, innovation and trial production for the early adopters; (2) expansion, possibly leading to a mass market; (3) maturity; and (4) stagnation and decline (Kotler, 1997; Porter, 1980; Rogers, 2003). Based on the events that have unfolded to date, Wi-Fi can be considered to have progressed through phase (2) and, depending on what is regarded as being included under the heading of Wi-Fi, may have entered phase (3).

The exploration and analysis of the dynamic development process of Wi-Fi is necessarily of a historical nature and includes a variety of explanatory variables, such as the technology, laws and regulations, values and norms, the strategies of the various firms, and the like. In the process various actors played roles that sometimes helped and sometimes hindered the development of Wi-Fi in becoming a success. The behaviour of actors concerning an innovation process is influenced largely by the institutional structures in their environment, such as laws and regulations. On the other hand, actors do have a certain degree of autonomy in terms of realising their own objectives, exploring new ways and changing the structures around them. Moreover, actors interact not only with the structures in their environment but also with each other. In doing so they share ideas and they learn, but they also compete and try to control the behaviour of others. To explore and analyse the dynamics of Wi-Fi we need to know about the behaviour of the different actors involved. In Figure 1.2 we present the different layers in the structural environment of the actors, with the arrows indicating the interactions. This model is based on that of Williamson (1998), and has been adapted by Koppenjan and Groenewegen for the purpose of institutional analysis in the context of sociotechnical systems (Koppenjan and Groenewegen, 2005). We follow North in his definition of institutions as 'humanly devised constraints that structure political, economic,

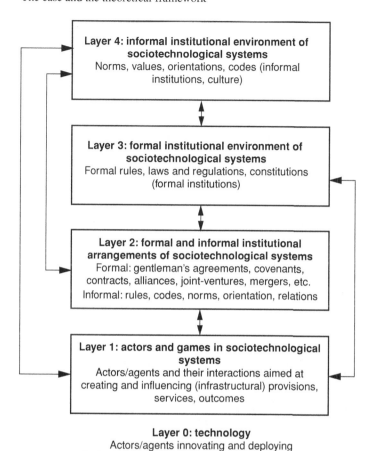

Figure 1.2 Five-layer model: levels of institutional analysis, technology enabled

and social interactions' and when he says that 'institutions consist of a set of moral, ethical, behavioural norms which define the contours and that constrain the way in which the rules and regulations are specified and enforcement is carried out' (North, 1990).

At the top of Figure 1.2, in layer 4, we find the so-called informal institutions, which influence the behaviour of actors. The culture in which the genesis of Wi-Fi was embedded has an impact on the motivation of actors and on their expectations of how the other private and public actors will behave. Ideas about universal service and the availability of technologies, such as Wi-Fi, to the wider community belong to the domain of informal institutions. At layer 3 we show the so-called formal institutions, which influence and direct the behaviour of actors. Laws about competition, corporations and corporate governance, for instance, are examples of explicit institutions that have an impact on the behaviour of actors. Layer 3 is typically the domain of public actors, such as the national parliament, ministries and public agencies. Layer 2 consists of the so-called institutional arrangements, being the institutions that private actors make to coordinate transactions between themselves. A distinction is made between the institutions that private actors create purposefully, such as contracts and organisations, and the ones that evolve informally, such as norms. At layer 1 we find the actors, who through their behaviour create the institutional structures, while being at the same time constrained by them. The arrows indicate the interactive relationships between the different layers.

Technology has played an important role in the development of Wi-Fi: the process of innovation is the central theme of this study. We have expanded the model to reflect technology at layer 0, which forms the underpinning for all the other layers, thereby reflecting the all-encompassing nature of technology. Technology is considered as being developed by actors/agents in layer 1 and in its application it impacts layers 2 through 4, and in its turn technology is itself shaped through these interactions.

For our analysis, the institutional environment – i.e. layers 3 and 4 – is considered to be endogenous. This does not imply that the institutional environment is considered to be static, bearing in mind that the Wi-Fi case study covers a period of approximately twenty-five years. The innovation trigger at the basis of the development of Wi-Fi can be construed as a 'parameter shift' occurring at layer 3, triggering changes in the institutional arrangements, and the creation of new arrangements between the actors involved.

Because of the multiplicity of explanatory variables involved at different levels of the analysis, it is clear that our study is of a multidisciplinary nature. At layer 1 the disciplines of history, anthropology and sociology are relevant. Layer 2 is the domain of political science and law, as well as economics (property rights, for instance). For the analysis of the institutional arrangements at layer 3 we consider institutional economics to be particularly relevant, while for the analysis of the interactions between the layers we make use of the insights of evolutionary economics. As can be seen, understanding and analysing the development process of Wi-Fi is a multidisciplinary affair requiring the application of different research perspectives, methodologies, theories and concepts.

1.3   Innovation and the landscape lens

When we aim to explore the dynamics between the elements of Figure 1.2 over time and we wish to describe and analyse the innovation process itself in

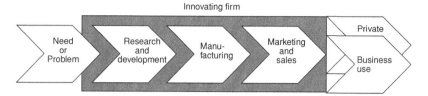

Figure 1.3 Sequential innovation process

particular, we are in need of a theoretical lens to provide us with the concepts to do so.

Innovation is a human phenomenon that occurs at all times and in all places. More recently, innovation has been recognised as the essential driver for continued economic growth and social development. In the words of Schumpeter: 'The fundamental impulse that sets and keeps the capitalist engine in motion comes from the consumer's goods, the new methods of production or transportation, the new markets, the new forms of industrial organization that capitalist enterprise creates' (Schumpeter, 1942). For this reason, researchers have been interested in identifying why innovation occurs and under what conditions. In our case, we are interested in the reasons and the preconditions that facilitated the genesis and the development of Wi-Fi. Wi-Fi is an innovation rather than an invention. Invention is considered to precede innovation and is often ascribed to serendipity: the accidental discovery of new ideas. Innovation is considered as knowledge put into practice to solve a perceived need or problem. How the innovation is perceived depends on the knowledge base of the onlooker. Rogers (2003) defines innovation as 'an idea, practice, or object that is perceived as new to an individual or another unit of adoption'. Even if the innovation is not 'new-new' it may have considerable value to the individual or organisation involved. Of importance in our context is the innovation development process, which Rogers defines as 'all the decisions, activities, and their impacts that occur from recognition of a need or problem, through research, development, and commercialization of an innovation by users, to its consequences'. This definition suggests an underlying sequential process: a perceived need or problem triggers an action by an entrepreneur, who allocates research and development (R&D) resources, to create a solution for the need or problem perceived, which is subsequently commercialised. See Figure 1.3 for an illustration of the flow.

While this may be the dominant form of innovation in our industrialised economy, it is certainly not the only form. Based on his empirical research, von Hippel (1988) replaces this 'manufacturer as innovator' assumption by four functional categories of innovators: (1) the users, (2) the manufacturers, (3) the

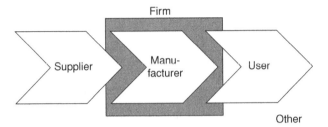

Figure 1.4 Sources of innovation

suppliers, and (4) 'others'. See Figure 1.4 for the relationship between these categories.

In the case studies supporting his research, von Hippel demonstrates that the innovators appear to be the actors that are best positioned to capture the temporary profits, or economic rents, from the innovative activities being undertaken. He observes, for instance, that, in the case of scientific instruments, the users are the main source of innovation; in engineering thermoplastics, the manufacturers are the source; in process equipment involving industrial gas, the gas suppliers are the innovators. In our Wi-Fi case we observe a shift in the locus of innovation, starting with the classical R&D model as it applies to the role of NCR in the innovation development process to the users involved in the creation of wireless neighbourhood area networks (NANs).

In our case we consider innovation, the innovation process and the resulting technological developments as the cumulative result of intentional behaviour on the part of actors. We thereby consider the innovation process to be an integral part of the overall organisational process of a firm, aimed at the production of goods and/or the delivery of services. As such, the innovation process is closely linked to the processes of manufacturing, sales and marketing, and it forms an important element in the strategy of the firm.

The firms that have business activities related to Wi-Fi can be considered to be part of an industry or industry segment. This industry is our next level of aggregation, which we use to capture the developments that all firms in the industry are facing, such as the rules of the competitive game, the process of standardisation and the laws and regulations regarding the use of radio frequency spectrum. The Wi-Fi industry is not a stand-alone industry, however, but an integral part of the broader ICT sector, with which it shares the (development of) the underlying information and communications technologies.

The perceived needs and problems that are addressed through the innovation process are, of course, determined by time and place. Our needs and problems reflect progress and the accumulation of knowledge. Hence, the available knowledge, technologies and tools that may be applied in the

Figure 1.5 Topography of technological evolution
Source: This figure appears in 'Technology guideposts and innovation avenues', in *Research Policy*; copyright © 1985, Elsevier; reprinted by permission of the publisher.

innovation development process provide the context within which solutions are pursued. In this respect, the past, both in the form of path dependency and in the form of paradigms (i.e. the way we tend to solve our problems), plays an important role. Innovations may appear coincidental. They are often a next step on a trajectory of technological development – a trajectory that is not necessarily continuous and certainly not linear. It may show turns and shifts, as well as discontinuities if paradigm shifts occur. It may show trajectories converging or branching off. The term 'innovation journey', as used by Van de Ven *et al.* (1999) to describe the dynamics of the innovation process within and among firms, and the 'landscape' metaphor, as introduced by Waddington in biology and applied by Sahal (1981, 1985) to describe the process of technological innovation, are appropriate ways to describe the development of Wi-Fi.[3] See also Figure 1.5.

In the landscape metaphor or topographical representation (Sahal, 1985; emphasis in original),

a developing object such as an infant technology is shown here as a ball. Starting in a low basin, the ball may roll along any one of the two valleys. It is chance that determines the specific valley chosen. Once a specific valley has been opted for, the ball can keep rolling on its own momentum until the next branch point is encountered at which stage chance once again predominates over necessity ... Beyond a certain stage, quantitative changes in the scale of an object are invariably transformed into certain qualitative changes with profound implications for its morphological, functional, and structural properties ... [T]he developing object can only ascend through the various slopes if its form is progressively modified. Eventually, it may reach one of the several hilltops if its form is perfected through a process of constant refinement. The higher the peak, the greater the perfection ... The overall topography itself can be altered by a wide variety of socio-economic forces ... The process of technological evolution is characterised not only by *specific innovation avenues* that concern individual industries ... but *generic innovation avenues* as well that cut across several industries ... [I]t is apparent that the

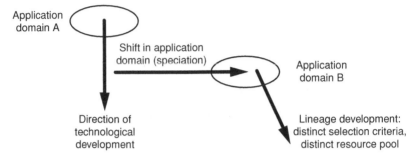

Figure 1.6 Speciation in technological development
Source: This figure appears in 'The slow pace of rapid technological change', in *Industrial and Corporate Change*; copyright © 1998, Oxford Journals; reprinted by permission of the publisher.

emergence of a new innovation avenue through *fusion* of two or more avenues or through *fission* of an existing avenue can give rise to sudden changes in the mode and tempo of technical progress.

The term 'necessity' in following a certain innovation avenue can be interpreted, in the terminology of Dosi (1982), as a technological trajectory or technological paradigm that guides the process of technological development. The latter emphasising the cognitive dimension, in a manner similar to the way in which scientific paradigms guide the process of scientific discovery, as elaborated by Kuhn (1962). In this context, Nelson and Winter (1977) use the term 'technological regime' – a term that is also used by Rip, Kemp and Geels to emphasise the social embeddedness of technological development (Geels, 2002; Rip and Kemp, 1998). The term 'chance' can be further elaborated, for example, by drawing a parallel with *speciation* in biology, whereby geographical separation may give rise to a new technological niche – as explained by Levinthal in an attempt to bridge incremental and radical views of technological change. See the illustration in Figure 1.6 (based on Levinthal, 1998, as quoted in Geels, 2002).[4]

In describing the innovation journey of Wi-Fi, we discuss the relevant aspects of the innovation process and use the 'landscape metaphor' and the concept of 'innovation avenues' to interpret the Wi-Fi developments at the level of the ICT sector, the highest aggregation level we consider in this case study. When it is deemed necessary, we may take a sidestep in order to investigate a specific aspect of the innovation journey using a particular theory or model, to be introduced.

Although we take it as a central theme that actors' behaviour is intentional, we submit that actors do not act in isolation but are socially embedded, and are a part of 'systems of interaction' that influence their behaviour (Boudon, 1981).[5]

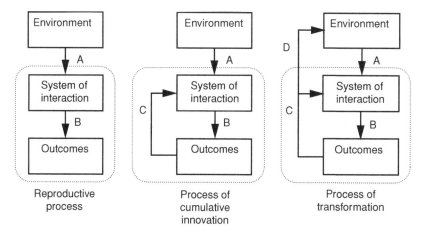

Figure 1.7 Processes of social change
Source: Adapted from Boudon (1981).

The 'system of interaction' represents the actors and the relations between them, also referred to as the structure of the situation (see Figure 1.7).

The environment includes the actors who are not directly involved in the system under consideration, but are influencing the behaviour of the system through causal link (A). In its most simple and stylised form, the 'system of interaction' leads to a reproductive process. In our case this refers to existing technical and organisational configurations and functions being continuously reproduced. If the outcome of the process is used as a feedback to the 'system of interaction' (C), however, an interactive learning loop is established and a process of cumulative innovation will be the result. The feedback will result in new technical configurations and functions. The guiding principles of the technological regime, considered to be part of the environment, are unchanged, however, and will keep technological development coordinated and cumulative.

The 'habits of thought' and 'habits of action' define the accepted ways that economic agents undertake search processes and exploit the learning trajectories for further development (van der Steen, 2001). If the outcome of the system under consideration also has an impact on the environment through feedback loop (D), a more comprehensive process of change may occur, including adjustments of the existing technological regime and processes of institutional transformation. In the Kuhnian sense, periods of normal science are interleaved with periods of transition from one scientific paradigm to another (Kuhn, 1962). In other words: the interactions shown in Figure 1.7 can result in different dynamics ranging from a reproduction of the system to a transformation (Denzau and North, 1994; Greif, 2006).

1.4   Theory and empirics

The historical case study is central to our analysis. We have discussed the framework we consider useful for studying the dynamics of a socio-economic system with a developing technology, such as Wi-Fi. We have presented the landscape metaphor as an appropriate lens by which to analyse the innovation process. In most historical analysis the researchers have to rely on archives and written documents. In our case we were in the fortunate position of having access not only to very well documented information but also to the actors that were involved in the development process. In this study, the exploration and analysis are provided by academic experts, based on contributions by representatives from the field who were involved 'first-hand' in the innovation journey of Wi-Fi, creating its global success. We are aware of the role that the theoretical framework can play in relation to the empirics we are studying: theories and concepts can 'construct' the reality. Because the researchers were able to confront their findings with the insights of many actors who were closely involved in the process, we found ourselves in the fortunate position of being able to check and to validate our findings.

1.5   Structure of the book

The book is original in that it is based on a combination of contributions from actors who were personally involved in the unfolding of events with scholarly contributions providing the interpretation of events based on related theory. In the account we go back to the year 1979, to Michael Marcus, the spread-spectrum project leader within the FCC; to Don Johnson, at NCR headquarters in Dayton, Ohio, in 1985; and to the members of the NCR team in Utrecht in the 1990s: Bruce Tuch, Cees Links, Vic Hayes and many others. This team became part of AT&T through its acquisition of NCR in 1991, and subsequently of Lucent Technologies and Agere Systems.

Their accounts of the genesis and development of Wi-Fi are arranged in a narrative that follows the product life cycle of Wi-Fi as it has emerged to date. Each phase in this development is introduced by an expert on the subject, who places the Wi-Fi development in its appropriate context and interprets the results in the context of the applicable theories. More practically, the expert also explores the implications and identifies the lessons for innovators, engineers, marketers, strategists and chief executives, as well as for government officials involved in developing innovation policies and regulatory policies to exploit the potential of information and communication technologies for economic and social development. Academic contributions to the book are provided by experts from Carnegie Mellon University (CMU, Pittsburgh, Pennsylvania), the Rheinisch Westfälische Technische Hochschule (RWTH) Aachen University (Germany), the Ecole Polytechnique Fédérale de Lausanne (EPFL,

Switzerland), Aalborg University (Denmark), the University of Twente and the University of Technology at Delft, both in the Netherlands.

In our narrative we follow the innovation journey as it unfolds, starting with NCR, the company that has been in the forefront of the developments that have resulted in the success of Wi-Fi. We touch upon rival products in the innovation phase and discuss competing approaches in the standardisation phase, such as HomeRF, an initiative driven by Intel, and HIPERLAN, promoted through the European Telecommunication Standards Institute (ETSI).

Part 1 of the book describes the innovation journey of Wi-Fi, initiated as it was by a change in regulatory policy, and the equipment manufacturers as the leading actors.

Chapter 2 starts with the decision by the US Federal Communications Commission on spectrum allocation for licence-exempt radio communication. It explains how NCR launched an R&D programme to take advantage of this opportunity. This early development is placed in the broader theoretical context of innovation, using the metaphor of the innovation landscape, and linkages to national and regional systems of innovation, and to knowledge transfer between universities and industry. In terms of the institutional environment, the political dimension of regulation is explored.

Chapter 3 discusses the strategic decision by NCR to break away from a position of following IBM and to assume a leadership role in establishing an open standard for wireless LANs. The chapter covers the development of the IEEE 802.11 family of standards, including the leadership role that NCR, AT&T and Lucent Technologies have assumed. The theoretical context is provided by the process of ICT standard setting, including the link between firm strategy and setting standards, and the changing institutional environment, including a discussion of the differences between the US and European standardisation systems, of open standards, the relation between stakeholders as well as coordination and competition in standardisation. Special attention is given to the role of the individual in setting standards.

Chapter 4 deals with the challenge that NCR faced in 'crossing the chasm' – the move from the early adopter phase to the phase of mass-market deployment. It discusses the lessons learned, from the first large-scale deployment in 1994 at the campus of Carnegie Mellon University onward. The theoretical context is provided by the product life cycle theory as interpreted by Moore in the 'bowling alley' metaphor, whereby the agreement with Apple, to provide the Apple AirPort at a price level of US$99 for the plug-in, represented the *head pin*, and the cooperation with Microsoft on the XP software and the establishment of the Wi-Fi Alliance the *whole product* dimension. The innovation context emphasises the aspect of diffusion. We reflect on the emergence and evolution of a new industry.

Chapter 5 discusses the move from networks in the private domain to networking in the public domain with the emergence of Wi-Fi-based 'hotspots'.

Hotspots represent new service opportunities for telecom operators and have led to the emergence of roaming providers. The context for this chapter is the innovation avenue metaphor, with a shift from product- to service-oriented innovation and the development of new business models for wireless internet service providers (ISPs).

Chapter 6 introduces Wi-Fi networks that have been built from the bottom up by communities of citizens. Wireless Leiden is used as a case example, followed by municipalities that have taken the initiative to create Wi-Fi networks as part of policies related to closing the 'digital divide', between those with and without access to internet services of a specified standard, and improving the 'economic fabric' of the city. The context for this chapter is, again, the innovation avenue metaphor, with a shift in the role of Wi-Fi from access to networking and the users as the source of innovation.

Part 2 of the book places the Wi-Fi innovation journey in a broader context by exploring five dimensions of particular interest.

Chapter 7 assesses the role that Wi-Fi can play in providing universal access in remote areas. The chapter investigates an example of a Wi-Fi community initiative in a developed country (Denmark), and five examples in developing countries (from Asia, Latin-America and Africa) aimed at providing access to the Internet at the so-called 'bottom of the pyramid'.

Chapter 8 explores the 'Dutch connection' to US-based NCR, AT&T, Lucent Technologies and Agere Systems. It is noteworthy that most of the development of Wi-Fi within this succession of companies took place in the Netherlands, even though the product was originally developed for the US market and the operation was directed from NCR's US headquarters. The chapter looks into the Wi-Fi legacy by following the knowledge trail from Philips Electronics to NCR, and the connection to spin-offs and start-ups and other innovation trajectories, such as Bluetooth and Zigbee. This perspective draws upon the notion of national innovation systems.

Chapter 9 takes the case of Wireless Leiden as the starting point to explore in more detail the role of the users in the process of innovation, and proposes 'the community' as a new source of innovation. This perspective draws upon theoretical strands of innovation studies and science and technology studies as academic disciplines.

Chapter 10 expounds the view that Wi-Fi represents the first example of a global success story in the use of the radio spectrum on a licence-exempt basis. It explores the origin and development of this licence-exempt use, and, moreover, it reviews the allocation of RF spectrum for Wi-Fi use across the globe and discusses the allocation of new radio spectrum to allow for growth. The perspective taken in this chapter is the relationship between technological and institutional developments, in particular the development of the radio spectrum governance paradigm.

Chapter 11's theme is the possible futures of Wi-Fi. Although the Wi-Fi activities within Agere Systems and its predecessor companies have been dissolved, the development efforts continue, as reflected, for instance, in the issuing of enhancements to the IEEE 802.11 standard on a regular basis. This perspective builds upon a micro-Delphi study in connection with the exploration of scenarios for a ubiquitous wireless world.

Chapter 12 provides a reflection on our research findings and derives implications for firm strategy formation and government policy making with respect to innovation and radio spectrum governance.

Part 3 of the book consists of a series of annexes: a glossary, a timeline of major events in the development of Wi-Fi, an overview of the IEEE 802.11 family of standards and an impression of the Wi-Fi ecosystem.

Notes

1 Prior to the establishment of dedicated national regulatory agencies as part of the telecom reform process, responsibility for the national regulatory function and for representation at the International Telecommunication Union (ITU) lay with government departments, which in this context were often referred to as administrations.
2 It should be noted that the FCC initiative to facilitate wider civil usage of spread-spectrum technologies, Docket no. 81–413, enabled not only Wi-Fi but also a generation of cordless telephones, and, more recently, Bluetooth and Zigbee (personal communication with Michael Marcus, 2009).
3 Sahal's research is aimed at developing an integral view of innovation processes. He concludes that important innovations result from the fact that every technology depends upon its size and structure. In the scaling up or scaling down, the relationship between size and structural requirements changes, which in turn severely limits the scope for further evolution. This triggers a wide variety of innovations – a process of learning by scaling (Sahal, 1985).
4 The notion of market niches in explaining and categorising radical technical change has been elaborated by Schot and Geels in terms of the dimensions of low and high protection/isolation and low and high stability of rules (Schot and Geels, 2007).
5 Examples of 'systems of interaction' include the family, the firm in which a human actor engages, a political party of which he/she is a member, and an organisation of volunteers.

References

Boudon, R. (1981). *De Logica van het Sociale: Een Inleiding tot het Sociologisch Denken* [original: *La logique du social: introduction à l'analyse sociologique*]. Alphen aan den Rijn, Netherlands: Samson.
Denzau, A. T., and D. C. North (1994). 'Shared mental models: ideologies and institutions'. *Kyklos*. **47** (1), 3–31.
Dosi, G. (1982). 'Technological paradigms and technological trajectories: a suggested interpretation of the determinants and directions of technical change'. *Research Policy*. **11** (3), 147–62.

Geels, F. (2002). 'Understanding the dynamics of technological transitions: a co-evolutionary and socio-technical analysis'. Dissertation. University of Twente, Enschede, the Netherlands.

Greif, A. (2006). *Institutions and the Path to the Modern Economy: Lessons from Medieval Trade*. Cambridge: Cambridge University Press.

Koppenjan, J. F. M., and J. P. M. Groenewegen (2005). 'Institutional design for complex technological systems'. *International Journal of Technology, Policy and Management*. **5** (3), 240–57.

Kotler, P. (1997). *Marketing Management: Analysis, Planning, Implementation, and Control*. Upper Saddle River, NJ: Prentice Hall.

Kuhn, T. S. (1962). *The Structure of Scientific Revolutions*. Chicago: University of Chicago Press.

Lemstra, W., V. Hayes and M. van der Steen (2009). 'Network modernization in the telecom sector: the case of Wi-Fi'. In R. W. Künneke, J. Groenewegen and J.-F. Auger (eds.). *The Governance of Network Industries: Institutions, Technology and Policy in Reregulated Infrastructures*. Cheltenham: Edward Elgar, chap. 6.

Levinthal, D. A. (1998). 'The slow pace of rapid technological change: gradualism and punctuation in technological change'. *Industrial and Corporate Change*. **7** (2), 217–47.

Nelson, R. R., and S. G. Winter (1977). 'In search of a useful theory of innovation'. *Research Policy*. **6** (1), 36–76.

North, D. C. (1990). *Institutions, Institutional Change and Economic Performance*. Cambridge: Cambridge University Press.

Porter, M. E. (1980). *Competitive Strategy: Techniques for Analyzing Industries and Competitors*. New York: Free Press.

Rip, A., and R. Kemp (1998). 'Towards a theory of socio-technical change'. In S. Rayner and E. L. Malone (eds.). *Human Choice and Climate Change*. Columbus, OH: Batelle Press, 329–401.

Rogers, E. M. (2003). *Diffusion of Innovations*. New York: Free Press.

Sahal, D. (1981). *Patterns of Technological Innovation*. Reading, MA: Addison-Wesley.
    (1985). 'Technological guideposts and innovation avenues'. *Research Policy*. **14** (2), 61–82.

Schot, J., and F. Geels (2007). 'Niches in evolutionary theories of technical change: a critical survey of the literature'. *Journal of Evolutionary Economics*. **17** (5), 605–22.

Schumpeter, J. A. (1942). *Capitalism, Socialism and Democracy*. New York: Harper-Perennial.

Van de Ven, A. H., D. E. Polley, R. Garud and S. Venkataraman (1999). *The Innovation Journey*. Oxford: Oxford University Press.

Van der Steen, M. (2001). 'Understanding the evolution of national systems of innovation: a theoretical analysis of institutional change'. Paper presented at the European Association for Evolutionary Political Economy conference 'The information society: understanding its institutions interdisciplinary'. Maastricht, 10 November.

Von Hippel, E. (1988). *The Sources of Innovation*. Oxford: Oxford University Press.

Williamson, O. E. (1998). 'Transaction cost economics: how it works; where it is headed'. *De Economist*. **146** (1), 23–58.

Yin, R. K. (1989). *Case Study Research: Design and Methods*. Newbury Park, CA: Sage.

Part 1

The Wi-Fi Journey

2 NCR: taking the cue provided by the FCC

Wolter Lemstra,
with contributions from Donald Johnson, Bruce Tuch
and Michael Marcus

2.1 The innovation trigger: the FCC Report and Order

Although different research perspectives may result in different starting points, a meaningful start for a wireless-based product such as Wi-Fi is to trace back the event or events that led to the allocation and assignment of radio frequency spectrum. In this case, it is the Report and Order adopted on 9 May 1985 by the US Federal Communications Commission[1] to authorise 'spread spectrum and other wideband emissions not presently provided for in the FCC Rules and Regulations' (see also Figure 2.1 for the coverage of the Report and Order; FCC, 1985).

The initiative by the FCC to open up the ISM spectrum for communications applications using spread-spectrum technology was in itself innovative, as most rule making is triggered by industry. This initiative had a different origin, as Marcus explains:

The political climate preceding the 1985 spread spectrum order was set by the Carter administration (1977 to 1981). Carter's programme was one of deregulation, which had already affected the airline, trucking and railroad industries. The White House facilitated a dialogue with regulators on basic concepts, and an interagency committee occasionally organised workshops for agencies to exchange ideas on deregulation. For example 'labelling' was considered a possible alternative to stricter regulation. For instance, the cigarette industry had to label its packages with the tar and nicotine contents, to be measured according to a new standard. The labelling made people conscious of the health risks, and the sales of high-tar cigarettes plummeted. This result would probably not have been reached if a regulation had been put in place with a set limit, since the political compromise necessary to get such a limit adopted would probably have resulted in a high limit for the tar and nicotine content.

The chairman of the FCC from October 1977 to February 1981, Charles Ferris, intended to extend the deregulation spirit to apply to the RF spectrum. He would like to end the practice whereby numerous requests for spectrum were brought forward, based on special cases of technology application. The motto was 'Let us unrestrict the restricted technologies'. To that end he hired as chief scientist at the FCC in 1979 Dr Stephen Lukasik, a physicist famous for having been the director of the Advanced Research Projects Agency (ARPA) from 1970, during the pioneering years of the ARPAnet.

21

802.4L/87-013
20 PAGES

Before the
Federal Communications Commission   FCC 85-245
Washington, D.C. 20554   35747

In the Matter of   )
)
)
Authorization of spread spectrum and other)   GEN DOCKET NO. 81-413
wideband emissions not presently provided)   —
for in the FCC Rules and Regulations.   )

FIRST REPORT AND ORDER

Adopted: May 9, 1985   Released: May 24, 1985
By the Commission:

INTRODUCTION AND SUMMARY

1.   Spread spectrum modulation is a wideband modulation which was
originally developed for military applications but which has
several interesting civil applications 1/. This technology has
been implicitly forbidden by the FCC rules with a few limited
exceptions. On June 30, 1981, the Commission adopted a Notice of
Inquiry ("Inquiry") 2/ in this proceeding seeking comments on a
rule structure that would permit civil use of this technology 3/.

1/ The spreading or dilution of the energy in spread spectrum
systems over   a wide bandwidth results in several possible
advantages: short range overlays on other emissions, resistance to
interference from other emissions, and low detectability. While it
is not anticipated that spread spectrum will replace other types of
modulations. in general, the unique characteristics of spread
spectrum offer important options for the communications system
designer.
2/   87 FCC 2d 876
3/   A companion Notice of Proposed Rulemaking was adopted in Docket
81-414 proposing use of spread spectrum in the Amateur Radio
Service and has been implemented, in part, in a Report and Order we
are adopting today.

Figure 2.1 FCC Report and Order on spread spectrum

At that time I was working for the Institute for Defense Analyses, which I had joined
in 1975. I was assigned to study options for electronic counter-countermeasures, a move
that was triggered by the 1973 Yom Kippur War in the Middle East, which had been
characterised by an unexpectedly large amount of communications warfare. In 1979,
during a closed meeting on electronic warfare held in Chicago, the delegates were seated
in alphabetical order, and it so happened that I was seated next to Dr Lukasik. I found
out that he was just about to leave Xerox to take up the post as chief scientist at the
FCC, having been asked by Ferris to identify new communications technologies that
were being blocked by anachronistic rules. I suggested that spread spectrum was such

a technology, and as a consequence I was invited by Lukasik to join the FCC to follow up on the idea.

The first order of business was the development of an action agenda for the chairman. The proposed agenda included three possible items to be 'unrestricted': spread spectrum, millimetre waves and adaptive antennae. On the first item, in December 1979 we contracted the MITRE Corporation to investigate the potential civil usage of spread spectrum. MITRE's report of 1980 resulted in the approval of two FCC notices of inquiry (NOIs) on spread-spectrum technology: Docket no. 81–413 for general use and Docket no. 81–414 for amateur radio use. Both were discussed and approved at an FCC meeting on 30 June 1981.[2]

2.1.1   The process of telecommunication reform

The deregulation of the telecommunication sector by the administration of Jimmy Carter (president 1977 to 1981) had its origin in the early 1970s, when AT&T's monopoly on telecommunications in the United States came under fire. This monopoly had been granted in the 1920s, a period in which telephone networks had emerged in the major US cities based on private entrepreneurial initiatives. Cities served by competing telephone companies remained, by and large, without interconnection, however. Moreover, rural areas were not properly served, as providing such a service was considered uneconomical. The value of providing all citizens with access to a fully interconnected telephone network was recognised by the US government, though, and to achieve this objective an agreement was made with the American Telephone and Telegraph Company to provide interconnection, called universal service, for which AT&T received in return a regulated private monopoly on providing telecommunication services (Fagan, 1975; Fischer, 1992; Melody, 2002).

In the late 1960s and early 1970s the development of new equipment, such as microwave technology, satellites, switching and computer terminal equipment and their applications, presented major challenges to the boundaries of the telecom industry monopoly, represented by AT&T and GTE (formerly the General Telephone and Electronics Corporation) (Melody, 1999). This led to the gradual removal of specific monopoly restrictions, allowing other firms to participate in the telecommunications marketplace. In 1968, through the Carterfone decision, the entry policy for the customer terminal market was formalised and based on compatibility and safety standards. In 1969 the FCC allowed competition to enter the long-distance services market, through its famous MCI decision. In 1980 the FCC's 'Computer Inquiry II' would lead to a structural separation of regulated and unregulated activities, with terminal equipment and enhanced services falling into the unregulated category. In 1982 an agreement was reached between the Department of Justice and AT&T whereby the long-distance operations, including the international operations, would be separated from the local exchange-based telephone business, and the local operating companies would be formed into seven independent regional holding companies. This agreement allowed AT&T to expand beyond the telecommunication business and paved the way for its entry into computers and computing (Melody, 2002) – an aspect to which we return later.

2.1.2   The origin of spread spectrum

In its notice of inquiry the FCC proposed the civil use of spread spectrum. Until 1981 this technique had remained officially classified as military technology (Mock, 2005). The invention of spread spectrum, in the form of frequency hopping (FH), dates back to 1942, when a patent was granted to actress Hedy Lamarr and composer George Antheil: US Patent no. 2,292,387, issued on 11 August, under the title 'Secret Communications System'. Lamarr, born as Hedwig Eva Maria Kiesler in 1913 in Vienna, had been married to Friedrich Mandl, an Austrian arms manufacturer, which had exposed her to many discussions regarding warfare. One of the issues discussed was the jamming of radio-guided torpedoes launched from submarines. In 1937 Kiesler left Austria for the United States, under a contract with Metro-Goldwyn-Mayer; it was here that she met with Antheil. Their combined insights into technology and music generated the idea of changing the carrier frequency on a regular basis, akin to changing the frequency when striking another key on the piano. The sequence of frequency shifts was to be known only by the transmitter and the receiver involved. This sequence was to be determined through punched holes in a paper roll, like those used in pianolas. By synchronising the receiver signal in the torpedo along the same roll, the communication would be hard to jam effectively because of its constant change of frequency.

Lamarr and Antheil presented their idea to the National Inventors Council, which had been established specifically to solicit ideas from the general public in support of US efforts in the Second World War. They subsequently donated their patent to the US military as a contribution to the war effort. The first practical application came after the war, however, in the mid-1950s, in sonobuoys used to locate submarines covertly (Mock, 2005). The first serial production of systems based on direct sequence spread spectrum most probably consisted of the Magnavox AN/ARC-50 and ARC-90 airborne systems, though it is highly likely that there are other early systems that have remained classified.[3]

Marcus continues his account of the regulatory developments:

The hostility of the US Intelligence Community to civil use of spread spectrum started ebbing at a meeting on spread-spectrum issues at the National Security Agency (NSA) in 1982. After I described the FCC proposals for civil use, a high-ranking officer of the NSA commented to the attendees that his wife had purchased a car with a radio that had a scanning possibility and preset selection of radio stations; that is in fact frequency hopping: '[S]o it is out of Pandora's box; let us not try to keep it there . . .'

The first comprehensive textbook on spread spectrum in the 'open' was the book by Dixon entitled *Spread Spectrum Systems*, published in 1975.[4] People were not free to use spread spectrum for civil applications, however, because the spectrum rules throughout the world required the conservative use of frequency spectrum.[5]

The FCC notice of inquiry did not propose any frequency band, yet it proposed to use spread spectrum as an 'underlay' within other bands – i.e. sharing the frequencies with other services.[6] The NOI triggered sixteen comments and twelve reply comments, most of which expressed fear of interference and the difficulty of tracing the source of interference. Only Hewlett-Packard (HP) and the IEEE Information Theory Society (IEEE-ITS) supported the idea. The IEEE-ITS support resulted from a challenge I made to the attendees at an IEEE-ITS workshop in a guest ranch in Wickenburg, Arizona, in 1983. I told the participants that they had spent a lot of time writing about the theory of spread spectrum, but if they wanted the technology to move from IEEE journal pages to actual use they should look at the FCC proposals and provide some useful feedback.

The responses by the FCC on the comments made by the public on the NOI were published in the so-called further notice of inquiry and notice of proposed rulemaking (NPRM), which was adopted on 21 May 1984. The NPRM proposed two rules changes: one for the licensed use of spread spectrum in the police bands and one for unlicensed use. The unlicensed proposal called for an overlay on the spectrum above 70 MHz at very low power (below −41 dBm, the power ratio in decibels of the measured power referenced to one milliwatt) and one for unspecified power limits in the three bands designated for ISM applications.[7]

2.1.3   The governance of radio frequency spectrum

Interestingly, the MITRE report that investigated the potential benefits, costs and risks of spread-spectrum communications and that led to the notice of inquiry did not identify a strong requirement or need on the part of industry for the assignment of spectrum for spread-spectrum applications. The report concludes that 'many potential spread spectrum applications are likely to be economically unattractive' and that other potential applications 'may be economically feasible, but may make poor use of the spectrum resources that they would require', and goes on that '[i]n certain applications, spread spectrum techniques can make more efficient use of the spectrum than the usual implementation of narrowband techniques . . . when the information bandwidth per user is low and the operating frequency is high' (MITRE Corporation, 1980). The main argument was based on the view that spread-spectrum systems are narrowband systems to which a higher level of complexity has been added to achieve a particular functionality, which in turn adds to the costs. In the analysis it was recognised that spread spectrum is inherently more resistant to interference. It also identified the difficulty of intercepting spread-spectrum signals, making monitoring harder, comparable to the monitoring of secure voice and secure data systems (MITRE Corporation, 1980).

These remarks should be interpreted in the context of the policies governing the radio frequency spectrum. In this respect the RF spectrum is often considered a 'natural' resource that is, in principle, accessible to every user. As a common pool resource, however, the RF spectrum is rivalrous: interference will occur if multiple users attempt to communicate at the same frequency, at the same time and in the same geographical area. Moreover, the spectrum resource is not infinite. Although technological progress has made the use of higher frequencies economically feasible, the propagation of radio waves diminishes at higher frequencies. As a result, higher frequencies are in principle less suitable for bridging longer distances. The governance of the RF spectrum has become a task for governments, with the objectives of ensuring an efficient allocation of spectrum and avoiding harmful interference. The governance paradigm that has emerged is based on assigning separate frequency bands to specific applications and (groups) of users, and to make users subject to a licensing regime. One of the first applications was ship-to-shore radio around 1900, to be followed by radio communication with aircraft. Radio broadcasting occurred on a daily basis from the early 1920s. An important use of radio frequency signals during the Second World War was radar. Soon after the war television broadcasting was introduced (ITU, 1965). In 1970, for the first time, the FCC set aside spectrum for cellular systems.

The MITRE report identified the industrial, scientific and medical bands as bands 'in which spread spectrum techniques may be able to improve the utilization of the spectrum ... [as these bands] are relatively unsuitable for applications requiring guaranteed high levels of performance. Indeed, since users of the ISM bands are not nominally protected from interference, it can be argued that any productive use of these bands frees other spectrum resources that are needed by applications requiring protection from interference' (MITRE Corporation, 1980). Typical applications in the ISM bands were garage door openers and retail security systems, and included the operation of microwave ovens. Hitherto no communications applications were permitted in the ISM bands. Most applications operate at relatively low power and at short distance. There were no commercial services operating in the ISM bands. Marcus continues his account:

This further notice triggered thirty-seven comments and fifteen reply-comments. Many of the respondents favoured the proposed authorisation of spread spectrum for low-power, limited-range communications devices. However, operators of frequency bands within the range of the rules were concerned about the overlay of spread-spectrum systems. Specifically, broadcasting groups and large consumer product manufacturers suggested serious degradation of television service. Some cordless phone manufacturers expressed concern that the proposed spread-spectrum authorisations could prejudice their petition for additional spectrum in the 47 MHz band. The FCC deferred all actions on all but the police radio service and the use of spread spectrum in the three bands designated for ISM applications: the 902 to 926 MHz, the 2,400 to 2,483.5 MHz and the 5,725 to 5,850 MHz bands. The limitation on peak power was set at a level of 1 Watt.[8]

This FCC ruling that would ultimately lead to the global success of Wi-Fi had an interesting final twist. After the release of the spread-spectrum authorisation, the whole top leadership of the Office of Science and Technology was exiled, possibly as a result of actions by industry in line with its concerns that the deregulation would make the FCC less responsive to major manufacturers, which wanted new technology to be made available only when it was convenient to them. In addition, an attempt was made to fire one deputy of Dr Bob Powers (the chief of the Office of Science and Technology), Margaret Reed, but she was able to arrange a transfer to another part of the FCC. The name of the Office of Science and Technology was changed into the Office of Engineering and Technology. Dr Powers took early retirement. Dr Marcus's position was eliminated and an attempt was made to dismiss him from the FCC. Procedural issues prevented him from ever being dismissed, but instead he was transferred to the enforcement department. Marcus concludes his account:

Thus, in the months following the spread-spectrum decision, three top managers of the Office of Science and Technology were removed, and the new organisation took no similar bold initiatives for almost a decade.

This sequence of events is an example of what is called 'regulatory capture': the ability of industry to influence the course of events within a regulatory agency in its favour. In this case, fortunately, it happened after the ruling was final.

In the case of spread spectrum, as well as with respect to the millimetre waves, some FCC staff members had opposed the rule changes out of fear that the new rules being adopted would never be used. Reality proved otherwise. The authorisations opened the way for innovation, because with the regulation in place companies were more willing to allocate investment capital to research and development.

2.1.4   Early civil applications of spread spectrum

From 1988 the first real civil applications of spread spectrum appeared in the form of local area networks, such as the Gambatte MIDI LAN, which became very popular with top rock musicians. A derivative of this system became used in nuclear power plants, under the name of MidiStar Pro (Marcus, 2000).

From the FCC database of equipment authorisations we can identify other early applicants. In 1988 there was Telesystems SLW of Canada, founded in 1987 with a product focus on wireless local area networks (WLANs)[9] (the company became Aironet Canada). In 1989 it was followed by: XCyte Inc., involved in measuring equipment; Cirronet, focused on industrial wireless

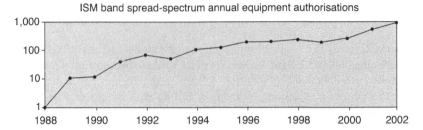

Figure 2.2 Spread-spectrum equipment authorisations, 1988–2002
Source: Marcus. Reprinted with the permission of the author.

applications and components; NYNEX, the regional Bell operating company; O'Neill Communications; Life Point System Inc.; and Agilis Corporation, which shifted its focus from computer manufacturing to WLAN systems. In 1990 the following companies applied for equipment authorisations: NCR; Intermec Technologies, active in the field of bar code equipment; Symbol Technologies, founded in 1975 with a focus on mobile data capture (the firm was acquired in 2007 by Motorola); and VeriFone Inc., founded in 1981 and active in the field of providing payment solutions (FCC, 2007). Other products included cordless phones and systems like a personal digital assistant (PDA). The FCC also approved unlicensed point-to-point microwave systems, such as AirLink T1. From 1990 onwards the number of equipment authorisations by the FCC rose significantly (see Figure 2.2).

By bringing spread-spectrum techniques into the civil domain, the FCC not only opened the way for Wi-Fi to emerge but also facilitated the developments leading to spread-spectrum application in the field of mobile telephony.

2.1.5   The link to mobile telephony

Mobile communications had been licensed for applications such as emergency services – police, ambulance and fire brigade – and for internal business use, such as taxis. This type of communication involved a fixed base station and mobile terminals. Although the concept of cellular systems had already been invented back in 1947 at Bell Labs, market interest did not begin to emerge until 1970, when, under industry pressure, the FCC set aside 75 MHz of bandwidth for use by cellular systems. The first commercial system, providing handover between the cells, was put into service in Saudi Arabia in September 1981.[10] It was based on the so-called NMT450 system (the Nordic Mobile Telephone system operating in the 450 MHz band), which had been developed and installed by Ericsson. The NMT network in Scandinavian countries would go live just one month later (Meurling and Jeans, 1994). In 1982 the FCC started to accept applications for cellular licences, and in 1983 the first

US cellular network, AMPS (Advanced Mobile Phone Service), was put into service by Illinois Bell in Chicago, operating at 800 MHz. These were all analogue systems, using frequency division multiple access (FDMA) to allow for simultaneous communications between the mobile users and the fixed base station. The first digital cellular systems were based on time division multiple access (TDMA). In the United States the so-called IS-54 standard was adopted in 1990 by the Telecommunications Industry Association (TIA). TDMA is also the basis for GSM (Global System for Mobile communications; originally from Groupe Spécial Mobile) services, launched in 1992 in Europe. The main driver behind the use of code division multiple access (CDMA), which uses the direct-sequence spread-spectrum technique, is Qualcomm, one of the telecommunications industry's greatest start-up success stories. The 'Quality Communications' company was established by Jacobs and Viterbi c.s. two months after the FCC Report and Order.[11] Although the R&O did not allow for the use of spread spectrum for land mobile services, it indicated that the FCC would be receptive to future rule changes to remove barriers to the use of spread spectrum. It had thereby provided a positive climate for investors in spread-spectrum-based technology.[12] Qualcomm filed for a patent on using CDMA in mobile communications application in 1986, and in 1988 it introduced the concept of cellular systems based on CDMA, leading to a field trial in 1989 by PacTel Cellular in San Diego. In 1992 Qualcomm signed a CDMA licence agreement with Nokia, at the time the world's second largest handset manufacturer. In July 1993 the TIA adopted CDMA as a North American standard, the so-called IS-95A. The first launch of a CDMA network was in Hong Kong in 1995, to be followed by PrimeCo launching commercial service in fifteen of the US states a year later. In 1998 the TIA endorsed CDMA2000 as the solution for third-generation (3G) mobile communication. In the following year Qualcomm and Ericsson reached a major agreement to cross-license CDMA (Mock, 2005).

2.2   The NCR response to the FCC Report and Order

A nagging issue for the NCR sales force was the lack of mobility in the commercial terminal product portfolio. Retail department stores, one of the main client groups of NCR, tended to reconfigure their sales floors on a regular basis, and the cost of rewiring the transaction terminals was a significant expense. To address this issue NCR had already conducted a study into the use of infrared light technology, but it quickly recognised that radio technology would work much better, 'if it was permitted, if we could make it work and if we could turn it into affordable products'. Don Johnson tells the story of how the FCC decisions influenced the company's thinking:

As senior engineer on the staff of the vice-president of corporate R&D, I advised on technology choices. The FCC had sometime earlier made radio-based local computer networking legal, using very low-power transmission, in the order of 1 mW (milliwatt). This had triggered the funding of an internal feasibility study. The initial stage of the study ruled out this very low-power variant, but it concluded that the ISM bands had potential. Hence funds were allocated to continue the study in more detail. At this stage the necessary funding was small, and remained within our normal spending range for exploratory work by headquarters.

2.2.1   NCR: the company

NCR Corporation was founded in 1879 as the National Manufacturing Company of Dayton, Ohio, by John H. Patterson to manufacture and sell the world's first mechanical cash register, which had been invented that year by James Ritty. In 1884 it was renamed National Cash Register Company. Patterson formed NCR into one of the first modern American companies, introducing aggressive new sales methods and business techniques. He established the first sales training school, in 1893, and a comprehensive social welfare programme for the factory workers. In 1906 the first cash register powered by an electric motor was designed by Charles Kettering. Thomas J. Watson, who would become the first chief executive officer (CEO) of IBM, worked his way up to general sales manager at NCR. The company went public in 1926 with an issue of US$55 million in stock. In 1953 it acquired Computer Research Corporation and created a specialised electronics division. In 1957 NCR introduced its first transistor-based computer, the NCR 304. In 1974 it commercialised the first bar code scanners. In 1982 NCR became involved in open systems architecture and introduced the UNIX-based TOWER 16/32 (NCR, 2007; Wikipedia, 2006). Around 1985 NCR became an international corporation, with revenue of around US$4 billion and an R&D budget estimated at US$300 million. Most of the revenues were realised in the United States, but Europe was an important export market, accounting for an estimated 25 per cent of revenues.

As a prelude to what comes next, NCR was acquired by AT&T in 1991 to boost its position in the computing industry. The government-induced break-up of AT&T in 1996 would lead to its re-establishment as a separate company in 1997, however. The wireless LAN activities thereupon moved to Lucent Technologies, the entity spun off from AT&T, the telecom operator, to assume the R&D and manufacturing of telecommunications equipment. In 2000 the WLAN activities transferred again, to Agere Systems, a new subsidiary of Lucent Technologies, with a focus on microelectronic devices, which became an independent company in 2001.

The purpose and mission of the corporate R&D organisation in Dayton was, first, to identify emerging technologies and, second, to promote advanced development and study in areas that would benefit many operating units. The objective was to avoid the duplication of efforts within the corporation, as well as promoting advanced studies that did not necessarily have an immediate application. All advanced development was performed in the individual operating units, and one of the roles of the R&D Division at headquarters was to determine which operating unit would conduct a particular investigation. The process was controlled through funding allocations. Understanding and keeping up to date with respect to the knowledge and resource base of the firm as it was operating globally constituted one of the key tasks, as it was essential to be able to justify and defend R&D funding decisions.

2.2.2   The link to the Netherlands

To adapt its products to specific requirements in place in Europe, NCR established its Systems Engineering Centre at Utrecht, in the Netherlands. The centre was part of the Communications Group within the Financial Systems Division and employed some sixty staff. There was a substantial software development team, working on making the company's financial systems compatible with those of IBM, and another group of experts worked on adapting telephone modem technologies to the European standards. In the process, the Utrecht centre became a centre of excellence in modem communication designs. One of the designs was a wired local area network called MIRLAN, which NCR deployed to wire up its cash machines in stores before the Ethernet system became the standard. The product was popular with NCR's customers and sold well, and the only way the company could achieve a cost reduction was to modify the design such that most of the functionality resided in an integrated circuit (IC). This was analogue design work for ICs, an area for which NCR did not have any skills base, and as a result it placed a recruitment advertisement. One of the respondents was Bruce Tuch, who went on to become the leader of Wi-Fi-related developments within NCR. He relates the story of his recruitment:

It was already four years that I had been working in the Netherlands, in one of the largest consumer electronic companies – Philips – and one of the few left outside Japan that actually was doing R&D for large-volume consumer electronics markets. Almost right out of university in the United States, this 'Brooklyn boy' moved to Europe, following his wife's opportunity to study veterinary medicine in Utrecht. Philips was a great place, since I wanted to apply my background to 'real electrical engineering', with communications and radio waves – a 'forgotten field', since in the 1980s all the electrical engineers gravitated towards the digital revolution. I wanted to learn more, Philips needed more talent willing to expand into 'analogue/RF design', and since the pool of talent available to do this was limited I could get my work permit from the Dutch government.

While I combined my work with getting my Dutch engineering degree at the Eindhoven University of Technology, which had to do with simulating radio frequency integrated circuits' behaviour with 'non-linearities' (in other words, predicting difficult circuits' behaviour), I really learned the most from the lifetime experience of my Philips RF colleagues, some of whom had been working in the field for many years and had gained their RF 'wisdom' by experience. They could really 'feel' what a circuit would do; yes, it could almost seem mystical: that 'black magician' who would lightly wave his hand over a circuit section, look at some display and determine how to fix things. I was at the bridge of this 'older art' and the new engineering generation, who tried to apply the rigour of analytic prediction as well but still loved to keep some of that feeling. While my commute to Eindhoven from Utrecht was doable, with the birth of our son, and both my wife and me being busy young parents, a nearby career opportunity was hard to refuse.

According to the advertisement in the paper, NCR was looking for an analogue design engineer to be located in Utrecht. I had just finished working on the second RF/analogue design with my Philips colleagues, an RF tuner integrated circuit that would replace most of the components in a television tuner; this was a real breakthrough-type product at the time, going up to the UHF (800 MHz) frequency channels. So, with this experience I felt as though I really knew something (I was still young then).

In the interview I was told about the cost reduction they needed for their wired local area network (MIRLAN). While interesting, the analogue design work was not 'cutting-edge RF'. There was a teaser, however; a new advanced development project might come in to take a look at the feasibility of wireless communications using radio. If I joined and designed the various product ICs needed and helped train the engineers in this area, the wireless communication project was the next step. So 1985 to 1986 became the period of normal analogue design for the different modem projects, with late 1986 to be the start of the feasibility study of the wireless LAN programme. The first people to be assigned full-time to the project were Maarten Visee, Hans van Driest and me.

2.3   The development of local area networks[13]

To place the developments of wireless LANs in perspective it is necessary to review, in summary form, the main stages in the development of wired LANs, which is, of course, directly linked to development in computing. This account is of particular interest for an understanding of the early stages of the Wi-Fi journey, especially the early innovation and start-up activity, as well as the struggle for a LAN standard.

From the early days computers had typically operated in stand-alone mode. An example of an early large-scale data network was the SAGE system (Semi-Automatic Ground Environment), which was installed by the US Air Force in 1958. This system used telephone lines to link radar stations and other devices across the United States to mainframe computers so as to provide centralised command and control. One of the first civilian wide area network (WAN) applications, installed in 1964 by American Airlines, was the SABRE system (Semi-Automatic Business-Related Environment), which was used to coordinate airline seat reservations. It connected over 1,200 terminals to the mainframe computer via 12,000 miles of telephone lines, making it a large-scale WAN application. The sharing of computer power through time sharing became the prevalent mode of operation in the early and mid-1970s, leading to the extensive use of wide-area terminal networks based on (dial-up) telephone lines (von Burg, 2001).

The sharing of supercomputer power as part of the US Department of Defense ARPA programme led to the development of the ARPAnet, which created the first wide-area computer-to-computer network, using leased telephone lines and minicomputers as the front end. In 1970 the first five nodes would be connected, primarily linking mainframe computers at university research centres, using packet switching. In contrast to circuit switching as used in telephony, whereby a two-way connection is established for the duration of the call, in the case of packet switching the information to be transmitted is divided into messages of fixed length, to which an address is added, thus forming the 'packet' that is subsequently transmitted on a store-and-forward basis through the network. The ARPAnet went on to evolve into the current-day Internet (Abbate, 1999; Lemstra, 2006; von Burg, 2001).

The introduction of the minicomputer in the late 1960s meant that it was becoming cost-effective for research departments within universities to own their computers rather than time-share a mainframe. The first IC-based computer, the PDP-10 from Digital Equipment Corporation (DEC), was introduced in 1968. At the University of California, David Farber became interested in linking these minicomputers to create a local distributed computing system. As these computers were going to be exchanging large amounts of data, this would require interconnection at much higher speeds than was necessary for text-based terminal communication. The local area network he built became known as the UC Irvine Ring. In 1971 this first LAN became operational, and by 1975 it connected computers, terminals, printers and a magnetic tape unit. The network operated on twisted pair cabling and on coaxial cable, at speeds of up to 2.3 Mbit/s (megabits per second). The stations were connected in a ring topology, and to manage the communication flow a token – a specific bit pattern – was transmitted continuously in one direction around the ring. If a station wished to transmit information it would 'seize' the token, change the bit pattern to 'busy' and add a destination address as well as the information to be transferred. At the destination the information would be retrieved and the token would be returned to the sender station, to be set 'free' again (von Burg, 2001).[14]

In a parallel development, the ARPA programme had also initiated research into the use of packet switching in land-based radio and satellite radio applications. As the noisy telephone lines on Hawaii appeared ill-suited for data transmission, Dr Norman Abramson at the University of Hawaii decided to try packet radio as an alternative to wire-based local area networking across the seven campuses and many research institutes. The resulting ALOHAnet used two radio channels, one to broadcast packets from the computer centre to the user stations and the other for the transmission from the user stations to the computer centre. The second channel would be subject to interference if two or more stations sent information at the same time. Rather than trying to prevent collision, the designers made sure the system could recover if a collision occurred, relying on the acknowledgement by the computer station of the packets being received in good order. If the user station did not receive an acknowledgement it would resend the information. To avoid the collision of two terminals and, potentially, endless retransmissions, the ALOHA protocol specified that the stations should use different waiting times before retransmitting: at random, but within a specified range (Abbate, 1999).

The ALOHA wireless LAN played an unexpected role in the development of the wired LAN, as a graduate student at Harvard University, Robert Metcalfe, was completing a PhD on packet-switching networks. He had been drawn into ARPAnet developments through his participation in project MAC at the Massachusetts Institute of Technology (MIT). In pursuing the theoretical aspect of his PhD he was introduced to the ALOHA network protocol, for which he devised a new waiting algorithm that would radically improve the throughput of the network under heavy load conditions.[15] In 1972, while still working on his PhD, Metcalfe accepted a job at the Xerox Palo Alto Research Center (PARC), and he was asked to design a system to connect the newly developed Alto workstations.[16] The Alto was part of Xerox's vision of creating a new 'architecture of information' for the office. This vision included the Alto 'personal' computer, equipped with a bit map monitor, a graphical user interface, a mouse and multitasking capability. The developments also included shared functions, such as a laser printer and a file server.

The requirements set out by Xerox for the local area network were that it had (1) to be capable of connecting hundreds of computers over hundreds of metres; (2) to operate at very high speed; (3) to use coaxial cable in order to meet the transmission requirements; and (4) to cost no more than 5 per cent of the cost of the personal computers it would connect. Based on his dissertation work, Metcalfe created a random-access broadcast system dubbed the Alto Aloha Network, soon to be renamed Ethernet. In this wired implementation, a station would 'listen to the wire', and when it found the wire to be silent it would initiate transmission. The principle applied became known as carrier sense multiple access with collision detection (CSMA/CD). The first version of Ethernet, introduced in 1973, would cover a distance of 1 kilometre, connect a maximum of 256 stations and operate at a speed of 2.94 Mbit/s (Abbate, 1999; von Burg, 2001).

Following these inventions by Farber and Metcalfe, a few firms started to commercialise proprietary LAN technologies. The leading firms were Network

Systems and Nestar (two start-ups), Zilog (a semiconductor firm) and Datapoint (a computer manufacturer). Network Systems, established in 1974, would pursue a mainframe LAN business addressing interconnectivity problems at fast-growing data centres, by providing a high-speed gateway function between proprietary systems. Nestar, founded in 1978 by researchers from IBM and Carnegie Mellon University, focused from the outset on linking microcomputers, and in 1980 introduced Cluster/One, aimed at the Apple II market (the Apple II had been introduced by Jobs and Steve Wozniak in 1977). Zilog, established by Intel alumni in 1974, applied a strategy of forward integration based on its successful communication chip, and developed Z-Net as part of its office system. Datapoint had been established in 1968 as a third-party manufacturer of computer terminals. Following its successful line of microprocessor-based terminals, which had become stand-alone business computers, they introduced a network-based distributed computing system called ARC. This system would become a direct competitor to the early Ethernet.[17] The products of the other companies floundered in the immature and rapidly changing market. As von Burg (2001) concludes: 'The commercialization efforts by the four pioneers . . . initiated the pre-dominant-design period. By 1980, they had created a small market but not yet an entire industry – nor had they set the standard.'

2.3.1   The creation of a LAN standard

In 1979 DEC, Intel and Xerox formed the DIX alliance, with the goal of establishing an industry-wide de facto LAN standard. DEC needed to link its new VAX computers in order to create a distributed computing environment. DEC liked the Ethernet solution, as it appeared to be possible to increase its throughput, and Metcalfe had suggested contacting Xerox to license the technology. The alliance opted for an open standard, on the grounds that this would increase the adoption of its LAN systems and increase the overall market. Moreover, the partners saw opportunities for augmenting the sale of other products. Furthermore, Xerox and DEC were pursuing an open strategy to attract third-party suppliers of Ethernet components, in particular IC manufacturers, Intel being their first supplier. According to von Burg (2001), the three firms complemented each other very nicely: 'Xerox had the technology; DEC provided market clout, credibility, and some Ethernet components; and Intel brought the chips, so vital in achieving steep price reductions.'

One of the earlier network standards, established under the leadership of Donald Loughry at HP, was approved in 1974 as IEEE 488, and was aimed at the remote control of programmable instruments in industrial processes. Recognising the distance limitations of this standard, Maris Graube at Tektronix started pushing for a new standard, and in 1979 submitted a project authorisation request to the IEEE; it was approved, and the first meeting of

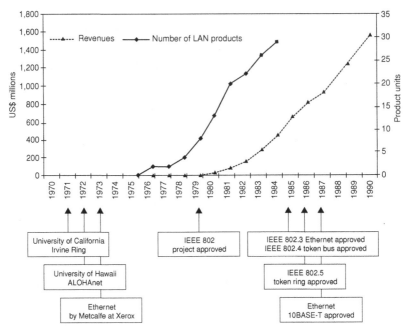

Figure 2.3 Developments in wired LANs
Source: This figure appears in 'The shaping of the IEEE 802.11 standard', in *Information Communication Technology Standardization for E-Business Sectors* (ed. Jakobs); copyright © 2009, IGI Global; reprinted by permission of the publisher.

IEEE 802 was convened in 1980. The participants were computer manufacturers, vendors of office automation products, vendors of factory automation systems and LAN start-ups, such as 3Com, established by Metcalfe in 1979, and Ungermann-Bass, a 1979 spin-off of Zilog. Because the various participants were all pursuing different objectives and could not agree on one single standard, the IEEE Standards Board ultimately approved three standards: in 1985 the IEEE 802.3 for Ethernet, primarily supported by the DIX alliance, HP, Data General, 3Com and Ungermann-Bass, and the IEEE 802.4 for Token Bus, supported by the vendors of factory automation systems; and in 1986 the IEEE 802.5 for Token Ring, with IBM as its main proponent. In 1987 HP initiated an extension effort to standardise a 10 Mbit/s version of Ethernet, which would use telephone wire rather than coaxial cable. In 1990 this so-called '10BASE-T' standard was approved by the IEEE Standards Board (von Burg, 2001). Figure 2.3 provides a timeline of the developments of wired LANs, highlighting the number of competing products; the two lines show the

LAN products being introduced and the revenues of the major LAN companies involved.[18]

What is interesting in this account of wired LAN developments is the role of the ALOHA network; it implies that the wired LAN was put on the radio-waves by Abramson, then returned to wire by Metcalfe, only to be put on the radiowaves again by Tuch.

2.4   NCR: providing the seed money for wireless LAN development

Turning away from the wired LAN landscape, it is time to resume the Wi-Fi journey, specifically the decision that had to be made at NCR head-quarters: where to allocate the task of carrying out the feasibility study on the application of spread-spectrum technology according the FCC rules and regulations. The decision to allocate the wireless LAN investigation to the Systems Engineering Centre at Utrecht was not a straightforward affair. In Don Johnson's words:

For me the choice of the Utrecht Engineering Centre for the execution of the technology investigation was an obvious one. Their signal-processing expertise and hardware design was, in my view, crucial for any radio-technology-based local area network. However, this choice was challenged by the R&D folks in the Retail Division. With retail terminals as the main immediate beneficiary of WLAN development, they claimed the right to execute the investigation. They challenged the superiority of the expertise in Utrecht and claimed a more cost-effective approach by doing the research in their location in Atlanta. In addition, the Microelectronics Division opposed the choice of Utrecht. They also challenged the Utrecht capability and felt that they should utilise an outside organisation to do the basic development. My organisation had to step in, and after an extensive battle I was able to convince other parties at the executive level that our choice had merit and was to be pursued.

The seed money from headquarters in Dayton kicked off a process whereby a Dutch facility started working on a feasibility study for an American company to assess whether a wireless radio could be developed for cash registers to be sold in the United States.

2.4.1   The WLAN feasibility study

The main objective of the feasibility study was to investigate the use of a different physical medium in the application of local area networking. Instead of wires, radio waves would be used for transmitting information. Copper wires, coaxial cable and (shielded) twisted pair differ from radio waves in their transmission properties and in the way the medium can be accessed. In terms of the Open Systems Interconnection (OSI) model, this implied that new designs were required at the physical (PHY) layer and at the medium access control

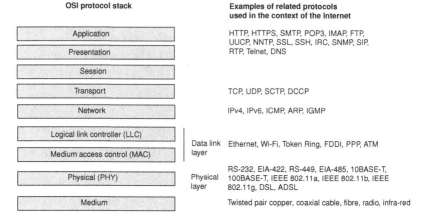

Figure 2.4 OSI protocol stack
Note: Refer to Annex 1 for explanation of acronyms.
Source: This figure appears in 'Network modernization in the telecom sector', in *The Governance of Network Industries* (ed. Künneke, Groenewegen and Auger); copyright © 2009, Edward Elgar publishing; reprinted by permission of the publisher.

(MAC) layer. See also Figure 2.4, which shows the layers of the OSI protocol stack in relation to examples of current-day protocols used in the context of the Internet. Any further impact on the higher layers of the stack (network through application) would also have to be assessed as part of the feasibility study.

NCR had already gained experience in building LANs. The first LAN was a 1.5 Mbit/s version, known as C-255, used for connecting checkout systems. MIRLAN was a more recent system, operating at 1 Mbit/s and using a bus system based on coaxial cable. The system was used extensively, being deployed, for instance, by Barclays Bank. MIRLAN was proposed as a candidate for standardisation in IEEE 802.

Tuch carries on the story of the feasibility study into the application of spread spectrum for wireless LANs:

The first part of the feasibility project was to determine what power levels were needed and under what rules such products could be certified by the FCC. At first it was clear that using low power rules (like the ones that cover devices such as radio-controlled toys) just would not meet the requirements of a true indoor wireless LAN. One needed to have communication between devices across the department store and at reasonable data rates. I recall the target was greater than 500 kbit/s, since most cash registers needed to get 'their firmware' downloaded in the morning, and with a large store you wanted this to be done quickly.

After it had been determined that the new FCC spread-spectrum rules would be used and the possible ranges had been assessed, more of the technical details of the system needed to be determined. The key question was: 'How can we get the highest data rates to make this really "feel" like a LAN system within these rules?' While frequency-hopping systems have some interesting diversity and multi-path characteristics, due to the FCC regulation the available bandwidth is limited, initially to 25 kHz (kilohertz), later 500 kHz; hence FH systems were data-rate-limited to approximately 250 kbit/s (kilobits per second). Our attention therefore became focused on direct sequence. Since this area was new for the commercial markets, the FCC labs that determined product compliance did not yet have their testing procedures in place.

One of the issues was the so-called processing gain requirements. This was the factor that you had to use to 'expand' the bandwidth above the bandwidth you would 'normally' need just to get your information data signal transmitted. The logic here is that the more 'spread' or processing gain the system has, the more the signal looks like noise to others, and the more capable the system is in rejecting other signals, so more coexistence would be possible in a non-licensed band. Of course, there is a trade-off between the data rates you want to achieve and the complexity of the total system, and thus the costs. I flew out to the Maryland FCC labs around October 1987. There we discussed how they would measure processing gain, which they mentioned '10x' (a 10-times processing gain) as the number in question. While I did not leave with anything in writing, I did get the feedback that we would need to spread the signal with a code sequence of length 10 (processing gain and code length are directly related) or greater (so each symbol sent in time would need to have ten times more transitions), but the modulation of the information on each symbol could be anything. This was important, since most spread-spectrum systems used much larger codes. I flew back to the Netherlands quite excited: we really could achieve over 1 Mbit/s, and, if we could get this done quickly, we would have a differentiated system (higher speeds) compared to others.

The team was small, and we set to work to get the processing gain parameters set. The system engineer on the project, Hans van Driest, came back after a weekend tinkering with his Sinclair computer (that was one of the first small home-programmable calculators/PCs) saying that he had 'found the code', which had a length of 11 (so just above the 10 required) and had the required properties that we had already determined from our indoor propagation studies.[19] I was quite excited when I saw the output results and knew immediately that this was 'the one'. This helped also to close on other research that had been started on the system cost aspects: what was the best approach to achieve the receiver function for spread spectrum? One option was to use integrated circuits with digital signal-processing techniques totally or to augment this with a component called a surface acoustic wave (SAW) filter to take on the 'heavy lifting' of doing the spread-spectrum processing. At the time SAW filters for this type of function were military components costing US$100 or more each! I knew that this could be done by normal silicon processing techniques that NCR had available in the Microelectronics Division; we just did not understand the design aspects. I contacted Professor Venema at the University of Technology in Delft, who was an expert in SAW devices, and started a research programme (NCR sponsored a PhD student, Jaap Haartsen) to design a 'SAW spread-spectrum demodulator' at different code lengths. This resulted in a working design (which we actually used in a wireless LAN demo unit) with a projected cost less than US$5. Nevertheless, at the code lengths of 11x (an 11-times processing gain) coupled with the advancement in integrated circuit technology required, the best approach was not to use this device in the product. Here was an example of research whose negative outcome was considered a positive result.

Haartsen, the PhD student from Delft, went on to work in the field of data communications, and became one of the originators of the Bluetooth technology at Ericsson (see also Chapter 8). Tuch continues:

We were ready! The feasibility outcome was a success with the product specifications in place. We were looking forward to starting the product development process. The NCR unit in the Netherlands was looking to get into new areas to improve the bottom line, given that some of the other products were at the end of their lives, and this wireless project seemed to be the next best bet. Nevertheless, it was not so easy, since it was determined that such a project was to be funded, and the business unit owners 'back home' wanted to own and develop the product. A small internal fight started, with product proposals from different groups, not all with the necessary transparency. The fact that we understood exactly the total system aspects and the FCC requirements and had actually built a demo system that worked showed that the Utrecht team was the best one for the job. It was not a bad thing, early in our 'learning curve', to have to show better technical results and be able also to communicate that to the business stakeholders, against the normal momentum of doing the development 'close to home'. This 'underdog' mentality would prove useful in the future 'battles' against external competition, even as a small group within a larger corporation.

At the time I had a lot of interaction with Don Johnson at NCR headquarters, which proved extremely useful in the allocation of the product development to 'Utrecht'. Don's background was in radio (he came from RCA), and he was someone who 'got it' within the company. As one breaks new ground, especially in an area that is quite new to the company, having the right entry into the life of the corporation, so that it can 'back you up' when things need to get started seriously (i.e. funded), is extremely helpful.

The first prototype developed as part of the feasibility study operated at 97 kbit/s.[20] The second generation, making use of surface acoustic wave filters, increased the data rate to c.500 kbit/s.[21] The (re-)discovery of an eleven-chip spreading code was the breakthrough towards the design of WLAN products operating at 2 Mbit/s.

2.5   Summary of the Wi-Fi journey: 1980–1987

The 'Summary of the Wi-Fi journey' section here, as throughout Part 1 of the book, summarises the Wi-Fi journey as it has unfolded in the chapter. The first lap of the journey can be recapped as follows.

The technological origin of Wi-Fi can be traced back to the invention of spread-spectrum techniques in 1942. Application of the technique in the civil domain became possible after a politically motivated decision by the FCC in 1985 to permit spread-spectrum-based communications in the ISM bands.

This new opportunity provided the spur for firms such as NCR to explore the technique for the use in wireless LANs – an application for which customer demand was recognised. The feasibility study was assigned to the R&D group of NCR in the Netherlands, based on its available expertise in the fields of both local-area networking and radio frequency technology.

2.6   Interpretation of the Wi-Fi case in the context of theory

As the Wi-Fi journey unfolds, in each chapter the developments are interpreted using the theories, concepts and models introduced in Chapter 1.

2.6.1   Innovation and the innovation landscape

Following the 'landscape' metaphor, Figure 2.5 shows the four main innovation avenues that have had an impact on wireless LAN developments (although they are depicted here as four independent avenues).[22] The central innovation avenue is related to computing. The emerging need for communication between computers over large distances has led to wide-area networking, based on the use of the existing public switched telephone network (PSTN) and/or leased lines. Communication needs between computers separated by short distances, as on university campuses and within corporations, in particular in the emerging automated office environments, have triggered a new innovation avenue – local-area networking. The technology used initially was 'token ring'. This avenue became fused (or, rather, infused) with packet-based technology – that is, linked to the avenue that generated today's Internet. The linkage came about through the development of the ALOHAnet, a packet-based radio LAN. Through the chance event of the PhD research project of Metcalfe, the ALOHA-related knowledge was injected back into the local-area networking avenue to generate Ethernet. The FCC decision to allow communications based on the civil application of spread spectrum in the ISM bands can be considered a landscape change, opening up a new avenue of wireless LAN development based on spread-spectrum techniques.

A new technological niche thereby emerges (Schot and Geels, 2007). In Figure 2.6 the interdependent innovation avenues are depicted in a stylised form.

Innovation process   In terms of the innovation process, this is a case of innovation rather than invention. The spread-spectrum principle and two of its application variants, frequency hopping and direct sequence, had already been invented, and applications existed in the military domain.

The developments within NCR are in line with the sequential model of inno-vation, whereby a firm perceives a customer need or market opportunity and

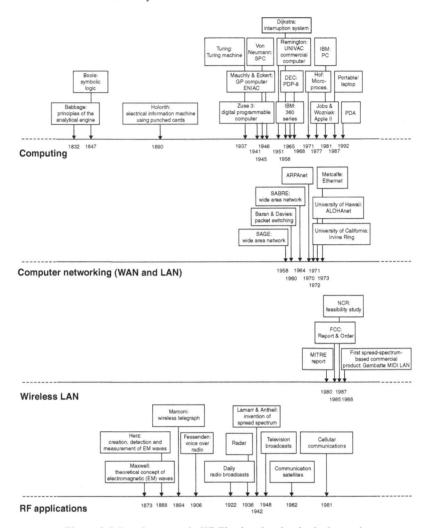

Figure 2.5 Developments in Wi-Fi-related technological strands

applies resources in its R&D department to the development of new solutions. The source of innovation in this case is NCR, the manufacturer of transaction terminals seeking more flexible ways of connecting cash registers to the computer networks of its clients. This applies in a similar vein to firms that apply spread-spectrum technology for data acquisition such as Symbol Technologies, Intermec Technologies, VeriFone. The major challenge is the application of the technology in products that are affordable in a commercial rather than a military setting.

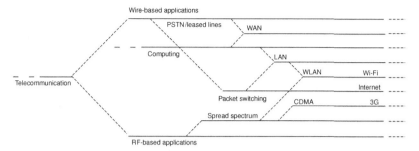

Figure 2.6 Relationship between Wi-Fi-related innovation avenues

Initially this is a clear case of product innovation, by firms applying a new technology to provide more flexible solutions to their clients, through the application of wireless data communication and wireless data capturing. From Chapter 6 onwards we will see an increasingly important role emerging for the end user in the innovation process.

National and regional systems of innovation   In studies seeking to explain the differences in the level of innovative activity between nations and to find guidance for policy formation, various scholars have explored the role of so-called national or regional systems of innovation (Lundvall, 1992; Nelson, 1993; Saxenian, 1994). According to Lundvall, an innovation system is consti-tuted by 'elements and relationships which interact in the production, diffusion and use of new, and economically useful, knowledge'. These innovation studies explore the role and importance of dimensions such as: industrial and centrally funded research; the role of policy in university–industry research collabora-tion, and in trade strategies; the role of institutions, for example with respect to intellectual property, to antitrust legislation, to labour-related legislation and the educational system; the role of the financial industry; the part played by networking and networks; the significance of (an entrepreneurial) culture; and the importance of access to markets. The national or regional innovation system is considered a social system, the central activity being constituted by learning as a social activity involving interactions between people. The innovation sys-tem is also dynamic, characterised by positive feedback and by reproduction (Lundvall, 1992).

Our case has a strong US national dimension, as the FCC is the first national regulatory authority (NRA) to allow civil spread-spectrum applications in the ISM bands. The firms initially involved in the application of spread spectrum were either American or Canadian. The fact that the Netherlands played an important role in the WLAN development is coincidental rather than structural. No Dutch government programmes that existed at the time can be identified as having had an important role in the course of events. What has been important in the decision-making process, however, is the comparative advantage of NCR's R&D entity in Utrecht in terms of its knowledge base, which was equal to the opportunity provided. It can also be argued that the RF expertise accumulated by Philips and the proximity of Philips' laboratories to the NCR offices in Utrecht facilitated developments – in other words, that the Dutch knowledge infrastructure did matter. At the very least it facilitated the acquisition of RF knowledge by NCR, in particular the acquisition of tacit knowledge through the hiring of staff from Philips. Moreover, the establishment of the NCR R&D centre in the Netherlands in the first place can be regarded as the result of a decision-making process comparing the conditions of alternative locations in Europe, from which it would appear that the Netherlands topped the list.[23]

Military–industrial complex   In explaining the high levels of innovative activity in the United States, many sources have pointed to the importance of the so-called military–industrial complex: the fact that military spending and government funding of, for instance, the aerospace sector would provide important spin-offs for the commercial sector. The example of micro-miniaturisation stimulating innovative developments in the semiconductor industry is often cited. Although spread-spectrum technology has been exploited within the military domain, in particular in the field of avionics, NCR has not benefited directly through participation in related military projects. NCR did benefit from the knowledge of spread-spectrum technology that became available in the public domain, however.[24]

ARPA linkage   Indirectly, the initiation and government funding of the ARPA programme has had an influence on developments in the LAN arena, in multiple instances: (1) in technology/research funding of packet-mode-based data communications; (2) in supporting the development of the ALOHA network; (3) in person, through Lukasik hiring Marcus to follow up on his idea of allowing the civil use of spread spectrum; (4) in person again, through Metcalfe, who became exposed to ARPA at MIT, and by Steve Crocker at ARPA providing him with papers on the ALOHA project as input for his PhD research project; and (5) through Robert Taylor, the initiator of the ARPAnet project who became the leader of the Computer Science Laboratory at Xerox PARC and hired Metcalfe to develop what would become Ethernet.

University–industry linkage   In representations of knowledge diffusion, the main direction of the flow is shown from industry research towards industry development, and from university research towards industry development. While the flow from research towards development can be observed, the flow from university research to industry development is not as obvious in the Wi-Fi case as it is in the case of Ethernet. The NCR development team did make use of specialised knowledge available at the Delft University of Technology, regarding surface acoustic wave filters, however. In subsequent chapters more interaction will be observed between NCR's Engineering Centre and universities.

2.6.2   Institutional environment and industry evolution

The most important institution in terms of triggering and influencing this early part of the development of Wi-Fi is the Federal Communications Commission, the United States' national regulatory agency. The FCC is an independent US government agency, directly responsible to Congress. The FCC was established by the Communications Act of 1934 and is charged with regulating interstate and international communications by radio, television, wire, satellite and cable. The FCC's jurisdiction covers the fifty states, the District of Columbia and US possessions (FCC, 2007).[25] The responsibility to Congress implies that the FCC's agenda is directly linked to the political climate in the Congress and that the FCC commissioners are political appointees.[26]

The WLAN innovation was triggered by a formal change in the institutional environment – i.e. in the regulatory regime of the radio frequency spectrum. As a common pool resource, the RF spectrum is managed by the government or a designated agency (the NRA) at the national level and coordinated at the international level through the International Telecommunications Union, as a part of the United Nations (UN) (ITU, 1965, 1998).

The main goal of the frequency management paradigm is to avoid harmful interference and to provide a fair allocation of the limited resource to a variety of uses and users – e.g. radio and television broadcasting, terrestrial and satellite communications, emergency services (police, fire, ambulance), the military and astronomy.

At first glance, the decision by the FCC to assign spectrum to applications for which no clear market demand was demonstrated appears strange, given that radio frequency spectrum is a resource in limited supply. The motivation was that of regulatory reform, of reducing the rules and regulations set by the government, with the aim of providing the industry with more freedom to innovate (layer 3 of the model as introduced in Chapter 1, impacting the institutional arrangements at layer 2). As an illustration, Figure 2.7 shows the major milestones in the process of telecom reform in the United States in relation to the political setting.

The assignment of spread spectrum to the existing ISM bands makes the decision far less controversial, however. It is one more application in an existing frequency band and in shared mode – i.e. without exclusivity and with

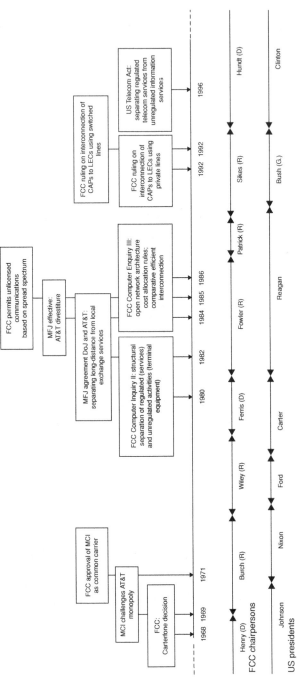

Figure 2.7 US telecommunication reform

Notes: MFJ is the Modification of Final Judgement ruling of 1982, between the Department of Justice (DoJ) and AT&T. CAPs are competitive access providers. LECs are local exchange carriers. D = Democrat, R = Republican.

limited protection against interference. As Marcus has observed on the lack of strong opposition to the assignment: 'Microwave ovens do not protest.' Moreover, there was not yet a strong perception of scarcity. The introduction of cellular systems in the United States was in its infancy: the FCC had started the acceptance of applications for cellular licences in 1982, and in 1983 the first cellular system had been introduced in Chicago. The mobile phone boom would not start until the early 1990s.

Another interesting aspect is that the technology to be used is prescribed as part of the FCC Rule and Order: spread spectrum – in either the frequency-hopping or direct-sequence variant. Moreover, requirements are set to facilitate coexistence within the ISM bands in terms of power levels and coding scheme. As the propagation of RF signals is dependent on the frequency band being used, and as frequency bands are assigned to specific applications and users or user groups, it is not uncommon for NRAs to prescribe the type of technology to be used for RF applications. This sets off the innovation process in a particular direction, however; it also assumes that there is adequate knowledge within the NRA to make the appropriate decisions.

Subsequent to the change in governance of the RF spectrum (at layer 3 in Figure 1.2), it was NCR operating as an economic actor (at layer 1) that optimised its resource allocations in the light of market demand and technological opportunities, and decided to invest R&D resources for exploring the feasibility of spread spectrum in the implementation of local area networks. Based on the availability of the knowledge required, it selected the most appropriate location for the execution of the feasibility study: its Engineering Centre in Utrecht.

Notes

1 The FCC is an independent US government agency, directly responsible to Congress. It was established by the Communications Act of 1934 and is charged with regulating interstate and international communications by radio, television, wire, satellite and cable. The FCC's jurisdiction covers the fifty states, the District of Columbia and US possessions (see 'About the FCC' at www.fcc.gov/aboutus.html (accessed 5 January 2007)).

2 When the FCC receives petitions for new rule making, or recognises a need to make a rule change, it has to organise a public consultation in the form of a notice of inquiry. The public at large are invited to comment within a set period, after which the FCC processes the comments, and the public are requested to provide comment on the comments – the so-called reply comments. All comments have to be addressed in the subsequent consultation round, the so-called notice of proposed rulemaking. In this paper, the FCC also provides the proposed new rules with the reasons for its choices. This round is also followed by a comment and reply comment period.

Again, the FCC has the obligation to address all comments and reply comments, and it publishes the results in a Report and Order (R&O). Sometimes a further notice of proposed rulemaking (FNPRM) is included when the Order is only partially completed. A comment and reply comment period automatically follows the FNPRM. Issues found in the Order can be appealed only in petitions for reconsideration.

3 Personal communication with Michael Marcus, 2007.

4 Spread spectrum includes a number of methods: frequency hopping, direct sequence or pseudo-noise (PN), time hopping, pulsed FM and hybrid spread -spectrum systems.

The FNPRM 81–413 provides the following definitions:

(t) Spread Spectrum Systems. A spread spectrum system is an information bearing communications system in which: (1) information is conveyed by modulation of a carrier by some conventional means; (2) the bandwidth is deliberately widened by means of a spreading function over that which would be needed to transmit the information alone. (In some spread spectrum systems, a portion of the information being conveyed by the system may be contained in the spreading function.)

(u) Direct Sequence Systems. A direct sequence system is a spread spectrum system in which the incoming information is usually digitised, if it is not already in a binary format, and modulo 2 added to a higher speed code sequence. The combined information and code are then used to modulate a [sic] RF carrier. Since the high speed code sequence dominates the modulating function, it is the direct cause of the wide spreading of the transmitted signal.

(v) Frequency Hopping Systems. A frequency hopping system is a spread spectrum system in which the carrier is modulated with the coded information in a conventional manner causing a conventional spreading of the RF energy about the carrier frequency. However, the frequency of the carrier is not fixed but changes at fixed intervals under the direction of a pseudorandom coded sequence. The wide RF bandwidth needed by such a system is not required by a spreading of the RF energy about the carrier but rather to accommodate the range of frequencies to which the carrier frequency can hop.

(w) Time Hopping Systems. A time hopping system is a spread spectrum system in which the period and duty cycle of a pulsed RF carrier are varied in a pseudorandom manner under the control of a coded sequence. Time hopping is often used effectively with frequency hopping to form a hybrid time-division, multiple-access (TDMA) spread spectrum system.

(x) Pulsed FM Systems. A pulsed FM system is a spread spectrum system in which a [sic] RF carrier is modulated with a fixed period and fixed duty cycle sequence. At the beginning of each transmitted pulse, the carrier frequency is frequency modulated causing an additional spreading of the carrier. The pattern of the frequency modulation will depend upon the spreading function which is chosen. In some systems the spreading function is a linear FM chirp sweep, sweeping either up or down in frequency.

(y) Hybrid Spread Spectrum Systems. Hybrid spread spectrum systems are those which use combinations of two or more types of direct sequence, frequency hopping, time hopping and pulsed FM modulation in order to achieve their wide occupied bandwidths.

5 Spread spectrum was therefore a modulation method that was not permitted. The FCC states the following (NPRM 81–143): 'Although most spread spectrum systems

are presently used in government applications, there are some non-government systems also in operation. In some instances, the existing Rules and Regulations allow such operation, in other cases, permission to operate has been obtained through special authorization. Under Section 90.209(b) and under footnote US217 in Section 2.106 of the Rules and Regulations, spread spectrum systems for radio location purposes can be licensed for operation in the 420–435 MHz [megahertz] band. Also, special authorization was given to the Amateur Radio Research and Development Corporation to conduct spread spectrum tests in the 50.0–54.0, 144–148 and 220–225 MHz bands. Under Part 25 of the Rules and Regulations which deals with Satellite Communications, licensees are only required to meet certain power attenuation standards and are not limited in operation by any specific emission designators. This, plus the wide bandwidth available in the 4.4–4.7 GHz [gigahertz] band, has enabled e.g. Equatorial Communications Company to use spread spectrum in its satellite communications.'

6 This underlay approach was similar to the approach the FCC adopted in 2003 for ultra-wideband (UWB), but in 1981 it was an idea ahead of its time.

7 The 'notice' part asked for further comments on the measurement techniques.

8 No limitations on the antenna gain were specified. The 1W limit was determined on the basis of a coverage area of one mile.

9 The product name was Arlan.

10 It was implemented as an extension to the 1977 Telephone Expansion Project to build a complete, new fixed telephone network for the Kingdom of Saudi Arabia, awarded to the Philips–Ericsson joint venture.

11 The precursor of Qualcomm was Linkabit, established by Jacobs, Viterbi and Klein-rock in 1968 as a consulting company. It was mainly involved in technology related to military and governmental contracts. Linkabit was acquired by M/A-COM in 1980. As M/A-COM was focused on exploiting proven technology, while Jacobs, Viterbi and Kleinrock were always working at the 'bleeding edge', Jacobs left the company in 1 April 1985.

12 This passage is based on a communication between Michael Marcus and Kevin Kelley, a former staff member of the FCC who became the head of the regulatory office of Qualcomm in Washington, DC.

13 This section is drawn primarily from the PhD dissertation by Urs von Burg, which was published in 2001 as a book under the title *The Triumph of Ethernet*.

14 This token ring principle would also be applied at Cambridge University in the so-called Cambridge Ring. Rather than using one token, this deployed the empty slot principle, providing stations more opportunities to send a message (von Burg, 2001).

15 Metcalfe proposed increasing the retransmission intervals in line with increasing traffic loads. For a more extensive discussion of the technical features, see Schwartz (1987: chap. 8, 'Polling and random access in data networks') and Tanenbaum (1996: chap. 4, 'The medium access sublayer').

16 The Alto was the unit that Steve Jobs saw in his December 1979 visit to PARC, and it provided him with the inspiration for the Apple Mac. The cost of the Alto was US$70,000. As Marcus observes: 'The genius of Jobs was keeping 80% of the value for 5% of the cost' (personal communication with Michael Marcus, 2009).

17 ARCnet had a head start of two to three years on Ethernet, which started shipping in 1979/80. It operated at comparable speeds – 2.5 Mbit/s – on a cable that was easy to install and allowed for the foolproof attachment of nodes. The cabling was often pre-installed, as IBM used the same wire for its terminal system. The ARC system was a token ring and operated on a hub technology. ARCnet had a price advantage over Ethernet: US$1,400 per node, against US$3,000–4,000 per node (von Burg, 2001: 96).

18 Included are the revenues from 3Com, Bridge Communications, Cabletron, Chipcom, Corvus, Excelan, Gateway, Interlan, Nestar, Network Systems, Novell, Proteon, SynOptics, Sytek, Ungermann-Bass and Vitalink. Excluded are companies such as Apple, Datapoint, DEC, IBM, Intel, Wang and Xerox, as no separate LAN revenues could be obtained. The product introduction dates are approximate (von Burg, 2001: 101, 218–19).

19 For those 'geeks' who want to know the code's property: the periodic and aperiodic autocorrelation function of this length 11 code is 'bounded' by one. As it happens, it turned out that this was an already known code called the Barker sequence, used in radar systems, and van Driest had simply rediscovered it.

20 Design Note 3 1987 by Tuch.

21 Design Note 8 1988 by Tuch.

22 The timeline is based primarily on ITU (1965), Kurzweil (1999) and von Burg (2001).

23 In 2003 the Dutch Ministry of Economic Affairs initiated a project to assess the Dutch position with respect to innovation and knowledge in the field of ICT. The author's contribution to this project involved an interview with Bruce Tuch, which can be considered the genesis of the Wi-Fi book project (Cap Gemini Ernst &Young, Strategy Academy and Zenc, 2004).

24 A more explicit case of a company benefiting from early involvement in military and government contracts related to spread spectrum is Qualcomm and its predecessor Linkabit (Mock, 2005).

25 The FCC has no jurisdiction over radio spectrum use by the federal government, which the Communications Act gives to the president, who has in turn delegated it to the National Telecommunications and Information Administration (NTIA) (private communication with Michael Marcus, 2009).

26 The FCC is directed by five commissioners appointed by the president and confirmed by the Senate for five-year terms, except when filling an unexpired term. The president designates one of the commissioners to serve as chairperson. Only three commissioners may be members of the same political party. None of them can have a financial interest in any FCC-related business (FCC, 2007).

References

Abbate, J. (1999). *Inventing the Internet*. Cambridge, MA: MIT Press.

Cap Gemini Ernst & Young, Strategy Academy and Zenc (2004). *ICT Innovation in Nederland: Een Strategische Analyse van het Nederlandse ICT-Innovatiesysteem*. The Hague: Ministry of Economic Affairs.

Fagan, M. D. E. (1975). *A History of Engineering and Science in the Bell System*, vol. I, *The Early Years (1875–1925)*. Murray Hill, NJ: Bell Telephone Laboratories.

FCC (1985). 'First Report and Order in the matter of authorization of spread spectrum and other wideband emissions not presently provided for in the FCC Rules and Regulations', General Docket no. 81–413. Washington, DC: FCC.

(2007). 'Equipment authorizations: DSS – Part 15, spread spectrum transmitter'. Available at www.fcc.gov (accessed 1 August 2007).

Fischer, C. S. (1992). *America Calling: A Social History of the Telephone to 1940*. Berkeley: University of California Press.

ITU (1965). *From Semaphore to Satellite: Celebrating the Centenary of the ITU*. Geneva: ITU.

(1998). *Radio Regulations*. Geneva: ITU.

Kurzweil, R. (1999). *The Age of Spiritual Machines: When Computers Exceed Human Intelligence*. New York: Penguin.

Lemstra, W. (2006). 'The Internet bubble and the impact on the development path of the telecommunication sector'. Dissertation. Department of Technology, Policy and Management, Delft University of Technology, Delft.

Lemstra, W., and V. Hayes (2009). 'The shaping of the IEEE 802.11 standard: the role of the innovating firm in the case of Wi-Fi'. In K. Jakobs (ed.). *Information Communication Technology Standardization for E-Business Sectors: Integrating Supply and Demand Factors*. Hershey, PA: IGI Global, 98–126.

Lemstra, W., V. Hayes and M. van der Steen (2009). 'Network modernization in the telecom sector: the case of Wi-Fi'. In R. W. Künneke, J. P. M. Groenewegen and J.-F. Auger (eds.). *The Governance of Network Industries: Institutions, Technology and Policy in Reregulated Infrastructures*. Cheltenham: Edward Elgar, chap. 6.

Lundvall, B.-A. (1992). *National Systems of Innovation: Towards a Theory of Innovation and Interactive Learning*. London: Pinter.

Marcus, M. (2000). 'Commercial spread spectrum background'. PowerPoint presentation, available at www.marcus-spectrum.com/documents/Orlando_000.ppt (accessed 28 June 2007).

Melody, W. H. (1999). 'Telecom reform: progress and prospects'. *Telecommunications Policy*. **23** (1), 7–34.

(2002). 'Designing utility regulation for 21st century markets'. In E. S. Miller and W. J. Samuels (eds.). *The Institutionalist Approach to Public Utility Regulation*. East Lansing: Michigan State University Press, 25–81.

Meurling, J., and R. Jeans (1994). *The Mobile Phone Book: The Invention of the Mobile Telephone Industry*. London: CommunicationsWeek International.

MITRE Corporation (1980). *Potential Use of Spread Spectrum Techniques in Non-government Applications*. Springfield, VA: National Technical Information Service.

Mock, D. (2005). *The Qualcomm Equation: How a Fledgling Telecom Company Forged a New Path to Big Profits and Market Dominance*. New York: AMACOM.

NCR (2007). 'About NCR – history'. Available at www.ncr.com/history/history.htm. (accessed 1 May 2007).

Nelson, R. R. (ed.) (1993). *National Innovation Systems: A Comparative Analysis*. Oxford: Oxford University Press.

Saxenian, A. (1994). *Regional Advantage: Culture and Competition in Silicon Valley and Route 128*. Cambridge, MA: Harvard University Press.

Schot, J., and Geels, F. (2007). 'Niches in evolutionary theories of technical change: a critical survey of the literature'. *Journal of Evolutionary Economics*. **17** (5), 605–22.

Schwartz, M. (1987). *Telecommunication Networks: Protocols, Modeling and Analysis*. Reading, MA: Addison-Wesley.

Tanenbaum, A. S. (1996). *Computer Networks*. Upper Saddle River, NJ: Prentice-Hall.

Von Burg, U. (2001). *The Triumph of Ethernet: Technological Communities and the Battle for the LAN Standard*. Stanford, CA: Stanford University Press.

Wikipedia (2006). 'NCR corporation'. Available at http://en.wikipedia.org/wiki/NCR_Corporation (accessed 1 May 2007).

3 Creating a wireless LAN standard: IEEE 802.11

Kai Jakobs, Wolter Lemstra and Vic Hayes,
with contributions from Bruce Tuch and Cees Links

3.1 The start of wireless LAN product development[1]

After the wireless LAN feasibility study had ended with positive results, the development team in Utrecht persuaded the Retail Systems Division, the internal customer, that it would be best if product development was also carried out by the same team. Inevitably, this outcome was not achieved without some internal 'turf battles' between the Financial Systems Division and the Retail Systems Division.[2] Again, the debate was decided on the basis of the availability of the necessary radio and communications expertise.

In the spring of 1988 the team set out to develop a wireless network interface card (wireless NIC) in order to create a wireless LAN, to be used in vertical applications in the retail markets that NCR was serving. The NIC would have to operate in the 902 to 928 MHz band, the lower band as assigned by the FCC for unlicensed use (FCC, 1985). This lower band was selected so as to provide the maximum possible range, as opposed to the ISM bands at 2.4 and 5 GHz, which have higher levels of attenuation. Another reason was to reduce the cost of the electronics, as at that time radio-processing components above 1 GHz were expensive, on account of the level of technology that was required and the relatively low volume of business.

A critical component of any LAN is the data link layer (DLL), as defined in the Open Systems Interconnection model (see Figure 2.4). With the approval of the IEEE Ethernet standard in 1985, the use of this OSI model had become common practice in the implementation of wired LANs, thanks to being pushed by end users and industry. The creation of a new medium access control protocol, as part of the DLL, was the focus of the development effort. The MAC controls the information flow on the multi-access channel. This is not a trivial affair, as this type of protocol is fairly complex, and the wireless dimension adds to the complexity. This is why, in order to limit costs and reduce the development time, the NCR team intended to leverage existing MAC designs as much as possible and to make use of existing protocol standards whenever it was practicable.

3.1.1   The role of standards within NCR

Within NCR, de facto standards had been a curse rather than a blessing, because they were being confronted with proprietary protocols. Although the company was a leading provider of point-of-sale terminals, most of the time these terminals had to be connected to a back office computing system, supplied more often than not by the leading mainframe provider, IBM. Having a dominant position in this market, IBM used proprietary protocols to connect terminal equipment to its mainframes and minicomputers. As a result, much of the protocol expertise of the Utrecht development team originated in its analysis and subsequent emulation of IBM protocols. When NCR had the opportunity to supply both the front and back office systems it allowed the use of proprietary protocols, so as to create competitive differentiation in the features it provided. For products outside its core business, however, the company prescribed the use of open standards. Bruce Tuch provides the rationale and the decision to go in any event for a standards-based approach:

Any proprietary system outside the scope of the core was considered to dilute the R&D efforts, and it could also open up new 'choke points' by other companies. Therefore the business units that attended to standards that were seen to be in the interest of NCR received funding through the corporate R&D organisation. Although our WLAN product was aimed at the vertical retail markets, and according to corporate rules would not require a standards-based interface, it was understood that if we worked towards a standard the total market in the future would be greater than the relatively small vertical retail niche. At that time we had no idea how much bigger this would really become!

Until the mid-1980s the position of NCR with regard to the making of standards can best be described as that of an 'observer' or 'adopter'. These are the two most passive of the four different categories of participation that can be distinguished based on the amount a company contributes to the creation of a new standard (classification adapted from: Updegrove, 2006):

(1) Observers   (2) Adopters   (3) Contributors   (4) Leaders

The main motivation of an *observer* for participating in standard-setting bodies (SSBs) is considered to be intelligence gathering.[3] They do not contribute to the creation of the standard, but want to be fully appraised of the development of the standard and the consequences if the standard is adopted. Their level of participation in standards meetings is guided by this need; typically, they either do not want or are unable to invest any significant resources in the effort. This group comprises mostly academics, consultants and system integrators. Representatives of the development team in Utrecht were *observers*, for instance, in the Dutch national standards institute (the NNI), in the International Organization for Standardization (ISO), the European Computer Manufacturers Association (ECMA) and the International Telecommunication Union – Telecommunication Standardization Sector (ITU-T), at that time known as the CCITT (International Telegraph and Telephone Consultative Committee).

As an *adopter*, a company is considered an active participant in the process of making standards. *Adopters* have a strong interest in understanding the intricacies of the implementation of the standard once it has been adopted, but they are not strong contributors to the development of the content of the standard. Large users, small and medium-sized (SME) vendors and manufacturers (as 'industry followers') are typically found in this category. In the 1970s and 1980s NCR was very active in ECMA, ITU–T, NNI, the American National Standards Institute (ANSI) (through headquarters – Don Johnson) and ISO to influence the final shape of the HDLC and X25 standards recommendations.

As a *contributor*, a company is an active participant in the process, and submits proposals aimed at the development of the content of the standard. Nonetheless, it is less interested in, or lacks the resources for, influencing the strategic direction of a standards body or industry consortium. Next to contributing to (parts of) the content, *contributors* also have a strong interest in understanding the intricacies of implementing the (full) standard once adopted. Innovating companies and manufacturers typically constitute this category. As a *contributor*, NCR assumed chairmanship positions in ECMA and ISO through Kees Houter.

The fourth category identified by Updegrove is the 'leader'. This consists of companies for which participation in a certain standard-setting activity is business critical. They may even, if required, create a new consortium to establish a platform for the standardisation work they consider to be crucial. They are prepared to make a large investment in such an activity. For these companies, the strategic benefit of participating in a given standards effort can far outweigh its costs. *Leaders* aim to control the strategy of an SSB,[4] rather than merely participate in its activities. Large vendors, manufacturers and service providers are typical representatives of this category. In the creation of the wired LAN standards, the DIX alliance and IBM were examples of *leaders* (see also Chapter 2, section 3.1).

Recognising the NCR strategy vis-à-vis the use of standards, the task at hand for the development team was, according to Tuch,

to find the right medium access control protocol, preferably one that was already standardised and implemented for a different medium, that could be used in our first wireless product.

3.1.2   In search of an existing MAC protocol

Finding an appropriate MAC was, in essence, a search for an existing MAC protocol already being implemented using a wireless medium, or to find a MAC implemented for another medium, such as twisted pair copper or coaxial cable, that could be adapted to wireless use. Tuch tells the story of this search, and how the link with the IEEE as a relevant standard-developing organisation came about:

I knew already of ALOHA, which was one of the first wireless radio protocols, and derivatives of this that morphed into Ethernet and later the IEEE 802.3 standard (see also Chapter 2, section 3). This was a CSMA/CD-based mechanism, which relied on the wired medium to be able to detect collisions. In a wireless environment we could not use this same mechanism, but given that this was already ALOHA-like and therefore 'wireless friendly' this was one of the development avenues we started to pursue. At the same time, while looking at the standards for LANs, another possible choice emerged: the medium access control used in the token bus standard, which was very recently approved as IEEE 802.4.

Being 'just a simple engineer', when I dived into the materials of the different standards organisations they seemed more like United Nations documents of engagement, and my eyes would roll. Luckily, NCR supported standard-making activities in various bodies. Vic Hayes was one of the experts who could guide one through this maze. It became clear that the standards body we needed to focus on was the IEEE, and in particular the '802' committee, given the market acceptance of this body for the standardisation of wired LANs. I also understood from Vic that, while working group 802.3 was still fully engaged with the next generation of Ethernet (going to 10 Mbit/s), the token bus group needed to add wireless as another medium for the standard to survive in the market. This was pushed by the industrial automation and control companies, which had very stringent requirements on the quality of service (QoS) because of their control applications: the time a data packet would need to get from the source to the destination had to be bounded by tight limits. Of course, this market was not as large as the generic LAN market that Ethernet was attacking, using a 'best try' more random mechanism. As a result, the total solution costs for token bus would remain high without enough silicon vendors getting into the game. It would also turn out, as Ethernet increased the data rates, that even its basic random nature would still have a tight enough bound to apply to these demanding industrial applications, and as a consequence token bus would lose even more market share.

We recognised that having an already established group within IEEE 802 to sponsor a new protocol layer was a much faster process than trying to start a new standard from scratch. From Vic, who had done the groundwork, I understood that there was an '802.4l' task group already working on a wireless variant driven by General Motors, but it seemed that it was 'losing steam'.[5]

The Institute of Electrical and Electronic Engineers has evolved into a US-based standard-developing organisation. The standardisation fields it covers ranges from power engineering standards through computer interface standards, such as the Ethernet, firewire and the wireless standards, to electromagnetic compatibility and the National Electrical Safety Code (NESC), which the IEEE publishes exclusively. The IEEE is a standard-developing organisation accredited by ANSI, and it has become a focal point for IT-related standardisation efforts.

At this point it is worthwhile to compare the United States and Europe in terms of their standardisation practices.

3.1.3 Differences in making standards

The United States and Europe have traditionally been the powerhouses in ICT standardisation.[6] The standard-setting environments of the two regions have very different characteristics, however. Whereas the United States favours an almost exclusively market-based, bottom-up approach to ICT standardisation, the European Commission (EC) uses standards as part of its regulatory policies – largely to achieve its objective of creating a common market in Europe – thus following a top-down approach.

In the United States there are over 250 ANSI-accredited national SDOs (ANSI, 2007a), and in Europe there are three European Standards Organisations (ESOs) plus thirty national standards bodies. These numbers highlight the two different approaches. The US system is highly decentralised and comprises organisations each of which typically serves one specific industry sector. Government agencies are encouraged to contribute actively to standard setting and to standards policy, in close cooperation with ANSI and the National Institute of Standards and Technology (NIST), which coordinates standards policy between the federal agencies (ANSI, 2007b). The US administration does not intervene in the process, however, and nor does it mandate any standards. Consequently, the individual agencies are free to select those standards that best meet their individual needs. In such a distributed environment, with largely autonomous actors, the maintenance of a coherent set of standards, with no conflicting specifications, is next to impossible. Accordingly, the United States standards strategy requires only that '[t]he process encourages coherence to avoid overlapping and conflicting standards' (ANSI, 2005).

The European approach differs in several respects. For one, the EC can (and does) issue standardisation mandates to the three ESOs (CEN, CENELEC and ETSI). Under the 'New Approach' to standardisation, 'legislative harmonisation is limited to essential safety requirements (or other requirements in the general interest) with which products put on the market must conform . . . ' (EC, 1985). These 'essential . . . requirements' are defined in directives; the ESOs are then charged with developing the harmonised European standards that specify how to meet them. In addition, not all standards are equal. European standards, while still strictly voluntary in nature, clearly enjoy priority over all other standards: '[T]he authorities are obliged to recognise that products manufactured in conformity with harmonised standards are presumed to conform to the essential requirements established by the Directive' (EC, 1985). Moreover, the EC has a clear preference for European standards, as in public procurement: 'If the producer does not manufacture in conformity with these [harmonised European] standards, he has an obligation to prove that his products conform to the essential requirements' (EC, 1985).

Obviously, in practice companies that wish to do business in European Union (EU) countries may consider the application of European standards not to be 100 per cent voluntary. Last, but certainly not least, the European Commission does have an influence over the European Standards Organisations. This may primarily be attributed to the fact that a significant percentage of the ESOs' funding comes from the EC (and this influence does not manifest itself exclusively as harmonised European standards). In the European Union, the EC also establishes the rules for the cooperation between the individual ESOs, on the one hand, and between ESOs and national bodies, on the other (EC, 1998). As a result, European standards are not in conflict with each other, nor are national standards in conflict with European ones.

The individual US-based SDOs are accredited by ANSI, which also coordinates their activities. For accreditation, the SDOs need to comply with ANSI's 'essential requirements' (ANSI, 2006), which lay down the characteristics of the standard-setting process that US national SDOs need to implement. A clear focus here is on process attributes such as openness and transparency, with particular importance assigned to 'due process'.[7] That 'the US standardization infrastructure is firmly rooted in American history and experience' (ANSI, 2007b) and that 'due process' is a central notion of the US constitution may help explain this assigned importance. Interestingly, neither the Comité Européen de Normalisation (CEN) 'Internal regulations' nor the European Telecommunications Standards Institute (ETSI) 'Directives' explicitly mention due process, although they do apply the associated mechanisms and procedures.

ANSI is also the only US representative on international and regional bodies (such as ISO and the International Electrotechnical Commision – IEC). In Europe, the ESOs basically represent regional mirror organisations of the three international bodies; see also Figure 3.1.

3.1.4   Engaging with the IEEE

While operating from the Netherlands the NCR development team started to engage with the US-based IEEE organisation to identify an appropriate MAC protocol, with the 802.4l task group being the first group that was targeted. Tuch continues his account:

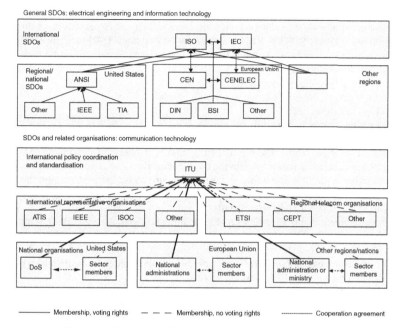

General SDOs: electrical engineering and information technology

SDOs and related organisations: communication technology

Figure 3.1 International relationships between SDOs, the United States and
the European Union
Note: Refer to Annex 1 for explanation of acronyms.

I joined Vic Hayes to a meeting of the 802.4l task group that was focused on the
application of the token bus protocol to the wireless media, using the token bus medium
access control protocol. The chair did not attend any more, but the executive secretary
was available and willing to convene the meeting in July 1988. In the November meeting
Vic was elected to take over the chair of this task group, with most of the early members
coming from a control industry background. For me, this was a real learning experience
in how standard-making works. In the early phase, when it is not yet seen as a large
market opportunity, it tends to be driven by engineers ('you get what you see' types),
who are diving into a technical puzzle. This group also included consultants/engineers,
who are very active, since the vertical specialised markets gave them enough business
opportunities to engage. As the market opportunity gets recognised and people start to
realise that this might become big, then we hit phase 2, and the real fun starts when
more engineering groups and marketing groups are all getting on board. The outcome
of the process is then being driven by totally different forces.

For the NCR team, the work on '802.4' started as phase 1, and this would
generate invaluable lessons as the team initiated phase 1 of '802.11', and later
became one of the key drivers of phase 2. At this point Vic Hayes takes over the
storyline, and recounts his experience in becoming involved in standard-making
within the IEEE.

As I attended for the first time a meeting of the IEEE standards association, I was struck by the peculiar way of conducting a meeting, even having ample experience with participation in ISO and the ITU's Radiocommunication Sector (ITU-R) meetings. All along the meeting, at specific points when there seemed to be an element of agreement, you would hear the following ritual.

Chair: 'I am ready to entertain a motion.'

One of the voting members: 'I move to adopt the agenda.'

Chair: 'Do I hear a second?'

Another voting member: 'Second!'

Chair: 'Is there any discussion? (Hearing no discussion) All in favour, please raise your hands.' The chair counts the raised hands, makes a note and continues: 'All opposing, please raise your hands.' Again the chair counts the raised hands and makes a note, continuing with: 'All abstaining, please raise your hands.' After the count, the chair continues with: 'The vote is X members supporting, Y members opposing and Z members abstaining. The motion passes (fails).'

In my second meeting at IEEE 802.4 I had to chair the task group, and working from imitating the ritual worked fine. I wanted to know more about the system, however, and looked in libraries and bookshops for guidance. The key to the solution appeared to be in the name of the process, *Robert's Rules of Order*, which appeared to be the mandatory way to conduct a meeting in IEEE working groups.

3.1.5   The rules of order in the IEEE

Robert's Rules of Order, as applied within the IEEE, describe the parliamentary procedures developed by a US Army engineer at the end of the nineteenth century. Being stationed at pioneer settlements, he felt embarrassed when asked, without warning, to preside over a meeting without knowing how. He started using a manual based on the rules and customs in conducting business in the British parliament and already being adjusted to American ideas. With his experience in civic and church organisations, he further developed the rules from the original sixteen pages. After his death his heirs continued the development, until today we have the tenth edition, consisting of 704 pages (Robert, 2000 [1876]).

With the book in place, formal assemblies could concentrate on the content of their business, freed from confusion and dispute over the rules governing the use of the different motions of parliamentary law. The rules of order carefully balance the rights of persons and subgroups – that is, they protect the rights of the majority, of the minority (especially a strong minority greater than one-third), of individual members, of absentees, and of all these together.

3.1.6   Robert's Rules of Order

Robert's Rules of Order specify which elements need to be defined in the by-laws of an organisation, what the roles and the tasks of the various officers are in an assembly, such as the chairman, secretary and treasurer, and the rights

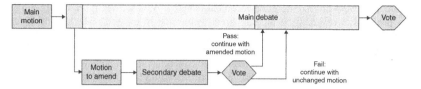

Figure 3.2 Example flow of motions in the IEEE

of ordinary members. It defines what the rules are that define the beginning and the end of a member's voting rights, and the required minimum number of members to be present for an assembly to make legitimate decisions.

The most fundamental rule is that all decisions have to be cast in (main) motions and that only one motion can be on the floor at any time. In the debate each member has no more than two turns to speak on the same motion, with each turn limited to a predetermined time, and when the debate is finished a vote is held. With only one motion permitted on the floor, a system of secondary motions is in place to be able to dispose temporarily of a motion, for instance when other, more pressing business needs to be conducted first, or to amend the motion when the debate indicates that the motion as stated does not meet the majority's need, or to adjourn the meeting. Secondary motions can take precedence over the main motions or other secondary motions in a hierarchy.

As an example, a member would take the floor and make a motion. Another member, interested in the topic, quickly raises his hand and calls: 'Second.' Now we have a main motion on the floor, and the chair entertains a debate. Another member senses that the text of the motion needs to be changed in order to make the motion more acceptable. When he obtains the floor he proposes a motion to amend, and, when seconded, the debate on the main motion yields to the debate on the motion to amend. When no one wants to add to the debate, the chair calls for the vote, and, depending on the result, the debate on the main motion continues with the debate on the same or the amended text of the motion. When the debate on the main motion is exhausted, the chair calls for the vote, and the business continues with the next item, either with a valid motion or a lost motion (see also Figure 3.2).

3.2   NCR involvement in IEEE 802.4: token bus

The involvement of the NCR development team in IEEE 802.4 proved to be of great value for its appreciation of the process of making standards. Tuch continues his account:

The 802.4l task group period was very stimulating. I enjoyed being one of the 'radio experts', being asked by all these already seasoned 'protocol' engineers about what was possible, and we were having great technical debates. As I learned more on how the 802.4 protocol 'worked' it became apparent to me that to try and make this fit with the wireless medium was like trying to use a boat to get across a swamp instead of a hovercraft. The protocol relied on 'tokens', which would be passed between client nodes, and thereby controlled the access to the medium. If a token was 'lost' then a time-consuming and complex recovery algorithm would kick in. Since the medium was wire and reliable, it was assumed that this would be a rare event. With wireless this assumption is not correct, especially in an unlicensed band in which different systems and networks can be in radio range of each other. The medium access protocol on a wireless medium should not be based on this assumption; moreover, it should also correct transmission failures, so that the end result is a reliable transfer of information.

One key philosophical point here, which relates to standards and market leverage, is important. Our product was to enter the vertical market segment for retail point-of-sale communications; it would do so by the creation of a wireless 'end node' connecting all the system components together by a LAN. Another internal goal was to expand this further into office markets not yet being addressed by NCR. Therefore, the applications running on top of this wireless LAN should appear the same to the end customer as if they had been implemented in a wired environment. Hence we had to retain as much as possible the existing protocol stack, both from an engineering development perspective and the customer application experience. Therefore it was vital to make sure we followed the standard interfaces as closely as possible within the OSI communication model. While the data link layer (including the medium access) would be different, as it directly linked to the wireless medium, the remainder of the protocol stack would have to be the same as in any other wired LAN, such as Ethernet. The medium access had to deal with a non-reliable medium in an efficient manner and also deliver data frames as reliable as any wired LAN to the next layer up the stack.

3.2.1   The need for a new MAC protocol

Having concluded that the token bus MAC protocol was not suitable for the purpose, Tuch started to talk with other members of '802.4', with the idea of moving to another medium access solution. One problem in the creation of a new MAC standard within the IEEE rules is the need to show that you are solving a different problem – one that the other MAC standards cannot solve. While this seemed pretty clear for the '802.4' token bus standard, the MAC used as part of '802.3' – the Ethernet standard – might still be adapted. One of the key issues was how to get 'collision detect' implemented using a wireless medium. During a late night 'brainstorming' session following an '802.4l' meeting, Mike Masleid (from Inland Steel) and Tuch worked out a mechanism that would be able to work on '802.3', in which the companies filed a joint patent (Tuch and Masleid, 1991). This solution was presented to the IEEE 802.3 Ethernet standards group, to solicit interest to start a new wireless working group. Vic Hayes relates the story:

NCR proposed the IEEE 802.3 working group for CSMA/CD local area networks to start a wireless extension to its MAC. First Bruce and I gave a two-and-a-half-hour tutorial to the 802.3 group (130 people). Then I led an ad hoc group of about nineteen people to assess the interest for a through-the-air extension of the standard. The result of a straw poll showed that two people would support working in the existing 802.3 working group, nine persons in a new working group and two persons to do both. Reporting this result back to the plenary meeting of 802.3, the meeting passed a motion to suggest to the executive committee deferring the authorisation of a new wireless working group until further study had been carried out; the initiation of a study group would be appropriate at this time.[8]

With the lack of interest in 802.3 established, the political stage was set for a 'starting from scratch' with a new wireless MAC standard, not hindered by any legacy issues.

3.3   Standards work within the IEEE

All standards work within the IEEE is performed within the IEEE Standards Association (IEEE-SA). IEEE members can obtain an additional membership of the SA for a small fee.[9] In the IEEE, organisation policy matters are decided within the board of governors, while standards matters are decided in the Standards Board. The Standards Board has a number of supporting subcommittees, the most important ones being NesCOM, the New Standards Committee, RevCOM, the Review Committee, and PatCOM, the Patent Committee (see also Figure 3.3 for the organisational structure of the IEEE-SA, highlighting the major organisational entities in the '802.11' wireless working group environment).

All standards work is started through a Project Authorization Request, to be approved by the Standards Board. NesCOM reviews all PARs and advises the board on the approval process.[10] PatCOM advises about the use of intellectual property. IEEE standards may contain patented material, provided that the patent owners have filed a letter stating that they are willing to provide, on request, licences for the use of their patented material against a reasonable fee, without discrimination. The working groups are required to solicit information at each meeting to report whether the draft standard contains patented material. If so, the chair has to solicit the aforementioned letter from the patent owner, and PatCOM then reviews the list of letters received. If, however, the patent holder has not filed the letter, the working group has to develop the specification in such a way that the patented material will not have to be utilised in the implementation of the standard. In the worst case, when no workaround is possible, the project will have to be terminated.

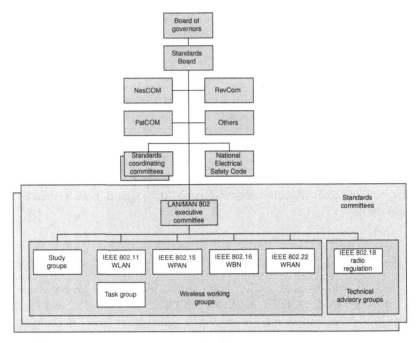

Figure 3.3 IEEE Standards Association structure

Once a proposed standard has been submitted to the Standards Board for approval, RevCOM reviews whether all the procedures have been duly executed, including that for potentially patented matter through PatCOM.

The actual technical work is performed in the standards committees. The coordinating committees deal with general subjects, such as terms and definitions, quantities, units and letter symbols. The standards committees have to be sponsored by one of the IEEE societies.

IEEE working groups are open to anyone to attend, as attendees do not have to be IEEE-SA members – i.e. any materially interested and affected parties can attend any standards development group meeting. A procedure for determining voting rights in the working group is usually established, however, to control the process of participation. This can range from being as simple as 'anyone can vote anytime' to more elaborate rules that allow someone to vote after attending a certain number of meetings (and the right of voting to be contingent on continued attendance). None of these voting rules would preclude an individual's right to participate and comment at any meeting, however.

In addition, all the results of the deliberations in IEEE standard-developing groups are publicly available, usually by means of having readily available minutes of meetings (the term 'minutes' here including members' submissions, agendas, actual minutes, ballot results and draft standards). In the paper era, one could order the documents at a copy service; more recently all documentation has been made available on the web.[11] Approved IEEE standards are available for a fee.[12]

3.3.1   Organisation of the standards work

Standards working groups are tasked with developing and maintaining standards on specific topics. Technical advisory groups advise standards working groups, but do not develop standards. Some have developed codes of practice. Study groups are established to investigate whether there is a need to engage in new projects, and, when the result is positive, to produce the paperwork to start such a project.

The executive committee oversees the overall work of the standards committees, and is in this case responsible for maintaining the IEEE 802 *Policies and Procedures Manual*. The membership includes all chairpersons of standards working groups and technical advisory groups.

To organise the work in the working group efficiently, experts are assigned into task groups for each topic. Each task group is responsible for executing the assigned task within a specific project.

Depending on the working group, individuals have to gain voting rights in each task group. In the 802.11 working group, at first the individual joins as an observer. He or she gains voting rights by the level of participation in the working group. Participation is defined as being in the meeting room for at least 75 per cent of the duration of a session, a session being defined as the meetings held during the course of a week of the conference. After having participated in two plenary sessions, the individual receives voting rights and becomes a member as soon as he/she attends the third plenary, so long as the sessions attended have taken place within four consecutive plenary sessions. There are two reasons for these requirements for becoming a member: to prevent any individual from simply walking in and exercising voting rights; and to ensure that the individual has gained an understanding of the rules and has obtained (some) topical knowledge before casting a vote.

After gaining membership status, members have to maintain this status by participating in at least two out of four consecutive meetings and returning two letter ballots out of each three consecutive letter ballots. These rules have been made so as to maintain the quorum level, as well as the letter ballot response level: a letter ballot is considered to fail if fewer than 50 per cent of the members return their vote.

The members of the executive committee guarantee their commitment in the following way:[13]

Any person to be confirmed by the Executive Committee shall, prior to confirmation by the EC, file with the Recording Secretary a letter of endorsement from their supporting entity (or themselves if self supporting). This letter is to document several key factors relative to their participation on the Executive Committee and is to be signed by both the Executive Committee member and an individual who has management responsibility for the prospective Committee member. This letter shall contain at least the following:

(a) statement of qualification based on technical expertise to fulfil the assignment,
(b) statement of support for providing necessary resources (e.g., time, travel expenses to meetings), and
(c) recognition that the individual is expected to act in accordance with the conditions stated in sub clause 7.1.3.1 Voting Guidance dealing with voting 'as both a professional and as an individual expert'.

3.4   The start of IEEE 802.11

The process for a new standardisation project within IEEE normally starts when an individual presents a proposal for a new project. A call for expressions of interest is then sent out, and, if sufficient interest[14] is generated, a study group is established with the task of studying the proposal's merits and coming up with a list of criteria.[15] When all the criteria can be met, the paperwork is submitted to the new standards committee, NesCOM, and once approval has been given a working group is established in order to prepare a draft. Hayes relays the course of events for the new MAC protocol:

Although the 802.3 motion had suggested the initiation of a study group, we strongly preferred to start directly with a new working group. Under the leadership of Bruce Tuch the individuals interested in establishing a wireless local area network standard quickly generated the necessary paperwork for the 'reassignment' of the 802.4l PAR to a new working group. I assumed the leadership for the process and guided this PAR through the IEEE organisation. On Thursday 13 July 1990 the IEEE 802 executive committee passed a motion, with only one negative vote, to establish a new working group IEEE 802.11; it considered the work done in IEEE 802.4l and the decision taken by IEEE 802.3 as the equivalent of running a study group.[16] Subject to the subsequent approval by the Standards Board the new 802.11 working group was born, and I was appointed as the interim chairperson.

3.4.1   NCR taking the lead

In September 1990, at the first meeting of the 802.11 working group, Hayes was elected as the chairman, and he was affirmed at the plenary meeting held in November for the period till the next March meeting, in 1992. As the outgoing chair of the 802.4l task group he had already led the initial work on the Project

Authorization Request. The work in the first year was the preparation of a definitive PAR, the writing of comments in response to FCC procedures and preparing a requirements document including an analysis of the necessary services. All this work had been executed in plenary format.

At the November 1991 meeting of the working group two task groups[17] were established, the MAC group and the PHY[18] group. Following the practice within IEEE 802.4, all individuals attending the task group meetings received voting privileges. Throughout the work on the base standard this position remained the same. The first assignment of the task groups was to send out the requests for proposals (RFPs) to establish the technological foundation for the MAC and the PHY standard to be developed.

On a case-by-case basis the subgroups made their own rules for what materials the proponents had to submit for the '802.11' membership in order for a well-informed decision to be made. Once the proposals were available, the two groups had the task of selecting the appropriate technology for the project. In most of the cases the task groups used a process of selection whereby, in each round of voting, the proposal with the lowest number of supporting votes would be removed from the list, until a proposal achieved majority support.[19] The proposal would then be submitted to the working group for approval as the technological basis for the draft standard.

3.4.2   The need to explain opposition in voting

To obtain results in a standard-setting body the mechanism that is used to obtain increasing support for a particular proposal is crucial. Within the IEEE, this is facilitated by the requirement that individuals opposing a proposal in a vote have to explain the reasons for their opposition. By making these reasons explicit the group as a collective is invited to find ways to resolve the issue, and if this process is successful it has the effect of broadening the support for the resulting proposal. This principle is applied at task group level as well as at working group level, where the draft is tested for submission to the Standards Board. Hayes explains the procedure:

Once the task group has a mature draft, it is put to the test of a working group letter ballot. The vote is on the question 'To send draft IEEE 802.11x version Y for sponsor letter ballot'. A working group letter ballot is sent out to the members and observers of the working group, requesting them to return their comments and their votes in writing within the set time.[20] The by-laws require that the response time shall be at least thirty days.[21] The members can have a choice from three options: (1) approve, with non-binding comments; (2) do not approve; and (3) abstain. 'Do not approve' votes are valid only when they are accompanied by comments saying how the group should change the draft standard so as to change the vote into an 'approve'. This way the group knows how a next draft could have a higher probability of being approved, and, more importantly, political votes can be identified and be disregarded in the process.

A letter ballot is valid if at least 50 per cent of the members have returned their ballots. The ballot is passed when 75 per cent of the sum of votes in the categories 'approve' and 'do not approve' have voted to approve. In a case of a fail, the task group is obliged to address all the votes and prepare a new draft based on the comments available. The new draft, as well as the unresolved 'do not approve' comments, are sent out for a next letter ballot.

Once the 75 per cent approval level has been reached, the new draft is sent out for a working group confirmation letter ballot. In a confirmation letter ballot, balloters may address and base their vote only on material that has been changed in the subjected draft standard, or they may vote 'do not approve' on the basis of the inclusion of an unresolved 'do not approve' comment. In this way, convergence is reached towards an approved draft standard.[22]

After the draft has been approved by the working group, the draft standard is sent out for a sponsor letter ballot under the auspices of the Standards Board. The sponsor letter ballot is composed of members of the IEEE Standards Association who have indicated that they want to be included in the ballot pool for the particular standard. For each draft standard a separate pool is composed. Once established, the membership of the pool is not changed. Most of the rules for the sponsor letter ballot are the same as for the working group letter ballot. The sponsor letter ballot is valid when 75 per cent of the members of the ballot pool have returned their vote and fewer than 30 per cent have abstained. Once the sponsor letter ballot has passed, the draft standard becomes an approved standard.

3.5   Competing proposals within IEEE 802.11

When used in a wireless environment the MAC standard needs to include (over and above the requirements for wireline applications) a 'method of association', to link the mobile station or terminal (computer, hand-held device) to one of the fixed base stations or access points within reach. A terminal device would listen on all available transmission channels to find which access points it can connect with. Subsequently it selects the best access point and transmission channel. When the terminal moves around the quality of the connection may degrade. At that moment it checks again, and if there is a better connection possible using another base station and/or channel a switchover is made. The terminal disassociates from the existing access point and reconnects with the new one.[23] The access points, acting as bridges between the wireline and the wireless network, are informed that the terminal has moved to another access point, and they update their routing tables to ensure that the traffic is routed accordingly.

Used in a wireless environment, the PHY standard would have to define the way the radio waves would have to be accessed, what modulation technique is to be used, the power management mechanism to be implemented and other aspects associated with the physical characteristics of the wireless medium.

3.5.1   The first battleground: IBM versus NCR/Symbol Technologies/Xircom

The first point of contention to emerge in the MAC task group concerned the principle to be used in assigning capacity to a terminal based on the shared use of the radio spectrum. A similar issue in the wired LAN arena had split the industry and led to the approval of three different and incompatible standards within the IEEE: Ethernet, token bus and token ring. For wireless LANs, IBM proposed a centralised approached based on a so-called point control function, while NCR (represented by Wim Diepstraten), together with Symbol Technologies and Xircom, submitted a proposal that supported a decentralised mechanism.[24] The merits of the two proposals were debated intensively. In the end, it was the proposal for a decentralised approach that won the vote, one of the reasons being that this protocol would support 'ad hoc' networking, whereby a terminal would be able to coordinate communications with another terminal independently. Unlike in the case of wired LANs, IBM did not pursue the development of an alternative standard.

3.5.2   The second battleground: frequency hopping versus direct sequence

The second area of contention related to the PHY. In its 1985 Report and Order the FCC had specified two different spread-spectrum modulation techniques that could be used: frequency hopping (FHSS) and direct sequence (DSSS) (see also Chapter 2, note 4). When the issue was put to a vote in the PHY task group, neither of the two modulation techniques obtained the requisite 75 per cent level of support.[25]

The main difference between the two technologies was, in essence, the way in which speed is perceived. FHSS was defined in one proposal as operating at varying speeds – 1, 1.5, 2, 2.5, 3, 3.5, 4 and 4.5 Mbit/s – but in practice it would operate at 1 Mbit/s given the operating environment and the technology available. The proposed standard specified 1 Mbit/s to be mandatory and 2 Mbit/s optional for FHSS. DSSS was defined at 1 and 2 Mbit/s, both mandatory; in practice it would operate at 2 Mbit/s at close range and at 1 Mbit/s for greater distances or under less favourable propagation conditions. At first glance this would appear to favour DSSS over FHSS. In the DSSS option, however, typically only three non-overlapping transmission channels would be available simultaneously. For the FHSS variant, various collocated access points could use different hop sequences. The FH proponents claimed that ten to fifteen access points could be collocated, each using a different sequence, with a resulting aggregate bit rate of ten to fifteen times 1 Mbit/s. Lucent Technologies showed in the trade press that the aggregate throughput would never exceed 4 Mbit/s when eleven access points are used, and even decreases when more than fourteen are used (Kamerman, 1996a, 1996b, 1997).[26] Given the state of the art in the 1995–9 timeframe, three collocated DSSS access points would provide a higher throughput than could be reached with more than eleven collocated FHSS access points.[27]

The proponents of FHSS also claimed that it was easier to implement, while DSSS held out the promise of a more robust system with a higher data rate. The FHSS camp feared that the required investment in silicon would be significant, while individuals in the DSSS camp tried to refute this argument on the basis of their experience in the implementation of pilot versions in silicon.

As neither of the two groups could secure the required level of support, the only way out was to include both modulation technologies in the standard. Thus it was that the adherents of each technique agreed to support the voting and approval process of the other option so that both options reached the required approval level and could be included in the standard.

3.5.3   The third battleground: HomeRF

The initiative for an alternative standard called HomeRF is said to have originated with Proxim, and it led to the establishment of an industry consortium called the HomeRF Working Group (HRFWG) in early 1997, with initial members Proxim, Intel, Microsoft, HP, Compaq and IBM (Negus and Petrick, 2008; Negus, Stephens and Lansford, 2001). The main driver for this development was the perceived inadequacy of the support for isochronous services – i.e. the use of telephony – in the IEEE 802.11 draft specification. At the beginning of 1999 the HRFWG claimed to have seventy plus members, with Intel as an important supporter (Lansford, 1999).[28] The HRFWG adopted the frequency hopping method as the basis for its standard.[29] The HomeRF Shared Wireless Access Protocol – Cordless Access (SWAP-CA) combined portions of the OpenAir frequency hopping PHY as developed by Proxim, the carrier sense multiple access with collision avoidance (CSMA/CA) packet data derived from the PHY of the 802.11 standard and TDMA-based voice support from the Digital European Cordless Telecommunications (DECT) standard. The connection point (base station) would provide the interface with the PSTN or the integrated services digital network (ISDN) for telephony services. The FH method adopted by the HRFWG supported a data rate of 1.6 Mbit/s. HomeRF was positioned as a low-cost solution, with a target price of US$200 for two PCs, having a relaxed PHY specification supporting both isochronous (connection-oriented) and asynchronous (connectionless) traffic. Isochronous traffic is centrally controlled from the control point, while asynchronous traffic is handled in an ad hoc peer-to-peer mode.[30]

The timeline envisaged by the HRFWG was highly ambitious, from a complete functional specification scheduled for the second quarter of 1998 to the launching of the first products in the second half of 1999. In April 2000 Intel announced its Anypoint wireless home networking and in November Proxim unveiled its Symphony HRF (Palo Wireless, 2003).

When the IEEE 802.11b project adopted an 11 Mbit/s data rate, based on a mathematical assertion that the method complied with the FCC rules accepting coding gain as a part of the processing gain (FCC, 1999), the HRFWG announced a second release of the specification for data rates of 6 Mbit/s up to 10 Mbit/s (Negus, Stephens and Lansford, 2001). This required the HRFWG to file a letter requesting an interpretation or waiver at the FCC permitting frequency-hopping devices to widen the channels from 1 MHz to 3 and 5 MHz, which it did on 11 November 1998.[31] Some of the members of the HRFWG, also being members of IEEE 802.11, disagreed with the move and filed letters claiming that the proposal was too heavy for a simple interpretation or waiver. The FCC agreed, and it released a notice of proposed rulemaking, called ET Docket no. 99–231, on 24 June 1999 (FCC, 1999). On 31 August 2000 the FCC released its first Report and Order (FCC, 2000), changing the FH rules, but announcing a second Report and Order while it awaited further measurements on the processing gain. Finally, on 11 May 2001, the FCC released a further notice of proposed rulemaking, which proposed to include in their rules a so called digital transmission system (DTS) that required the transmission to be within 1 W (30 dBm – i.e. 30 decibels (dB), with 0 dB at 1 milliwatt) total power with a power spectral density of 8 dBm for each 3 kHz and a relaxation of the FH rules so that FH devices would be able to hop at frequencies not occupied by DTSs. Both changes opened the way for less interference between FH devices and DTSs, as well as the use of OFDM (orthogonal frequency division multiplexing) modulation, thus opening the way for the enhancement of IEEE 802.11g.

The HomeRF battle in the 802.11 working group was fierce. Hayes provides as an illustration some anecdotal evidence:

The battle went so far that an officer of the IEEE Electromagnetic Compatibility (EMC) committee (who also happened to be an employee of a company with high stakes in the HomeRF work) called me after the September 1999 meeting of IEEE 802.11 coercing me to stop submitting IEEE 802.11 reply comments to the FCC pending approval by that committee, based on the IEEE rules according to that person. I knew the rules of the IEEE very well to state that each group within the IEEE had the freedom to submit papers to the US government, provided the IEEE–USA had approved it. The person was not able to direct me to any evidence that we had to receive approval from the EMC committee. Waiting for the approval of that committee would have been killing for the filing of our comments, as the deadline would have passed.

Despite the support of major players in the industry, the HomeRF initiative failed. According to Jim Lansford, in a personal communication dating from 2007, the reasons for the failure were twofold:[32]

(1) because none of the HRFWG members other than Proxim were developing PHY silicon, they were forced to abandon a PHY that was similar to 802.11 FH and switch to the OpenAir PHY developed by Proxim. Many companies in the HomeRF Working Group felt that this made the standard a proprietary system; and

(2) the adoption of 802.11b in 1999 and its support by several silicon vendors (including Harris and Agere Systems) drove prices down relatively quickly compared to the single silicon source for HomeRF. The HRFWG had assumed that FH products would always be cheaper than DS products, but market competition invalidated that assumption.[33]

Tuch's conclusion, expressed in a personal communication in 2009, is that, in comparison with IEEE 802.11, the HomeRF initiative was 'too little, too late':

The proposed HomeRF standard supported only 1.6 Mbit/s, with the goal to be able to go to a 10 Mbit/s data rate in the future, when the FCC approved the new rule-making proposals. The fact that HomeRF also supported voice services was not a 'market need'; voice was not driving the usage model. Getting the IEEE 802.11b standard at 11 Mbit/s accepted in 1999 was the key nail in the HomeRF coffin.

According to Marcus, again in a 2009 personal communication, a key factor in the demise of HomeRF was the legal strategy deployed by the Wireless Ethernet Compatibility Alliance (later the Wi-Fi Alliance) of delaying Docket no. 99–321, in which the HomeRF Working Group sought a relaxation of the FCC rules. By the time the ruling came out, it was too late.[34]

The HomeRF group was officially disbanded in January 2003 (Shim, 2003).

3.5.4   The fourth battleground: HIPERLAN

Following the FCC's 1985 decision, an ad hoc group on radio LANs (RLANs) within the Conférence des Administrations Européennes des Postes et Télécommunications (CEPT), or European Conference of Postal and Telecommunications Administrations, the body responsible for the harmonisation of spectrum use in Europe, recommended that the 2.4 GHz band destined for ISM applications should be opened for the use of RLAN devices, and it requested ETSI, the body responsible for the development of telecommunication standards in Europe, to develop the necessary standard to define the transmission rules and the measurement standard.[35] In 1991 CEPT assigned the 2.4 GHz

ISM band for RLAN use; on a non-protective and non-interference basis, without the need for an end user licence (CEPT, 1991). In 1993 ETSI approved the measurement standard (ETSI, 1993). This paved the way towards the global allocation of spectrum for wireless LANs.

Once this milestone had been reached the ad hoc group moved on to the next task: searching the radio spectrum for the next free band to accommodate RLANs by studying the allocation rules from 2.5 GHz upwards. The first opportunity occurred at 5,150 to 5,300 MHz, with an optional extension to 5,350 MHz. As often happens in Europe, this portion of the spectrum was earmarked for devices adhering to a specific interoperability standard, in this case the standard tagged HIPERLAN (for high-performance radio local area network), yet to be developed. This decision was ratified by CEPT in 1992 (CEPT, 1992). This band allocation was not combined with ISM applications, and hence there was no need to spread the signal, as in DSSS or FHSS, to create a very robust transmission.

Within ETSI, an ad hoc RLAN group initiated the establishment of Technical Committee ETSI-RES 10 for the development of the HIPERLAN standard. HIPERLAN was aimed at providing high-speed (24 Mbit/s typical data rate) radio local area network communications in the 5 GHz band compatible with wired LANs based on Ethernet and token ring standards.[36] HIPERLAN was aimed to cover a range of 50 m and to support asynchronous and synchronous applications.[37] Restricted user mobility was supported within the local service area only. The specification included the PHY[38] and MAC, and a new sub-layer called channel access and control (CAC) managing the access request to the channels based on priority. Major contributors to the development of the standard were Plessey, Symbionics, Roke Manor, Telia, Apple Europe, NCR, Daimler Benz and the universities of Aachen and Bristol, with the Dutch Ministry for Transport and Public Works acting in an important liaison capacity between CEPT, ETSI and Dutch industry.

Following the establishment of the IEEE 802.11 working group for wireless local area networks in July 1990, Hayes was invited to participate as industry representative in the CEPT project team on RLAN, and in the ETSI Radio Equipment and Systems (ETSI-RES) ad hoc committee on RLAN. This provided the NCR team (and, upon the 1991 acquisition, the AT&T team) in Utrecht with a unique position from which to leverage its activities in the IEEE and ETSI, and to align as far as (politically) possible the activities in the two standard-setting bodies. Again the company volunteered to provide the chairperson, and Jan Kruys became the second chair of ETSI-RES 10. The committee published its first technical specification, HIPERLAN/1, in 1997 (ETSI, 1998; CEPT, 1999).

A second version, HIPERLAN/2, was developed as part of the ETSI-BRAN (Broadband Radio Access Networks) project to provide much higher speeds (up to 54 Mbit/s data rate) for communication in the 5 GHz band, between portable computing devices and broadband asynchronous transfer mode (ATM) and Internet Protocol (IP) networks.[39] This version supported multimedia applications, with emphasis on quality of service aspects. The typical operating environment was indoors. Restricted user mobility was supported within the local service area; wide area mobility (e.g. roaming) was foreseen, but the development of a standard was considered to be outside the scope of the BRAN project. A new type of use has emerged more recently: HIPERLAN/2 as an access network for the Universal Mobile Telecommunications System (UMTS). In this type of use, HIPERLANs would be used both indoors and outdoors, and would be controlled by a licensed network operator.[40] This new requirement would increase the need for a spectrum designation that would allow outdoor use by a subset of HIPERLAN devices. HIPERLAN/2 is a centrally controlled system. This means that all communication is made between a central point, called the access point, and the mobile terminals. The protocol covers the PHY[41] and the MAC. The protocol supports multiple applications and provides for unicast, multicast and broadcast transmissions. A HIPER-LAN2 Global Forum was established to support its deployment, supported by, for example, Bosch, Dell, Ericsson, Nokia, Telia and TI (Palo Wireless, 2003).

During the development of HIPERLAN/2, ETSI-BRAN and IEEE 802.11 were liaising closely, with the unique result that the IEEE 802.11a and the HIPERLAN/2 modulation schemes are both OFDM with almost equal specifications.[42] The MAC protocols remained distinct, as HIPERLAN placed much more emphasis on synchronous applications and the related QoS.

Neither the HIPERLAN/1 standard completed in 1997 nor the HIPER-LAN/2 standard completed in 2004 has become a success.[43] Although Alvarion, Motorola and SICE Communications were involved in early product introductions, the level of acceptance remained so low that there was effectively no competition in the market, such that customers had to choose between products based on either of the two rival standards, IEEE 802.11 and HIPERLAN.

HIPERLAN/2 was optimised for isochronous services, and hence more layers of the OSI protocol stack were affected and needed to be specified, complicating the implementation in comparison with IEEE 802.11. HIPER-LAN/2 is a centralised protocol with a master that controls the other stations. In the IEEE 802.11 protocol there is no need for a recognised 'master and slave', as each device can function as both the base station and the mobile station. As was the case with HomeRF, HIPERLAN/2 also had to compete with a much more matured IEEE 802.11 standard, for which devices had been developed that had already reached a price that was too low to compete with effectively.

3.5.5   The fifth battleground: Lucent Technologies versus Harris versus Micrilor

Following the approval of the 100 Mbit/s Ethernet standard in 1993, high-speed wired LAN products had been introduced onto the market. By the end of 1997 it was becoming clear to everybody in the '802.11' community that higher-speed wireless LANs would also be required. The goal was to implement a 10^+ Mbit/s variant in the 2.4 GHz band and a 50^+ Mbit/s variant in the lower 5 GHz band. The decision was made to keep the MAC the same for both frequency bands. The PHY would have to be different given the different bands; moreover, fewer constraints applied to the use of the 5 GHz band.

The least contentious was the 802.11a variant in the 5 GHz band. There were two main proposals: one from BreezeCom (later Alvarion), and one from Lucent Technologies (represented by Richard van Nee) and NTT, based on OFDM.[44] The voting was won by the Lucent Technologies and NTT combination, leading to a 54 Mbit/s standard.

The voting for the IEEE 802.11b PHY was very divisive and combative, and the depth of feeling was such that the 802.11 working group was on the brink of being torn apart. The main contenders were Harris and Lucent Technologies, and a proposal from an outsider, Micrilor (a start-up company with very good radio knowledge), supported by Clarion, which had serious plans to enter the wireless LAN market. Cees Links[45] recalls the course of events:

When these three remaining proposals were left and subjected to the next round of voting, the Lucent Technologies proposal was voted out. What happened then is hard to describe, and challenged the democratic rules of the IEEE. In the voting Micrilor came out with twenty-nine votes and Harris with twenty-eight votes, with one vote for neither of the two proposals and no abstentions. According to one set of rules, Micrilor had won the vote, but this was immediately contested, as Micrilor did not have a majority of the votes: twenty-nine out of fifty-eight votes is not 'more than 50 per cent'. A violent discussion started to unfold on the interpretation of the outcome of the vote, with many real and emotional arguments floating around.

Then Jeff Abramowitz, the 3Com product manager for wireless LANs, stood up and moved a motion in which he contested the whole voting procedure. According to the rules of the IEEE, an IEEE member engineer should vote for the best technical proposal, and in his assessment, despite the voting having been 'closed', the reality of the voting was that the individual members had voted along 'party' lines – that is, along the line of the company for which they worked. This was true to a great extent, but he phrased his motion in such a way that it was obvious that he was suggesting that the Harris proposal should be declared the winner, as the voting in favour of Micrilor had become an anti-Harris vote. It became clear that 3Com was a Harris supporter. The chaos this motion created was incredible, and the whole meeting went down in flames.

There was a degree of truth in the 3Com statement that most of the Lucent Technologies supporters had decided to side with Micrilor, as otherwise Harris and its supporters would have an unfair advantage in the marketplace, as they already had progressed substantially in their development efforts. In the same week that the IEEE meeting took place, representatives of Lucent Technologies and Harris sat together and acknowledged that a compromise solution had to be reached. Subsequently, Jim Zyren of Harris and Richard van Nee of Lucent Technologies worked out a new radio transmission scheme, different from anything that had been proposed before, called complementary code keying (CCK). The two parties could agree on this alternative proposal, as it would provide improved performance compared to the original Harris proposal and reduced complexity compared to the original Lucent Technologies proposal.[46] Because this suggestion conferred no advantage (or disadvantage) to any other party, the joint proposal was accepted at the next meeting of the working group, six weeks later, resulting in the IEEE 802.11b standard.[47]

3.6   Formal approval of IEEE 802.11 standard

At the November 1993 meeting the foundation technology of the MAC was selected. The first letter ballot on the draft standard was started at the November 1994 meeting. In total, four ballots were needed to reach the required level of 75 per cent support.

The sponsor letter ballot was issued in August 1996, and after two recirculation ballots the draft standard was submitted to the Standards Activities Board (SAB) in August 1997, to be approved at their September meeting and to be published on 10 December 1997 as IEEE 802.11 – 1997 edition, covering frequency hopping at a (mandatory) data rate of 1 Mbit/s and an optional 2 Mbit/s (which was never implemented), and direct sequence at 1 and 2 Mbit/s (both mandatory).[48]

3.6.1   *Approval of the first extensions: IEEE 802.11a and 11b*

With a working group now experienced in developing a standard and all members eager to increase the supported data rate, a study group was established at the November 1996 meeting. Two projects were established, to make extensions to the standard: project 802.11a, for an extension of the standard to support higher data rates in the 5 GHz band, which received its SAB approval in August 1997; and project 802.11b, for an extension of the standard to support higher data rates in the 2.4 GHz band, to be approved in December 1997.[49]

Both were balloted at working group level in November 1998, and then recirculated twice to start the sponsor ballot in April 1999. Following two recirculation ballots, both were submitted to the SAB in August 1999. IEEE 802.11a was officially published on 30 December 1999, covering data rates up to 54 Mbit/s in the 5 GHz band. IEEE 802.11b was published on 20 January 2000, covering an 11 Mbit/s data rate in the 2.4 GHz band.

In parallel with the 802.11a and 11b projects the group also undertook the task of revising the 802.11–1997 standard, with the objective of leading it through the ISO/IEC process in order for it to become adopted as an international standard.

3.6.2   The ISO ratification of the standard

With the European Community planning to limit purchases to products that conformed to harmonised standards (HSs), and the Japanese having similar rules, working group 802.11 decided in 1995 to submit the standard for ISO adoption. In July a proposal for a new work item was submitted to ISO. As an example of the standard-to-be, draft 2 was attached to the proposal. In November 1996 draft 5 was submitted to ISO, which was adopted as draft standard 8802 part 11.

Draft 5 was the subject of the IEEE sponsor ballot process, and standard 8802–11 became the subject of balloting among the international member bodies of the ISO/IEC committee, known as Joint Technical Committee 1 (JTC 1). An additional task therefore arose, namely the synchronisation of the two approval procedures, to the best extent possible. As the IEEE had approved the final version of the standard, the final changes between draft 5 and the approved version were submitted to ISO as comments from the US member body. They were all accepted. The Japanese delegates also came up with comments, however, because their regulations required all radio stations to send out their 'call sign'. This issue was solved in a very pragmatic way, by adding to the text the words 'Some countries impose specific requirements for radio equipment in addition to those specified in this standard' and 'The FHSS PHY shall conform with regulations for out-of-band spurious emissions'.

Following the careful synchronisation of the processes within the two organisations, the revision of IEEE Standard 802.11–1997 was published on 10 August 1999, with the designation ISO/IEC 8802–11:1999 (see Annex 3 for an overview of the IEEE 802.11 family of standards).

3.7   Reflections on the standardisation process in the IEEE

3.7.1   Reflections on participation

After having chaired working group 802.11 for ten years, the maximum period allowed by the IEEE rules and regulations, Hayes offers these thoughts on the role of the participants in the shaping of the wireless LAN standard:

The majority of participants in the 802.11 working group and task groups were sponsored by companies interested in manufacturing and selling devices that needed wireless connectivity, such as bar code readers, cash registers, bank terminals and, later, laptops. They assumed different roles in line with their corporations' objectives. An important category of participant was the consulting companies. Robert O'Hara, one of the 'single person' consultancy companies, assumed the role of the technical editorship of the standard. He turned out to be a very reliable contributor to the work.

In the first couple of years, first in the task group 802.4l and later in the working group 802.11, we had the benefit of having two active user organisations in our membership, General Motors Oshawa, a car manufacturer based in Canada, and Inland Steel, a steel plant south of Chicago. Both needed a dependable wireless system to support their manufacturing operations. Unfortunately, after years of support, they resigned; the time it took to make a standard and obtain a viable product must have been too long. Later, representatives from Boeing participated and exposed the membership to real user concerns and needs.

We also had participation from the academic community, as well as from government agencies, contributing to the channel assignment and to watch our activities related to encryption.

In the beginning of our work, we did not have much information about the propagation characteristics of indoor radio at the frequencies we were interested in. NCR brought in measurement results from within a retail store. From the academic side we received input based on a recent PhD dissertation on indoor radio.[50] Our two user community sponsors (General Motors Oshawa and Inland Steel) provided funding to perform a measurement test at a car manufacturer, and a representative from the NTIA[51] provided reports on his related work.

Over time, the participant level of the working group increased when new technology could be proposed and selected, only to decrease again when the draft standard had to be made ready for the final approval – a period characterised by the crossing of the 't's and the dotting of the 'i's (see also Figure 3.4). Alternatively, might the decline be a result of participants pressed to get their products into production?

During my chairmanship, the members of IEEE 802.11 were very reluctant to schedule parallel meetings; everyone wanted to be at each meeting in order to maintain the knowledge of the technology, as well as to be able to influence the contents. After 2000 the number of task groups grew rapidly, so it would be unreasonable to schedule a single track. Hence the participation grew from an average of 100 to 400, as attendees had to involve their colleagues to oversee all the work that was going on (see Figure 3.5).

Figure 3.6 shows the number of contributions from each company that submitted ten or more papers from the start of IEEE 802.11 in 1990 till the end of 1999. The count in Figure 3.6 includes the documents provided for administrative purposes, such as meeting minutes, agendas, ballot results and planning presentations. With 531 contributions, representing 23 per cent of the total and almost four times as many as the next company in the sequence, the leadership role that NCR, and subsequently AT&T and Lucent Technologies, assumed in the development of the IEEE 802.11 standard becomes obvious.

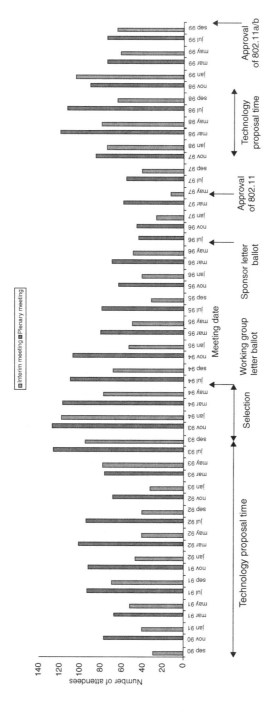

Figure 3.4 Attendee level at IEEE 802.11 meetings

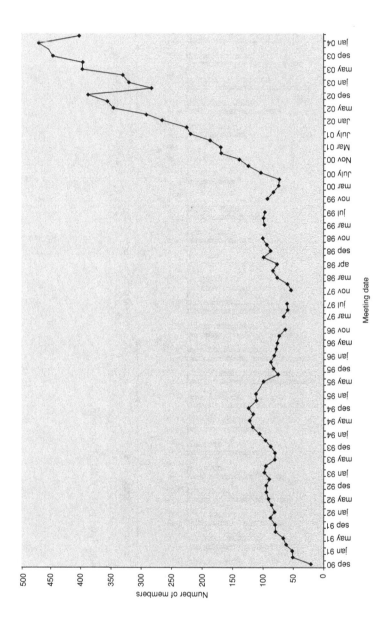

Figure 3.5. Attendance at IEEE 802.11 meetings over time

Source: This figure appears in 'Network modernization in the telecom sector', in *The Governance of Network Industries* (ed. Künneke, Groenewegen and Auger); copyright © 2009, Edward Elgar Publishing; reprinted by permission of the publisher.

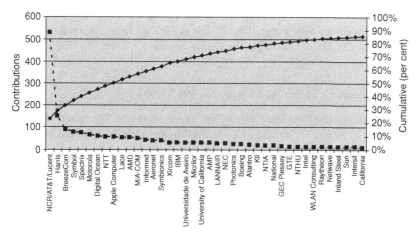

Figure 3.6. Overview of contributions to IEEE 802.11
Source: This figure appears in 'The shaping of the IEEE 802.11 standard', in
*Information Communication Technology Standardization for E-Business
Sectors* (ed. Jakobs); copyright © 2009, IGI Global; reprinted by permission
of the publisher.

3.7.2   Reflecting on the standard-making process

Hayes provides comments on his experience during his tenure as chairperson
on the standard-making process:

I applied the rules very strictly, because I was aware of the fact that millions of dollars
were at stake for the members, and the only way to protect the individual against
allegation is to play by the rules.

The rule of the IEEE 802.11 working group was that voting at working group level
was limited to members only, and at subgroup level all attendees could vote. At one time
this was (mis)used by a professor who voted his patented modulation scheme in two out
of three PHY task groups (one task group for each of the three modulation techniques:
frequency hopping, direct sequence and infrared), bringing in sufficient students to
obtain the 50 per cent level of support at the subgroup level to 'submit the proposal
to the Working Group'. At working group level, however, the request of the subgroup
to get approval for inclusion into the draft standard failed, because here the working
group members could vote, which included the members working in the MAC subgroup.
On several occasions I received threats that the incumbent would appeal either at the
IEEE 802 executive committee or at a court of justice. Because the professor received
the attention during meetings warranted by the *Robert's Rules of Order* and the votes
were authentically taken, however, there was no base for his case.

Nevertheless, with that experience, the rule of IEEE 802.11 was revised to limit voting
to the membership at all levels of the working group except for study groups, much the
same as they were in other working groups. In fact, when the selection procedure on the
MAC took place, the group decided to hold secret votes, so that individuals were not
exposed to company scrutiny.[52]

It is worth noting that, from the first involvement of the NCR team in the standard-making activity within IEEE 802.4l in 1988 until the approval of IEEE 802.11a/b in 1999, a period of eleven years elapsed.

3.8   Summary of the Wi-Fi journey: 1987–1999

Following the positive result of the feasibility study, the NCR team in Utrecht started the product development of a 1 to 2 Mbit/s wireless LAN in the autumn of 1987. The strategy was to use as much as possible of the existing OSI protocol stack, replacing only parts directly related to the wireless medium. As no suitable MAC protocol could be identified, the IEEE 802.11 working group was initiated to develop a new PHY and MAC standard in 1990. The MAC task group discussed the merits of central (IBM) versus distributed control architecture (NCR/Symbol Technologies/Xircom), a debate that was won by NCR and partners. The PHY task group could not decide between the two spread spectrum options, frequency hopping and direct sequence, and therefore both became part of the standard. In 1997 the IEEE 802.11 standard for 1 to 2 Mbit/s operating in the 2.4 GHz band was approved, to be adopted by ISO as International Standard 8802 part 11 in 1999.

In 1997, to provide support for synchronous services, such as telephony, an industry consortium around Proxim, with the support of Intel, started to push the HomeRF proposal, which was based on frequency hopping. In parallel, ETSI initiated the development of the HIPERLAN standard. Both options were defeated, essentially because of the success of IEEE 802.11.

Meanwhile, work had started on a 10^+ Mbit/s version in the 2.4 GHz band, to become IEEE 802.11b, and a 50^+ Mbit/s version in the 5 GHz band, to become IEEE 802.11a. The MAC protocol remained the same, and for the 802.11a the Lucent Technologies/NTT proposal for OFDM was selected.[53] The choice of a new PHY for 802.11b was extremely contentious, with competing proposals from Harris, Lucent Technologies and Micrilor. Ultimately, a new proposal jointly developed by Lucent Technologies and Harris won the day. The IEEE 802.11a/b standards were approved in 1999, and subsequently ratified by ISO.

3.9   Interpretation of the Wi-Fi case in the context of theory

In this section we interpret this period of the Wi-Fi journey and focus on the strategic behaviour of the firm in relation to the process of standard making. In line with the theoretical framework outlined in Chapter 1, we touch upon the innovation dimension and look at the institutional environment, in particular the standard-setting bodies in the United States and Europe.

3.9.1   Firm strategy and standard-making

True strategic issues tend to be paradoxical in nature. One of the many paradoxes an entrepreneur or strategist is confronted with in practice is whether, in order to become successful, the firm should comply with the existing 'rules of the game' in an industry or break these rules so as to create a competitive advantage by establishing new rules, possibly introducing a new competitive game. De Wit and Meyer (2004) observe that a firm wishing to break the existing rules and intending to establish a leadership position based on a new set of rules has to

> move beyond a compelling vision, and work out a new competitive business model. If this new model is put into operation and seems to offer a competitive advantage, this can attract sufficient customers and support to gain 'critical mass' and break through as a viable alternative to the older business model. To shape the industry, the firm will also need to develop the new competences and standards required to make the new business model function properly.

Moreover, they observe, following Hamel and Prahalad (1994), that 'changing the rules rarely happens overnight. Rather, it can take years, figuring out which rules can be broken and which cannot. It can be a marathon, trying to get the business model right, while building competences and support. Therefore, organizations require perseverance and commitment if they are to be successful as industry shapers.' This characterisation seems to describe perfectly the situation that NCR/AT&T/Lucent Technologies was facing in the market for wireless LANs. As often occurs, however, the strategic intent is far less deliberate than it may appear in hindsight. Becoming a leader in this industry was an emergent process, unfolding as the development progressed, albeit based on the compelling logic of creating an open standard.

3.9.2   The strategic considerations in standard making

Aiming at a leadership position in a standard-setting body is not always a prerequisite for a company to reach its strategic objectives. 'Why participate at all?' is a very valid question, in particular for some stakeholders. After all, standardisation is a costly business and time-consuming, and the return on investment is uncertain in many cases, OSI being an especially disastrous case in point. Large vendors and manufacturers may want to open up new markets, and system integrators may try and push their own technical ideas (or thwart competing specifications); but what about the users? For them, there are few direct, tangible benefits in active participation in standard setting. They may reap major benefits from well-designed standards addressing real needs, however, as illustrated in the WLAN case by the participation of GM

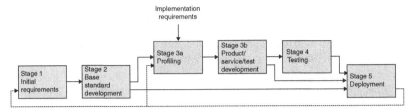

Figure 3.7 The standards life cycle
Source: Adapted from Reilly (1994).

and Inland Steel in the beginning and Boeing later. The role of the users in setting standards is primarily one of contributing real-world requirements, and of providing practical experience (see Jakobs, 2002, for a more detailed discussion).

For those firms that want to influence the process in one way or another, there is ample evidence that direct participation in the process should be the approach of choice (see, for example, Jakobs, Procter and Williams, 2001), subject to available financial and human resources. Smaller companies in particular tend to face resource constraints. In these cases, participation via umbrella organisations is an option, as is participation at the national level.

The choice of the appropriate standards forum is the next question to be addressed. While the standards bodies have developed a degree of specialisation, similar systems may well be standardised in parallel by different regional SSBs, and participation in all relevant activities is well beyond the means of all but the biggest players. The correct choice of standards forum is crucial, however, as being saddled with a non-standard technology will at the very least incur considerable cost – i.e. additional development costs for vendors and, eventually, switching costs for users.

The final question is 'When should we participate?'. In most cases 'the standardisation process' is viewed as a single element, incapable of further subdivision. The standards life cycle depicted in Figure 3.7 suggests otherwise, however. Participation in profile development, for example, would be an option if the major concern is the interoperability of implementations.[54] There is little point in participating in profiling if the base standard does not meet the requirements in the first place, however.

From the above, and based on Updegrove (2006), we may classify participation into five categories related to the individual stakeholders' motivations for participation in the standard-making process (see also the elaboration in section 3.1.1): (1) observers, (2) adopters, (3) opponents, (4) contributors and (5) leaders. The category 'opponents' has been added to acknowledge that the objective of participation may be one of delaying or diverting the process, so as, for instance, to protect a profitable market position.

Depending on the objective being pursued – whether the creation of a (successful) standard, the creation of a market, influencing the direction of development, the sharing of development costs or simply the gathering of intelligence – a firm should analyse the appropriateness of the standard-setting bodies for alignment with its strategic objectives. Major considerations in this respect are the governance regime of the standards body and the position it takes towards intellectual property rights (IPR). See also Table 3.1 for the linkages between strategic goals and SSB characteristics.

As already mentioned, making standards is a process that requires long-term commitment in order to bring it to a successful conclusion. Figure 3.8 shows a typical timeline for the standard-making process and the related product life cycle, based on experience obtained within the IEEE (Carlo, 2007). It should be noted that some standards reach peak volume after ten years, others after five years, and some only after a much longer period of time, of, say, twenty years.[55]

3.9.3   Institutional environment and industry evolution

In this section the standard-setting world is reviewed from an institutional perspective, in which institutions are considered to be 'a system of rules that structure the course of actions that a set of actors may choose . . . whereby these rules are accepted by those involved, used in practice and have a certain degree of durability' (Koppenjan and Groenewegen, 2005).

3.10   The evolving world of ICT standard setting

Over the past four decades the world of ICT standardisation has changed dramatically, from the simple, straightforward and rather static situation of the 1970s, depicted in Figure 3.9, to the complex web of standard-setting bodies of today, as shown in Figure 3.10.

The development of ICT standards in the 1970s was carried out almost exclusively by formal standard-developing organisations. It was also characterised by a clear distinction between the then CCITT, in charge of telecommunications standards, on the one hand, and a set of organisations developing information technology (IT) standards, on the other. CCITT was, basically, run by the national postal, telegraph and telephone (PTT) companies, which still enjoyed a monopoly position in their respective countries. ISO was in charge of almost all other IT-related standardisation activities. The various national bodies developed their own specific standards, but also contributed to the work of ISO and CEN, the European committee for standardisation, which itself cooperated with ISO.

Table 3.1 *Strategic goals in relation to standard making*

To create a (successful) standard	*Governance* Does it provide for strong influence on the part of interested players? Or is it more 'egalitarian'?
	Finance Are the finances sound? Will the SSB have the stamina to survive the process? Does it depend heavily on individual entities/contributors?
	IPR policy Can I put my IPR portfolio to good use? Do I hold 'essential' IPR?
	Reputation Is the SSB well respected in the area in question?
	Membership Are there potential allies/opponents? Is adequate technical expertise available, at both corporate and individual level?
	Key player involvement Is the combined market power adequate? Are relevant stakeholders represented? Are important stakeholders absent?
	Timing How long will it take to develop a standard? Will the window of opportunity be met?
	Process characteristics Can the process be used against me – e.g., to delay the standard? For how long? What are the decision mechanisms?
	Products Does the SSB offer an appropriate type of deliverable?
	Dissemination Will the specifications (and, possibly, reference implementations) be available for free?
In addition: to create a market	*IPR policy* Will the IPR policy eventually put off users who are afraid of high licensing fees? Will it deter holders of important IPR from joining?
	Competition Are there competing consortia? Are competitors likely to emerge, or are all relevant players members?
	Membership levels Does the highest membership level available guarantee the necessary level of influence? Who else is at this level? Are leading users represented in the 'upper' levels?
	Key players Who are the active players, and which roles do their representatives assume (individual capacity/company rep.)? Are the 'right' companies represented? Are all relevant stakeholders represented? Are leading users on board? Are any key players missing? Is the combined market power adequate?
To influence standard development	*Governance* Does it provide adequate influence for smaller players as well?
	Membership Who else is involved? Is adequate technical expertise available, at both corporate and individual level? Who are the 'active' members?
	Key players Are the important players on board? Who are potentially strong opponents or allies?
	Individuals' capacity Do I need to know the individual reps. and their views, and the roles they are likely to assume?
	Required level of consensus Is it possible to exploit the consensus requirement in order to delay the process or to cripple the outcome?
To share development costs	*Membership* Are enough (important) members with similar interests on board, at an adequate membership level (to indicate sufficient interest)?
To gather (specific/early) intelligence	*Governance* Is a level available that offers a good return on investment – i.e. one that gives access to all relevant information without costing a fortune?

Source: Based on Updegrove (2006).

Typical standards activity

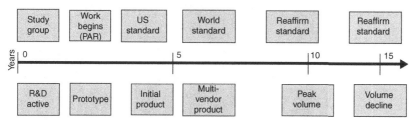

Typical product market activity

Figure 3.8 Standards and product timelines

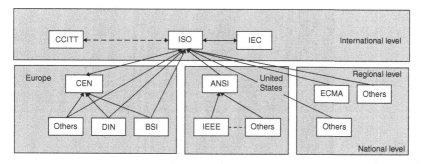

Figure 3.9. The ICT standardisation universe in the 1970s (simplified)

Over time, several trends contributed to the increasingly complex ICT standardisation environment that can be observed today:
- the growing importance of information technology relative to communication technology;
- the liberalisation of the telecommunications market;
- the emergence of regional standards bodies;
- the globalisation of markets;
- in Europe, the objective of creating a common market in telecommunications; and
- the (still ongoing) convergence of the formerly distinct markets for telecommunications and information technology.

In addition, and perhaps most notably, standards consortia emerged as a new phenomenon. Well-known examples today include, for instance, the World Wide Web Consortium (W3C), the Organization for the Advancement of Structured Information Standards (OASIS) and the Object Management Group (OMG). For a number of years, especially in the 1990s, new consortia emerged at an almost alarming rate (Cargill, 1995). This was, on the one hand, in

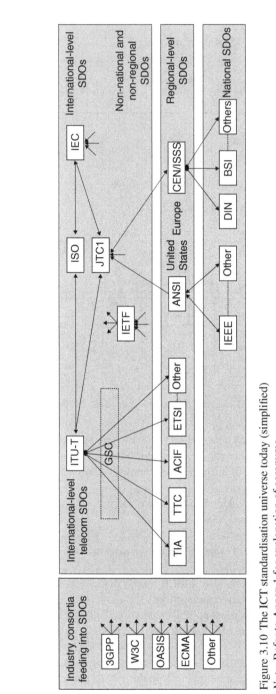

Figure 3.10 The ICT standardisation universe today (simplified)
Note: Refer to Annex 1 for explanation of acronyms.

response to the enormous rapidity of technical development in ICT and in e-business systems; traditional SDOs were widely considered as not being able to cope with the required speed (Besen, 1995; Cargill, 1995).[56] On the other hand, consortium standards could be used as a means to create markets through standards, in areas in which no SDOs were active, or in which their – then cumbersome – processes were too slow. In such cases, a standards consortium, as a group of companies, would have greater credibility, know-how and resources than a single company. In addition, consortium members could share the costs of developing standards. In many areas, such as the World Wide Web, consortia have marginalised SDOs.[57] In other sectors, consortia and SDOs coexist (for example, ECMA is contributing considerably to ISO's data interchange standards, and several OASIS standards on webXML have been accepted as ISO standards). Today, the boundaries between consortia and SDOs are becoming increasingly blurred, with many consortium by-laws hardly distinguishable from those of SDOs, and with many SDOs adding 'consortium-like' processes to their portfolios (see also Chapter 8 section 3 below).

The Internet's standards body, the Internet Engineering Task Force (IETF), played a somewhat special role thanks to the unprecedented importance of the Internet in today's economy. For many years the IETF was not accepted as a standard-setting body, and its output, the Internet Standards, was not recognised by government procurement regulations (Werle, 2002). This has now changed.[58] Moreover, the IETF may be regarded as the role model for many large consortia, primarily for the W3C. In fact, many have considered the IETF's process to be superior to those of the formal SDOs (Crocker, 1993; Monteiro, Hanseth and Hatling, 1994; Solomon and Rutkowski, 1992).[59]

To increase the complexity of the situation further, a proliferation of sector-specific standards has taken place recently in Europe, especially in the e-business domain (in the United States, sector-specific standardisation has long been the norm).

3.10.1 The notion of 'open standards'

The directive by NCR headquarters to follow an open standards approach in the development of non-core products created some ambiguity for the developers, as the term 'open' had not been defined properly and, as a result, had acquired different meanings for different people. More recently, the standard-setting community has defined an 'open' standard in various but similar ways, one of which originates from the ICT Standard Board (ICTSB):[60] 'An open standard . . . should be:

- developed and/or affirmed in a transparent process open to all relevant players, including industry, consumers and regulatory authorities . . . ;
- either free of . . . IPR concerns, or licensable on a (fair), reasonable and non-discriminatory ((F)RAND) basis;

- driven by stakeholders, and user requirements must be fully reflected;
- publicly available (but not necessarily free of charge);
- maintained.'

An interesting element here is the need to reflect user requirements fully. While this may be hard to enforce in practice (see, for example, Jakobs, Procter and Williams, 1998), the incorporation of (reasonable) user requirements is undoubtedly a crucial characteristic of an open standard.

Another more recent interpretation of 'open' originates from the open source software (OSS) community. This definition would require an open standard to (IDABC [Interoperable Delivery of European e-government services to public Administrations, Businesses and Citizens], 2008):

- be adopted and maintained by a not-for-profit organisation;
- be developed on the basis of an open decision-making procedure available to all interested parties;
- be freely available; and
- make irrevocably available any associated IPR on a royalty-free basis.

The discussions that emerged about (a slightly different predecessor of) this definition revolved in particular around the requirement for IPR availability on a 'royalty-free' basis. The fact that one study that published such a definition was commissioned by the European Commission helps to explain the ensuing public outcry. In the first place, this requirement excludes the products of the vast majority of both formal SDOs and industry consortia from the list of producers of open standards. With very few exceptions (e.g. the more recently established W3C being a very prominent one), standard-setting bodies typically ask for IPR to be included in a standard to be made available on a (fair), reasonable and non-discriminatory basis.[61] In addition, a recent study has revealed that it remains rather unclear even to those managing SSBs how this rule should actually be implemented. In general, it is reported that the licence fee should not be higher than 1 per cent of the final product price (Blind, Thumm, Bierhals *et al.*, 2002).

Furthermore, this IPR requirement is also likely to deter many IPR holders from participating in standard setting. Even applying (F)RAND can lead to this 'adverse' selection process (Blind and Thumm, 2004) – i.e. the withdrawal of IPR holders. Rather than giving up their IPR they may consider following other more worthwhile avenues in order to reap the benefits from their intellectual property. In general, any initiative to define open standards as royalty-free should consider an in-depth analysis of the consequences of ETSI's unsuccessful attempt to change its licensing scheme to allow for compulsory licensing (Iversen, 1999). Although consumers and users may benefit in the short run, the incentives to invest in R&D would dry up in the long run. The United States even complained that such a rule would lead to the expropriation of its knowledge assets.

The absence in these definitions of a requirement for due process is a striking aspect. After all, this is one of the cornerstones of all SDOs' processes, and it is also included in the processes adopted by many standards consortia. Due process is more than just 'an open decision-making procedure available to all interested parties' in that it also incorporates an appeal authority.[62]

3.10.2   Relations between stakeholders

The procedures adopted by the individual SSBs may differ with respect to a number of process criteria. In particular, the criteria upon which voting power is assigned to members differ. The options range from 'one country/company/individual – one vote' (applied by, for example, ISO, the W3C and the IEEE) to rather elaborate schemes with different membership levels that allow companies to 'buy' voting power. In these cases, the 'price' (i.e. the membership fee) typically also depends on the size or revenue of the company. ETSI and the OMG use such a scheme.

At least the former approach, which is essentially egalitarian in nature, suggests that the degree of control over, and influence on, the standard-setting process is distributed more or less equally between the different types of stakeholders. This, in turn, yields the model of the standardisation process that is depicted in Figure 3.11.

The figure shows the 'ideal democratic' situation, with all stakeholders having a (more or less equal) say in the standard-setting process. This – relatively technocratic – model underlies many SSBs' rules and processes. Unfortunately, it ignores organisational and social aspects, and does not assume any links or interrelations between the different stakeholders.

As a consequence, this 'ideal' scenario is far removed from reality – at least, according to some earlier research (see, for example, Jakobs, 2004). In fact, it appears that, to date, IT standards development has been almost exclusively technology-driven, with the standards produced reflecting solely providers' and implementers' priorities – for example, the ability to implement rather than the usability. This can be attributed largely to the fact that the relevant standardisation committees have typically been dominated by engineers representing manufacturers and service providers (Jakobs, Procter and Williams, 2001).

Obviously, there are also relationships between these various stakeholders outside the standard-setting process, the most obvious one being the customer–supplier relationship. These relations may well have considerable impact on activities and conduct with regard to standardisation on both sides.

Those entities that form the 'Third Estate' in setting standards are a different case altogether. Although they represent the vast majority of stakeholders, these groups have extremely little say in the standard-setting process. This

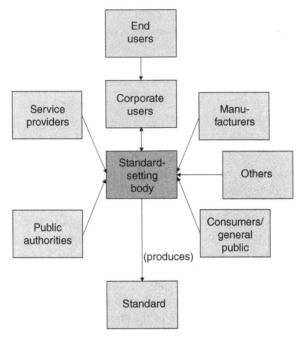

Figure 3.11 A simple model of the standard-setting process
Source: Adapted from Egyedi, Jakobs and Monteiro (2003).

holds despite the fact that organisations such as ANEC[63] (for consumers) and NORMAPME[64] (for SMEs) are actively participating in selected standards working groups on behalf of their respective constituencies. Figure 3.12 depicts the actual situation more realistically.

Notably, the figure highlights two phenomena. First, manufacturers and service providers – deliberately or not – seem to act as a sort of 'buffer' between corporate users and standards committees (Jakobs, 2004), in that they filter their customers' requirements. Moreover, in cooperation with the users, they provide customised solutions to meet their customers' needs. This way, potentially they compromise to some extent the idea of many ICT standards – i.e. to provide interoperability.

Second, some sort of invisible 'shield' keeps the standardisation's 'Third Estate' away from the working groups. This 'shield' is, to a large extent, a result of a lack of financial resources – actively contributing to standard setting being a costly business (Spring and Weiss, 1995), frequently combined with inadequate knowledge about the value of standards in general, and of the potential value of active contributions to standard setting in particular.

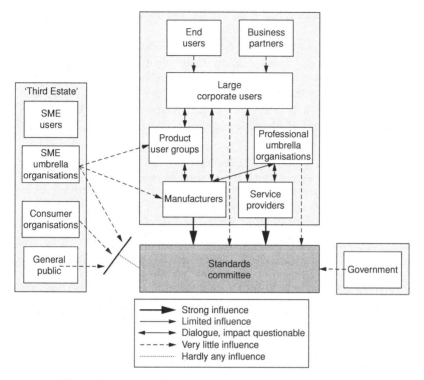

Figure 3.12 The relations between stakeholders in standardisation
Source: Adapted from Jakobs (2004).

3.10.3   *Coordination and competition in standardisation*

Standardisation is, basically, a mechanism for coordination (Werle, 2001). Not unlike research, standard setting serves as a platform for cooperation between companies that are otherwise competitors. This function of standardisation is largely independent of the nature of the actual platform – that is, it does not make a big difference whether negotiation and cooperation occur within a formal SDO or an industry consortium. Provided the objective and basic content of the standard have been agreed upfront, cooperation during the execution of the work is the rule. Notably, industrial players want a 'level playing field' in which no competitor has a clear advantage over its peers. When the players involved see the selection of the objectives and content as a zero-sum game, however, cooperation suffers, because players are unwilling to sacrifice anything for the overall good. Mature SDOs will tend to work on the basis of the non-zero-sum game model, because the players realise that increasing the cake is sometimes as good as, or better than, increasing their own slice. The implication is that pre-competitive standardisation is mostly wishful thinking in areas with large market potential.

In some cases, a new standard is based on new technology that has no large presence in the market. In such cases, although there is a level playing field (as with the development of the 5 GHz wireless LAN standards), competition within and between SSBs plays a major role. With reference to the battle between HIPERLAN and IEEE 802.11, the chairperson of the HIPERLAN committee at the time made the following observations:

Much of the divergence between ETSI-BRAN and IEEE 802.11 regarding HIPERLAN is due to differences in styles of thinking and working – and managing – between the United States and Europe. US society is permeated by the 'need to compete' at any level and on any subject, whereas Europeans tend to look for consensus. The outcomes of these processes are not necessarily very different in their technical quality, nor does one deliver more quickly than the other, but the way in which the two models deal with the outside world is very different: the competition model tends to focus people on beating their co-players and external events tend to be less relevant. The consensus model, on the other hand, is more open to external influences. That 802.11 accepted the same approach to OFDM as ETSI-BRAN has much to do with the fact, in addition to the same proposal being made in both groups, there was no strong competing scheme from within 802.11. It is also true that there was significant technical 'feedback' from the IEEE to BRAN, and this is consistent with the more competitive style of the former.

Both styles can lead to long processes with questionable output; there is no panacea except for good management. That brings up the last point: effective management requires decision making and the competitive style prevalent in the US makes that people are more open to taking decisions – usually in the expectation of profiting one way or another. The consensus model encourages people to avoid decision making: a wrong outcome will haunt the one who pushed the decision, whereas a good outcome will not benefit anyone in particular. To paraphrase a popular saying: 'Success has many fathers, failure just one.'[65]

The complex structure of the web of SSBs described above suggests a considerable amount of fragmentation and overlap of standard-setting activities. In many cases, therefore, some coordination of SSBs' activities would be desirable, as would be a distribution of labour.

Today, various forms of cooperation between SSBs may be found. In the realm of SDOs, 'horizontal' cooperation between the international SDOs (ITU, ISO, IEC) is regulated by a dedicated guide for cooperation between ITU-T and ISO-IEC's Joint Technical Committee 1 (ITU-T, 2002). Similarly, the CEN/CENELEC/ETSI Joint Presidents' Group (JPG) coordinates the standardisation policies of the ESOs based on a basic cooperation agreement. Moreover, Directive 98/34/EC mandates that conflicting standards in the European Union have to be withdrawn (European Commission, 1998).

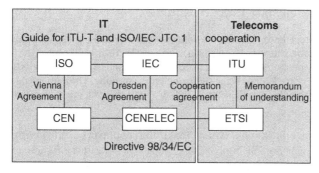

Figure 3.13. Cooperation and coordination agreements between European and international SDOs
Source: Adapted from Jakobs and Mora (2008).

'Vertical' cooperation between ESOs and the international bodies is governed by individual documents. Here, the major need for cooperation and coordination is primarily sector-specific (IT, telecommunications): the 'Vienna Agreement'[66] provides the rules for cooperation between CEN and ISO; analogously, the 'Dresden Agreement'[67] governs relations between IEC and CENELEC. See also Figure 3.13.

In general, the 'vertical' agreements and memorandums of understanding (MoUs) define various levels of cooperation and coordination, albeit with varying degrees of specificity. Nonetheless, cooperation between CEN and ISO, and CENELEC and IEC, has been very successful, primarily through joint working groups.

The partnership projects[68] organised by ETSI represent a different approach to coordination. Covering both SDOs and consortia, these projects coordinate a group of regional SDOs and industry consortia working towards a common objective. The '3rd Generation Partnership Project' (3GPP) is a current and prominent example.

3.10.4   The role of the individual

In standard-setting bodies, at either national level or regional level, membership is typically vested in a company, a consumer organisation, an industrial organisation, a government agency or, in case of regional-level bodies, a national standards body. At the IEEE, however, the membership is vested in the individual. On the one hand, from the perspective of the firm this raises the 'principle–agent' question, and from the perspective of the standards body it raises the question of whether membership assignment to the individual actually works to the benefit of the standardisation process.

On the latter question, Hayes comments:

I do believe so. I have had several valuable members who changed employer, yet continued to participate in the work, even maintaining an office. Of course, the individual is sponsored by his employer to participate in the work and has a bias towards the studies and analysis done back home when preparing for the meeting. The individual has a stake in the well-being of his company, so he will certainly take that into consideration when casting his vote.

On the former question, it is clear that different players exert varying degrees of influence over an SSB's processes, depending not just on their respective levels of interest in a new standard but also on rather more mundane aspects, such as the depth of their pockets, and their market power. At the end of the day, however, a standard's specification results from the efforts of the members of an SSB's working group. Consequently, these individuals' motivations, attitudes and views are very likely to have an influence on their contributions to the standard-setting process, and thus on its outcome.

Various factors, which do not necessarily bear a relation to the technology to be standardised, are channelled into an SSB's working groups, and shape the process outcome. Jakobs, Procter and Williams (2000) argue that the respective corporate environments of the working groups' members' employers, for instance, play a major role here. The different visions of how a technology should be used, and the ideas of how this can be achieved, are shaped by these local environments, which therefore also exert an impact on the standard-isation work. This holds especially in the case of anticipatory standards, which specify new services from scratch, and thus offer the opportunity to incorporate to some degree the particular presumptions of the (more outspoken) members of the originating working group. Nevertheless, a reactive standard will likewise transpose the environment from which it originally emerged – i.e. the corporate environment of the inventor who specified the system upon which the standard will be based.

To find out which such non-technical factors actually do play a role, and thus to gain a better understanding as to why a standard emerges the way it does, we need to have a closer look inside working groups.[69] In a relatively small qualitative study of factors that influence the standard-setting process at working group level within ISO and ITU-T, Jakobs, Procter and Williams (2001) show that a working group's decisions are taken for a variety of reasons, a proposal's technical merits being but one of them. For example, about one out of three respondents from ISO observed that it is individuals who are most powerful. One respondent said:

Oddly enough, it's been my experience that individuals dominate ISO. Sometimes the individual will have a powerful multinational corporation or government/national interest on their side, but the bully pulpit is controlled by individuals, and only those with a strong sense of purpose survive.

Much in line with the above observation, many respondents from ISO and ITU stressed that speaking out at meetings for or against a proposal is the most important single factor influencing technical decisions. As one put it:

For any given technical decision, the presence of supporters/opponents weighs heavily, for in practice, unless there is someone or some organisation that champions a solution and pushes it forward, it does not get as much consideration/exposure as alternate [sic] solutions. That is, group members typically do not delve into researching solutions that someone happened to send us unless such solutions at first glance seem to be overwhelmingly good. More likely, the members push the solutions that they already understand.

Along similar lines, the influence of those who are prepared to put in extra work should not be underestimated. These two aspects are probably linked: those with strong views are more likely to be inclined to invest time and effort to get their views through. One respondent summed it up:

Often the group 'leaders' (including formal editors, and strong personalities who are not formal leaders) have tremendous influence. (This is not necessarily bad.)

Another factor identified as influential – though, overall, it was said to be of lower importance – is a proposal's technical merit; underlying company interests may also have to be taken into account. These are two respondents' comments:

Unless you are at the meeting, your view is not taken into account (no matter how technically correct it may be). This is the overwhelming factor that decides the content of the standard. Company interests (political influence at the voting level) is [sic] the next priority. Technical merit is of little importance – standards are usually a poor compromise of many strong views.

The technical viability of a decision does carry great weight. As almost all members at the technical committee meeting level are engineers, the technical prowess of the solution, tied with the credibility (knowledge) of the person presenting it, are [sic] very influential. On occasion, a company which already has a product back in their labs will also prove to be a formidable opponent.

The above observations stress the importance of the non-technical aspects of the standardisation process. Clearly, these aspects are strongly linked to the individual working groups' members' attitudes and approaches.

3.10.5   The individual in the case of IEEE 802.11

In the IEEE, membership – including voting rights – is assigned to the individual, as opposed to, for example, a company. Hence, here as well a closer look at the roles, views and motivations of working group members is of interest: do working group members actually act on the basis of their personal views and perceptions, or do other factors also play a role? To this end, a questionnaire comprising sixteen open-ended questions was distributed to a number of individuals who played an important role during the development of the IEEE 802.11 set of standards (primarily of 802.11a/b). The findings from this survey should be taken as a snapshot – the idea being to shed some light on different aspects associated with the IEEE's 'individual membership' approach.

Almost all the respondents have a strictly technical background, with job titles such as 'communication engineer' or 'system architect'. They were all very active in the process, and typically attended almost all the meetings (which gave them almost permanent voting rights), yet only a very few had previous experience in standards development. Clearly, the initial motivations for attendance differed, but interest in the technology dominates (which is no big surprise, considering the respondents' engineering background). In addition, with many engineers in the working groups, one might be inclined to suspect the technical characteristics of a specification to be of overriding importance. Here as well, though, the physical presence of a proposal's supporters played a crucial role, and is widely seen as being more important than its technical merits. In this context, the observation that existing implementations might well have a detrimental effect on a proposal's chances of being accepted is interesting. One respondent said:

Main factors are definitely supporters/opponents present during discussion, and their reputation would play a role.

As another respondent put it:

Technical merits are important but never the most important. Implementability, time to market (for all), fairness are equally important to drive decisions.

Obviously, the desire not to favour one company (the implementer) over others plays a role, too. This – rather striking – aspect surfaced quite frequently.

Solutions already implemented did play a strong role, but could also be a strong reason to change things, to level the playing field (by forcing changes for certain vendors that already had an implementation).

Another comment was:

I have never seen that a decision is taken that is in the benefit of only one company (because it already has solutions/products).

Even more strongly expressed was this view:

No four organisations can make 802.11 do anything.

Even if the latter may be a slight exaggeration, these comments suggest that (many) members of the 802.11 groups were not prepared to let their work be overly dominated by corporate interests, and also that they were actively acting against any such dominance.

To a considerable extent, developing standards is about the distribution, and the use, of power. In the case of the 802.11 group, for obvious reasons, power lay primarily with large chip manufacturers. With their vested interest in the technology, they were prepared to invest heavily in R&D efforts, and to send numerous representatives widely respected in the industry to the working group meetings. These individuals came armed with good proposals (the results of the R&D efforts), for which they could make a strong case. Strong corporate interest, good proposals and respected and knowledgeable proponents would seem to be a winning combination. It was stated that, of these three elements, one alone would not suffice; whether or not two would remains an open issue. In the words of one respondent:

Influence in the working group is a combination [of, e.g., powerful organisation, deep pockets, strong technical proposals, active/respected representatives], but the companies that were the strongest in the market also put most effort in the standard by means of number of people, proposals, technical knowledge, experience in the field. But there are also examples of small companies with very smart/respected representatives who took and got a lot of bandwidth.

In addition, finding allies and forming alliances is an integral part of the game. Not least, this was triggered by the IEEE balloting process, which requires a 75 per cent level of support for a proposal to enter the next stage of the process.

This harsh reality is a bit of a contradiction to the attempts not to let the process be overly influenced by particular companies. Necessarily, those companies that have the strongest interest in the topic, and that are therefore likely to be the most active in the process, are the same ones that are the most likely also to have prototype implementations ready.

Voting behaviour is very good indicator whether or not working group members act as 'individuals' as opposed to company representatives. In the 802.11 case, respondents agreed that normally, but certainly not automatically, representatives of a company would vote in unison. One said:

Most acted in unison based on their affiliation, and usually because they had a vested interest in their proposal or position succeeding. [...] But I also remember when individuals voted differently than [sic] others with the same affiliation. Sometimes these alternative views were represented because of strong personal philosophy on the [engineering or moral] issue at hand. Other times people would purposely vote opposite to their affiliation to 'appear' fair-minded.

Contrary behaviour can be explained by the IEEE rules (according to the same respondent). In this case, it cannot really be considered to be 'individual' behaviour but, rather, tactical conduct:

Other times they would vote contrarily when it could be predicted, or sometimes just in case, the vote would confirm that alternate [*sic*] position anyway. That would ensure that the company had at least one vote on the prevailing side so that individual could later make a motion for reconsideration – again, that's another political ploy.

Along similar lines, respondents widely agreed that, occasionally, an individual would follow his/her own agenda. In most cases, this would happen to push a specification that was perceived as technically superior:

He always votes and promotes excellence in the standard and votes generally (95 per cent of the time) as an informed individual concerned for producing the best technical specifications. Because of his stance and clarity of positions in all matters on the standard, he is very highly regarded.

In addition, a member's change of job might go hand in hand with a change of views; the same could hold for a consultant changing clients:

Easier to see when a company gets acquired – the need to protect Bluetooth was not on Airgo's mind, but Qualcomm cares about Bluetooth.

Clashes of egos are a frequent occurrence, and may relate to either personal or corporate views – e.g. if a company depends on a certain technology to be standardised. This is little surprise, as 'being outspoken' and 'having a sense of purpose' are essential attributes for successful standard setters:

Some people are very insecure, or just plain argumentative. I observed several loud shouting matches on the meeting floor, and I heard about (but did not witness) an incident prior to the start of my participation where a particular argument resulted in a fist fight. *Robert's Rules* were more formally applied after that, I think.[70]

The survey responses form a somewhat ambivalent picture. On the one hand, it seems that the majority of members of the 802.11 working groups have a very strong sense of fairness; they try not to allow a single powerful company, or a group of them, to dominate the process, and they may consider existing pilot implementations as an unfair advantage and, accordingly, reject the associated proposal. On the other hand, it is safe to say that the majority of the leading figures come from exactly such powerful companies; they have the means and the motivation to invest heavily in the standard-setting process, as the return on investment may be significant. In addition, their employees are likely to be motivated to assume formal roles in the process (chair, secretary, technical editor, etc.), thus getting additional influence.

Overall, it seems that working group members cast their votes at least with a view towards their respective employers' business interests. Exceptions to this seem to be not so infrequent, however, and typically aim at technically superior solutions. Likewise, the reports about working group members adapting their point of view to the one held by their current employer do not hint at strong personal opinions (rather, at pragmatism). Thus, here again we do not see a

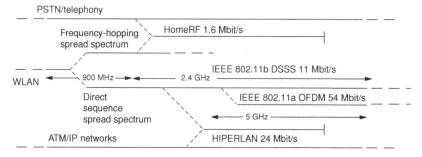

Figure 3.14 WLAN innovation avenues, 1987–99

homogeneous picture (of course, it is hard to vote against your employer's interests when you see people being fired for having done exactly that; another course of events not entirely unheard of, according to some respondents). Then again, the apparently fairly frequent clashes of egos imply strong feelings about a proposal (although there may be other reasons involved as well).

All in all, we do not believe that the IEEE's 'individual' membership makes a big difference. People act differently; some may interpret 'individual' membership as carte blanche to push their own proposals, while others will still act exclusively on behalf of their employers, both regardless of the official membership rules.

3.11   Innovation and the innovation landscape

With reference to the innovation avenues introduced in Chapter 1, and applied to WLAN in Chapter 2 (see in particular Figure 2.6), we can observe that in the period 1997 to 1999 the WLAN avenue saw many branching points. From the very start we should distinguish within the WLAN innovation avenue between the two modulation variants: frequency hopping and direct sequence.[71] Subsequently, we see the emergence of isochronous applications next to the main stream of asynchronous applications, in the form of competing concepts such as HomeRF and HIPERLAN that are aimed to support telephony and other real-time-sensitive applications. On the spectrum dimension, we see the WLANs migrate from the 915 MHz band to the 2.4 GHz and 5 GHz bands. The main avenue becomes the 2.4 GHz band, with global allocations of spectrum and very successful product implementations at 11 Mbit/s, up from initial product introductions supporting 1 to 2 Mbit/s (see also Chapter 4). To compete effectively with the wired LANs, which have migrated from 10 to 100 Mbit/s, we see WLANs providing for speeds up to 54 Mbit/s in the 5 GHz band, where they do not have to compete with ISM applications. In Figure 3.14 these developments are mapped as innovation avenues, highways and byways.

Notes

1 An earlier version of the material of this chapter has been published in summary form in *Information Communication Technology Standardization for E-Business Sectors: Integrating Supply and Demand Factors*, edited by Jakobs (Lemstra and Hayes, 2009).

2 Initially the Retail Systems Division outsourced a token-bus-derived development activity to Spread Spectrum Sciences, later Omnipoint, only to be disappointed with the result and to return to the 'internal' WLAN source.

3 Ronald Brockmann, a participant in the '802.11' negotiations and co-founder of a WLAN start-up, has observed that participating in a standards body is one of the best ways of learning about a new technology (see also Chapter 8).

4 This term is used to denote both formal standard-developing organisations (SDOs) and standards consortia.

5 According to the Project Authorization Request (PAR), this task group was originally denoted 802.4c, which through a transcription error became 802.4l.

6 This situation may change soon, though, with the increasing influence of Asian countries, especially China.

7 'Due process means that any person (organization, company, government agency, individual, etc.) with a direct and material interest has a right to participate by: a) expressing a position and its basis, b) having that position considered, and c) having the right to appeal. Due process allows for equity and fair play' (ANSI, 2006).

8 IEEE 802.3 minutes, July 1990.

9 The bulk of the income of the association is generated from the sales of the standards.

10 All active PARs are posted on the Internet at http://standards.ieee.org/board/nes/approved.html.

11 mentor.ieee.org/802.11/documents. With other standards bodies, the documents are typically available only to the members.

12 The IEEE 802 standards are available free of charge, however, in pdf format one year after the publication date. This has been made possible by assigning a large portion of the registration fee for the plenary IEEE 802 meetings to the IEEE standards department. In principle, draft IEEE standards are also available to the public, but at a fee. There was a reluctance to make draft standards available, supposedly because people not present at meetings could easily misunderstand the draft and build to an incorrect specification.

13 Section 7.1.2 of the IEEE Project 802 'LAN MAN Standards Committee (LMSC) policies and procedures' manual, which is available at http://standards.ieee.org/board/aud/LMSC.pdf.

14 What exactly 'sufficient' means is not defined.

15 It was an IEEE 802 requirement to meet five criteria. They are defined in clause 17.5 of the *IEEE Project 802 LAN MAN Standards Committee (LMSC) Sponsor Policies and Procedures* manual at http://ieee802.org/policies-and-procedures.pdf.

16 At the end of this agenda item the 802.4 chair announced that the working group intended to go into hibernation (IEEE 802.0 minutes 13 July 1990).

17 The actual designation of the groups was 'subgroups', because a task group is normally related to a project, whereas we had one project but needed to assign the work to smaller groups. The term 'task group' will be used as the designation in this chapter.

18 The PHY is the layer concerned with the physical transport of a raw bit stream, subject to the type of medium being used (see Figure 2.4).

19 In this instance the stipulation that a 75 per cent majority had to be reached was abandoned at the task group level, so as to speed up the process, but it remained in force at the working group level.

20 Only members can vote.

21 See *IEEE Project 802 Policies and Procedures* manual; http://ieee802.org/policies-and-procedures.pdf.

22 Each time a technical change is made in the draft standard, the draft has to be subjected to a confirmation letter ballot. Only then is the draft finally ready for the next stage, when no technical change has been made in the production of the next draft standard.

23 The objective is to make a 'soft' switchover, without the application or the user being aware that a change has been made.

24 Symbol Technologies was known for its data collection terminal equipment, with specific strength in infrared bar code reading. Xircom was known in the market for its 'pocket LAN' adapters, which allowed computers to be connected to a network using a printer port. In 1999 Xircom was acquired by Intel.

25 The proponents of direct sequence included NCR, Harris (from 1994), Symbol Technologies (until 1993), Toshiba, Telxon/Telesystems and LACE. The contributions from NCR to the task group were made and defended by Jan Boer. The proponents of frequency hopping included Motorola, Symbol Technologies (from 1993), IBM, California Microwave Corporation, Apple, GEC Plessey, Symbionics and Lannair.

26 Recall that in 1991 NCR was acquired by AT&T, the incumbent US telecommunications operator. In 1983, in settling an antitrust court case, the company spun off seven regional holding companies. AT&T remained as the provider of long-distance and international services. The company also retained Bell Labs, the famous research entity, and its manufacturing activities. The settlement allowed AT&T to expand abroad, which led to a joint venture with Philips Electronics in the field of public telecommunication equipment in 1984. In 1996, to solve the channel conflict between AT&T the operator and AT&T the equipment vendor, the company decided to split into three independent companies: AT&T – the operator of long-distance and international communication services; Lucent Technologies – the equipment division, which included Bell Labs; and NCR, the computing business – to become an independent entity again. In this move the WaveLAN activities moved from AT&T Global Information Systems to Lucent Technologies.

27 The aggregate data rate includes the inefficiencies due to latencies in medium access, overhead in transmit frames, loss due to errors and overlapping channels in FHSS.

28 Companies that were involved in product development included: Butterfly Communications, Compaq, HP, IBM, Intel, iReady, Microsoft, Motorola, OTC Telecom, Proxim, RF Monolithics, Samsung and Symbionics (Lansford, 1999).

29 According to Marcus, a consideration for choosing FH might have been that the eleven-chip PN code defined in IEEE 802.11 direct sequence was questioned by some members of the FCC Office of Engineering and Technology with respect to whether it was in full compliance with the FCC rules.

30 HomeRF features that were claimed were: good support for voice and data by using both TDMA and CSMA/CA access mechanisms; support for four high-quality voice

connections with 32 kbit/s adaptive differential pulse code modulation (ADPCM); high data throughput at 1.6 Mbit/s; three levels of encryption – none/basic/robust; power management for isochronous and asynchronous modes; and a 24 bit network identity (Negus, Stephens and Lansford, 2001).

31 These would entail power reductions of 68 per cent and 80 per cent, respectively. Note that most of the IEEE 802.11 devices operate on a power level of less than 10 per cent of the maximum allowed level.

32 Lansford was co-chair of the Technical Committee for the HomeRF industry working group and wireless system architect with Intel Corporation.

33 This notion was said to be confirmed in a personal statement by David King, the CEO of Proxim, admitting that the Lucent Technologies' deal with Apple was the real blow to HomeRF.

34 See also Negus and Petrick (2008) for a detailed discussion of HomeRF in the context of WLAN developments.

35 Note that, in Europe, the 900 MHz band is used for GSM services.

36 IEEE 802.3 and IEEE 802.5; ISO 8802.3 and ISO 8802.5.

37 Audio at 32 kbit/s, 10 nanosecond (ns) latency; video 2 Mbit/s, 100 ns latency.

38 The PHY allowed for frequency-shift keying (FSK) and Gaussian minimum-shift keying (GMSK) modulation.

39 In the period from 1996 to 1998 the Fifth Framework of the EU research pro-gramme contained a project called 'Magic Wand' that aimed at – and succeeded in – developing a demonstrator of wireless ATM technology based on OFDM radios that motivated a number of European players to take up the challenge of developing HIPERLAN/2.

40 The specification was aimed at creating a free-forming mesh-type wireless network that had the capability to connect to other networks, for instance wired networks.

41 The PHY covers BPSK, QPSK, 16QAM and 64QAM modulation (see Annex 1 for definitions).

42 The only differences are minor, related to the use of ATM by HIPERLAN/2 and CSMA/CA by IEEE 802.11.

43 A number of Japanese companies became interested in HIPERLAN/2, and initiated a parallel effort under the name of MMAC (multimedia mobile access communications).

44 The rules were changed in 2002 into a spectrum density and maximum total power specification versus a spreading gain specification, opening up the possibility of also using OFDM in the 2.4 GHz band (FCC, 2002).

45 At the time Cees Links was product line manager of WLAN products.

46 Personal communication with Tuch, 2009.

47 Two years later Micrilor was acquired by Proxim, whereby it obtained a strong patent portfolio.

48 Soon after the SAB approval, products that conformed with either 1 Mbit/s FH or 2 Mbit/s DS began to appear on the market. The third option, based on infrared, never made it into actual hardware.

49 Note that 802.11a and 802.11b were included in a consolidated standard in 2005.

50 'Characterization of UHF multipath channels', by Theodore S. Rappaport and Clare D. MacGillem, Engineering Research Center for Intelligent Manufacturing Systems,

School for Engineering, Purdue University, West Lafayette, Indiana 47907, TR-ERC 88–12, June 1988.
51 See www.ntia.doc.gov.
52 The *IEEE 802 Policies and Procedures* manual had a clause that prescribed that, when the chair detected block voting, he had to count the votes of the company as one. In practice, this rule was ineffective, because there was no accurate definition of block voting. The current version of the *Policies and Procedures* manual no longer includes that rule.
53 On the basis of participation of the Utrecht Engineering Centre, in particular Richard van Nee, in the European 'Magic Wand' project, OFDM was positioned for the 802.11a standard (see also van Nee and Prasad, 2000).
54 Profiling is used to select a set of attributes of a base standard that meets a certain application need. The need for profiling is sometimes considered a sign of a weakness, as the base standard can include many options, often as a result of compromises in the decision-making process.
55 Personal communication from Donald Loughry, 2009.
56 Whether or not this view is justified is a matter of debate. For a slightly different view, see, for example, Jakobs (2002) and Sherif (2003).
57 In Europe, the IEEE has been perceived by many as a consortium, although it is an ANSI-accredited US national standards body.
58 For example, in 1994 the United States abandoned GOSIP, the 'Government Open Systems Interconnection Profile', thus acknowledging the 'victory' of the Transmission Control Protocol/Internet Protocol (TCP/IP) protocol suite. The popularity of the World Wide Web was perhaps the final nail in OSI's coffin.
59 See Jakobs (2003) for a perhaps less biased discussion of this view.
60 The ICTSB is 'an initiative from the three recognized European standards organizations and specification providers to co-ordinate specification activities in the field of Information and Communications Technologies' (www.ictsb.org).
61 They do this, however, without going into too much detail about what exactly (F)RAND means.
62 Historically, the definition of 'due process' has included notice and hearing, allowing the defendant to speak and state his/her case, the right of appeal, judicial process, fairness, reasonableness, impartiality, equality, common law and agreed-upon usage (the acid test of due process: see Gray and Bodson, 1995) and equal protection in law.
63 The European Association for the Co-ordination of Consumer Representation in Standardisation.
64 The European Office of Crafts, Trades and Small and Medium-sized Enterprises for Standardisation.
65 Both the IEEE and BRAN work according to a consensus. In BRAN it is by asking if there is any objection to accepting (something not specifically defined), and it is 'decided' when nobody dares to raise his/her voice, whereas in the IEEE the decision phrase is documented and each member is invited to cast a vote; the decision is taken when a well-defined support level is reached.
66 See www.cen.eu/boss/supporting/reference+documents/vienna+agreement/vienna+agreement.asp.

67 See www.iec.ch/about/partners/agreements/cenelec-e.htm.
68 'Where appropriate, ETSI will base its activities on Partnership Projects committed to basic principles such as openness, clear Intellectual Property Rights (IPR) policy and financial co-responsibility, to be established with partners of any kind (global and regional, Standards Development Organizations (SDOs) and Fora, etc.).' See www.etsi.org/etsi_galaxy/worldwide/partnership/partnership_a.htm.
69 Somewhat strangely, the literature has thus far largely ignored this topic. Only a few findings have been published (Jakobs, Procter and Williams, 2001; Spring and Weiss, 1995).
70 This particular comment is a respondent's observation in connection with a working group other than 802.11.
71 To be complete with respect to the IEEE802.11 standard, an infrared variant should also be mentioned.

References

ANSI (2005). *United States Standards Strategy*. Washington, DC: American National Standards Institute. Available at http://publicaa.ansi.org/sites/apdl/Documents/Standards%20Activities/NSSC/USSS-2005%20-%20FINAL.pdf (accessed 18 March 2009).

(2006). *ANSI Essential Requirements: Due Process Requirements for American National Standards*. Washington, DC: American National Standards Institute. Available at http://publicaa.ansi.org/sites/apdl/Documents/Standards%20Activities/American%20National%20Standards/Procedures,%20Guides,%20and%20Forms/ER0106.doc (accessed 18 March 2009).

(2007a). *Accredited Standards Developers*. Washington, DC: American National Standards Institute. Available at http://publicaa.ansi.org/sites/apdl/Documents/Standards%20Activities/American%20National%20Standards/ANSI%20Accredited%20Standards%20Developers/AUG07SDO.pdf (accessed 18 March 2009).

(2007b). *Overview of the US Standardization System* (2nd edn.). Washington, DC: American National Standards Institute. Available at http://publicaa.ansi.org/sites/apdl/Documents/News%20and%20Publications/Brochures/U.S.%20Standardization%20System-07.pdf (accessed 18 March 2009).

Besen, F. M. (1995). 'The standards process in telecommunication and information technology'. In R. W. Hawkins, R. Mansell and J. Skea (eds.). *Standards, Innovation and Competitiveness: The Politics and Economics of Standards in Natural and Technical Environments*. Cheltenham: Edward Elgar, 136–46.

Blind, K., and N. Thumm (2004). 'Interdependencies between intellectual property protection and standardisation strategies'. *Research Policy*. **33** (10), 1583–98.

Blind, K., N. Thumm, R. Bierhals, K. Hossein, E. Iversen, R. van Reekum and B. Rixius. (2002). *Study on the Interaction between Standardisation and Intellectual Property Rights*. Brussels: European Commission.

Cargill, C. F. (1995). *Open Systems Standardization: A Business Approach*. Upper Saddle River, NJ: Prentice Hall.

Carlo, J. (2007). 'IEEE 802: yesterday, today and tomorrow'. Paper presented at the IEEE Steinmetz Award for the 'Father of Wi-Fi'. Delft, 2 February.

CEPT (1991). 'Wide band data transmission systems using spread-spectrum technology in the 2.5 GHz band', Recommendation T/R 10–01. Copenhagen: CEPT.

(1992). 'Harmonised radio frequency bands for high performance radio local area networks (HIPERLANs) in the 5 GHz and 17 GHz frequency range', Recommendation T/R 22–06. Copenhagen: CEPT.

(1999). *Compatibility Studies Related to the Possible Extension Band for Hiperlan at 5 GHz*, ERC Report no. 72. Copenhagen: CEPT.

Crocker, D. (1993). 'Making standards the IETF way'. *ACM Standard View.* **1** (1), 48–56.

De Wit, B., and R. Meyer (2004). *Strategy: Process, Content, Context – An International Perspective.* London: Thomson.

EC (1985). *Technical Harmonisation and Standardisation: A New Approach*, COM(1985)19 final. Brussels: European Commission.

(1998). 'Directive 98/34/EC of the European Parliament and of the Council of 22 June 1998 laying down a procedure for the provision of information in the field of technical standards and regulations'. *Official Journal.* L 204, 37–48.

Egyedi, T., K. Jakobs and E. Monteiro (2003). *Helping SDOs to Reach Users.* Aachen: RWTH Aachen University.

ETSI (1993). 'Wideband transmission systems; technical characteristics and test conditions for data transmission equipment operating in the 2.4 GHz ISM band and using spread spectrum modulation techniques', ETS 300 328 Radio Equipment and Systems. Sophia-Antipolis: ETSI.

(1998). 'HIgh PErformance Radio Local Area Network (HIPERLAN), type 1 functional specification', ETS 300 652 Radio Equipment and Systems. Sophia-Antipolis: ETSI.

FCC (1985). 'First Report and Order in the matter of authorization of spread spectrum and other wideband emissions not presently provided for in the FCC Rules and Regulations', General Docket no. 81–413. Washington, DC: Federal Communications Commission.

(1999). 'Amendment of part 15 of the commission's rules regarding spread spectrum devices: notice of proposed rulemaking, released June 24, 1999', ET [Office of Engineering and Technology] Docket no. 99–231. Washington, DC: Federal Communications Commission. Available at www.fcc.gov/searchtools.html (accessed 8 February 2008).

(2000). 'Amendment of part 15 of the commission's rules regarding spread spectrum devices: first Report and Order, released August 31, 2000', ET Docket no. 99–231. Washington, DC: Federal Communications Commission. Available at www.fcc.gov/searchtools.html (accessed 8 February 2008).

(2002). 'Amendment of part 15 of the commission's rules regarding spread spectrum devices; second Report and Order, released May 30, 2002', ET Docket no. 99–231. Washington, DC: Federal Communications Commission. Available at www.fcc.gov/searchtools.html (accessed 8 February 2008).

Gray, E. M., and D. Bodson (1995). 'Preserving due process in standards work'. *StandardView.* **3** (4), 130–9.

Hamel, G., and C. K. Prahalad (1994). *Competing for the Future: Breakthrough Strategies for Seizing Control of Your Industry and Creating the Markets of Tomorrow.* Boston: Harvard Business School Press.

IDABC (2008). 'Draft document as basis for EIF 2.0'. Available at http://ec.europa.eu/ idabc/servlets/Doc?id=31597 (accessed 18 March 2009).

ITU-T (2002). *Guide for ITU-T and ISO/IEC JTC 1 Cooperation*. Geneva: ITU. Available at www.itu.int/rec/dologin.asp?lang=e&id=T-REC-A.23–200111-I!AnnA! PDF-E&type=items (accessed 8 February 2008).

Iversen, E. J. (1999). 'Standardization and intellectual property rights: ETSI's controversial search for new IPR procedures'. In IEEE. *Proceedings of the First International Conference on Standardization and Innovation in Information Technology*. New York: IEEE Press, 55–63.

Jakobs, K. (2002). 'A proposal for an alternative standards setting process'. *IEEE Communications Magazine*. **40** (7), 118–23.

   (2003). 'A closer look at the Internet's standards setting process'. In IADIS [International Association for Development of the Information Society]. *Proceedings of the IADIS International Conference 'WWW/Internet 2003'*. Lisbon: IADIS Press, 557–64.

   (2004). '(E-business and ICT) standardisation and SME users: mutually exclusive?' In IADIS. *Proceedings of the Multi-Conference on Business Information Systems*. Göttingen: Cuvillier Verlag, 101–16.

Jakobs, K., and M. Mora (2008). 'Co-ordinating rule setters: co-operation in ICT standards setting'. In International Conference on Information Resources Management. *Information Resources Management: International Conference, 2008*. Red Hook, NY: Curran Associates, chap. 17.

Jakobs, K., R. Procter and R. Williams (1998). 'Telecommunication standardization: do we really need the user?' In IEEE. *Telecommunications, 1998: Sixth IEEE Conference on Telecommunications*. New York: IEEE Press, 165–9.

   (2000). 'Standardization, innovation and implementation of information technology'. In L. B. Rasmussen, C. Beardon and S. Munari (eds.). *Computers and Networks in the Age of Globalization: Proceedings of the Fifth Human Choice and Computers International Conference*. Dordrecht: Kluwer Academic, 201–18.

   (2001). 'The making of standards: looking inside the work groups'. *IEEE Communications Magazine*. **39** (4), 102–7.

Kamerman, A. (1996a). 'Selecting spread-spectrum specs to deploy wireless LANs'. *Asian Electronics Engineer*. **10** (5).

   (1996b). 'Spread-spectrum techniques drive WLAN performance'. *Microwaves and RF*. **35** (9), 109–14.

   (1997). 'Application note: spread-spectrum schemes for microwave-frequency WLANs'. *Microwave Journal*. **40** (2) 80–90.

Koppenjan, J. F. M., and J. P. M. Groenewegen (2005). 'Institutional design for complex technological systems'. *International Journal of Technology, Policy and Management*. **5** (3), 240–57.

Lansford, J. (1999). *HomeRF: Bringing Wireless Connectivity Home*. Santa Clara, CA: Intel.

Lemstra, W., and V. Hayes (2009). 'The shaping of the IEEE 802.11 standard: the role of the innovating firm in the case of Wi-Fi'. In K. Jakobs (ed.). *Information Communication Technology Standardization for E-Business Sectors: Integrating Supply and Demand Factors*. Hershey, PA: IGI Global, 98–126.

Lemstra, W., V. Hayes and M. van der Steen (2009). 'Network modernization in the telecom sector: the case of Wi-Fi'. In R. W. Künneke, J. Groenewegen and J.-F. Auger (eds.). *The Governance of Network Industries: Institutions, Technology and Policy in Reregulated Infrastructures*. Cheltenham: Edward Elgar, chap. 6.

Monteiro, E., O. Hanseth and M. Hatling (1994). *Standardisation of Information Infrastructure: Where Is the Flexibility?*, Technical Report no. 18/94. Trondheim: University of Trondheim.

Negus, K. J., and A. Petrick (2008). 'History of wireless local area networks (WLANs) in the unlicensed bands'. Paper presented at the conference 'The evolution of unlicensed wireless policy'. Arlington, VA, 4 April.

Negus, K. J., A. P. Stephens and J. Lansford (2001). 'HomeRF: wireless networking for the connected home'. *IEEE Personal Communications*. **8** (1), 72–4.

Palo Wireless (2003). 'HomeRF overview and market positioning'. Available at www.palowireless.com/homerf/homerf8.asp (accessed 7 August 2007).

Reilly, A. K. (1994). 'A US perspective on standards development'. *IEEE Communications Magazine*. **32** (1), 30–6.

Robert, H. M. (2000 [1876]). *Robert's Rules of Order: Newly Revised*. Cambridge, MA: DaCapo Press.

Sherif, M. H. (2003). 'When is standardization slow?' *International Journal of IT Standards and Standardization Research*. **1** (1), 19–32.

Shim, R. (2003). 'HomeRF Working Group disbands'. New York: CNET. Available at http://news.com.com/2102–1039_3–979611.html (accessed 7 August 2007).

Solomon, R. J., and A. M. Rutkowski (1992). 'Standards-making for IT: old versus new models'. Paper presented at the conference on the economic dimension of standards: 'Users and governments in IT standardization'. Tokyo, 18 November.

Spring, M. B., and M. B. H. Weiss (1995). 'Financing the standards development process'. In B. Kahin and J. Abbate (eds.). *Standards Policy for Information Infrastructure*. Cambridge, MA: MIT Press, 289–320.

Tuch, B. T., and M. A. Masleid (1991). *Wireless Information Transmission System*. Alexandria, VA: US Patent and Trademark Office.

Updegrove, A. (2006). 'Participating In standard setting organizations: value propositions, roles and strategies'. *Consortium Standards Bulletin*. **5** (9). Available at www.consortiuminfo.org/bulletins/oct06/php.

Van Nee, R., and R. Prasad (2000). *OFDM for Wireless Multimedia Communications*. Norwood, MA: Artech House.

Werle, R. (2001). 'Institutional aspects of standardization: jurisdictional conflicts and the choice of standardization organizations'. *Journal of European Public Policy*. **8** (3), 392–410.

(2002). 'Lessons learnt from the Internet: hands off, hands on, or what role of public policy in Europe?' *Druzboslovne Razprave* [*Journal of Social Science Studies*]. **18**, 63–82.

4   Crossing the chasm: the Apple AirPort

Wolter Lemstra,
with contributions from Cees Links, Alex Hills,
Vic Hayes, Dorothy Stanley, Albert Heijl and Bruce Tuch

4.1   Crossing the chasm

'Changing the rules rarely happens overnight' is a characterisation that certainly applies to NCR and the Wi-Fi journey; or, in the words of Martin Bradley, general manager at NCR: 'Bringing new technologies to market takes time, and, whatever time in your estimate it will take, it will take longer.' Although the value aspect of deploying a wireless LAN appears an attractive enough proposition – obviating the need for the expensive cabling systems required for a wired LAN – the initial sales efforts showed that the introduction of the new technology was not the smooth ride suggested by the stylised technology adoption curves presented in marketing textbooks.

In this respect, Moore (1991) points to the difference in the process between continuous and discontinuous innovations.[1] Continuous innovations are often incremental and do not require consumers to change their habits. Discontinuous innovations, on the other hand, demand significant changes not only on the part of the consumer but also in the related infrastructure. While recognising that companies have the objective of subsequently capturing each group of buyers, from the early adopters to the laggards, Moore emphasises the differences between five buyer groups and companies' need to adjust their marketing and sales effort to each group. The alternative is that they 'lose momentum, [and] miss the transition to the next segment, thereby never to gain the promised land of profit-margin leadership in the middle of the bell curve' (Moore, 1991).

Moore points in particular to the 'gap' or 'chasm' that exists between the requirements that have to be satisfied for the category of early adopters and those that are related to the category of the early majority, the beginning of the mass market (emphasis in original):

What the early adopter is buying ... is some kind of *change agent*. By being the first to implement this change in their industry, the early adopters expect to get a jump on the competition, whether from lower product costs, faster time to market, more complete customer service, or some other business advantage ... By contrast, the early majority want to buy a *productivity improvement* for existing operations. They are looking to minimize the discontinuity with old ways ... They want technology to enhance, not

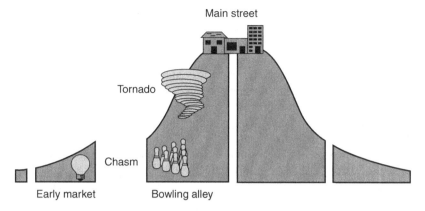

Figure 4.1 Crossing the chasm
Source: This figure appears in *Living on the Fault Line*; copyright © 2002, Geoffrey A. Moore; reprinted by permission of the author.

overthrow, the established ways of doing business. And above all, they do not want to debug somebody else's product. By the time they adopt it, they want it to work properly and to integrate appropriately with their existing technology base.

The pragmatists represented by the early majority want the 'whole product', which has become defined as 'the minimum set of products and services necessary to ensure that the target customer will achieve his or her compelling reasons to buy' (Moore, 1995). As a result, the successful strategy to cross the chasm is 'to identify with a beachhead of pragmatic customers in a mainstream market segment and to accelerate the formation of 100 percent of their whole product'. Moore uses the metaphor of the *bowling alley* and the *head pin* to relate to this niche market expansion strategy: a careful selection of the initial market segment, conquering this segment by providing a whole product and subsequently moving to the adjacent segments, building on the references obtained in the first segment.

In the technology adoption life cycle, Moore distinguishes six zones, which can be characterised as follows (Moore, 1995) (see also Figure 4.1).

(1) *The early market*: a time of great excitement, when customers are technology enthusiasts and visionaries looking to be first to get on board with the new paradigm.

(2) *The chasm*: a time of great despair, when the early market's interest wanes but the mainstream market is still not comfortable with the immaturity of the solutions available.

(3) *The bowling alley*: a period of niche-based adoption in advance of the general marketplace, driven by compelling customer needs and the willingness of vendors to craft niche-specific solutions.

(4) *The tornado*: a period of mass-market adoption, when the general market-place switches over to the new infrastructure paradigm.
(5) *Main street*: a period of after-market development, when the base infrastructure has been deployed and the goal now is to flesh out its potential.
(6) *End of life*: this can come all too soon in high-tech products, because of the semiconductor engine driving price/performance to unheard-of levels, enabling wholly new paradigms to come to market and supplant the leaders, which themselves had only just arrived.

We can now resume our account of the Wi-Fi journey based on the stages or zones identified by Moore, and move from the 'innovator' stage described in Chapters 2 and 3 to a description of the developments in the 'early market' and the 'chasm', and then, using the 'bowling alley', move into the 'tornado'.

4.2   The early market

The decision by NCR to exploit the new business opportunity through the development of an open standard in cooperation with others was an important step in realising its WLAN vision. Although partners can be aligned through the standardisation process, real products are required to convince potential customers of the benefits that wireless LANs provide. Market research was initiated by NCR to establish the right product-positioning strategy. Focus group meetings of IT experts representing targeted customer segments were organised in New York, Chicago and Los Angeles to discuss the concept of wireless LANs and to identify the potential 'pros' and 'cons'. These sessions were complemented with a quantitative study, involving the interviewing of 150 companies by telephone. This study was completed with ten in-depth face-to-face interviews.

The outcome in general was positive. The representatives agreed that the (re)wiring of buildings was cumbersome and expensive, with a cost estimated at between US$200 and 1,500 per 'drop'; and only a very few companies had applied a 'structured wiring plan'. The lack of expertise was also mentioned as an issue. The connection of PC adapters to the coaxial cable and localising faults in the early Ethernet systems were both known to be awkward procedures. Lower overall costs were identified as the key feature of wireless LANs.

4.2.1   The product launch

Based on the market intelligence obtained and on its contributions to the IEEE standardisation process, but ahead of a formal standards approval, NCR launched its first WaveLAN product for the US market at Networld in Dallas in September 1990. The product operated at 915 MHz and used one

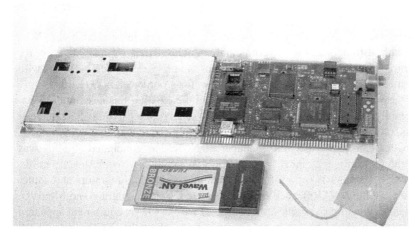

Figure 4.2 First and subsequent NCR WLAN products for the US market

communication channel providing a bandwidth of 2 Mbit/s. It was a desktop PC plug-in board, essentially a radio-based network interface card (NIC), and it required an external antenna (see also Figure 4.2; the box at the right bottom shows the external antenna). At the other end of the radio connection was another NIC, providing the link to the existing wired infrastructure.

The general product release was in May 1991, after radio certification and manufacturing start-up issues had been cleared and resolved.[2] Prospective customers appeared to be fascinated by the technology, but the benefits were perceived as marginal and the price as too high. At the product launch the price was set at US$1,390 per card, which included the Novell Netware driver.[3] This compared favourably with the competing wireless LAN product of Motorola, the Altair. For the NCR development team the Altair had been the benchmark. Motorola had opted to implement a product in the 18 GHz band, involving a different technology, that was inherently more expensive, however, and this made it virtually impossible to reach a cost base lower than US$1,000.[4] Moreover, it would be very difficult, if not impossible, to scale down the product to make it portable (Tuch, 2009).[5] For comparison purposes, an ARCNet wired LAN card was sold at US$300, an Ethernet card at US$495 and a Token Ring card at US$645. Given the difference in implementation, however, only a total cost of ownership (TCO) analysis would provide a fair comparison, including the cabling costs on one side and the costs of WLAN cards at the server side on the other. Although this improved the case significantly, within a short period of time NCR would lower the price of the PC plug-in to US$995.

4.2.2   The sales channel

The wireless LAN product was introduced first to existing customers of NCR, to retail customers and to governmental agencies. Trials were set up with, for example, J. C. Penney's and Sears. One of the early sales successes was with Chemical Bank in Raleigh, North Carolina, for an order of 1,000 cards.

These efforts quickly identified a flaw in the existing business model. Traditionally, NCR had operated in the 'direct sales' mode, selling checkout systems, minicomputers, etc. to large accounts in horizontal and vertical markets. As Cees Links, product line manager at NCR, has concluded: '[T]his was not the appropriate channel for something as small as a wireless LAN card.' Hence, the emphasis was shifted to distributors, system integrators and value-added resellers (VARs), such as Computerland, Softsel, Ingram and Micro/D. Although this improved sales, the selling of wireless LAN equipment appeared to be complex, and despite many marketing efforts by NCR, including a prepackaged 'Network in a box', the sales volume remained low.[6]

NCR had yet another option that could be pursued: the original equipment manufacturer (OEM) sales channel. The OEM sales force was already used to sell products from the Semiconductor Division to companies such as IBM, Apple, Compaq, Toshiba and Digital. To the list were added Nokia, Sony, Samsung, Dell and Siemens, but they all made very little response to the sales efforts – with the exception of Toshiba, which initially cooperated on portions of the MAC protocol, although no further cooperation evolved. Sometimes companies responded by sending a representative to the IEEE 802.11 meetings. According to Cees Links, an interesting lesson could be learned:[7]

Several of these computer companies were quite interested; but that was it. Nothing happened. Among the PC vendors there appeared to be a strong herd mentality, and very few were willing to take the step into something new. This is remarkable, as they all claimed to be innovative and to provide thought leadership. The exception was Apple. Unfortunately, Apple was already working with Motorola, but not with the Altair product line.[8] They were applying a frequency-hopping version of spread spectrum while the NCR product used the direct-sequence version, and for some reason Apple had an 'internal hang-up' on DSSS and declared FHSS to be the technology of choice, claiming that it was more resistant to interference.

NCR approached not just PC companies but networking companies as well. 3Com was not interested, in effect asking NCR to leave the company alone until there was an IEEE standard. Xircom seemed similarly uninterested, although it was much more interested the year afterwards, by which time it had launched its own internal development programme. The initial success came with Pure-data, a successful Ethernet card supplier. The result was ambivalent, however, as one of the first customers it pursued was Canada Revenue, the Canadian tax authorities, which was also pursued by NCR's direct sales force. Consequently, the first 'channel conflict' had emerged already. Then Digital Equipment Corporation became interested in cooperation, strongly supported by its CEO, Ken Olson. This company focused on the access point side of the business, and would launch its version as 'RoamAbout'. Over the years DEC became a serious competitor, resulting in some serious channel conflicts as a consequence of the two-prong strategy. NEC in Japan, and Solectek in the United States, became the two most successful partners in the OEM channel.

An unexpected opportunity appeared in the first year after the product launch: the need for outdoor point-to-point connections. Links continues his account of events:

In fact, more than a half of the leads coming in were for outdoor applications, despite the fact that the product was designed for indoor networking – in an office, in a store, in a warehouse or factory.[9] What customers really liked to use the product for was to connect to the building on the other side of the street, or further downtown. Fortunately, our design was modular; the omnidirectional antenna, designed for indoor use, could easily be replaced with a directional antenna and if necessary could include an 'antenna booster'. VARs, such as Persoft and Hiperlink, did a lot of pioneering work and started businesses on the basis of a long-range value proposition, and achieved amazing results. Anecdotal stories talked about connecting buildings across fifty miles in Kansas. Most of the initial enthusiasm of customers came from this type of application, as not only was it significantly cheaper than leasing a T1 line,[10] it was under their own control and more quickly installed.

During the course of 1991 it became clear that wireless technology was interesting to the market, but that the product appeared to be incomplete in the view of prospective customers. Links continues his account:

In principle, the WaveLAN[11] card was intended to replace the cable between the PC and the main computer or central server in the computer room. In many cases, however, the computer room was too far away, even on another floor. We developed many ideas to solve this distance problem: repeaters, 'leaky cable', passive antenna amplifiers. None of them was considered feasible except for the concept of a base station, initially called an access point (AP). The functionality of the AP includes transmitter, receiver, antenna and a bridge to route packets to and from the wired network infrastructure – essentially, the Ethernet. We realised we would need multiple APs to cover larger buildings, to be connected to the wired LAN infrastructure, plus the capability of roaming (also called 'hand-off') between the APs. When walking around in a building with a portable/laptop you should remain connected, and when coming within the range of another access point the communication session should not be interrupted as a result of the switchover.

The concept was easy to describe and could readily be adopted, given its similarity with cellular communication. The implementation looked relatively easy, as the client stations, whether PC or laptop, could keep track of the signal strength of each AP within reach and switch the connection to the AP with the best transmission performance. The R&D effort increased significantly, however, and became comparable to the efforts involved in the development of the NIC, when the system had to be 'scaled up'.

4.2.3   Security concerns

The use of radio waves in wireless LANs raised the issue of security. Uncertainty about the level of security provided raised doubts in the minds of prospective customers, which in turn frustrated WLAN adoption. It is much easier to eavesdrop on a wireless system than on a wired system that is buried in the ground, or that uses optical rather than electrical signals. From the outset WaveLAN included as an option a data encryption security (DES) chip, based on a fully documented algorithm available in the public domain. This DES chip was developed by a Dutch company and manufactured in France. It appeared that the implementation and distribution of this algorithm was controlled by the US National Security Agency, however. After many deliberations, NCR was allowed to include the chip without restrictions in its shipments to the United States and Canada. Shipments to financial institutions (mainly banks) in other countries would be subject to export controls: as long as the financial institution was in a country that was not blacklisted, such as Libya, North Korea or South Yemen, the chips could be provided to these institutions.

The use of spread-spectrum technology also attracted the attention of the NSA, and its Dutch equivalent. One of the concerns of these agencies is their ability to monitor communications if national security issues are involved. The use of the low spreading code of eleven chips per bit made this issue melt away quickly.

For other non-financial customers, NCR developed a DES-based algorithm with reduced complexity. This algorithm was screened and approved by the NSA, and implemented under the name of advanced encryption security (AES). This chip was used until the IEEE standard was implemented, which included the so-called wired equivalent privacy (WEP) algorithm, providing a basic authentication and encryption method.

4.2.4   Getting the product market combination right

To improve the results of their sales efforts, the NCR team emphasised the total cost of ownership of WaveLAN in replacing cable. Although the argument was persuasive, many prospective purchasers hesitated to undertake the change because of the significant upfront investment required. The case could be argued more successfully if the WLAN supported mobile applications; but the early products were too bulky and required too much power to be feasible for portable devices.

Getting the product right was further complicated by the different computing environments that prospective customers had. There existed many networking flavours, all requiring different software drivers. Next to Microsoft and Novell, which were battling for market leadership, there was, for instance, Banyan Vines. To complicate matters further, moreover, IBM introduced a new hardware interface, the Microchannel bus, to replace the AT (advanced technology) bus.

The good news was that the market did exhibit price elasticity: lower prices did lead to an increase in volume. Volumes remained low, however, as most deals involved ten to twenty cards, with contracts for 1,000 cards or more being the exception. Larger projects were pursued with the major high street stores, such as J. C. Penney's, Littlewoods, Younkers, House of Fraser, Victoria's Secret, Stop & Shop and Wal-Mart. The results were mixed at best, though; for instance, J. C. Penney's contracted for three department stores an average of six APs and eighty point-of-sale terminals.

The combination of WaveLAN and outdoor communications continued to be very compelling. The reach of the card was extended by using 'power amplifiers', which boosted the output power well beyond the maximum prescribed by the FCC. As in these point-to-point applications, directional antennae were used; the potential harmful interference was relatively low. The FCC did attempt to reinforce compliance with the regulation, however, by prescribing a special antenna connector for these applications, available only through recognised outlets.

Selling packaged solutions, sometimes in combination with other NCR products, was another way of going to market that was being pursued. For American Airlines, a pre-configured travel agency computer system was proposed, but no contract was closed. In the banking sector, attempts were more successful with the so-called 'replicated branch', which included a centralised staging and testing of the computer system of a bank branch office. The system would subsequently be trucked to the site and be installed overnight. Before customers started coming in the next day the whole system would be replaced, without disruption and running instantaneously.

Another market opportunity that emerged involved the 'tablet', the computer without a keyboard. Turning the tablet into a mobile device was the clear target of the companies pursuing wireless LAN business. Apple pioneered the technology as part of its personal digital assistant (PDA) programme. NCR was also involved, as were Fujitsu and Grid, and start-ups such as EO and Momenta. In 1992 Bill Gates and Steve Balmer visited NCR in support of a collaborative effort on the operating system for the tablet computer. This opportunity was used to present and discuss wireless LANs as well. The market did not appear to be ready for the tablet, however: the tablet was bulky and the handwriting technology was considered to be insufficiently mature and too slow in execution. The meeting did not result in any wireless LAN business with Microsoft either.

It was around this time that wireless wide area networks also emerged. It all started with an internal network going public: the Ardis network, used by Motorola and IBM technicians. In an effort to improve economies of scale, Ardis invited other companies to develop modems for use with the Ardis network. NCR declined the invitation, maintaining its focus on wireless LAN. The cellular digital packet data (CDPD) initiative by McGaw, to add data communication to the cellular voice network, also falls into this category.[12] Collaboration was proposed by McCaw, but declined by NCR on the grounds that the business case could not be made profitable. Moreover, there were no clear, perceived synergies with the WLAN developments.

4.2.5   The market outside the United States

There were early applications of WLANs in Europe as well. A typical case was the installation at the European Container Terminal (ECT) in Rotterdam, the Netherlands, for communication with automated stacking cranes and automated guided vehicles. Albert Heijl, formerly with the ECT and currently working at Agentschap Telecom,[13] tells the story:

In 1986 a licence was granted for an adaptive data communication system using the assignment for voice-based radio, occupying 0.5 MHz bandwidth in the 410 to 430 MHz band and providing an effective data rate of 12,000 bit/s. With the capacity in this band being limited, growth had to be accommodated in the newly allocated 2.4 GHz band. To address the concerns of potential interference among multiple applications in this band, a working group was formed with representatives of the Ministry of Transport and industry – including ECT, NCR, NOB (the Dutch broadcasting organisation), PTT Research, NEDAP (a Netherlands-based organisation supplying information systems) and Radio Holland (interested in RF identification and tagging). Following extensive interference testing by PTT Research, it was concluded that the coexistence of radio label systems, mobile video links and radio LANs was feasible. ECT followed through with the deployment testing of a frequency-hopping system, which it considered to be more robust for its purposes given the highly 'reflective' nature of a container terminal.[14]

After their initial successes in the US market the NCR sales and marketing teams started to explore more vigorously the opportunities for WLANs 'abroad'. Unfortunately, in Europe the 900 MHz band was assigned for the use of GSM, the European digital cellular communication system. As the licences for GSM were granted to network operators on an exclusive basis, it was incompatible with the licence-exempt regime of WLANs. Soon after the establishment of working group IEEE 802.11 in 1990, however, an ad hoc group was formed within CEPT[15] charged with preparing the 'Recommendation' for the use of the 2.4 GHz ISM band for WLANs in Europe. This group consisted of representatives of the responsible ministries and agencies in the United Kingdom, the Netherlands and Sweden. Cees Links continues his account on the related sales and marketing efforts:

NCR started to push on two fronts: on the one hand, a lobbying effort for the assignment of spectrum; and, on the other hand, a marketing effort to create customer awareness. The latter involved publishing a set of articles on the wireless Ethernet and how it had established itself in the United States – an approach that would be replicated by NCR in Japan. The situation was not as trivial as the denotation '2.4 GHz band' suggests. In the United States this refers to the band from 2,400 to 2,473.5 MHz, in Australia from 2,000 to 2,450 MHz and in Japan from 2,474 to 2,484 MHz. Within Europe different countries had different rules: France allowed the use of 2.4 GHz only in the seventy major cities, as the military also used the band. In Italy the band was in principle licence-free, but for data communication a licence fee was required.

Initial opposition to the harmonisation of the 2.4 GHz band for wireless LANs in Europe came from an unexpected source: Olivetti, which had a vested interest in DECT and considered wireless LANs a potential competitor. Interestingly, as Olivetti withdrew from the market the licence fee for data communication was also dropped by the Italian government.

In 1992 the lobbying efforts achieved success, as the European Union officially assigned the 2.4 GHz ISM band for the use of wireless LANs. Moreover, the CEPT team identified higher-frequency bands for potential wireless LAN application. In July 1994 it assigned the 5,150 to 5,250 MHz band and the 17.1 to 17.3 GHz band, with a potential extension with the 5,250 to 5,300 MHz band in the future. This spectrum was reserved for devices operating according to the HIPERLAN standard being developed by ETSI (see also Chapter 3).

Now that the major industrial countries had allowed wireless LAN devices, virtually all other states followed their lead and allowed the use of WLANs in the 2.4 GHz band. Those countries that had close relations with the United States followed the rules as defined by the FCC, such as a maximum of 1 W transmitted power with a maximum antenna gain of factor four and a minimum 'processing gain' of ten for direct sequence transmitters. Those countries that had more in the way of ties with Europe followed the rules set by the CEPT 'Recommendation', such as a maximum of 100 mW output power, including antenna gain, and a power density requirement of maximum 10 mW/MHz, instead of a processing gain requirement.

4.2.6   Global versus local products

The differences between the early successes in the 915 MHz US market and the 'international' market adopting 2.4 GHz raised the strategic question of whether to manufacture a global product or localised products. The FCC

Report and Order had assigned three ISM bands for WLAN use, and hence the 2.4 GHz band was also available in the United States. The 915 MHz lower-frequency range had the advantage of a larger reach, as the attenuation of radio waves increases with frequency. In the 2.4 GHz band more spectrum had been assigned, however, and hence more channels could be accommodated and used simultaneously, thereby increasing the system's performance. In the 915 MHz band only one channel could be accommodated. While, on the one hand, a global product would be more cost-effective, production costs at 2.4 GHz would be higher than at 915 MHz. Moreover, as the products would provide the same functionality, it would be difficult to differentiate them in pricing.

The decision was, essentially, determined by market forces. Competitors that were marketing products only in the 2.4 GHz band pushed the advantage of more channels, which gave the customers the impression that the 2.4 GHz product was providing a higher data rate. With the illusion of higher speed, the issue of a shorter range became a moot point. As Links observes:

This shift in the market implied a further setback for the WLAN business case. The shift to a 2.4 GHz product would further erode the margins, which were already very tight: at or below 10 per cent, whereas 30 per cent was desirable. The cost of a 2.4 GHz radio was estimated to be US$350 or more. To combine a competitive market price with a reasonable margin, the costs should come down to US$250 or less. Aggressive cost reduction efforts would have to be started immediately, and hence the integration of functionality into a smaller chipset – although there was one advantage: we would not have to spend a lot of marketing dollars in moving the early adopters from the 'old' 915 MHz product to the 'new' 2.4 GHz product.

A new form of competition in the 2.4 GHz band came from an unexpected internal source. Part of the 1982 agreement between the US Department of Justice and AT&T implied that, with the break-up of the telecommunications company, AT&T would be allowed to diversify into the computing business. To strengthen its position, AT&T acquired NCR in 1991 for US$7.4 billion, to extend the product line and to provide the company with the necessary sales and marketing savvy that the former utility company was lacking. The original idea of Bob Allen, CEO of AT&T, was that NCR would assume the leadership role of the Computer Systems Division; in practice, however, AT&T divisional management started to run NCR.

The AT&T Consumer Products Division looked at the 2.4 GHz band for a new generation of digital cordless phones. According to Links:

Research by consumer products had shown that the 2.4 GHz band was very appropriate; only some wireless LAN applications interfered. The design requirement was therefore to 'blast WaveLAN out of the band'. It is clear that, with this type of colleague, you do not need any competitors. A lot of intense discussions followed, and AT&T argued that if it did not take the opportunity somebody else would. Proposals to arrive at a win-win solution or to co-market wireless voice and wireless data were rejected. Fortunately, this programme encountered trouble, as the development team could not realise the targeted cost level, and ultimately the programme was cancelled. This case reminded us all that the use of the ISM band for wireless LANs is not 'protected'.

In 1993 AT&T released the 2.4 GHz WaveLAN PC adapter for the global market. It operated at a data transfer rate of 2 Mbit/s and provided thirteen different channels that could be pre-selected within the assigned band. The card was connected to an external antenna. It was also in 1993 that the form factor of the 915 MHz US product was improved through the release of a Personal Computer Memory Card International Association (PCMCIA) card version. The 2.4 GHz version of the card, for the global market, followed in 1995.

4.2.7   Carnegie Mellon University project 'Wireless Andrew'

In 1993 AT&T successfully concluded its first contract for the large-scale installation of WaveLAN, at the Carnegie Mellon University in Pittsburgh. The project involved the establishment of access points to serve some 10,000 students, faculty and staff moving about the university campus. Having CMU as a client provided a perfect test bed for large-scale deployment. Moreover, the experts and expertise available within the academic environment would make CMU a perfect partner in pushing the WaveLAN product to the next level. CMU could also become a lead customer providing access to the campus segment of the LAN market.

Dr Alex Hills, distinguished service professor of engineering and public policy, conceived project 'Wireless Andrew' in 1993, naming it after Andrew Carnegie and Andrew Mellon, and he led the project until 1999. The implementation started in 1994, as a research network funded by the National Science Foundation to support Carnegie Mellon's wireless research initiative; originally it provided coverage in seven campus buildings. Later it was expanded to serve all academic and administrative buildings on the campus.[16] In 2006 there were close to 19,000 wireless cards registered to Carnegie Mellon users. The network now uses over 1,000 access points to cover seventy-six buildings, comprising a total floor area of approximately 4 million square feet, as well as outside areas. Wireless Andrew is built on the university's wired network infrastructure, which in 1994 provided 10 Mbit/s service, while in 2007 100 Mbit/s and gigabit Ethernet service were provided to the desktop. Professor Hills provides a first-hand account:[17]

The main challenge for the Wireless Andrew project team was the large-scale deployment of wireless LAN technology; it was the largest deployment of its kind. While general product specifications and performance characteristics were available from the supplier, no specific guidance was provided on how to deploy the product in a university campus setting. We could confirm that good-quality transmission could be established between the network adapter (NA) or network interface card in the PC and the access point at more than 300 metres in an open environment, but observed that this range was reduced to 20 to 60 metres in office environments. Wood, plaster and glass are not serious barriers to the wireless LAN radio transmissions, but brick and concrete walls can be significant barriers; the greatest obstacle to radio transmissions commonly found in office environments is metal, such as in desks, filing cabinets, reinforced concrete and lift shafts.

Structure of Wireless Andrew

We installed a new IEEE 802.3 Ethernet backbone network on the campus to connect the APs in each building with the rest of the campus wired network through a dedicated switch in the central campus network facility. Each AP is connected to an IEEE 802.3 10BASE-T hub in a building's remote wiring closet near the AP. These hubs, in turn, are connected to a switch in the building's main distribution wiring closet, which is, in turn, connected to the switch in the university's central network facility. This central switch is connected to a router, also in the central network facility, which forms the link between the wireless backbone and the remainder of the campus data network. This structure allows us to operate the high-speed wireless network independently of the campus network and to disconnect the two if necessary. The structure also allows us to separate traffic on the wireless LAN backbone network from traffic on the rest of the network; the router connecting the wireless backbone to the rest of the campus network filters packets based on destination address and passes packets to and from the wireless backbone only as needed. Figure 4.3 shows how the large-scale wireless LAN network is connected to the campus network.

Design challenges

The challenges in building such a large wireless network are designing the network so that the coverage blankets the campus and so that adequate capacity is provided to handle the traffic load generated by the campus community. The design essentially includes two components: selection of AP location, and the assignment of radio frequencies to APs. In laying out a multiple-AP wireless LAN installation, care must be taken to ensure that adequate radio coverage will be provided throughout the service area by carefully locating the APs. Experience shows that the layout must be based on measurements, not just on 'rule-of-thumb' calculations. These measurements involve the extensive testing and careful consideration of radio propagation issues when the service area is as large as an entire campus (Bennington and Bartel, 1997).

The layout and construction of buildings determine the coverage area of each AP, but network performance is also an issue, as an AP and the (mobile) computers within its coverage area share the finite amount of bandwidth available. The CSMA/CA protocol that is used makes radio interference between APs and NAs operating on the same radio channel a particular challenge: if one AP can hear another AP or if it can hear a distant NA, it will defer, just as it would defer to a mobile NA transmitting within

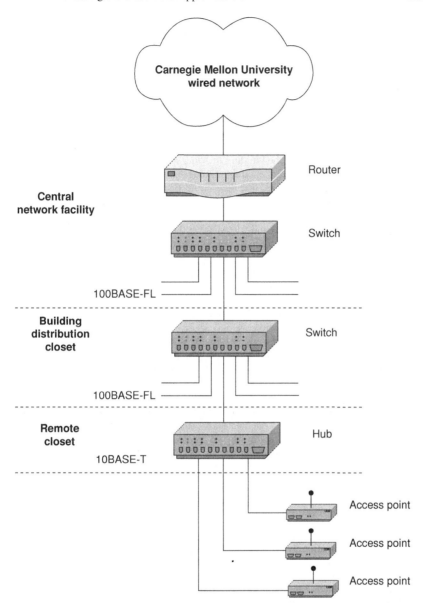

Figure 4.3 The structure of Wireless Andrew
Source: This figure appears in 'Large-scale wireless LAN design', in *IEEE Communications Magazine*; copyright © 2001, IEEE; reprinted by permission of the publisher.

its coverage area. Interference between adjacent APs therefore degrades performance. Similarly, if a mobile NA can be heard by more than one AP, all these APs will defer (Chhaya and Gupta, 1996). Accordingly, the APs should be spaced far apart so as to avoid coverage overlap between APs operating on the same radio channel (co-channel overlap). Another reason to space the APs as far apart as possible is to minimise the cost of equipment and installation. In selecting AP locations, however, coverage gaps must also be avoided.

We have found that approximations are inadequate in doing this type of design. Rather, each building design must be based on careful signal strength measurements. This is particularly challenging given that the building is a three-dimensional space, and an AP located on one floor of the building provides signal coverage to adjacent floors of the same building, and perhaps to other buildings as well.

After the APs have been located and their coverage areas measured, radio channels are assigned to the APs. Eleven DSSS radio channels are available in the 2.400 to 2.4835 GHz band used in North America, but, of these, there are three that have minimal spectral overlap. These are channels 1, 6 and 11. APs can therefore operate on three separate non-interfering channels. Further, some network adapters can switch between channels in order to talk with the AP providing the best signal strength or the one with the lightest traffic load. The use of multiple channels can be very helpful in minimising co-channel overlap, which would otherwise degrade performance. Making these frequency assignments is essentially a map-colouring problem, and there are various algorithms that provide optimal or near-optimal assignment of the three radio channels, given a particular set of AP placements and coverage areas.

The design must also consider service to areas with high and low densities of users. If many users of mobile computers are located in a small area (a high-density area – particularly classrooms and lecture halls, with high concentrations of mostly students), it may be necessary to use special design techniques. Most parts of a campus will be low-density areas, however.[18] The use of multiple radio channels can allow the use of multiple APs to provide coverage in the same physical space. The exact capacity improvement is dependent on the algorithm used by the mobile NA to select an AP. A load-balancing algorithm will provide the greatest capacity increase, while an algorithm which selects the strongest AP signal will not provide as great an increase.

Design procedure

Because radio propagation inside a building is frequently anomalous and seldom completely predictable, the design of an indoor wireless installation must be an iterative one. Our design procedure includes five steps.
(1) Initial selection of access point locations.
(2) Testing and redesign, which consists of adjusting the access point locations based on signal strength measurements.
(3) Creation of a coverage map.
(4) Assignment of frequencies to APs.
(5) Auditing, which consists of documenting the AP locations and a final set of signal strength measurements at the frequencies selected.

Design tool

In order to help with the design process, we have developed a computer-based tool that assists with AP placement and frequency assignment. The tool allows the user to measure AP coverage areas by merely walking around the target space. It generates coverage maps, showing the coverage areas of all APs. It also gives the optimal frequency assignments for this set of coverage patterns, allows the user to use 'drag and drop' to relocate APs virtually and predicts a new set of coverage patterns for the virtually relocated APs. We have found this tool to be extremely helpful in efficiently designing wireless LAN installations.[19]

Under the leadership of Professor Hills, the Wireless Andrew team confronted and resolved many other issues, such as those concerning security, network management and maintenance; the integration with cellular and PCS (personal communications service) networks; training; and the development of university policies needed for the successful operation of the wireless network.[20]

4.2.8   The competition on speed in LANs

In the field of ICT, competition is first and foremost about bandwidth, which relates not just to the amount of data that can be transported per unit of time, but also to the response time involved. High bandwidth means high transport volumes and rapid response times. The developments in the LAN world are a good example. The first version of Ethernet, demonstrated in 1973, operated at a data transfer rate of 2.9 Mbit/s. In 1981 products were introduced at 10 Mbit/s using 'thick' coaxial cable (the so-called 10BASE5 version), followed in 1982 with a version for 'thin' coaxial cable (10BASE2). In 1985 Synoptics introduced a 10 Mbit/s version for use on shielded twisted pair (STP) cable, and in 1986 AT&T introduced a 1 Mbit/s version for telephone wire (i.e. non-STP cable), to which Synoptics responded in 1987 with a 10 Mbit/s version for telephone wire. This set in motion the standardisation of the 10BASE-T version of Ethernet, which was approved in 1990. The 100 Mbit/s version was approved in 1993 (100BASE-T) (von Burg, 2001).[21] This sequence of events also shows the importance of being able to use the existing cable infrastructure for increasingly high bandwidths.

When the wireless LAN products were conceived the LAN market using telephony cable was dominated by Omninet, operating at 1 Mbit/s, and ARCNet, at 2 Mbit/s. When wireless LAN products were actually introduced, however, operating at 2 Mbit/s, Ethernet LANs were already operating at 10 Mbit/s, and widely deployed. This made the WLAN value proposition increasingly difficult to sell. As a piece of good news, it also implied that the prevailing wired network to which the WLAN would have to interface would be a

10 Mbit/s Ethernet. This would obviate the need to interface directly with a variety of computer systems, although, in penetrating IBM-dominated computing environments, compatibility with token ring would remain essential.

4.3   The chasm

Summarising the situation in early 1997, Links concludes:

While the early product development period, 1987 to 1991, had been cumbersome, the period 1991 to 1994, involving the general availability of the WaveLAN product and a major marketing and sales effort, was not much better. We had essentially 'doubled our bets' by adding a 2.4 GHz product, but there were no real profits in sight. After the first period we had a wireless LAN card; after the second period we had a wireless LAN system. Thus we could bridge into a wired environment, and we could roam through buildings while staying connected. After the first period we had a US-only product; after the second we had a worldwide product.

This was all encouraging in terms of progress. The cost was still too high, however, and the data rate of 2 Mbit/s was too low compared with wired LANs. Moreover, the market acceptance of wireless LANs was still very low. There were serious concerns raised about the lack of a standard. All companies – the major ones (Proxim, Aironet and now AT&T) and the many smaller ones (including BreezeCom, WaveAccess, Xircom) – had different products. All of them were telling prospective customers why they were the best and what was wrong with the technology of the competitor. The consequence of all this was that prospective customers did not trust anybody – 'Data was precious, and radio waves were weird' – so the prevailing attitude was 'Wait and see'. It was clear that what we needed were standards, higher speeds and lower costs.

In the period 1995 to 1997 the wireless LAN industry was struggling to keep afloat. In my assessment, the companies were only marginally profitable, and overpowered by the hype around cellular. The cellular phone industry did not understand LANs and was about to make the same mistake as their wired predecessors had made with ISDN, assuming that data was just a variation of voice. Having become part of the big AT&T through the acquisition of NCR in 1991, we had become part of Lucent Technologies in 1996, and thereby a marginal activity in the scheme of the multi-billion-dollar public telecommunications equipment business.

Note that, to solve the channel conflict between AT&T the operator and AT&T the equipment vendor, the company decided to split into three independent companies: AT&T – the operator of long-distance and international communication services; Lucent Technologies – the equipment division, which included Bell Labs; and NCR – the computing business, to become an independent entity again. In this move the WaveLAN activities moved from AT&T Global Information Systems to Lucent Technologies.

The telecommunications industry, represented by, for example, Alcatel, Ericsson, Lucent Technologies, Motorola, Nokia, Nortel and Siemens, was riding the cellular wave and already looking for the 'next big thing'. Although many executives were expecting wireless data to be important, these public networking companies were not used to working with unlicensed spectrum; in fact, they were not used to the Ethernet protocol either. These companies were network-centric and not PC-centric. Optical fibre attracted most of their investments, and 3G (UMTS in Europe) was to be the next 'promise'.

By 1997 our investments in establishing a standard for wireless LANs culminated in the approval of IEEE 802.11, which covered 1 and 2 Mbit/s, frequency hopping and direct sequence spread spectrum operating at 2.4 GHz. In April 1998, as Lucent Technologies, we announced our IEEE-802.11-compliant WaveLAN product – a PC-card with an integrated antenna – to be introduced at the Networld+InterOP show in Las Vegas (see Figure 4.2).

By then we had all read the books by Geoffrey Moore, *Crossing the Chasm* and *Inside the Tornado*. If there was one case of technology-driven innovation that was clearly showing the difficulty of 'crossing the chasm', it had to be wireless LAN.[22] I would conclude that we had explored all possible market segments that could have become our 'beachhead', although, so far, we had failed to deliver in full on the 'whole product' concept. We finally had a standard-based product available, though.

4.3.1   *Increasing the data rate: the turbo version*

As the products of the various manufacturers were all based on the same open standard, this allowed for very little product differentiation. It is regularly observed in these circumstances that manufacturers try to enhance the functionality of the standard product in order to generate differentiation. In communication systems, this is often effected by increasing the data rate by providing a 'turbo option'. This was indeed the strategy pursued by the Lucent Technologies team, as the IEEE 802.11 working group began to focus on improving on the standard in the areas of security and quality of service. For that purpose, Bruce Tuch engaged the support of Bell Labs scientist and mathematician Israel bar-David, who went on to spend his sabbatical year in Utrecht so as to support the design of a 10 Mbit/s version. The theorist Israel worked closely with system engineer Rajeev Krishnamoorthy on the practical aspects of the algorithms. This gave birth to an 8 Mbit/s pulse position modulation (PPM) technique. As soon as the product development for this differentiated turbo product (chipset and NIC) was completed it was ready for market introduction.[23]

Things were not standing still in the IEEE standards arena, however, and the strong forward momentum did not end with the completion of the 2 Mbit/s version of the standard in 1997. Following the approval by the IEEE of the 100 Mbit/s Ethernet standard in 1993, high-speed wired LAN products had been introduced into the market, and during the final editing of the IEEE 802.11–1997 version of the wireless LAN standard it became clear to everybody in the '802.11' community that higher-data-rate wireless LANs would also be required. The goal that was set was to extend the performance and the range of applications in the 2.4 GHz band, and specify a higher-data-rate wireless access technology suitable for data, voice and image information services in the lower 5 GHz band.

This result forced Lucent Technologies to change its strategy hastily from the pursuit of a proprietary 'turbo' solution to supporting a standards-based high-data-rate version of IEEE 802.11. The good news was that Vic Hayes had remained the chair of working group 802.11, and the team could quickly resume its full contribution to the standards effort by proposing PPM for 802.11b in the 2.4 GHz band, enabling it to influence the outcome, as well as submitting an OFDM proposal – together with Nippon Telegraph and Telephone (NTT) of Japan – for the 802.11a standard in the 5 GHz band.

4.4   The bowling alley

In the course of 1998 senior management at Lucent Technologies started questioning the results of the wireless LAN project – after only two years' involvement and with less than complete knowledge of what had been spent in the preceding decade by AT&T and NCR. Slowly but surely resources were moved to other more promising radio projects, such as wireless local loop (WLL). WLL was an RF-based alternative for the copper cable connecting the customer's premises to the telephone exchange. To meet fast-growing demand at diverse and unforeseen locations, a wireless solution was considered to be much quicker, more flexible and more cost-effective.[24] Nonetheless, the sales team kept pushing WaveLAN. The fortunes of WaveLAN – and, for that matter, WLANs in general – took a turn for the better following an unexpected call from Apple headquarters, simply stating 'Steve Jobs wants to have a meeting with Rich McGinn about wireless LANs' (McGinn was at that time the CEO of Lucent Technologies).

4.4.1   The Apple AirPort

Jobs, who had returned to Apple as 'interim CEO' to reinvigorate the company at the end of 1996, was looking for a differentiating feature for the new iBook, and wireless connectivity attracted his renewed interest.[25] Steve Jobs brought Dick Allen back to the company, who had run its earlier wireless programme. Allen was asked to look for the 'best in class' supplier for integration of the wireless technology in the iBook. After leaving Apple, Allen had founded Photonics, a start-up involved in wireless connectivity based on infrared light technology. Bruce Tuch recalls his interactions with Dick Allen:[26]

It was the time we had our first IEEE-802.11-standard-based 2 Mbit/s product out in the market. It was the 'evangelical' phase, to get the message out that wireless LAN would 'change the way you do business'. I was on a panel giving my pitch, and emphasised the fact that radio waves were the only 'real solution' that would meet the user needs. Dick of course disagreed, and we had some nice public debates, but it was always with mutual respect on- and offstage. Photonics eventually closed down the infrared activities.

Infrared never made it due to the physics; you just could not get through the walls, let alone floors, and the sunlight through the windows even hurt the transmission range in open space. Dick also attended the IEEE 802.11 meetings, with a keen interest in the radio-technology-based standard; I remember lots of discussions on the RF propagation models I submitted to IEEE working group 802.11. 'Hey, Dick, you can see this really does go through walls as well' would be the tease. I had my 'hands full' in getting the development machine moving full force to get our 11 Mbit/s version going, and there was still competition from different technologies – HomeRF, Bluetooth WLAN, all at 1 to 2 Mbit/s – making it all the more critical to get 11 Mbit/s in the minds of the market, as the data rate needed to play the game. Getting this into the mainstream was important, and Apple appeared just at the right time. Dick Allen knew that the 11 Mbit/s standard was close and product development ongoing; if Apple worked closely with its 'chosen supplier', in parallel with the next-generation development, Apple could be the first to market with an 802.11b 11 Mbit/s integrated wireless notebook. This is typical for Apple, especially with 'Steve being back', showing leadership in sexy new applications. Dick and I spoke, and he also knew that we were 'best in class' in terms of our radio development so far, and we were making contributions to the 802.11b programme. I did not know it then, but Dick got things moving at the highest levels in the company, which resulted in Steve Jobs instructing his staff to contact the CEO of Lucent Technologies, Rich McGinn, to arrange a talk about wireless LANs.

As a consequence, Links, running the WaveLAN business at Lucent Technologies, received a call to come over to meet with McGinn's staff, to discuss the proposed meeting with Apple. Links provides the details of the meeting:

The request by Steve to meet Rich was an intriguing one, considering that Lucent Technologies was about ten times the size of Apple. More challenging for us, though, was the fact that Rich had hardly been exposed to WaveLAN; his major concern was closing multi-billion-dollar deals with the large US 'telcos'. To get his staff to agree to the meeting we had to beef up the agenda with some topics of interest for Lucent to discuss, such as digital subscriber line (DSL). The meeting date was set for 20 April 1998, and a pre-meeting took place in the Peppermill opposite the Apple headquarters in Cupertino (in California). As was known, Rich immediately took the initiative by firing off a range of questions: 'How much are we going to sell?'; 'Explain to me what these wireless LANs are'; and 'Why is Apple interested?'. We reviewed the presentation we were planning to give, and then: 'Let's go!' Rich impressed me in the way he was able to use the right words at the right moment in the meeting, as if he had already believed in the wireless LAN business for years, and had been personally pushing the technology – which he had only just learned about.

The meeting in the Apple boardroom was an interesting one. Lucent Technologies brought some of the most senior managers to the meeting (including John Dickson, the head of the Semiconductor Division), and so did Apple. Cordialities were exchanged, business cards handed out, etc. The meeting started at 2:00 p.m., the companies at either side of the table; the Lucent representatives were wearing suits and ties, but the Apple delegation had shown up Californian-style. No Steve Jobs, though; the atmosphere became somewhat awkward: Steve had been delayed. Then Steve walked in,

Californian-style too, walked over to the Lucent side and shook hands with everyone, needing no introduction.

Steve started talking – 'Wireless LANs are the greatest thing on earth, this is what Apple wants' – for about ten minutes straight. I believe Rich tried a few comments; no traction. Then Steve asked: 'Are there any questions?' I tried to show a few slides: key wins, market positioning, product offering, value creation, etc. Presenting slides with Steve Jobs is actually quite easy: you put up the slide, and he will do the talking, not necessarily related to the slide; then he asks for the next slide.

Rich McGinn chimed in with a few words; he thought 1999 would be the big year for DSL: 'Will Apple be ready?' (That is: 'Will Apple PCs have DSL?') Steve Jobs: 'Probably not next year, maybe the year after; depends on whether there is one standard worldwide...' Turning the conversation back to wireless LANs: 'We need the radio card for US$50, and I want to sell at US$99.' Then Steve apologised; he had to leave. Standing up, he said 'Hi!' and went. The room fell silent.

This is unmistakably an example of two different worlds meeting. For Jobs, the job was done; for Lucent Technologies, the work was only starting. The target was audacious, because in early 1998 the cost level of the cards was still above US$100. The chipsets for the next round of cost reductions had been designed, but it was not clear whether the target set by Apple could be met by the spring of 1999. In the following months several rounds of negotiations took place to obtain agreement on the product definition. Apple wanted a special interface, and it also wanted three versions of the access point: low-, medium- and high-end versions. Furthermore, the price was the subject of some tough negotiations. The outcome was a cost-plus target, whereby Apple would support Lucent in obtaining the best possible deals from its suppliers. A complicating matter was that the initial agreement had been based on the existing 2 Mbit/s product. The standard-making process had advanced substantially, however, and the 11 Mbit/s version was expected to become available in 1999. The proper timing of the next product release was critical. Apple wanted to go directly to the 11 Mbit/s version but did not want to accept a higher price for the increased data rate. It became an all-or-nothing negotiation.

Another change of heart occurred when the original agreement of supplying one wireless card for each notebook was reinterpreted by Apple as meaning that each notebook would be equipped with a radio card bay and in-built antenna. Moreover, just before the release of the product, Apple changed its requirement regarding the AP functionality. Initially the agreement had included the AP for home environments – i.e. without the roaming feature. As Apple was also targeting schools with its new product, it wished to see the roaming feature included in the AP that would be part of the Apple AirPort package. Lucent Technologies had implemented this feature in a high-end, and thus more expensive, version of the AP. Again, an all-or-nothing type of negotiations was the result.

Figure 4.4 Apple AirPort access point
Courtesy Frans Florentinus.

The product was launched at Macworld on 21 July 1999 as the Apple AirPort, with the PCMCIA card priced at US$99 and the access point at US$299 (see Figure 4.4).

At this price level the 11 Mbit/s wireless LANs could compete effectively with the 10 Mbit/s wired Ethernet. The industry was shocked. Links recalls:

We were accused of 'buying' the market and that we were losing money on every card sold. We weren't, though. The mechanism we used was 'forward'-pricing the product. With the volume going up the costs would also come down quickly, and the market share gained would bring in the margin. That is the theory; well, it worked in practice, and it worked very well, as it would turn out in the following years.

4.4.2   Microsoft XP

Dell was the first PC vendor to follow the trend set by Apple. Links recounts the story:

I received an e-mail that happened to have in its tail an original discussion with Michael Dell, who was furious about the fact that he had been beaten by Apple – although he had been offered the opportunity. Going through my notes I can confirm I had called Michael Dell personally in 1992 to propose cooperation. In fact, in 1993 Dell had tested our WaveLAN product as well as products from the competition, but, as the company stated, it was not convinced that a market existed for this type of technology.

In comparison with Apple, the cooperation with Dell had an additional complicating factor: that company used the Microsoft operating system (OS). As a consequence, Lucent Technologies was faced with another hurdle.

As Microsoft had become overloaded with requests to resolve interface issues, it had instituted a new certification procedure called Wireless Hardware Quality Labs (WHQL, pronounced as 'wickel') testing. All vendors of peripheral equipment had to obtain the stamp of approval through WHQL to avoid customers calling for support, as their PCs would show at start-up a warning message declaring that the machine was running uncertified software. Unfortunately, some requirements in the certification programme were incompatible with the operation of wireless LANs. This required Lucent Technologies to work closely with Microsoft to resolve these issues. Initially some compromises were made and waivers obtained to expedite market deployment. The cooperation involved working with the team of Jawad Khaki, vice-president at Microsoft in charge of Windows OS networking, to create new software to support wireless LANs proper, to be included in the upcoming release of Microsoft XP in 2001 (Agere Systems, 2001).[27]

Once this task had been carried out, the world's two leading PC operating systems now had in-built features to support wireless LANs, and hence another dimension of the 'whole product' concept had been resolved. The Apple AirPort had become the beachhead, the 'head pin'. The cooperation with Microsoft ensured that other PC vendors could now follow. With the success of the Apple AirPort the chasm had been crossed effectively; the company was now entering the 'tornado zone'.

4.5   Inside the tornado

In the terminology of Moore, the 'tornado zone' in the technology adoption life cycle refers to the period of mass-market adoption, when the general marketplace switches over to the new infrastructural paradigm (see also Figure 4.1). To understand the tornado-like dynamics, he emphasises the role of the infrastructure or technical buyers – '[the] people in charge of deploying and maintaining our basic support systems. These people are charged with providing reliable and efficient infrastructure by virtue of which we can transact, analyze, monitor, create, communicate, collaborate, and so forth' (Moore, 1995). Although Moore's focus is on the role of IT managers and the adoption of a new generation of computing equipment or a new software release, a parallel can be drawn with the adoption of wireless LAN technology by PC vendors, thereby providing infrastructural functionality to the end users. Moore describes the dilemma that IT managers face as 'balancing alpha and beta risk, being defined as any pair of risks that are inversely proportional to each other' – in this case, the risk of switching too early versus switching too late. For a long time, he claims, the alpha risk exceeds the beta risk; then 'the herd is at peace'. As the paradigm shift approaches, however, the alpha and beta risk move towards each other, creating the instability that precedes the flashpoint change in the marketplace. Moore describes the underlying herd behaviour as follows:

(1) 'When it is time to move, let us all move together.'

Pragmatists want all to move at once to minimise the risk of moving either too early or too late. When the herd migrates, the industry must follow, and thus no one gets caught out without support. In addition, whatever protocols get adopted at that time will be the go-forward de facto standards.

(2) 'When we pick the vendor to lead us to the new paradigm, let us all pick the same one.'

Picking a common vendor, which has the side effect of driving that company to becoming the market leader, ensures a clear reference point for the de facto standards. Moreover, pragmatists like to stay on the beaten path. They know that market leaders are always the safe buy, always get the best third-party support, and they know they can always find people who have experience in that technology.

(3) 'Once the move starts, the sooner we get it over with the better.'

The goal in any infrastructure swap-out is to collapse the transition time in order to minimise the disruption for end users and the stress of having to maintain parallel infrastructures, not to mention having to build temporary bridges between them. The sooner everyone can be settled into the new home, the better.

In parallel with Dell, other computer vendors – such as Toshiba, Compaq, HP and IBM – were approached to discuss wireless LAN solutions. On the networking company side, Lucent Technologies worked very closely with 3Com to integrate its products into the 3Com product line, to the point of discussing the potential acquisition of the WaveLAN business by 3Com. The relationship soured, however, and 3Com started to work with the competitors Intersil and Symbol Technologies. Nevertheless, within a year all other PC vendors had followed the example set by Apple. Agere Systems had made virtually a clean sweep of the wireless LAN market for PCs.

It was during this period, in 2000, that, in another episode of corporate transformation, Agere Systems was incorporated as a subsidiary of Lucent Technologies, assuming the activities of the former Microelectronics Division, and including WaveLAN.[28]

This new period posed new challenges. Ramping up the volume on the manufacturing side became the key challenge, which implied lead time reduction, improving inventory management and optimising test capabilities. Tuch provides the insights:

The company had worked for over a decade with Universal Scientific Inc. (USI), a Taiwanese manufacturing organisation. It had assisted us in the manufacturing start-up process; it had invested in manufacturing capabilities while we invested in R&D. In the process USI had become the world's largest wireless LAN card manufacturer.

As an illustration of the progress we made, in the early days the radio part of the card had about fifteen test points and involved manual calibration. Today the cards are fully tested through software. The early cards had about 300 components, which fell first to thirty, and then further to ten; all the result of moving from a production level of 100 cards per week in 1991 to 100,000 cards per week in 2001.

4.5.1   The home market

With the success of the Apple AirPort the wireless LAN product had moved to a new market segment: the home.[29] It required a rethinking of the WaveLAN product positioning. As Links recalls:

The move to the home implied providing internet connectivity, with the Internet as a river of information that flows through society and into which everybody can tap at any moment in time. This is why the new name for the redefined product line became 'ORiNOCO', after a river in Venezuela that according to ancient history had on its bank the city of El Dorado, where everything was made of gold. ORiNOCO represented wireless connectivity to the Internet, in the office, in the home and in 'hotspots'.

The home environment is very different from the corporate set-up, however, which is able to call upon IT departments with personnel skilled in new hardware and software installations and in the application of Microsoft tools. The initial home deployment generated a flurry of support calls, which implied that more work had to be done to make the product 'self-install'. It also made it clear that the cooperation with Microsoft on XP, to be launched in 2001, was business-critical.

4.5.2   Wireless Ethernet Compatibility Alliance

With the approval of the IEEE 802.11 standard a number of implementation variants were allowed, as a result of the FCC Report and Order that included the two spread spectrum variants, frequency hopping and direct sequence. This could in theory lead to two companies claiming to be compliant with the standard even while their products were incompatible. This situation forced the leading wireless LAN companies to collaborate – an effort that Nokia joined as well. Agere Systems was already part of the wireless LAN Association (WLANA), but this organisation was dominated by Proxim and its OEM customers, and previous attempts to make the organisation more neutral had failed. A partnership with competitor Harris/Intersil, supplier to 3Com, Aironet and Symbol Technologies, therefore appeared the best alternative. The Wireless Ethernet Compatibility Alliance (WECA) started operation in 1999 as a non-profit organisation driving the adoption of a single DSSS-based worldwide standard for high-speed wireless local area networking. Governed by a small board, WECA quickly established an interoperability testing procedure and a seal of compliance, the Wi-Fi (Wireless Fidelity) logo. In 2002 it changed its name to the Wi-Fi Alliance, in order to acknowledge the power of the Wi-Fi brand. As of July 2007 the organisation had certified the interoperability of over 3,500 products (Wi-Fi Alliance, 2007).

4.5.3   Resolving security issues

The security of wireless LANs has remained an ongoing concern. With the approval of the IEEE 802.11–1997 standard the wired equivalent privacy (WEP) algorithm was introduced, providing a basic authentication and encryption method. WEP was designed in the 1990s and was deliberately weak, so as to remain within the confines of existing export requirements. WEP encryption is based on RC4, the most widely used software stream cipher in cryptography, which uses a forty-bit key together with a twenty-four-bit random initialisation vector. The authentication provides for two modes of operation: 'open system' and 'shared key'. The first facilitates access in the 'public' domain, the latter for closed networks (Ohrtman and Roeder, 2003).

In late 1999 and early 2000 some initial attacks on WEP were identified and made public, just at the time that WLAN technology was becoming popular, thus becoming a fertile area of investigation for security researchers and an attractive target for hackers. Studies by Borisov, Goldberg and Wagner (1999) and Walker (2000) discussed the vulnerabilities of WEP.[30] The results of the research findings, presented at the eighth annual workshop on selected areas in cryptography in August 2000, in particular *Weaknesses in the Key Scheduling Algorithm of RC4*' (Fluhrer, Mantin and Shamir, 2001), enabled easy-to-mount passive attacks on WEP.[31] The lack of wireless LAN security was a threat to the continued adoption of IEEE-802.11-based equipment, and, while some businesses deployed WLAN technology in combination with virtual private network (VPN) software and proprietary security solutions, many prospective customers deferred deployment.

Industry responded with the development of an IEEE-802.11-standard-based solution, with interoperability certification developed by the WECA. Dorothy Stanley, who participated in the development of the IEEE 802.11i security amendment, representing Agere Systems, recounts the story:

IEEE 802.11 members were aware of the weaknesses of WEP, and in September 1999 approved the formation of a study group to develop a Project Authorization Request for MAC enhancements, including quality of service and security. As a result of the study group's work, formation of the IEEE 802.11e task group (TGe) was approved in March 2000. Initially the TGe PAR included an investigation into MAC enhancements for both QoS and security. Interestingly, the early meetings had many more attendees with an interest in the QoS area than in security solutions. Hence the PAR was split in April 2001, and the IEEE 802.11i task group was formed to develop a standard for security enhancement solutions. The early discussions in IEEE 802.11i focused on the need for both strong cryptographic methods and strong end user authentication.

The IEEE 802.11i members decided to use existing, state-of-the-art, proven ciphers and cryptographic protocols. The Advanced Encryption Standard was an easy choice, as it had been selected as the winner of the National Institute of Standards and Technology 'bake-off'.[32] The more controversial question was which mode within the MAC was to be used in combination with AES. After lengthy discussions over the need for a solution that would be simple to implement, non-encumbered and that could be approved for Federal Information Processing Standards (FIPS) use, the proposal using the 'counter with CBC-MAC' (CCM) mode in combination with AES was accepted.[33]

The consensus within IEEE 802.11i was that both new equipment, which implemented hardware changes to support AES, and the installed base of WEP-capable equipment needed to be supported. Therefore the Temporal Key Integrity Protocol (TKIP) solution was developed, to be deployed on existing WEP-capable, but hardware-limited, equipment.[34] The design lifetime of TKIP was intended to be five years; provided that no viable attacks were found and mounted against TKIP for this period, allowing time for WEP-capable equipment to be upgraded as needed, and then to be replaced by CCMP-capable equipment. TKIP has met this design goal – from 2002 to now. Today virtually all Wi-Fi devices that are produced support the AES/CCMP technology.

The technical choices for end user authentication were, essentially, (1) a Kerberos-based solution and (2) an IEEE 802.1X and Extensible Authentication Protocol (EAP) combined solution. Originally the IEEE 802.1X standard was developed for wired networks, and extensions were needed to support wireless network applications. Ultimately, the combination of IEEE 802.1X and EAP was selected because it allowed flexibility in the use of authentication credential types – such as passwords, digital certificates, SIM cards, etc. The requirements on EAP methods for use in wireless LAN applications have been developed in collaboration with the Internet Engineering Task Force, and documented in IETF RFC (request for comments) 4017.

The IEEE 802.11i amendment was published in June 2004, and since then it has been integrated into the 2007 version of the IEEE 802.11 standard. Prior to the availability of this standard, the opportunity was taken by vendors to fill the market need for secure WLANs with proprietary solutions, including VPN overlay solutions, and layer 2 solutions that were snapshots of early versions of TKIP.[35]

The WECA/Wi-Fi Alliance developed Wi-Fi protected access (WPA) and WPA2, supporting TKIP and AES-CCMP, respectively, to provide the industry with a multi-vendor, standard-based security solution.[36] WPA2 is based on the approved IEEE 802.11i standard, and provides government-grade security by implementing the so-called NIST-FIPS-140–2-compliant AES encryption algorithm. Both WPA and WPA2 can be enabled in two versions: personal and enterprise. WPA2 – personal protects unauthorised network access by utilising a set-up password or pre-shared key. WPA2 – enterprise provides end user authentication using IEEE-802.1X-based EAP methods. WPA2 is backward-compatible with WPA.

With these security improvements in place, it is surprising that some users appear to be reluctant to upgrade their legacy equipment and are still using WEP in their WLAN deployments. Unbelievably, there are organisations that are still supporting WEP, and trying to give it a longer life.[37] This provides hackers with opportunities to 'optimise' attacks on WEP, leveraging known weaknesses in the algorithm.[38] Nevertheless, the supply side of the industry is moving away from WEP. WEP is no longer required by the Wi-Fi Alliance as part of WPA2 certification. If the equipment offered for testing supports WEP, it is tested for interoperability, but there is no requirement for its inclusion in new releases of Wi-Fi-compatible equipment.

4.6   The penultimate success: Centrino

By the end of 2001 Agere had reached the summit as a supplier of Wi-Fi products, with a market share of approximately 50 per cent, inclusive of the OEM channel. By that time the annual size of the market had grown close to the US$1 billion level.

A growing market inevitably attracts competition, however, and not all opportunities turned into contracts for Agere Systems. For instance, Microsoft issued a tender to equip its complete Redmond campus with access points, to which (among others) Cisco, Aironet, 3Com and Agere Systems responded. The contract was awarded to Aironet. Cisco had become interested in the wireless LAN business, as would become apparent later when Aironet was acquired by Cisco. Another success for Cisco was the acquisition of a big project at Boeing. Boeing was already an important customer of Cisco, and it was able to leverage this position in its favour, despite the very positive evaluation of the ORiNOCO product.

The increasing success of Wi-Fi also highlighted the channel conflicts. In the words of Links:

Through our OEM channel we were competing with our own product, ORiNOCO. In having our own equipment brand, OEM customers had the impression that we favoured our own products – for example, in terms of releasing new functionality. Moreover, our close cooperation with USI in Taiwan made it difficult for us to work with other Taiwanese offshore developers and manufacturers (ODMs), such as Ambit, Compal, Alphatop and Gemtek, the outsourcing partners of the PC vendors. These ODMs are important to us as not only the manufacturing but also the development is subcontracted by the PC vendors to these ODMs.

By the end of 2001 it was clear that the industry was moving into another phase. With the broad acceptance of Wi-Fi it was clear that the wireless LAN functionality would be progressively integrated into the various computer and networking products. The competition would shift from the plug-in cards to the chipsets, as was confirmed by the moves of, for instance, Intersil, Broadcom, Infineon and AMD. As a consequence, the ORiNOCO brand and the related infrastructure products (access points, residential gateways and outdoor routers) were separated organisationally from the chip activities. USI, the world's largest wireless LAN card producer, was going to be transformed, from a manufacturing subcontractor to an ODM specialised in wireless LANs. In 2002 Agere Systems sold the ORiNOCO business unit to Proxim in a friendly takeover valued at US$65 million.

Proxim's claim to fame had been HomeRF, as the company had managed to line up several large companies behind the concept, Intel, Siemens and Motorola being the most important ones. HomeRF was effectively defeated with the introduction of the Apple AirPort and its US$99 price.[39] Subsequently it embraced the IEEE 802.11 standard and boosted the business by acquiring Farallon, followed by the acquisition of the ORiNOCO business unit.

Agere Systems continued to develop the wireless LAN technology and turned it into new chipsets. It also sold the technology to other chipset providers to allow the integration with other input-output (I/O) technologies.

Meanwhile, Intel had expanded its WLAN expertise by acquiring Xircom in 1999. In 2003 Intel launched the Centrino chipset, with built-in Wi-Fi functionality for mobile computers.[40] This launch was supported by a US$300 million marketing campaign, essentially moving the success of the 'Intel inside' promotion to a 'Wi-Fi inside' campaign.

This marks the penultimate success of Wi-Fi, having moved from PC adapters, through plug-ins and integrated chipsets, to functionality that has become part of the hardware core of laptop computers. This also moves the industry into another era and ends the period of the speciality suppliers.[41] As a result, Agere Systems discontinued its wireless LAN activities in 2004. The remaining WLAN expertise transitioned 'in person' to other firms, in particular to Motorola, a company active in the field of WiMAX (worldwide interoperability for microwave access) – another member of the Wi-Fi family.

4.7   Summary of the Wi-Fi journey: 1987–2003

Following the positive outcome in 1987 of the feasibility study into spread-spectrum technology, NCR started the development of a wireless LAN product. The first 2 Mbit/s product was launched in the US market in 1990, operating in the 915 MHz band. The initial sales effort was aimed at the NCR customer base, but lack of success led to its expansion to include PC and network systems vendors. Ultimately a three-pronged sales strategy evolved, which included the direct, the indirect and the OEM channels. The product evolved from a one-on-one replacement of cable to a genuine wireless LAN system, with access points supporting roaming. To reach the global market the product was standardised at 2.4 GHz, and the competition with Ethernet resulted in an 11 Mbit/s version.

The volume breakthrough came as a result of a strategic collaboration with Apple, in 1999, to launch the Apple AirPort with a PC card priced at US$99. Other PC vendors follow suit within a year. The introduction of the WECA

Alliance that year (later the Wi-Fi Alliance) drove the industry towards the adoption of one standard and led to compatible products. Strategic collaboration with Microsoft provided for wireless LAN support in XP, launched in 2001. That year the WaveLAN product line reached its peak, with a market share of some 50 per cent. The Wi-Fi functionality was progressively integrated, culminating in the launch of the Centrino platform by Intel in 2003. Meanwhile, the Utrecht Systems Engineering Centre that started the innovation journey at NCR had, through successive corporate transformations, become part of AT&T (following the acquisition in 1991), of Lucent Technologies (in 1996) and of Agere Systems (in 2000). In 2002 the infrastructure unit was acquired by Proxim, and the chip technology unit was dissolved in 2004.

4.8   Interpretation of the Wi-Fi case in the context of theory

In this section we interpret this leg of the innovation journey in line with the theoretical perspectives introduced in Chapter 1, namely the innovation landscape, the innovation process and the institutional environment. In this section we also expand the notion of innovation diffusion to cover network-related products. Moreover, we introduce and use the perspective of industry evolution in relation to the management of the firm.

4.8.1   Innovation and the innovation landscape

The landscape as depicted in Figures 2.5 and 2.6 is also applicable to this stage of the journey. As we use the metaphor of innovation avenues, highways and byways, a refinement of the wireless LAN innovation avenue can be made in terms of its use of radio frequency spectrum. The initial deployments took place in the United States in the 915 MHz band, while the mass market developed on the basis of the 2.4 GHz band, globally. The 5 GHz band is available for further expansion. In terms of innovation, the higher-frequency bands require the application of different and more complex technologies.

In this chapter we have seen a first linkage emerging between the innovation avenues of WLANs and the Internet, for which the resolution of security issues leads to the development of requirements in cooperation with security experts of the Internet Engineering Task Force, and documented following the IETF rules of engagement.

Innovation process   The pattern we typically see after the invention of a product is for the next step in the innovation process to be a 'proof of concept', in the form of a working model, to be followed by a first generation of products. Use is usually made of readily available design and production techniques. Following market testing a next generation of products is initiated, with an

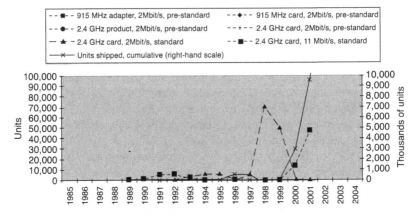

Figure 4.5 A series of WaveLAN product introductions

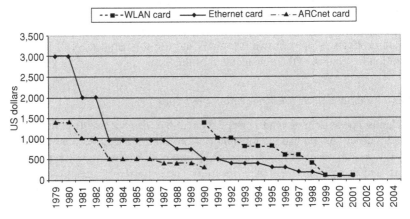

Figure 4.6 Price decline for LAN and WLAN cards

emphasis on reducing the costs and enhancing functionality as demanded by the market. This generates a sequence of product introductions, with increasing volume and progressively lower prices. The resulting pattern in the case of WaveLAN is shown in Figures 4.5 and 4.6.[42]

This pattern is typical for the pre-diffusion phases (innovation and adaptation phases) of products in high-tech sectors. From extensive case study research, Ortt *et al.* (2009) show that the innovation phase for telecommunications, media and internet products averages 8.9 years, and the adaptation phase 6.4 years. For electronic equipment, the averages are 7.2 and 12.0 years, respectively. The cases show a significant dispersion, with instances of very short cycles and instances with pre-diffusion periods of twice the average. Knowledge of the pre-diffusion pattern is considered crucial for the commercialisation strategy to be chosen (Ortt *et al.*, 2009).

The Apple AirPort deal has forced the price of WLANs to converge with those of wired LANs, in all probability more rapidly than otherwise would have happened.[43] In the process the data rate has increased fivefold, of WLANs from 2 Mbit/s to 11 Mbit/s, and of LANs from 2 Mbit/s to 10 Mbit/s.

Innovation diffusion   Rogers identifies five attributes of innovation that influence the adoption of new technology and products and hence the diffusion of innovations. According to his research, these five dimensions explain most of the variance in the rate of adoption, from 49 to 87 per cent (Rogers, 2003):

(1) *Relative advantage*: the degree to which the innovation is perceived to be better than the idea it supersedes. This may be measured in economic terms, but social factors also play an important role.

(2) *Compatibility*: the degree to which an innovation is perceived as being consistent with the existing values, past experience and needs.

(3) *Complexity*: the degree to which the innovation is perceived as difficult to understand and use.

(4) *Trialability*: the degree to which the innovation can be experimented with on a limited basis.

(5) *Observability*: the degree to which the results of the innovation are visible to others.

For the Wi-Fi case, this related to (1) the advantage relative to Ethernet as the wired alternative, which, as has been seen, required a total cost of ownership rational to justify the initial higher price of wireless LAN; (2) in principle there is a high degree of compatibility between wired and wireless solutions, but (3) as the medium used is different the complexities surrounding the use of radio frequencies – e.g. security and RF planning – played an important role; (4) the degree to which WLANs can be trialled is comparable to LANs; as is (5) the observability, although it can be argued that more companies were active in the early days of LAN development, providing greater product exposure than was the case for WLANs. From this 'analysis in retrospect' we might conclude a high degree of similarity, and hence anticipate a similar uptake to that for wired LANs, with the use of RF as the uncertain factor.

Next to these five perceived attributes of innovation, Rogers distinguishes three types of decisions with respect to the adoption of innovation: (1) optional or individual; (2) collective; and (3) demanded through authority. The reasoning is that if the choice is an individual one adoption can be more rapid than when organisations are involved. The decision logic suggested by Moore for infrastructure-related innovation (see section 4.5) confirms the delayed take-off, but emphasises the acceleration in the adoption that is the result of collective action.

As other variables influencing the process of adoption, Rogers distinguishes: (1) the communication channels being used – e.g. the role of the mass media; (2) the nature of the social system in which the innovation is introduced – e.g. its norms, degree of network interconnectedness; and (3) the extent to which change agents play a role.[44] Initially the wireless LAN product was aimed at the business market; through the cooperation with Apple the consumer market was addressed, and hence there arose the benefit of mass media attention. The US market is known to be technology-savvy and thus the product fitted well into this environment, and as part of the ICT revolution it rode the wave of PC and internet growth. This applied also, albeit to different degrees, to the global markets that were being pursued, primarily Europe and Japan. Apple, the 'head pin' in Moore's metaphor, can be considered the 'change agent' in the model provided by Rogers: providing wireless LANs with their high-tech and marketing-savvy image, as well as moving them into the home environment.

In reflecting on the diffusion of a network-related product, an important concept is 'critical mass', or the point after which further diffusion becomes self-sustaining (Rogers, 2003). Within networks or network industries, this concept relates to what economists call the 'network effect', or increasing returns to scale in consumption (Economides, 2003).[45] A market is considered to have network effects when the value to a buyer of an extra unit is higher when more units are sold, or expected to be sold, *ceteris paribus*.[46] Network effects arise because of complementarities, which can be either direct or indirect. The telecom network is a prime example of direct positive network effects, where the addition of one new user adds $2n$ new communication possibilities to the existing n users.[47] Indirect network effects can also occur in one-way networks, such as in the case of complementary goods.[48] The relationship between mobile standards and compatible handsets is a typical example. The network effect leads to a positive feedback loop that is constrained only by the downward slope of the demand curve (Economides, 2003). As a result, the diffusion of a new good with network effects is much more rapid.

In our case, direct complementarities relate to access points (at home or at 'hotspots') and wireless-LAN-enabled PCs/laptops. Indirect complementarities play a more important role, however – i.e. the diffusion of PCs and the diffusion of the Internet, in particular in the home. PCs, including laptops, are the devices that a wireless LAN connects to each other and to the Internet. Figure 4.7 shows the penetration of PCs and the Internet in US homes (ITU, 2006). The Internet facilitates communication between PCs, for example through e-mail, and facilitates the retrieval of information stored at web hosts.

In Figure 4.8, the diffusion of wireless LANs is shown in comparison with the diffusion of PCs and internet hosts. For comparison, the diffusion data on wired LANs and cellular phones is also reflected. It is worth noting that our ability to communicate at any place and any time using cellular devices has

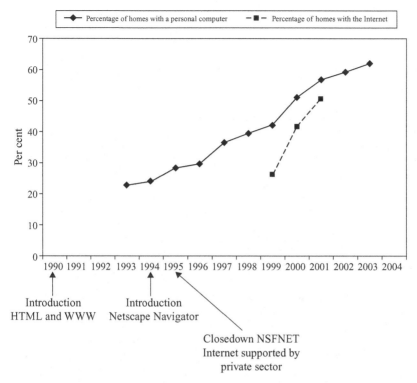

Figure 4.7 Penetration of PCs and the Internet into US homes

stimulated the need for 'mobile data' next to 'mobile voice' – a trend enforced by an increasingly mobile workforce.

According to Economides, network effects may also originate from the expectations of agents (e.g. in their anticipation of platform dominance) or be stimulated through coordination among agents (e.g. by producers coordinating standards efforts or by buyers teaming up) (Economides, 2003). A comparison can also be made with the adoption model for infrastructure-related products by Moore, as summarised and applied in this chapter (Moore, 1991, 1995).

In our case, standardisation plays an important role in product acceptance and subsequent diffusion. Moreover, 'buyers are teaming up' in the sense that all PC vendors followed within a year the example set by Apple in terms of including wireless LAN functionality in their products. Once the 'whole' product is available – i.e. compliance with a standard, compatibility among equipment from different vendors and a resolution of the security issues – the market starts to develop properly.

Sources of innovation   The involvement of the user in the shaping of technology, in particular in the case of emerging new functionalities, is

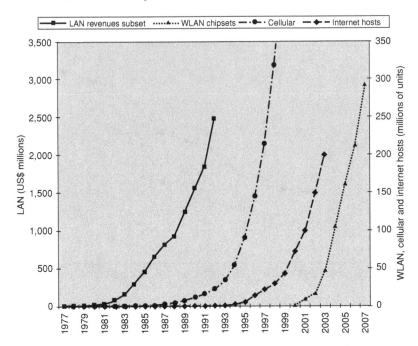

Figure 4.8 Diffusion of LAN, WLAN, cellular and internet hosts
Note: The cellular and internet host data reflects the installed base, while the LAN data reflects annual revenues and the WLAN data annual chipset shipments.

referred to in science and technology studies as the coevolution of technology and the user context (Geels, 2002).[49] The technology is shaped in a process of 'learning by using', whereby the interactions are crucial, although in the process the usage may change.

In testing the early market we see the customer emerging as a source of innovation, in our case through project 'Wireless Andrew' at the Carnegie Mellon University. Field experience from the project was fed back to AT&T on large-scale deployment issues, such as network management and maintenance. Moreover, the customer developed support tools for the placement of access points and the related RF planning. In a later stage of the development there are the PC vendors, which influenced the innovation process by requiring specific functionality and by influencing the form factor of the products. We can also observe a change in the use of WLANs, from being confined to the enterprise to including the home. (In Chapters 6 and 7 we see end users emerging as a source of innovation.)

4.8.2   The institutional environment

From a coevolution perspective, scholars have emphasised the simultaneous shaping of technology and institutions in a configuration that works. The different perspectives being applied lead to a different emphasis: large-scale technical systems theory describes how system builders mould technologies, economics, regulation and user preferences; actor network theory emphasises the more abstract aspects of translation, enrollment and alignment; while social construction of technology theory argues that 'cognitive, social and material elements are gradually woven into a technological frame as social groups and technical artefacts stabilise' (Geels, 2002).[50]

In the context of security, the National Security Agency comes into play, as does the National Institute of Standards and Technology and the Federal Information Processing Standards body. It appears that products using encryption technology are subject to export restrictions set by the US government. Encryption thereby shows its two sided, somewhat paradoxical nature: on the one hand, the user data should be protected as best as possible against sniffing (intentional and illegal eavesdropping); and, on the other hand, for national security reasons government agencies should, when duly authorised, be able to monitor data communication traffic.

The Internet Architecture Board (IAB) and the Internet Engineering Task Force are two of the most important institutions guiding the development of the Internet. A convergence of interests has made the experts work together in the interests of security.

4.8.3   The industry evolution

De Wit and Meyer (2004) define an industry as 'a group of firms making a similar type of product or employing a similar set of value-adding processes or resources'.[51] Using product similarity as our criterion, we may conclude that a wireless LAN industry has emerged, with firms such as NCR, Proxim and Symbol Technologies competing for the customer business. Using Porter's (1980) model for industry analysis with Wheelen and Hunger (1983) for the social, economic, political and technological dimensions (see Figure 4.9), we can identify in the initial configuration offshore developers and manufacturers as the supplier.[52] The main customers are the enterprises implementing wireless LANs at their premises, consisting of access points and PC plug-ins.

In this chapter we have seen the development of WLAN to become synonymous with Wi-Fi. This sheds light in particular on the rivalry between the existing firms. Before the IEEE 802.11 standard became available the equipment vendors were competing with wireless LAN products using proprietary protocols. This caused a severe fragmentation of the market at an early stage, while it was struggling to boost volume. As we have seen in Chapter 3, these

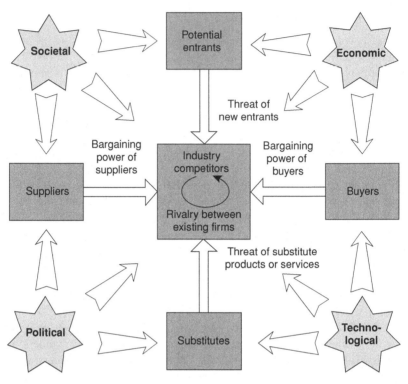

Figure 4.9 Framework for industry analysis (Porter–Wheelen–Hunger)

same vendors collaborated and competed in the IEEE standards arena to develop a common standard. Once the standard was available it became apparent that the two major options included in the standard (frequency hopping and direct sequence) could still frustrate the development of the market. In a collaborative effort the WECA established a common platform and a set of compatibility tests that would reassure customers that when they bought Wi-Fi-certified equipment from one vendor it would be compatible with Wi-Fi-certified equipment from another vendor. Subsequently vendors competed with compatible products, primarily on price and quality.

In the evolution of the industry, 'integration' is the name of the game: integration in terms of cost reduction and cramming more functionality onto a single chip, as well as the integration of the WLAN functionality into the peripheral devices being connected to the WLAN, in particular PCs. The technology focus shifted from PC adapters to PC cards, to chipsets and, ultimately, to wireless access technologies and protocols. The customer shifted thereby from the enterprise, as the end user, to the PC vendor and, ultimately, to the integrated circuit (IC) vendor.

The firm[53] If we consider strategic management as the process linking the firm to its environment, NCR faced a number of strategic challenges that were paradoxical in nature, most notably the question of whether it should remain an industry follower and adapt as well as possible to the environment dominated by IBM, or create an environment that best suited the firm. With wireless LAN representing a new innovation avenue to NCR, and with the deliberate choice to create an open standard, the company had placed itself into a leadership role in the emerging WLAN industry. In breaking with the old rules it had to discover the new rules that would govern the competitive game in the WLAN industry. Starting from an inside-out perspective, as the technology was a given, the challenge became one of discovering the new rules in the marketplace. A lengthy and evolutionary process of 'learning by doing' followed, to find the right product–market combinations as well as the best channel to market. The 'whole product' concept appeared to be critical in the move from the early market to the mass market. Strategic collaboration with partners in the value network proved to be essential for mass-market adoption: in creating an open standard, in driving for compatible products, in ensuring PC software support, in finding the head pin of the bowling alley. Ultimately, a global market was established, with global products as the result.

The challenges the WaveLAN group faced in the marketplace were exacerbated by the corporate transformation, from NCR, to AT&T, to Lucent Technologies to Agere Systems. In the NCR period the WaveLAN product addressed an issue raised by NCR customers. The WaveLAN product was, in essence, complementary to the company's main product line. With the acquisition by AT&T the focus switched to computing, although networking technology lay at the core of the AT&T business. Within AT&T, however, the focus was on voice communication rather than data communication, and the public networking customers were more important than enterprise customers.

With the trivestiture, the WaveLAN activities moved to Lucent Technologies and became part of the wireless networking business unit. While a technological synergy could be argued, the focus in Lucent was on public networking and customers who exploited the RF spectrum on an exclusive basis. Although Lucent Technologies had an Enterprise Division its focus was on private automatic branch exchange (PABX) activities. This unit was moved to the Avaya subsidiary, which would subsequently be divested. The transfer of the WaveLAN activities to Agere Systems, the former Microelectronics Division, emphasised the importance of technology, and not of product. Exacerbating the challenges for the Utrecht engineering team was the fact that, in each corporate transformation, the sales force had to be built anew – an effort that typically takes one to two years.

During its lifetime the WaveLAN business was too small to take an independent position within the corporation, and hence it became subject to an uncertain corporate journey. As the unit was small, however, it remained below the radar of senior management most of the time, and so it could survive the long gestation period from product design in 1987 until mass-market take-off in 2000.

Our case also illustrates the fact that the 'peaking' of a firm does not necessarily have to coincide with either the peaking of the product, the peaking of the industry or the peaking of the underlying technology.

Notes

1 The author is Geoffrey A. Moore; the so-called 'Moore's Law' derives from Gordon E. Moore.
2 In June 1991, at the first Virginia technical symposium on wireless personal communications, Bruce Tuch would present his invited paper, 'An engineer's story of WaveLAN'. At that time wireless LANs were still referred to as cordless LANs (Tuch, 1991).
3 Novell Netware was the prevailing network operating system at the time.
4 Operation in the 18 GHz band required a licence from the FCC, which was obtained by contacting the FCC and registering the application, upon which a specific frequency range would be assigned for its operation (personal communication from Tuch, 2009).
5 Personal communication from Tuch, 2009.
6 The sales efforts were further complicated by the fierce battle between the Microsoft Lan Manager and Novell Netware for market leadership.
7 In addition to the citations, information provided by Links has been used extensively in the development of the main storyline of this chapter.
8 At its Schaumburg location in Illinois, Motorola was working on wireless LANs operating in the 18 GHz band. The product was known as Altair.
9 Although a surprise to the sales team of NCR, outdoor applications had been foreseen by the FCC in its rule making (Marcus, 2007).
10 A T1 line refers to a wired digital connection of 1.5 Mbit/s; the equivalent of an E1 of 2 Mbit/s in Europe. In addition, the use of a T1 line would require multiplexing equipment.
11 The WaveLAN product name originated with Tino Scholman of the Utrecht Engineering Centre, and was introduced in the market with the 1993 release of the 2.4 GHz product for the global market.
12 CDPD can be considered a precursor of today's GPRS (general packet radio service).
13 Agentschap Telecom is the NRA with responsibility for the implementation of RF spectrum policy in the Netherlands.
14 Personal communication from Albert Heijl, 2008. The product was supplied by LANAIR/BreezeCom. The system was put into service in 1996, and it continues to serve 300 to 350 mobile stations through eighty access points covering an area of 4 km^2.
15 Following the establishment of ETSI, CEPT is responsible only for the harmonisation of the radio spectrum in Europe and other countries that have ratified a memorandum of understanding. Administrations that signed the MoU have agreed to implement the 'Recommendation' of the CEPT.

16 The National Science Foundation grant for the project was US$500,000, with the objective of helping create a 'laboratory for wireless researchers'. Four vendors were considered to be in a competitive process, and ultimately AT&T was selected as the supplier. Initially the pre-standard 915 MHz WaveLAN product was installed, and this was used until 1997. In that year 'Wireless Andrew II' was announced, to cover the entire campus, and it used the 2.4 GHz full-production standard-based product. This new network replaced the old one.

17 In addition to personal communications, this account has been based on earlier publications by the architect of project Wireless Andrew (Hills, 1999, 2001; Hills and Johnson, 1996; Hills and Schlegel, 2004). Additional information is provided by Bennington and Bartel (1997).

18 Two design layout techniques that are useful in high-density situations are increasing receiver threshold settings and using multiple radio channels. Some wireless LAN products allow one to set the receiver threshold, thus controlling the size of the coverage area of the AP. A coverage-oriented design should use the minimum receiver threshold setting, maximising the size of the coverage area of each AP. When capacity issues are considered, however, one may wish to use higher AP receiver threshold settings in high-density areas, reducing the coverage area of each AP.

19 The Rollabout tool was commercialised by Helium Networks, a Pittsburgh company, and is covered by a number of patents. The product, now called Site Scout, is still sold commercially (see also Hills and Schlegel, 2004).

20 In more recent studies, the usage of campus-wide wireless networks has been reported: for example, at Stanford University's computer science department, with seventy-four users in one building, over a twelve-week observation period (Tang and Baker, 2000); at Dartmouth College, New Hampshire, with some 2,000 users and 476 APs spread over 161 buildings, during an eleven-week period (Kotz and Essien, 2005); and a related study of the Metricom Ricochet metropolitan-area network in the United States, with 24,773 clients and 14,053 APs, over a seven-week period (Tang and Baker, 2002).

21 According to Links, the importance given to the perception of speed became very apparent with the success of the Xircom Ethernet port adapter. While providing on the network side a connection to the Ethernet operating at 10 Mbit/s, it would connect to the computer via the Centronics port, which had a maximum throughput of 700 kbit/s.

22 In 1990 NCR had hired a company called Regis McKenna to assist in the product launch of WaveLAN. This contract came to an abrupt halt when it appeared that another office of Regis McKenna was supporting Motorola in the launch of its rival product, Altair.

23 Personal communication with Tuch, 2009.

24 Practical issues frustrated this proposal, however. The system, operating at 3.4 GHz, required a line-of-sight link between the transceivers at either end of the connection. At the customer's premises it required outdoor placement and careful alignment with the central station.

25 Apple had considered wireless connectivity to be essential to the success of its laptops and PDA business. In early 1990 Apple petitioned the FCC to allocate 40 MHz of spectrum in the 1,850 to 1,990 MHz band earmarked for new technologies, in particular PCS, for a new radio service called Data-PCS. In the autumn of 1993 this request was accommodated, except that the band was used by microwave users.

Although relocation with compensation was agreed upon, there was no effective model for managing the relocation. Apple also filed a petition for rule making in 1995 for an allocation of 300 MHz in the 5 GHz band, linked to the National Information Infrastructure (NII) initiative in the Clinton–Gore period. In 1997 the FCC created the Unlicensed NII band within the existing 5 GHz ISM band (Goldberg, 2008).

26 Personal communication with Tuch, 2009.

27 In the cooperation with Microsoft, the strategic importance of IEEE 802.11 being restricted to the PHY and MAC layer showed in the relative ease of implementation within a PC operating system environment (personal communication with Tuch, 2009).

28 Avaya was the other subsidiary that was created, assuming the business communications systems activities. Lucent Technologies would continue to focus on public communications systems.

29 This also applied to the educational market, a prime target of Apple.

30 Brockmann, formerly No Wires Needed, pointed to a 1995 draft paper by Andrew Roos at Vironox Software Laboratories, posted at the sci.crypt newsgroup with the title 'A class of weak keys in the RC4 stream cipher'. See also Chapter 8.

31 See also http://sourceforge.net/projects/airsnort.

32 This advanced encryption standard was totally different from the functionality that NCR introduced under the name of AES in the early product versions in combination with DES.

33 CCM with AES was developed by Russ Housley (RSA Laboratories), Niels Ferguson (MacFergus BV) and Doug Whiting (Hifn) and is specified in RFC 3610; see www.ietf.org/rfc/rfc3610.txt.

34 Key contributors to TKIP were Russ Housley, Niels Ferguson and Doug Whiting, together with Jesse Walker (Intel).

35 For example, No Wires Needed introduced AirLock security as a product differentiator, using a Diffie–Hellman session key and a 128-bit RC5.

36 More information on WPA is available at www.wi-fi.org/files/kc_10_WPA% 20QandA_12–30–04.pdf.

37 See https://edge.arubanetworks.com/blog/2007/04/airdefense-perpetuates-flawed-protocols.

38 See http://arstechnica.com/news.ars/post/20070404-new-attack-cracks-wep-in-record-time.html.

39 See Chapter 3 for an account of the battles between Wi-Fi, HomeRF and HIPERLAN.

40 Centrino is a platform marketing initiative covering a particular combination of central processing unit (CPU), mainboard chipset and wireless network interface in the design of laptop PCs. Intel claimed that systems equipped with these technologies should deliver better performance, longer battery life and broad wireless network operability. Following the 2003 Carmel platform release, Intel has released the Sonoma platform in 2005, the Napa platform in 2006 and the Santa Rosa platform in 2007. The Wi-Fi functionality supported in the latter includes IEEE 802.11 a/b/g/draft-n; see the Wikipedia entry 'Centrino', at http://en.wikipedia.org (accessed 17 August 2007).

41 While Intel would take a leading position in providing Wi-Fi functionality in laptops, Broadcom would become the leading provider of Wi-Fi chips to be included in gateways and routers.

42 The data points have been derived from von Burg (2001) and a personal communication from Links in 2007, with interpolations and extrapolations being applied.

43 According to Ronald Brockmann, Harris/Intersil had also been in negotiations with Apple, but apparently refused to accept the terms set by Apple.

44 Rogers distinguishes eight types of diffusion research with, as main dependent variable, (1) the earliness of knowing about innovations; (2) the rate of adoption of different innovations in a social system; (3) innovativeness; (4) opinion leadership; (5) diffusion networks; (6) the rate of adoption in different social systems; (7) communication channel use; and (8) consequences of innovation. Each of these perspectives may add explanatory power to a particular case being researched (Rogers, 2003).

45 Arthur (1994, 1996) has already pointed to the effects of increasing returns and path dependence in the economy. Network effects can also be observed in credit card networks, ATM networks, computerised reservation systems, railroads, airlines and health care (Katz and Shapiro, 1998).

46 This is in contrast to the case of non-network goods, for which the willingness to pay for the last unit of a good is considered to decrease with the number of units sold (Economides, 2003).

47 Consider a two-way (in terms of call set-up direction) network of n users. A communication 'good' is defined as either the origination or the reception of a communication. Thus the nth user represents a total of $2n(n-1)$ 'goods'. Each additional user thus adds $2n$ new 'goods' (Economides, 2003).

48 Consider m VCR players compatible with n VHS video tapes generating mn composite 'goods'. An extra (compatible) VHS video increases the demand for the complementary 'good' VCR recorder, and vice versa.

49 Geels distinguishes multiple theories in this context: large technical systems theory, actor network theory and social construction of technology theory.

50 The focus by Geels is on understanding the dynamics of (large-scale) technological transitions.

51 It should be noted that strategists like to challenge existing definitions of an industry in order to create new business opportunities. Moreover, while an economist may consider Swatch, Rolex and Citizen watches all to be part of the watch industry, a strategist may consider Swatch to be in the fashion accessory industry, Rolex in the luxury goods industry and Citizen in the watch industry (personal communication with Bob de Wit, 2006).

52 For companies without internal semiconductor production capabilities, the semiconductor manufacturers should also be considered as suppliers.

53 This section builds on de Wit and Meyer, 2005.

References

Agere Systems (2001). 'Agere Systems to work with Microsoft to promote PC users' new freedom to roam'. Allentown, PA: Agere Systems.

Arthur, W. B. (1994). *Increasing Returns and Path Dependence in the Economy*. Ann Arbor: University of Michigan Press.

(1996). 'Increasing returns and the new world of business'. *Harvard Business Review*. **74** (4), 100–9.

Bennington, B. J., and C. R. Bartel (1997). 'Wireless Andrew: experience building a high-speed, campus-wide wireless data network'. In ACM [Association for Computing Machinery]. *Proceedings of the Third Annual International Conference on Mobile Computing and Networking*. New York: ACM, 55–65.

Borisov, N., I. Goldberg and D. Wagner (1999). '802.11 security'. www.isaac.cs. berkeley.edu/isaac/wep-faq.html (accessed 30 January 2007).

Chhaya, H. S., and S. Gupta. (1996). 'Performance of synchronous data transfer methods of IEEE 802.11 MAC protocol'. *IEEE Personal Communications*. **3** (5), 8–15.

De Wit, B., and R. Meyer (2004). *Strategy: Process, Content, Context – An International Perspective*. London: Thomson.

(2005). *Strategy Synthesis: Resolving Strategy Paradoxes to Create Competitive Advantage*. London: Thomson.

Economides, N. (2003). 'Competition policy in network industries: an introduction'. Research Paper no. 03-10. New York: Center for Law and Business, New York University.

Fluhrer, S., S. Mantin and A. Shamir (2001). *Weaknesses in the Key Scheduling Algorithm of RC4*. San Jose, CA: Cisco.

Geels, F. (2002). 'Understanding the dynamics of technological transitions: a co-evolutionary and socio-technical analysis'. Dissertation. University of Twente, Enschede, the Netherlands.

Goldberg, H. (2008). 'Grazing on the commons: the emergence of Part 15'. Paper presented at the conference 'The genesis of unlicensed wireless policy'. Arlington, VA, 4 April.

Hills, A. (1999). 'Wireless Andrew'. *IEEE Spectrum*. **36** (6), 49–53.

(2001). 'Large-scale wireless LAN design'. *IEEE Communications Magazine*. **39** (11), 98–107.

Hills, A., and D. B. Johnson (1996). 'A wireless data network infrastructure at Carnegie Mellon University'. *IEEE Personal Communications*. **3** (1), 56–63.

Hills, A., and J. Schlegel (2004). 'Rollabout: a wireless design tool'. *IEEE Communications*. **42** (2), 132–8.

ITU (2006). *World Communications/ICT Development Report: Measuring ICT for Social and Economic Development*. Geneva: International Telecommunication Union. Available at www.itu.org (accessed 16 February 2006).

Katz, M. L., and C. Shapiro (1998). 'Antitrust in software markets'. In J. A. Eisenach and T. M. Lenard (eds.). *Competition, Innovation and the Microsoft Monopoly: Antitrust in the Digital Marketplace*. New York: Kluwer Academic, 29–81.

Kotz, D., and K. Essien (2005). 'Analysis of a campus-wide wireless network'. *Wireless Networks*. **11** (1–2), 115–33.

Moore, G. A. (1991). *Crossing the Chasm: Marketing and Selling High-tech Products to Mainstream Customers*. New York: HarperCollins.

(1995). *Inside the Tornado: Marketing Strategies from Silicon Valley's Cutting Edge*. New York: HarperCollins.

(2002). *Living on the Fault Line: Managing for Shareholder Value in Any Economy*. New York: HarperCollins.

Ohrtman, F., and K. Roeder (2003). *Wi-Fi Handbook: Building 802.11b Wireless Networks*. New York: McGraw-Hill.

Ortt, J. R., S. Tabatabaie, G. Alva, G. Balini and Y. Setiawan (2009). 'From invention to large-scale diffusion in five high-tech industries'. Paper presented at the eighteenth international conference on management of technology. Orlando, 7 April.

Porter, M. E. (1980). *Competitive Strategy: Techniques for Analyzing Industries and Competitors*. New York: Free Press.

Rogers, E. M. (2003). *Diffusion of Innovations*. New York: Free Press.

Tang, D., and M. Baker (2000). 'Analysis of a local-area wireless network'. In ACM. *Proceedings of the Sixth Annual International Conference on Mobile Computing and Networking*. New York: ACM, 1–10.

   (2002). 'Analysis of a metropolitan-area wireless network'. *Wireless Networks*. **8** (2–3), 107–20.

Tuch, B. (1991). 'An engineer's story of WaveLAN'. Paper presented at the Virginia Polytechnic Institute and State University's first symposium on wireless personal communications. Blacksburg, VA, 3 June.

Von Burg, U. (2001). *The Triumph of Ethernet: Technological Communities and the Battle for the LAN Standard*. Stanford, CA: Stanford University Press.

Walker, J. (2000). *Unsafe at Any Key Size: An Analysis of the WEP Encapsulation*. Hillsboro, OR: Intel.

Wheelen, T. L., and D. J. Hunger (1983). *Strategic Management and Business Policy*. Reading, MA: Addison-Wesley.

Wi-Fi Alliance (2007). 'Get to know the alliance'. Austin, TX: Wi-Fi Alliance. Available at www.wi-fi.org (accessed 16 August 2007).

5   Hotspots: the Starbucks initiative

Wolter Lemstra and Els van de Kar,
with contributions from Gerd-Jan de Leeuw
and Leo Brand

5.1   Introduction: Starbucks

'Travel at blazing speeds on the Internet – all from the comfort of your favorite cozy chair' (Starbucks, 2007). This headline illustrates the next step in the development of Wi-Fi: from its original application within the enterprise, then subsequently moving into the home, it has been the Starbucks initiative to provide wireless access to the Internet in its coffee shops that has set up Wi-Fi as the preferred means of accessing the Internet in public areas. For Starbucks, it was the prospect of attracting more customers and keeping them longer in the coffeehouse, in particular after the rush hour, that made investments in the new service an attractive proposition.

In January 2001 Starbucks, MobileStar and Microsoft announced that they had forged a strategic relationship in order to create a high-speed, connected environment in Starbucks locations across North America. The service would be provided by MobileStar, a wireless ISP established in 1996 with a focus on providing high-speed internet access for business travellers in 'hotspots' such as airports, hotels, convention centres, restaurants and other public places in the United States. MobileStar would install access points in the Starbucks locations and connect these locations to the Internet using T1 lines.[1] Microsoft was to provide the portal so as to facilitate an easy log-on procedure (Microsoft, 2001).

MobileStar set out using a proprietary frequency-hopping spread-spectrum product supplied by Proxim, and subsequently moved to an IEEE-802.11-compliant direct-sequence-based product. In May 2001 Compaq announced that it would enhance the proposition by providing Starbucks locations with Hewlett-Packard iPAQ hand-helds to assist customers in accessing the Internet. This plan was rolled out in a number of major US cities. By the end of the year MobileStar had equipped some 500 Starbucks locations, but it had also run into financial difficulties. With the collapse of the stockmarket, following the bursting of the internet/telecom bubble, and the events of 11 September severely limiting business travel, the company had been forced to cease trading in October 2001. The assets were subsequently acquired by VoiceStream, a cellular communications company that had been bought by T-Mobile in 2001. By February 2002 the service at Starbucks was operating under the T-Mobile 'HotSpot' brand. This acquisition made T-Mobile the largest hotspot provider in the United States.

In early 2002 Starbucks launched a major expansion plan to provide wireless access at 'T1' speed in 800 coffee shops in the United States and 400 in Europe, to be extended to 2,000 in total by the end of the year. In this extension plan, Starbucks cooperated with T-Mobile as service provider and HP to provide access software, in particular the wireless connection manager, which facilitates easy configuration management for notebooks or PDAs not running on the Microsoft XP operating system (Arar, 2002; Singer, 2002).[2] In 2003 Howard Schultz, the CEO of Starbucks, claimed that the partnership with T-Mobile had contributed to a 27 per cent increase in revenue in June 2003 over June 2002, and that customers spent approximately forty-five minutes per session using hotspot access (O'Shea, 2003).[3] In the face of increasing competition and in order to stimulate usage, the prices of the T-Mobile 'HotSpot' service were sharply reduced in 2003 (Griffith, 2003b).[4] In July 2004 Starbucks announced further successes: that 3,100 coffeehouses were offering Wi-Fi-based internet access,[5] and that T-Mobile 'HotSpot' subscribers visited Starbucks more often – on average eight times per month – and spent on average one hour per session, while 90 per cent of accesses took place during off-peak hours. Moreover, exclusive access to entertainment content was being provided at the Starbucks locations (Business Wire, 2004), which was expanded through an exclusive partnership between Starbucks and Apple to preview, buy and download music from the iTunes Wi-Fi Music Store, launching in October 2007 (Apple, 2007a).

This example of Starbucks illustrates how, in private locations, Wi-Fi access is used in support of the business model of the location owner. The concept of providing internet access at hotspots using WLANs dates back to 1993. According to a popular account, Wi-Fi access in public places was first conceived by Brett Stewart while he was working on the IEEE 802.11 MAC at AMD (Fleishman, 2002). (In all probability, others came up with the same idea in the same time frame, considering the many start-ups that emerged pursuing wireless access services in public places.)[6] To implement his idea, the company Plancom was established in 1995, changing its name to Wayport in 1996. In that year Wayport equipped its first hotel lobby and bar with wireless access.[7] By 2003 Wayport was serving some of the major hotel brands: Embassy, Four Seasons, Sheraton, Summerfield, Westin and Wyndham. Wayport has become a pioneer in digitising retail outlets and developing Wi-Fi-based applications for retail venues, such as McDonald's and Starbucks, helping the chains to reduce costs and/or enhance their services.

Thus it was that the initial successes were achieved in hotels and at airports, while, as described above, the mass market was unlocked by Starbucks' provision of Wi-Fi-based services to the wider public. This development led to the emergence of wireless ISPs (WISPs), of which many were soon acquired by incumbent operators: Wayport, for instance, was acquired by AT&T in 2008. Creating a successful WISP business requires focus and/or an extension of the service portfolio to meet the demands of specific market segments, such as the hospitality industry. By applying a roaming model, aggregators and clearing houses are increasing convenience to 'hotspot' users and providing back-office services to location owners. Finding 'hotspots' is facilitated through websites providing listings across multiple providers. WISPs are providing premium services on trains and aeroplanes. An alternative business model based on revenue sharing has been introduced under the name of FON (from the company FON Wireless). Increasingly, Wi-Fi functionality is added to mobile devices, allowing for convergence between Wi-Fi and cellular services.

In this chapter we describe the emergence of the 'hotspot' business, and illustrate it with the Swisscom case. Next, we describe the hotspot business models and their developments.

5.2   Creating a hotspot business

The relatively low cost of the Wi-Fi access point equipment represented a low market entry barrier, and consequently the opportunity was taken by many start-ups to enter the hotspot business and become a wireless internet service provider. A few early examples in the United States are Deep Blue Wireless, FatPort, iBahn, NetNearU, SurfandSip and Wayport.[8]

5.2.1   The Swisscom case

An example of an incumbent telecommunications operator in Europe that recognised the opportunity early on is Swisscom Eurospot, with the business guests of the hospitality industry as its primary target. Leo Brand, CEO of Swisscom Hospitality, provides a first-hand account of the developments:[9]

In 2002 Eurospot was established as a subsidiary of Swisscom AG. To expand our footprint quickly we acquired a range of start-up companies, including Megabeam Ltd and WLAN AG, both in Germany, and Aervik, in the Netherlands. By the end of 2004 Eurospot had established 1,930 sites with approximately 60,000 access points in ten European countries, and we had 800 more sites under contract. In our home country, Switzerland, we have over 1,000 hotspots and we consider Wi-Fi as an alternative form of access to fixed and mobile service offerings, while, abroad, we use it for market entry and compete head-on with the incumbent operators.

In the early days of Wi-Fi, hotspot providers were confronted with the fact that not all users had Wi-Fi-enabled laptops, and some organisations, such as banks, did not allow their employees to use Wi-Fi at hotspots for security reasons. To address these issues and stimulate the usage of our hotspot locations, we added wireless bridges in hotel guest rooms to enable all laptop users to connect to our services. This also opened an alternative billing channel, using the property management systems of the hotels, with room number and guest identity becoming available.

The use of wireless (Wi-Fi) and wireline enabled the provision of public services, such as high-speed internet access, Internet Protocol television, voice over Internet Protocol (VoIP), etc., to be combined with venue-specific applications, to be managed over one converged network. This reduced the total cost of ownership of providing these services for the location owner. Combining these public applications into a hospitality service package made our offering financially attractive, which would have been difficult to do if these services had been offered on a stand-alone basis. Examples of converged services we provide are the ability to connect via Wi-Fi with Session Initiation Protocol (SIP) client software to the hotel network and enable voice calling over the hotel network so as to avoid roaming costs; taxi ordering, room service ordering, etc. from the mobile device; and the printing of boarding passes from the wireless device to the printer at reception or in the business centre. Swisscom is bringing contextual Wi-Fi services to venues by enabling location-based applications using Wi-Fi-enabled devices, such as iPhones or other PDAs. This is important, considering that the sales volume of Wi-Fi-enabled phones surpassed the sales volume of laptops in 2008, leading to a new phase of 'always on' mobile WLAN services.

A number of WISPs, including Swisscom, started to offer additional services over the wireless overlays in these venues. For example, we added business centre PCs, digital signage and group meeting services over these cost-effective Wi-Fi networks and generated new revenue streams. Moreover, we developed a unique guest experience based on Web 2.0 technology by introducing value added service to the communications offering. We provide access to more than 600 digital newspapers within minutes of their release for printing (which allows downloading by the user), localised weather forecasts and real-time flight information, as well as unlimited free worldwide calling. Even though there are companies that offer (some of) these services free of charge to their guests, over 50 per cent of our guests, across all star categories of hotels served by Swisscom, purchase these premium services, providing the company with a healthy average revenue per user.

Swisscom continuously develops its hospitality service portfolio in line with our envisaged strategy of becoming the global market leader in managed services for the hospitality industry. Today there are two to three IP devices in each hotel room; in the near future we expect twenty to thirty IP-enabled devices. To manage the complexity of this ecosystem (with service-level agreement per device, security protocols, etc.), hotels and other venue owners will need specialised support. To meet these needs, we have changed Swisscom Hospitality into a (W)LAN service provider managing networks and applications as an enterprise solution.

Other incumbents providing Wi-Fi-based hotspot service in Europe include Belgacom, Bouygues Telecom, BT Openzone, Eircom, KPN (through the acquisition of HubHop), Lattelekom, Orange, PTWIFI, SFR, Sonera wGate, T-Com, TDC, Telecom Italia, Telefonica, Telia HomeRun, T-Mobile, Turk Telecom and Vodafone. Incumbents in the United States providing Wi-Fi-based access include AT&T_Wi-Fi and Verizon; and incumbents in Asia are

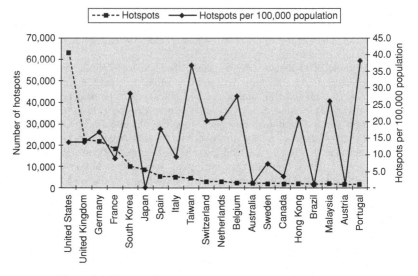

Figure 5.1 Hotspots by country
Sources: JiWire (2007), based on US Census Bureau (2006).

KT Nespot, NTT DoCoMo, PCCW, SingTel, Softbank, Telecom New Zealand and Telstra (WLAN Report, 2007).

We may conclude that all incumbent operators have become engaged in Wi-Fi, very often having obtained their footprint through the acquisition of existing players.

5.2.2   Hotspot statistics

As of April 2009 JiWire's Wi-Fi directory listed a total of 256,147 hotspots in 140 countries (see also de Leeuw, 2007). Boingo was quoted by the Wi-Fi Alliance as having identified the addressable market in the United States at 2 million potential locations, consisting of: 212 convention centres, 3,032 train stations, 5,352 airports, 53,500 hotels, 72,720 business centres, 202,600 petrol stations, 480,298 restaurants, bars and cafés and 1,111,300 retail stores. Gartner estimated that in 2002 there were 59 million mobile workers in the United States who were potential clients of hotspot operators (Wi-Fi Alliance, 2004a).

In 2007, according to JiWire, the top five countries in terms of the number of hotspots were the United States, the United Kingdom, Germany, France and South Korea, although in terms of hotspots per head of population Portugal was in the lead, with thirty-eight hotspots per 100,000 inhabitants, followed by Taiwan (with thirty-seven) and South Korea (with twenty-eight).[10] See also Figure 5.1.

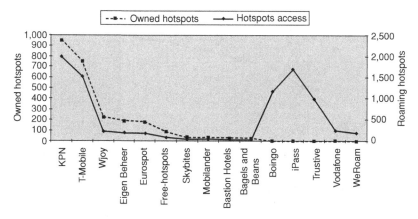

Figure 5.2 Hotspot providers in the Netherlands, 2007
Source: Based on data provided by de Leeuw in a personal communication, 2007.

To provide some insight into the hotspot market, Figure 5.2 shows as an illustration the distribution of hotspots by provider in the Netherlands in 2007. A total of 2,634 hotspots were registered through the site 'hotspotsvinden', with incumbent operators KPN and T-Mobile owning 58 per cent of the total (left-hand axis). Through roaming agreements, KPN provided access to 75 per cent of the market, iPass to 64 per cent and Boingo to 44 per cent (right-hand axis). In addition, 3,900 FON routers are identified, though no information is available as to whether these 'Foneras' were all open to the public (see section 5.3.2).

In Figure 5.3 the distribution of hotspots is shown by major type of location or activity. In this data set, hotels, restaurants and cafés represent 63 per cent of the total of 2,634 hotspots in the Netherlands.

An important factor in the quality of service that is provided at hotspots is the number of access points (antennae) that are deployed. Although at the start WISPs focused on just a few APs per venue, during the years that followed all WISPs started to expand the coverage per location, with ratios of one AP for every five to seven rooms in the case of hotels. As the usage increased and the need for bandwidth exploded in hotels, with usage more or less doubling every six to nine months, well-financed players such as Swisscom started to add wired backbone networks in order to optimise the delivery of high-speed internet access.[11]

5.3   Hotspot business models

The business model of a hotspot operator or wireless ISP has, essentially, two primary 'flavours': (1) the wireless access network is exploited for a profit;

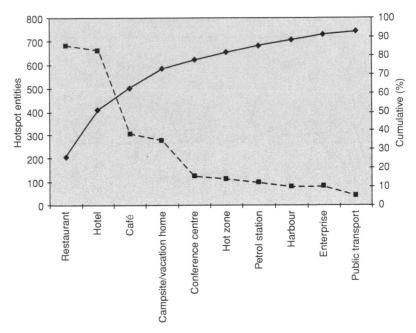

Figure 5.3 Hotspot distribution by location or activity in the Netherlands
Source: Based on data provided by de Leeuw in a personal communication, 2007.

or (2) the network is exploited to stimulate the core business of the location owner. In practice, a blend of the two extremes can be observed. As operating a telecommunications network and service is not the core business of location owners, hotspot operators have stepped in to provide the service. As the location owner and hotspot operators are mutually dependent, a wide variety of business models have emerged, including a variant in which the operator installs, owns and exploits the hotspot and compensates the location owner for the 'rights of way' to the location. An example is the already mentioned Swisscom Eurospot, which develops exclusive partnerships with hoteliers whereby the company assumes the capital and operating expenditure for providing the services and shares the revenue with the location owner (Gastaldo, 2004). Boingo, as an example, has a slightly different business model, as it brings together the networks of many location owners and provides the marketing, the technical support, the end user software and the billing, while the location owners either build and operate the networks themselves or engage a third-party network provider to assume these functions (Boingo Wireless, 2002). Through cooperation with product vendors, Boingo also offers location owners contemplating the creation of a hotspot the opportunity of a 'WISP-in-a-box' (Boingo Wireless, 2007c).

In the following sections we discuss the business model in more detail, by addressing the value proposition, the revenue model, the value network of actors and some technological aspects.

5.3.1   Value proposition

A wireless ISP may choose to serve the hotspot market in general or opt for pursuing certain market segments. The primary target of Swisscom Eurospot, for instance, is the hospitality industry – hotels and conference centres – while T-Mobile targets the broader market and aligns Wi-Fi access with the strategic objectives of its mobile network activities. Certain WISPs opt for a national or regional footprint, while others pursue business across the globe. In addition, the quality of the location matters in terms of the revenues that can be generated. As a result, the hotspot business is characterised primarily by 'competition for the market' and, secondarily, by 'competition in the market'.

To obtain a connection to the Internet while travelling one can simply open up the notebook and see what networks are available and provide open access. Alternatively, one can travel more purposefully and determine in advance which coffee shop, restaurant or hotel provides public access to the Internet. Hotspot operators provide listings of hotspot locations they serve through their websites. To make life more easy, however, 'hotspot finders' have emerged that collate information about hotspots from a wide range of providers and provide this free of charge to prospective users. They invite hotspot providers to submit information on hotspot locations so that they can be included in their directories.

As can be seen, different value propositions exist. We now discuss some of the variation, looking at FON and at premium offerings.

5.3.2   FON

Between the use of Wi-Fi for free in the home and for a fee in hotspots, a new model was introduced by Varsavsky in 2006 under the name of FON. The company has its headquarters in Madrid, and is funded by Sequoia Capital, Index Ventures, Google and eBay.[12] The business model of FON is aimed at establishing privately owned hotspots worldwide under the slogan 'Make a little money with your WiFi and roam the world for FREE'. It is based on acquiring a wireless router and access point called 'la Fonera', which splits the network access capacity into two streams, one for personal use and one for public use.[13] FON distinguishes three types of users: 'Bills', 'Linuses' and 'Aliens'. The 'Bills' charge for providing access, while also paying for obtaining access to any other Foneros network. The 'Linuses' open their network for free, to visiting 'Bills' as well. 'Aliens' are non-Foneros or customers from outside the community, who may use the FON spots by signing up through eBay's PayPal online payment service.[14] The revenue from opening up the FON access point is split fifty-fifty between the FON organisation and the 'Fonera' owner. Additional revenues can be made through advertising as part of the sign-in (Crane, 2007; FON, 2007).

5.3.3   Premium hotspots

Obtaining or creating a captive audience is an important objective of the sales and marketing function. For Wi-Fi hotspot operators, these represent locations such as trains and planes where users spend a considerable amount of time. In 2003, based on FCC and Federal Aviation Administration (FAA) approvals, Boeing in cooperation with Lufthansa and Cisco trialled on-board Wi-Fi service on Boeing 747 flights between Frankfurt and Washington, launching the service more widely in 2004 (Griffith, 2003a; ZDNet, 2004a). It was also in 2003 that British Airways trialled the service between London and New York. By 2006 the 'Connexion' service was offered on other intercontinental routes as well, for instance by SAS and Singapore Airlines.[15] The Wi-Fi on-board hotspot is connected to the Internet using a geostationary satellite connection with a 20 Mbit/s downlink and 1 Mbit/s uplink. At the end of 2004 the FCC approved the use of the 800 MHz band, already used for the in-flight phone service, to provide connection to the Internet (MSNBC, 2004). This allows for direct connections between aeroplanes and a terrestrial network. The related auction was won by Aircell in 2006, with commercial services starting in 2008 (Anderson, 2007).[16] In 2006 Boeing closed down the 'Connexion' service, however. Different reasons have been suggested for its failure, including the fact that Boeing took upon itself the task of selling the service to travellers (Pollack, 2006).

Wi-Fi services have been tested on trains, in the United Kingdom, for instance, in 2004 by Icomera for railway operator Great North Eastern Railway (GNER) serving the east coast mainline, and by hotspot operators Broadreach and Virgin on the west coast mainline (Twist, 2004).[17] In early 2005 Thalys, a French high-speed train service, started testing an on-board Wi-Fi service, using a satellite link to connect to the Internet. The tests were concluded successfully, and a tendering process was used to select a partner for the installation and exploitation of a commercial service, starting at the end of 2007 and covering the Thalys network (Clubic.com, 2006). In Japan the Shinkansen 'bullet trains', currently equipped with an analogue system using a 'leaky coaxial cable' along the tracks and providing basic communications as well as a radio channel that is rebroadcast in the train, are in the coming years to be upgraded to a digital system, which is to provide Wi-Fi-based internet access (Williams, 2006).

The deployment of Wi-Fi-based services is reported either to be under way or planned for trains in the United States, Canada, the Netherlands, Italy, Sweden, Switzerland, Portugal, Spain, China, South Korea and India.

5.3.4   Revenue model

WISPs commonly offer a menu of pricing options for Wi-Fi customers, including some combination of usage fees, fixed fees and service fees. Moreover, two principal payment options are offered: prepaid and post-paid. The fixed fees cover the basic service charges and are usually purchased by (part of) the hour or by the day, either as a rolling twenty-four-hour period from the time of purchase or as a fixed daily charge. Monthly plans and year plans are also on offer. Usage fees may apply that take into account the number of bytes of usage, or the time spent online. Service fees may account for the quality of service provided, for example the bandwidth provided, or the type of service being provided, such as e-mail, virtual private network (VPN) or streaming video and VoIP (Langeveld, 2005; Wi-Fi Alliance, 2004a).

Alternative pricing schemes exist whereby access is offered at a reduced fee or for free. An example of the former is FON, for which a lower fee is obtained through participation (see section 5.3.2.). Location owners may provide lower fees or provide the service for free as part of their business model in order to attract customers. Moreover, advertising is used as a source of income, allowing the service to be provided free of charge.

5.3.5   Value network of actors: aggregators and clearing houses

As indicated, the hotspot business is characterised by competition 'for the market' rather than 'in the market'. As a consequence, a particular hotspot is typically served by only one provider. This poses additional problems for the user. Next to dealing with different log-in procedures, it implies that the value of a subscription is limited by the number of hotspots served by a particular provider. To resolve this problem, aggregators and clearing houses have emerged that provide hotspot users with the benefit of a single sign-on, while taking care of all the necessary back-office activity required for authentication and authorisation, as well as accounting and settlement. Typical providers of these services, which enable roaming on the part of the end users, are Boingo, iPass, Trustive and Picopoint, which uses the name GBIA (Global Broadband Internet Access).[18] Some of these providers focus on a single country or region; others aim to serve the global business traveller. To extend their reach, roaming providers establish contractual arrangements with many other hotspot providers. In Figure 5.4 a generic roaming model using post-paid billing is depicted (Wi-Fi Alliance, 2004c).[19]

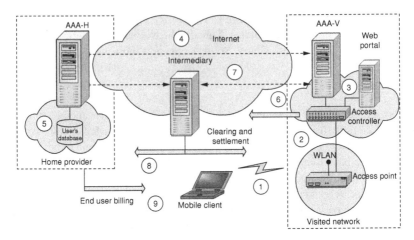

Figure 5.4 Generic roaming model
Notes: AAA-H = home provider of a computer system performing authentication, authorisation and accounting (AAA) servies. AAA-V = AAA proxy server located within the visited network.

A typical hotspot communication session based on roaming may run as follows. At the hotspot the user connects to the local access point (1), which uses the access controller (2) to present the user with a log-on script from a web portal (3) as a universal access method (UAM). Based on the user identity, the authentication, authorisation and accounting proxy server supporting the visited network is invoked (AAA-V) to contact the AAA function of the home provider (AAA-H) (4) to query the user's database (5). Following a successful execution of the authentication procedure, the user is provided with access to the Internet (6). At the end of the session the visited network informs the home provider or an intermediary of the session details (7) so as to permit financial clearing (8) and the settlement of the bill (9).[20]

The roaming provider typically provides the functions in the AAA-V 'cloud' in support of the visited network as well as the 'intermediary' function for clearing and settlement. In the case in which the roaming provider presents the user with a 'single bill', it also assumes the home provider function. As an aggregator, the roaming provider will typically provide marketing and technical assistance aimed at the (potential) end users and in support of the associated venue and hotspot providers, all aimed at bringing fragmented networks together and improving utilisation (Boingo Wireless, 2002).[21] To expand the roaming business more rapidly, providers such as Boingo offer a 'Hot-Spot-in-a-Box' and a 'MetroZone' for deployment by municipalities (Boingo Wireless, 2007a, 2007c)[22] (see also Chapter 6 on Wi-Fi-based community initiatives).

5.3.6   Technological aspects

The Wi-Fi Alliance supports the enabling of public access through certification programmes and the development of standards to promote interoperability and to enable roaming, by providing deployment guidelines for public access with enhanced security and by the development of a framework for sound business models that will enable the growth of the industry (Wi-Fi Alliance, 2004a, 2004c). The convergence of Wi-Fi and cellular services offers additional business opportunities.

5.3.7   Convergence of Wi-Fi and cellular services

With Wi-Fi-enabled devices supporting voice communications through VoIP and cellular networks supporting data communications using packets, the convergence of these two wireless services becomes a logical next step in their development. Wi-Fi–mobile convergence (WMC) implies a combination of Wi-Fi, providing wireless broadband connectivity in the local area of the home, the enterprise and in public hotspots, with mobile cellular networks, providing wide-area coverage, but often with a more limited throughput (Wi-Fi Alliance, 2006). By combining the access to both infrastructures, the functionality of each can be provided through a single terminal, with automatic switchover. Data communication and voice communication services can be supported on both networks, albeit subject to cellular operators supporting VoIP.

To support converged applications, three key issues have been addressed and resolved by the industry.

- *Support for isochronous services.* Support for real-time or latency-sensitive applications such as voice, video and audio streaming, or interactive gaming, is facilitated through the capability to distinguish different classes of applications and associated traffic streams requiring different QoS levels as part of IEEE 802.11e – enhancements to the MAC layer – approved in 2005. This addendum to the standard allows a distinction in four access classes – voice, video, best effort and background – which are used to prioritise and manage the traffic flows so as to ensure that the related applications are assigned the necessary network resources (Wi-Fi Alliance, 2004b).[23]
- *Power-saving mechanism.* To extend the battery life of mobile Wi-Fi devices, in particular VoIP-capable devices, the IEEE 802.11e addendum includes advanced power management functionality. The original IEEE 802.11 standard includes a power-saving mechanism that allows the client station to become inactive, or 'doze', when there is no traffic. Therefore the access point will buffer the data frames for each client and deliver the frames when the client is 'awake' (Wi-Fi Alliance, 2005). The advanced power management function included in IEEE 802.11e resolves the increased latency typically

associated with the power-up/down cycle, moreover; using a trigger-and-deliver mechanism, it allows downlink data frames to be sent together in a rapid sequence, thereby reducing overheads, and it allows latency-sensitive applications to trigger the access point more frequently.

- *Security of public access.* In the case of a wired LAN, users assume that the access equipment they connect to is under the control of a service provider they know, and hence they tend to trust the connection for transferring authentication information, such as the subscriber identifier and password. In principle, however, anyone can deploy a Wi-Fi hotspot with a familiar wireless LAN identifier or service set identifier (SSID). This familiar SSID does not ensure that the user will be connected to equipment operated by a service provider he/she can trust. Therefore, for public access, special emphasis is placed on mutual authentication to ensure that the user is connected to a trusted network prior to disclosing credential information for the purposes of network access. The use of the Extensible Authentication Protocol supports the use of password, token-based and SIM-card-based methods, as well as 3GPPP/3GPPP2 methods, making it compatible with authentication methods used in cellular networks. WPA2, as a subset of IEEE 802.11i, supports this pre-authentication procedure, facilitating secure access and fast roaming (Wi-Fi Alliance, 2004c).

The convergence of cellular and Wi-Fi services provides the user, in principle, with the best of all worlds: maximum data throughput at the lowest costs, with seamless coverage. For operators it provides opportunities to improve spectrum utilisation and in-building coverage. Moreover, lower costs may be translated into lower prices and an increase of fixed to mobile substitution (Wi-Fi Alliance, 2006). To facilitate market development, the Wi-Fi Alliance provides certification for Wi-Fi multimedia products in lockstep with the standardisation efforts within the IEEE.

The introduction of multifunctional cellular phones that are Wi-Fi-compatible also provides new business opportunities for hotspot operators, and introduces the home as a new hotspot. Various operators have been trialling the service; in the United States, for example, AT&T Singular Wireless, Sprint Nextel and T-Mobile under the label 'HotSpot @Home' in Seattle, using phones from Nokia and Samsung. T-Mobile launched the service nationwide in the United States in July 2007.[24] In Europe the service has been tested by, for example, British Telecom, Telecom Italia and Orange (Sharma, 2007). In July 2007 the range of Wi-Fi-compatible phones was extended with the introduction of the iPhone in the United States by Apple (Apple, 2007c).[25] Moreover, in September Apple presented the new iPod line, which includes the iPod Touch with Wi-Fi functionality to facilitate easy and quick downloads of iTunes over the Internet – that is, without the need for a PC to interface with the net (Apple, 2007b; Crum, 2007).

5.4   Summary of the Wi-Fi journey: 1993–2008

The concept of providing internet access at hotspots using WLANs dates back to 1993. Initial successes were achieved in hotels and at airports, while the mass market was unlocked by Starbucks providing Wi-Fi-based services to the wider public. This development led to the emergence of wireless ISPs, which were soon acquired by incumbent operators. Creating a successful WISP business requires focus and/or an extension of the service portfolio to meet the demands of specific market segments, such as the hospitality industry. By applying a roaming model, aggregators and clearing houses increase the convenience to hotspot users and provide back-office services to location owners. Finding hotspots is facilitated through websites providing listings across multiple providers. More and more, WISPs provide services on trains and aeroplanes. An alternative business model based on revenue sharing has been introduced under the name of FON. Increasingly, Wi-Fi functionality is being added to mobile devices, facilitating convergence between Wi-Fi and cellular services and markets.

5.5   Interpretation of the Wi-Fi case in the context of theory

In this section we interpret this lap of the innovation journey following the perspectives introduced in Chapter 1, namely the innovation landscape, the innovation process and the institutional environment. We continue to use the industry evolution and the management of the firm perspectives as introduced in Chapter 4.

5.5.1   Innovation and the innovation landscape

In providing access to the Internet at home and in the office, Wi-Fi links again with the internet innovation avenue, which becomes reinforced by providing internet access at 'hotspots'. In the process, Wi-Fi has moved from indoor and stationary use to outdoor and nomadic use. In terms of application, it can be seen that Wi-Fi is becoming a competitor and a complementor to data communication enabled via cellular networks. The resulting development of the innovation landscape is illustrated in Figure 5.5.[26]

Innovation process and sources of innovation   In developing towards 'hotspots', Wi-Fi has become the access technology of choice in the business model of the wireless ISP, comparable to DSL in the model of the wired ISP. Consequently, Wi-Fi has entered the domain of service innovation.

As the nomadic user cannot be identified any more through the network connection being used, new functionality is required in terms of authentication

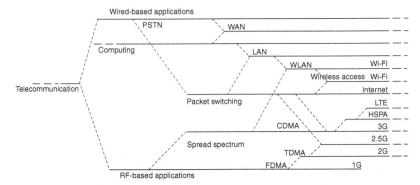

Figure 5.5 Cellular and Wi-Fi-related innovation avenues
Note: Refer to Annex 1 for explanation of acronyms.

and authorisation. In addition, as the service is provided for a fee, accounting functionality also needs to be added. This new application area does therefore affect the communication functionality of Wi-Fi as defined in the IEEE 802.11 standards. Providing secure access has led to the introduction of Extensible Authentication Protocol as part of the IEEE 802.11i security-related extension effort (see also Chapter 4 section 5.3).

Moreover, the nomadic use has directed attention towards extending the battery life of mobile devices, and hence a change in the communications protocol through the IEEE802.11e extension. Furthermore, in support of the increasing use of real-time-sensitive applications on the Internet, such as voice, audio and video streaming, enhancements have been made to the MAC layer, and they have also become part of the 802.11e extension to the standard.

These innovations are an integral part of the evolution of the IEEE standard under the auspices of working group 802.11. As such, they have been driven primarily by the Wi-Fi product manufacturers acknowledging the new application areas of Wi-Fi.

Innovation diffusion   With the emergence of 'hotspots' the utility of Wi-Fi has been further increased, stimulating its diffusion. Having started as a point-to-point wiring replacement technology, Wi-Fi has evolved towards providing wireless LAN functionality, first in a static mode, later with roaming features. As part of the 'hotspots', Wi-Fi has now moved from a free service within the business environment and the home to a fee-based service as part of a WISP business model. In the process Wi-Fi is moving from indoor use only to include outdoor use. The integration of Wi-Fi in cellular devices makes it an almost universal means of access for data communication in stationary and nomadic mode alike.

As a consequence, the diffusion of Wi-Fi is not linked to PCs and laptops any more but to mobile devices in general, significantly expanding the addressable market.

5.5.2 Institutional environment

In the transition from private to public use, the institutional environment for the use of Wi-Fi has changed. To the extent that ISPs are considered telecommunications providers under the law, so are WISPs. This may range from being subject to levies that fund the national regulatory agency to being responsible for the implementation of the European Union data retention directive. For applications of Wi-Fi on board transport vehicles, the appropriate authorities have become involved, such as the Federal Aviation Administration in the United States in the case of use on aircraft.

5.5.3 Industry evolution

In terms of telecommunication industry evolution, having Wi-Fi at public 'hotspots' implies the application of a new technology enabling the entry of new firms, which added further intensity to the pre-existing rivalry in the domain of mobile data communications. If we consider the developments over time, we observe first specialisation, in terms of the emergence of wireless ISPs, followed by consolidation, as many of the WISP start-ups were acquired by the established operators. In this way, incumbent operators quickly gained a footprint in this new market segment – a development consistent with the dynamic market theory of de Jong (1996).

With the emergence of the WISPs, Wi-Fi entered the services industry, whereby the service providers became important buyers of access points, becoming part of a service infrastructure that included authentication, authorisation and accounting servers, and interconnection with internet backbone networks, including peering arrangements. Although quality of service aspects have been addressed in the IEEE 802.11e extension, Wi-Fi operates on a licence-exempt non-protective basis. The actual level of service depends on the density of APs in relation to the number of simultaneous users and the data transfer needs of the applications they are running.

For incumbent operators not active in the cellular market, the combination of fixed and Wi-Fi provides for a limited mobility offering; a case in point is British Telecom's OpenZone.

For mobile device manufacturers, Wi-Fi forms a new functionality that can be integrated into existing business and will stimulate the sale of new devices in a market that is becoming increasingly dependent on replacement sales.

Notes

1 T1 lines provide a 1.5 Mbit/s connection to the backbone network.
2 The service was offered after a free trial for US$49.99 per month, with unlimited national access for a flat fee of US$2.99 for a fifteen-minute session. In addition, prepaid plans were available at US$20 for 120 minutes nationwide or US$50 for 300 minutes.
3 By 2003 T-Mobile operated 2,100 Wi-Fi 'hotspots' in the United States. The lion's share was taken by the Starbucks outlets, further examples including Kinko's copy shops and Borders Books stores.
4 The rate was cut to unlimited access for US$29.99, without a cap on data transfer, based on a subscription of one year. The pay-as-you-go plan came in at US$2.99 for the first fifteen minutes, US$0.25 per minute thereafter up to an hour and US$0.10 per minute after the hour.
5 These 3,100 were out of 4,700 T-Mobile 'HotSpots' in total in the United States, covering Borders Books and Music, FedEx Kinko's Office and Print Centers, Hyatt hotels and resorts, airport business lounges of American, Delta, United Airlines and US Airways.
6 That new ideas are claimed by multiple persons at about the same time is a well-known phenomenon. For instance, a bitter fight emerged between Alexander Graham Bell and Elisha Gray on inventing the telephone; apparently Bell filed his patent application in Boston just hours before Gray did in Chicago. Their inventions had been preceded by a version of the telephone made by Philipp Reis of Bad Homburg, Germany, in 1860; and in Italy it was Antonio Meucci who, in 1857, created some form of voice communication apparatus.
7 They used BreezeCom equipment, which was based on frequency hopping.
8 More recent examples are Airwave Adventures, Butler Networks, Coach Connect, Cometa, Harbor Link Network, Hotpoint Wireless and Panera Bread. Current examples in Europe are A1, airmedis, AkiWifi, bitbuzz, the Cloud, dna, Elecktrosmog, GANAG, Golden Telecom Wi-Fi, HiPort, Hotspot Deutschland, Komstar, Kubi, Meteor, Monzoon, Passman, Rover Rabbit, SparkNet, Swisscom Eurospot, Telenet/Sinfilo and TheNet. Examples of hotspot operators in Asia are Airzed, Asia Starhub, Azure, Beenet, CafeNet, CBN, Chungwha, iPrimus and Maxis (WLAN Report, 2007).
9 Personal communication from Leo Brand, 2009; see also Gastaldo (2004).
10 This ranking remained the same in early 2009.
11 This has been done using coaxial, CAT3 VDSL (very-high-speed digital subscriber line) and CAT5/6 cabling. Personal communication from Leo Brand, 2009.
12 Varsavsky was also the founder of Viatel and Jazztel, new entrants in the telecommunications market.
13 In 2007 'la Fonera' was advertised at US$39.99 per month. In a dedicated campaign, 'la Fonera' was offered for free when living next to a Starbucks coffeehouse.
14 In 2007 the advertised rate for 'Bills' and 'Aliens' was US$3 for a twenty-four-hour connection.
15 The service is priced at US$9.95 per hour, or US$29.95 for the duration of the flight (Broache, 2006).
16 The licence was acquired for US$31.3 million.

17 GNER is offering the service for free in first class and for £4.96 per hour in standard class. The service uses a satellite downlink and the mobile phone network for the uplink to the Internet (ZDNet, 2004b).

18 In 2005 Boingo served 20,000 hotspots under its own brand. Picopoint claimed to serve over 100 mobile carriers, ISPs and hotspot operators, covering 10,000 hotspots. Trustive serves about 8,000 hotspots globally; in the Netherlands it serves KPN, Mobilander and WinQ as providers (de Leeuw, 2005).

19 Other billing options include pre-paid billing and direct to the home provider.

20 It should be noted that the components depicted are functional and reflect a logical relationship; in reality, for instance, the access controller, web portal and AAA server may be shared between multiple hotspots (for further details, see Wi-Fi Alliance, 2004c).

21 Boingo provides services in cooperation with network provider partners such as Wayport, iBahn, SurfandSip, NetNearU, Deep Blue Wireless and Fatport (Boingo Wireless, 2007b).

22 These solutions are offered in cooperation with partners Pronto Networks and Tropos Networks.

23 Wi-Fi Multimedia (WMM) is based on the IETF's differentiated services (diffserv) architecture. The packets are labelled with either IETF DSCP (differentiated services code point) headers or IEEE 802.1d tags. The access categories are derived from IEEE 802.1d.

24 For the trial, T-Mobile customers paid US$20 in addition to their monthly cellular phone subscription, and an additional US$5 for adding another family member. At the launch the service was advertised at US$9.99 on individual charging plans and US$19.99 on family plans with up to five handsets (Pogue, 2007).

25 The iPhone was launched with an AT&T service plan starting at US$59.99, including Visual Voicemail and Unlimited Data (e-mail and web) or iPhone Data Plan as an add-on to existing qualifying rate plans.

26 For an assessment of Wi-Fi and 3G as access technologies, see Lehr and McKnight (2003). For a comparative longitudinal case study of Wi-Fi and cellular developments, see Lemstra and Hayes (2009).

References

Anderson, N. (2007). 'WiFi (again) flies the friendly skies'. Ars Technica; http://arstechnica.com/news.ars/post/20070403-wifi-again-flies-the-friendly-skies.html (accessed 5 September 2007).

Apple (2007a). 'Apple and Starbucks announce music partnership'. Cupertino, CA: Apple. Available at www.apple.com/pr/library/2007/09/05starbucks.html (accessed 26 September 2007).

(2007b). 'Apple unveils the iTunes Wi-Fi music store'. Cupertino, CA: Apple. Available at www.apple.com/pr/library/2007/09/05itunes.html (accessed 26 September 2007).

(2007c). 'iPhone premieres this Friday night at Apple retail stores'. Cupertino, CA: Apple. Available at www.apple.com/iphone/pr/20070628iphone.html (accessed 5 September 2007).

Arar, Y. (2002). 'Starbucks expands wireless internet offering'. Hemel Hempstead: PC World. Available at www.pcworld.com/printable/article/id,104237/printable.html (accessed 29 August 2007).

Boingo Wireless (2002). 'Network providers pdf'. Los Angeles: Boingo Wireless.

(2007a). 'Boingo ready MetroZone pilot pack'. Los Angeles: Boingo Wireless. Available at www.boingo.com/hso/metrozone.html (accessed 30 August 2007).

(2007b). 'Hotels'. Los Angeles: Boingo Wireless. Available at www.boingo.com/hso/hotels.html (accessed 30 August 2007).

(2007c). 'WISP-in-a-box'. Los Angeles: Boingo Wireless. Available at www.boingo.com/hso/wisp.html (accessed 30 August 2007).

Broache, A. (2006). 'Wi-Fi: coming soon on board US airplanes'. San Francisco: CNET News; http://news.cnet.com/2102–7351_3–6080252.html (accessed 5 September 2007).

Business Wire (2004). 'Starbucks builds continued success with T-Mobile HotSpot'. Seattle: Business Wire. Available at http://home.businesswire.com/portal/site/home/index.jsp?epi-content=NEWS_VIEW (accessed 30 August 2007).

Clubic.com (2006). 'Thalys: de WiFi dans le train d'íci la fin 2007'. Clubic.com; www.clubic.com/actualite-37267-thalys-wifi-train-fin-2007.html (accessed 5 September 2007).

Crane, M. (2007). 'Stealing Starbuck's Wi-Fi customers'. New York: Forbes. Available at www.forbes.com/2007/02/23/fonbucks-wifi-starbucks-ent_cx_mc_0226fonbucks_print.html (accessed 28 August 2007).

Crum, R. (2007). 'Apple revamps entire iPod line'. New York: MarketWatch. Available at www.marketwatch.com/news/story/apple-adds-touch-screen-wi-fi/story.aspx (accessed 5 September 2007).

De Jong, H. W. (1996). *Dynamisch Markttheorie* [*Dynamic Market Theory*]. Weteringbrug, Netherlands: Edclusa.

De Leeuw, G.-J. (2005). *De Nederlands Wi-Fi Markt in 2005*. Delft: Delft University of Technology.

(2007). *A Snapshot of the Wi-Fi World in 2007*. Delft: Delft University of Technology.

Fleishman, G. (2002). 'Wi-Fi timeline'. Wi-Fi Net News; http://wifinetnews.com/archives/001315.html (accessed 31 May 2006).

FON (2007). 'What's Fon?'. Madrid: FON. Available at www.fon.com/en/info/whatsFon (accessed 30 August 2007).

Gastaldo, F. (2004). 'Swisscom Eurospot and the WiFi market'. Paper presented at the Swisscom investor conference. Paris, 7 October.

Griffith, E. (2003a). 'Lufthansa and Cisco put Wi-Fi in the plane'. Foster City, CA: Wi-Fi Planet. Available at www.wi-fiplanet.com/news/print.php/1570531 (accessed 5 September 2007).

(2003b). 'T-Mobile cut price of Wi-Fi'. Foster City, CA: Wi-Fi Planet. Available at www.wi-fiplanet.com/news/print.php/1855971 (accessed 29 August 2007).

JiWire (2007). 'Hospot directory'. San Francisco: JiWire. Available at www.jiwire.com/hotspots-hot-spot-directory-browse-by-country.htm (accessed 12 September 2007).

Langeveld, M. (2005). *Number of Wi-Fi Hotspots Is Poor Indicator of Success*. Research Brief. Houten, Netherlands: TelecomPaper.

Lehr, W., and L. W. McKnight (2003). 'Wireless internet access: 3G vs. WiFi?'. *Telecommunications Policy.* **27** (5–6), 351–70.

Lemstra, W., and V. Hayes (2009). 'License exempt: Wi-Fi complement to 3G'. *Telematics and Informatics.* **26** (3), 227–39.

Microsoft (2001). 'MobileStar to provide high-speed wireless internet access and infrastructure'. Redmond, WA: Microsoft. Available at www.microsoft.com/presspass/press/2001/jan01/01–03starbuckspr.mspx?pf=true (accessed 29 August 2007).

MSNBC (2004). 'High-speed net access coming to planes'. New York: MSNBC; www.msnbc.msn.com/id/6717750 (accessed 5 September 2007).

O'Shea, D. (2003). 'Starbucks says Wi-Fi's a hit'. Chicago: TelephonyOnline. Available at www.printthis.clckability.com/pt/cpt?action=cpt&title=Starbucks+Wi-Fi+access (accessed 29 August 2007).

Pogue, D. (2007). 'IPhone-Free cellphone news'. *New York Times*, 5 July. Available at www.nytimes.com/2007/07/05/technology/circuits/05pogue.html (accessed 5 September 2007).

Pollack, P. (2006). 'Boeing drops its Connexion'. Ars Technica; http://arstechnica.com/news.ars/post20060817–7536.html (accessed 5 September 2007).

Sharma, A. (2007). 'How Wi-Fi can extend T-Mobile's range'. *Wall Street Journal*, 3 May. Available at http://online.wsj.com/public/article_print/SB1178159383-77190497.html (accessed 29 August 2007).

Singer, M. (2002). 'Starbucks serves up Wi-Fi access'. Foster City, CA: Internetnews.com. Available at http://siliconvalley.internet.com/news/print.php/1450471 (accessed 29 August 2007).

Starbucks (2007). 'Highspeed wireless internet access'. Available at www.starbucks.com/retail/wireless.asp (accessed 28 August 2007).

Twist, J. (2004). 'Wireless web reaches out in 2004'. London: BBC. Available at http://newsvote.bbc.co.uk/mpapps/pagetools/print/new.bbc.co.uk/2/hi/technology/3341 (accessed 3 September 2007).

US Census Bureau (2006). 'Population'. Washington, DC: US Census Bureau. Available at www.census.gov/ipc/www/idb/ranks.html (accessed 12 September 2007).

Wi-Fi Alliance (2004a). *Enabling the Future of Wi-Fi Public Access.* Austin, TX: Wi-Fi Alliance.

(2004b). *Wi-Fi Certified for WMM: Support for Multimedia Applications with Quality of Service in Wi-Fi Networks.* Austin, TX: Wi-Fi Alliance.

(2004c). *WPA Deployment Guidelines for Public Access Wi-Fi Networks.* Austin, TX: Wi-Fi Alliance.

(2005). *WMM Power Save for Mobile and Portable Wi-Fi Certified Devices.* Austin, TX: Wi-Fi Alliance.

(2006). *Wi-Fi Mobile Convergence: The Role of Wi-Fi Certified.* Austin, TX: Wi-Fi Alliance.

Williams, M. (2006). 'Japan's bullet trains to get Wi-Fi'. Haarlem, Netherlands: Webwereld; www.webwereld.nl/articles/41796/japan-s-bullet-trains-to-get-wi-fi.html (accessed 5 September 2007).

WLAN Report (2007). *WISP Guide Worldwide.* Munich: WLAN Report.

ZDNet (2004a). 'Lufthansa broadband poised to take flight'. San Francisco: ZDNet; www.zdnet.co.uk/misc/print/0,1000000169,39149469–39001101c,00.htm (accessed 5 September 2007).

(2004b). 'Wi-Fi sends train passengers rushing to first class'. San Francisco: ZDNet; www.zdnet.co.uk/misc/print/0,1000000169,39167279–39001101x,00.htm (accessed 5 September 2007).

6 Wi-Fi-based community networks: Wireless Leiden

Wolter Lemstra and Leo Van Audenhove,
with contributions from Huub Schuurmans,
Marten Vijn and Gerard Mourits

6.1 Wireless neighbourhood area networks

Wireless internet service providers typically exploit Wi-Fi technology to provide internet access services for a profit, or, in the case of location owners exploiting 'hotspots', the objective may be to stimulate the revenues of the core business. Next to these commercially oriented organisations, groups of volunteers have emerged that use Wi-Fi to provide internet access either for free or at very low cost. The shared internet access, often accompanied by direct communications between community members in the form of an intranet, is provided on the basis of interconnected Wi-Fi access points forming a wireless neighbourhood area network (WNAN).[1]

These communities of volunteers tend to be motivated by their enthusiasm to explore the possibilities of new technologies and their wish to demonstrate their technological savvy. These groups of Wi-Fi volunteers are in many ways similar to the early 'Homebrew Computer Club' that emerged in Silicon Valley when the first do-it-yourself computer kits came on the market in the mid 1970s (Freiberger and Swaine, 1984). Members would come together to trade computer parts and exchange schematics and programming tips.[2] A typical example of a Wi-Fi community in the Netherlands is 'Wireless Leiden', a group of volunteers that started in 2001 and has built a neighbourhood area network that has reached 100 nodes, covering most of the city of Leiden (some 160,000 inhabitants) and neighbouring villages – an area of about 500 square km (van Drunen *et al.*, 2003; Vijn and Mourits, 2005).

Based on an investigation conducted in the spring of 2006, there were eighty-eight NAN initiatives in the Netherlands then, of which the Wireless Leiden NAN was the largest.[3] A study by Schreurs (2006) has revealed that there are, or have been, many more initiatives than there are networks that are providing an actual service. One plausible reason concerns the nature of these schemes: for the most part they are the work of loosely organised groups of volunteers whose involvement in the Wi-Fi community initiatives has to compete with their day job commitments. Without strong economic incentives,

175

therefore, such projects tend to take a long time to realise, if they ever are at all.

Nevertheless, there is ample evidence that these Wi-Fi-based NANs are important from an economic and social perspective, in particular (1) in areas in developed countries where incumbent telecom operators fail to provide broadband internet access (a typical example is the peninsula of Djursland in Denmark; see Chapter 7 for a description) and (2) in developing country areas where the investment capital is often lacking to provide the inhabitants with even the most basic communication services, such as telephony (typical examples come from the rural areas in developing countries, as in India, Venezuela and South Africa, of which illustrative case stories are presented and discussed in Chapter 7). The case of Wireless Leiden is of interest for several reasons: because of its early start and its significant size, and also for the engineering and the hardware and software development that were carried out to make Wi-Fi networking possible, and the entrepreneurial activities that it generated.[4] Reflecting this significance, we explore the Wireless Leiden case in some detail, and subsequently the municipal Wi-Fi activities that have emerged, in particular in the United States. We also assess the benefits they can bring to the communities involved.

6.2   The case of Wireless Leiden

The Wireless Leiden neighbourhood area network is the result of an initiative by Jasper Koolhaas, a technical director at one of the early ISPs in the Netherlands, together with Marten Vijn, who met at a 'Linux install party' organised by HCC-Leiden, the local branch of the Hobby Computer Club, in October 2001. The idea was to create a wireless network that would cover the city of Leiden. Following an initial exploration of the feasibility of the idea, the two gathered together six more volunteers within a few weeks, all with very diverse backgrounds, including two individuals with a technical background and expertise in the operation of amateur radio. The first three nodes were contributed by three of the volunteers; the fourth node was the result of efforts by Huub Schuurmans, who introduced the concept of 'sponsored' nodes.

Schuurmans, a former scientific attaché for the Ministry of Economic Affairs who founded the Netherlands Office for Science and Technology in Silicon Valley, and who had been involved with the management of innovation and development at oil company Royal Dutch Shell, assumed the public relations (PR) and public affairs function for the group of volunteers. He explains the purpose of the network:[5]

The network is not a collection of isolated 'hotspots' but consists of wirelessly interconnected nodes. These nodes are the access points to the network for houses, schools and offices in their direct surroundings. In addition, mobile users and visitors with a laptop can connect freely without registration. To connect to the Internet via the network, it is not necessary that each and every node has an internet connection. In theory, one gateway would suffice; currently, several gateways[6] are operational. Individual users can also (selectively) share their internet connection not only with their direct neighbours but also with people on the other side of town. Apart from internet access (at present the most used service), this local network provides easy and free access for all, whether for making a private connection, for delivering one's own information and services over the network or for experimenting with new applications.

Through the organisation of volunteers, the Wireless Leiden network is strongly embedded in the economic and social structure of the city of Leiden. Companies that, for instance, like to link their offices across the city or to their home sponsor the network by providing the equipment for a network node at their premises, which subsequently operates under their name. Other firms provide communication equipment in kind, or provide facilities for the group of volunteers to meet on a regular basis. The municipality supports the group by providing locations to place nodes and antennae. For one local church the Wireless Leiden network provides live broadcasts of church services, and in return it is allowed to place an antenna on the church tower.[7] The network also provides inexpensive communication between schools in the city, and provides access to the Internet at the library and at the library bus that serves the city neighbourhood.

6.2.1   The technical challenges

One of the first challenges the group faced in building the network is that Wi-Fi is designed as a network access solution and not as a network node. The Wireless Leiden community resolved this issue by creating Wi-Fi-based backbone routes which connect PC-based network nodes supporting Transmission Control Protocol/Internet Protocol (TCP/IP), thereby creating an intranet. One of the first major applications on the network became a major challenge: the live video broadcasting of the Rapenburg Concert in September 2002. This triggered a switch from Linux to the use of FreeBSD software (Vijn, Mourits and van 't Hart, 2007). Recognising that the reliability of the network depends on the proper functioning of the nodes, which are often located at places that are difficult to access, the procedure to create a node would be standardised and partly automated in the form of a 'node factory' (see Chapter 9 for a more detailed account of the (re-)engineering performed by the volunteers of Wireless Leiden).

6.2.2   The organisation

Right from the start a culture of mutual trust developed, as the volunteers focused on collaboration in delivering results. With technical issues progressively being solved, new organisational issues started to emerge as the group of volunteers grew in size and the network expanded. Schuurmans reflects on the choice and the development of the organisational structure:

Wireless Leiden became a non-profit foundation in 2002, operating with professional volunteers and focusing on the network infrastructure.[8] We believed this to be essential for the success of the project. The project is founded on enthusiasm, organisational ability and broad support among the local community. Expenses are kept low by the use of inexpensive hardware, open standards, open source software and, first and foremost, volunteers – in a cooperative, non-profit and planned approach.

A group of professional volunteers with experience in and knowledge of a whole range of disciplines, such as radio technology, network planning, innovation management and public relations, forms the core of Wireless Leiden.

Once a month the board of the foundation meets and discusses progress under the themes of general management, finance, technology development and technology implementation. The volunteers are associated with one or more of these areas (Vijn, Mourits and van 't Hart, 2007). Schuurmans continues his account:

Formally, we have established a foundation, rather than an association with members, in order to enable quick decision making and minimise red tape. Since we do not have commercial interests, we can easily cooperate with commercial and non-commercial parties alike. We stimulate and facilitate commercial activities around our network by others and as spin-offs. Several new companies have indeed been started up. The unique character of our approach was recognised when the foundation received the 2003 Vosko Award for network pioneers.

We publish our experiences and the know-how we have developed on our website, www.wirelessleiden.nl (currently mainly in Dutch). True to the open source philosophy, we do not expect others to 'reinvent the wheel'. All our software, technological and organisational knowledge is freely available to others under an open source licence. We encourage serious and enthusiastic people in other cities to copy our project and provide feedback. Copying the Wireless Leiden model appears to be more difficult than expected, however, the main challenge being organisational.

The communication infrastructure deployed by the volunteers includes: mailing lists by topical area (such as users, volunteers, technology, projects, advisory board, node planning); a wiki; instant messaging (Jabber); and a revision control system (Subversion). As the node building is a repetitive task, the technical experts designed checklists for the site survey teams, followed by procedures for the building of the nodes. This allows volunteers without a technical background to participate actively in expanding the network. Monthly meetings are held to transfer information, which have grown from ten to twenty volunteers to 150 participants when users started to join. These large-scale meetings were made possible when 'de Burcht' centre started to sponsor the meetings in kind (Vijn, Mourits and van 't Hart, 2007).[9] Schuurmans continues his account:

The expenses of a Wi-Fi network can be minimal, partly because no licence costs have to be paid. A cooperative, non-profit approach also enables free access to strategic locations for placing the nodes and the antennae. In contrast, a for-profit company would be asked to pay for rooftop access. With a large number of nodes the operating costs would have been prohibitive. Almost all our expenses are for investment in hardware for the nodes, and we have been successful in securing sponsors to pay for the nodes that they need for their own use, and in exchange the node bears their name, which works quite well. Cooperating within the Wireless Leiden framework almost always results in win-win situations.

Our approach has been, first, to realise a basic network infrastructure, aiming to cover the whole city. During the roll-out phase we have concentrated mainly on professional users:

• companies needing a virtual private network to link to their employees at home;
• schools with several locations;
• the public library, with several locations and stops for the library bus; and
• homes for the elderly (interconnected administrative systems, with a connection with the library and churches).

Although individual users were not a primary target group, the network was soon discovered by such users who wanted to make a connection to the Wireless Leiden network from their homes, mainly to get free, and relatively fast, internet access. To prevent abuse, only web traffic ('port 80') is allowed.

Many small villages surrounding Leiden joined the Wireless Leiden initiative, mainly because there was no fast internet connection available other than that provided via Wireless Leiden.

In addition, meetings were organised with these neighbouring localities to share experiences: the villages in question are Leiderdorp, Jacobswoude and Rijnswoude, and, further out, Hoofddorp and Zoetermeer (Vijn, Mourits and van 't Hart, 2007).

6.2.3 Operating within the law

A recurrent theme in board meetings has been that of liability. What if volunteers accidentally damage property while placing a node on the rooftop of a municipal building? What if, due to a storm, damage is caused by an antenna to the building or to passers-by? What role should the Wireless Leiden Foundation assume vis-à-vis the volunteers? Financial insurance can protect an organisation in this respect, but this requires in turn a basic level of formalisation of the relationship between the foundation and its volunteers. In 2004 the 'vrijwilligersverklaring' (declaration of the volunteer) was introduced to enforce compliance with safety and health procedures.

Another issue that arose was the distributed ownership of the nodes that collectively form the Wireless Leiden network, whereby nodes may be placed by volunteers or through sponsorship. What if a volunteer decides to remove his/her node from the network? Given the nature of a Wi-Fi-based network, no performance guarantees can or will be provided, even though for companies to become interested in joining the network as sponsors some level of confidence in the performance of the network is required – an issue that relates not only to equipment performance but also to the 'collective' ensuring that the network is functioning properly. With regard to this concern in a WNAN setting, informal relationships take on the function of formal relationships. Knowing the organisation and knowing the individuals involved has built the necessary level of trust required with regard to companies, sponsors, the municipality and other stakeholders.

Another form of liability that the organisation identified could result from malevolent use of the network. What if a user started to distribute illegal content? In principle the network is open and there is no central registry of users, so there is no central control either. Could the foundation still be held liable for the acts of volunteers and visitors? At the time it was understood that, in the United States, WNAN initiatives had to restructure, or had even collapsed, on account of the threat of the organisation – and thereby its members – becoming liable for activities outside its control. Moreover, would the organisation be obliged to work with law enforcement agencies on this matter? Would it become obliged to arrange for monitoring facilities in the way that the telecom operators and internet service providers are? This would add significantly to the expenses of the low-cost operation of the Wireless Leiden network.[10] The underlying question was: when would Wireless Leiden be considered an operator according to the Netherlands' Telecommunications Act?

From its inception the principle was that the Wireless Leiden network would be built for and by Leiden's citizens. A communications infrastructure would be provided using Wi-Fi and internet-related technologies. The foundation would not provide any services over the network, but would allow others to do so. Moreover, the network would be operated within the confines of the law. In an effort to address and resolve the aforementioned issues, brainstorming meetings were held: in the spring of 2003 with experts at the Delft University of Technology, and in the autumn with representatives of the Ministry of Economic Affairs and of OPTA, the national telecoms regulatory agency, to discuss the options. The latter meeting was held in the context of the government-initiated 'Broadband Action Programme', which had as one of its objectives the removal of legal and regulatory barriers to the development of broadband.

From the brainstorming sessions it became clear that the dividing line between a private network and a public network had shifted from the perimeter of a facility as the boundary between public and private networks, as it had been in the past, to the interface between the networks, as it was now under the new telecommunications legislation. The recommendations developed by the group included the following: make a clear definition of purpose;

acknowledge that Wireless Leiden was innovative and, accordingly, request/ claim the required experimental space; keep the threshold for participation as low as possible; define how privacy-sensitive information is to be handled; define the boundaries in technical, organisational and legal dimensions; communicate well; and do not aim to become an ISP, as this would involve a significant set of obligations to be fulfilled (Lemstra, 2003).

Another legal topic the Wireless Leiden community had to address was that of the ownership and distribution rights of the specific software that was being developed, including the software to provide the PCs, that formed the hardware core of the network nodes, with the appropriate routing functionality. On the one hand, the FreeBSD operating system was used, and the individuals leading the software development had a strong background in the open source movement; on the other hand, key volunteers were employed by large IT firms, and therefore were subject to more restrictive codes of conduct.[11] The main options discussed were whether to adopt the BSD licence or the GNU General Public License.[12] The decision of the board was to follow the BSD licensing regime. This operating principle was also covered in the 'vrijwilligersverklaring'.[13]

6.2.4   The competition

From the earliest days the Wireless Leiden volunteers were acutely aware that the use of Wi-Fi is non-exclusive, and thus another group could start an alternative network in the city. Recognising that this would seriously impact the performance of the Wireless Leiden network, the operating principle that was adopted was to cooperate with all interested parties. In the words of Schuurmans:

Wi-Fi uses a free frequency band: anybody can use it. Of course, this advantage is also a disadvantage, as one person's signal is another person's noise, so there is the risk of Wi-Fi failing due to its very success. A coordinated approach is therefore required. Furthermore, a coherent network is much more valuable for all users compared to individual wireless solutions. Our approach aims to make it more attractive for all interested parties to join the network, rather than trying to deploy Wi-Fi on their own; hence our appeal to companies, the university, the city government, schools, organisations and citizens to join.

In providing communications between the volunteers and to occasional visitors, the Wireless Leiden network competes with established communication infrastructures and services provided by the incumbent operators. The emergence of this new infrastructure has not been considered a major threat to their operations, however; there have not been specific marketing or sales actions aimed at the Leiden citizens, nor have actions been taken in the regulatory or policy domain. As indicated earlier, the Ministry of Economic Affairs considers the emergence of Wi-Fi-based networks to be a healthy sign of innovation in the sector. OPTA is well aware of the development, but has not yet seen any reason to intervene.

6.2.5   *The reasons for success*

The implementation of the Wireless Leiden network with 100 nodes can be considered a major achievement for an organisation of approximately 100 volunteers of which just fifteen can be considered the 'hard core'. As the group grew, maintaining its cohesion became an organisational challenge. As one volunteer put it: 'With every new engineer joining another degree of [intellectual] freedom is added to the system' (van Drunen *et al.*, 2003). Managing such a large and diverse group in an open manner, and without a command and control structure, can be difficult at times. Another observation typifies the challenges that have been faced: '[O]n the non-technical level the more religious ideas between, e.g., the different operating systems or engineering solutions on a specific topic are a problem to cope with. A heterogeneous set-up with different operating systems will gain a broader acceptance within the group and probably builds a more robust network, but will be much more difficult to manage' (van Drunen *et al.*, 2003).

Looking back over the past five years, Schuurmans concludes that Wireless Leiden has been successful because of a combination of factors:

- the availability of a variety of technical and organisational competences, setting ambitious goals and a challenging time frame;
- having a first-mover advantage: back in 2002/3 wireless technology was new and exciting, and it was relatively easy to obtain media attention;
- enjoying good relationships with the local community and business;
- standardising hardware and software, and looking for long-term, sustainable and scalable solutions; and
- having a self-organising capability, with no dependence on subsidies, and focusing on the real needs of real customers.

6.2.6   *Future direction*

Since the foundation of Wireless Leiden in 2002, however, there have been important changes in the environment: broadband internet access through asymmetric digital subscriber line (ADSL) and cable modems and the use of domestic Wi-Fi have become ubiquitous. Moreover, the objectives of the early techno-enthusiasts have been fulfilled with the establishment of the network. Keeping the network running requires a different attitude and different motivation on the part of volunteers. Deep knowledge of the technology remains essential, nevertheless; one volunteer expressed his concern in these words (Vijn, Mourits and van 't Hart, 2007):

Je hebt mensen die het begrijpen en je hebt mensen die een kunstje leren. Op het moment dat mensen een kunstje geleerd hebben en denken dat zij het begrijpen gaat het mis. Als deze mensen ook nog een aansturende rol in de organisatie krijgen, begeeft de organisatie zich op een hellend vlak.

Freely translated, this means:

There are people who understand it and there are people who learn a trick. When the people who learned the trick think that they understand it, things go wrong. If these people also take a managerial role, the organisation is at risk.

Adding to the challenge, in 2006, after nearly five years' involvement as a voluntary leader, the last of the original pioneers retired from the board of the foundation.

Meanwhile, Wireless Leiden has become highly visible, and according to Maarten van der Plas, economic adviser to the civil servants at the city's council offices, it has become a highly valuable asset in the positioning of Leiden as a high-tech city. The continuity of the Wireless Leiden network has become important to the municipality.

Moreover, professional parties have shown an interest in using the network for developing new, wireless applications, such as location-based services. The Wi-Fi network of Wireless Leiden offers a unique possibility for developing and testing new techniques and applications. This is the reason that a close working relationship has developed with several research institutions, such as the Centre for Technology and Innovation Management (CeTIM) at Leiden, the Institute for Societal Innovation (IMI), the Hogeschool Leiden and Leiden University.

Professionals require a reliable, responsive organisation as a partner, however, and this important realisation has occasioned Wireless Leiden to rethink its strategy. Schuurmans takes up the story:

We have been rethinking our strategy[14] and have concluded that – given the availability of affordable fixed internet access – the main attractions of a wireless network are:
- freely available internet access for relatively short-term use (e.g. tourists, visiting businesspeople, people settling into a new house or office);
- low-cost internet access for low-income groups;
- location-based services, using the network to provide up-to-date information and communication at a specific location; and
- streaming of video, requiring high bandwidth upstream capacity.

At the same time, it has become apparent that it is very difficult to maintain a reliable service with volunteers alone. Unlike, for instance, open source software development projects, a large wireless network requires permanent monitoring and maintenance. For that purpose, Wireless Leiden has had since its early days a basic monitoring system.

To improve the responsiveness to disruptions, a more professional maintenance system is required. Plans for such an organisation are under development with the Hogeschool Leiden. The goal is to establish a knowledge centre for wireless communications at the hogeschool and to use the network for educational and R&D purposes. We are also working on several joint projects for improvement of the network and developing new applications.

From the beginning the innovative character of Wireless Leiden has been very appealing to volunteers. We see this as an essential part of any future development as well. The network will provide a large, real-life environment for education and experimentation and for the development and testing of new wireless applications. This fits well into the new approach for stimulating ICT innovations in the European Union: Wireless Leiden as a 'living lab'. Living labs are a new concept for R&D and innovation to boost the Lisbon strategy for employment and growth in the European Union (Living Labs, 2007). In the EU context, Wireless Leiden has become part of the Knowledge Workers Living Lab, headquartered in Munich. With CeTIM, Leiden University, the Hogeschool Leiden and several local companies we are working on the development of location-based services.

We expect that working with well-established organisations and grasping the opportunities for innovation will provide a sustainable basis for Wireless Leiden to remain an exciting environment for professional volunteers and students and provide added value for the local community.

6.3   Municipal networks

Meanwhile, the value that wireless networking can bring to a city is being broadly recognised. Providing wireless municipal broadband access has become a major theme in the United States. For example, in Boston, Philadelphia and Portland (Oregon), networks are under construction for which Microsoft is providing content and services with the objective of boosting online traffic and advertising revenues. This is following the example of Google in San Francisco, where it is building a network in cooperation with Earthlink (Hudson, 2010; Kharif, 2006). In Mountain View, California, Google covered the city with a free outdoor wireless service as part of its community outreach programme (Stratix, 2006). Another San Francisco Bay Area initiative involves San Mateo County for services to some thirty-five communities in the four counties covering Silicon Valley. Santa Clara and Cupertino, two other Silicon Valley communities, have taken an independent initiative. According to a count by Tapia, over 100 cities announced plans for municipal wireless in 2005 (Tapia, Stone and Maitland, 2005). In a count made in 2007 de Leeuw identified 415 projects in the United States: of these, ninety-two were regional or citywide initiatives, sixty-eight were city 'hotzones', forty were for municipal or public safety only use and 215 were planned deployments (de Leeuw, 2009).

The provisioning of citywide Wi-Fi-based connectivity is seen as a way for local governments to improve the availability and affordability of broadband access. Municipalities thereby have the opportunity to leverage their role as consumer when considering becoming a supplier of broadband access. The reasons that are given for municipalities pursuing the opportunity to enter the market for wireless broadband service provision include the following (Hudson, 2010; Tapia, Stone and Maitland, 2005; Weiss and Huang, 2007):

- capitalising on the opportunity to fill the gap in available and affordable (wired) broadband access, when private firms fail to provide services or offer services at a price considered to be too high;
- creating a 'third pipe' next to DSL and cable so as to improve competition;
- making the city more competitive in attracting business;
- improving intra- and intergovernmental communications, thereby enhancing the quality of employees' working lives;
- widening the availability of wireless technology at low cost, without the need for a licence; and
- taking the opportunity to offer services at lower costs of deployment, such as through the ownership of rights of way, the use of municipal premises and leveraging internal use of the network.

The role of governments in municipal wireless projects may vary, from being a facilitator (in taking a municipal Wi-Fi idea to an operational Wi-Fi service), through a role as anchor user or anchor tenant (the latter in providing access to facilities) to becoming a full-fledged operator (by investing in and managing a municipal Wi-Fi network) (Weiss and Huang, 2007).[15]

The operator role of a local government in providing wireless broadband access has led to intense debates as to whether these public initiatives infringe on the private interests of the incumbent telecom and cable operators and whether public funds may be used (Lehr, Sirbu and Gillett, 2006). Incumbent operators have lobbied vigorously at the US state level to prohibit or severely limit municipal broadband, in particular as larger cities such as Philadelphia, San Francisco and Minneapolis have become interested in municipal wireless projects (Hudson, 2010). This interest of municipalities in Wi-Fi deployment has resulted in additional law making at state level to regulate if and how municipalities can enter the wireless service provider sphere, notwithstanding the strong evidence that competition has improved communication services (Hudson, 2010; Tapia, Stone and Maitland, 2005).

In a comparative study, including European initiatives, van Audenhove *et al.* (2007) conclude that local government motives to engage in wireless network deployment include:

- policies related to the 'digital divide';
- city renewal;
- stimulating innovation;
- stimulating tourism; and
- improving the 'economic fabric' of the city.[16]

In comparison, the European initiatives are more oriented towards 'hotspots' and 'hotzones' and do not necessarily aim at full-city coverage – an attitude that may be influenced by uncertainty on the critical position of the European Commission regarding these initiatives with respect to the potential distortion of competition and state aid.

In addressing these concerns, Ballon *et al.* (2007) have analysed the underlying business models with varying degrees of public and private involvement with respect to network ownership and service provisioning. They adapt the typology provided by Bar and Park (2006) to fit the real-life cases in Europe and the United States. They distinguish between network ownership and service provisioning. On the network ownership side, four players and their respective roles can be distinguished (Ballon *et al.*, 2007).

(1) *Private player*: the network is operated on the basis of a contractual arrangement in the form of a licence, concession, etc. The municipality contributes by providing access to sites, existing backbones, financial support, etc.

(2) *Public player*: the municipality owns the network and operates the network.

(3) *Open site*: the municipality provides open access to sites for the construction of works.

(4) *Community player*: the network is operated by a community of individuals and/or organisations.

On the service provisioning side, four players and their respective roles can also be distinguished.

(1) *Private player*: one private player provides access to services on the network.

(2) *Public player*: a public or non-profit actor provides access to services on the network.

(3) *Wholesale*: various private players build on a wholesale access offer and provide services to end users.

(4) *No specific ISP*: there is no specific party providing access to end user services – e.g. because only point-to-point data links are provided.

In the context of concerns over fair competition and limited public funds, the study reveals that the authorities opt for a trade-off between minimising their inputs for establishing and operating a wireless city network, in terms of investments and risk, and maximising their influence for reaching specific policy goals. From the study of twenty-eight initiatives, six combinations of ownership and service provisioning emerge (Ballon *et al.*, 2007).[17]

(1) Private concessions for the network ownership and service provisioning; applied or proposed in Bristol, Cardiff, London and Paris.

(2) Private concession of the network combined with a wholesale-based service provisioning; used mainly in the United States – in Philadelphia, Portland, Sacramento and San Francisco.

(3) Public ownership of the network combined with wholesale provisioning; applied in Stockholm and Boston.

(4) Fully public model; applied only in the case of St Cloud, Minnesota.

In addition, two more open models can be discerned.

(5) An 'open site' model is employed in Paris and Bologna, in which the city grants open access to public sites and/or to its backbone network for private providers to exploit.

(6) The community model is applied, in different flavours, to Wireless Leiden in the Netherlands and Turku in Finland.

The different objectives and business models lead to different pricing schemes being applied for different categories of users: free access; free access to specific target groups; free access with advertising; free access with restrictions; paid access; and access restricted to government personnel. For projects in which fee-based internet access is provided, these range from US$14.95 to US$31.95 per month, with data rates ranging from 768 kbit/s to 5 Mbit/s.

Municipal networks are considered to provide a low-cost alternative to fixed networks, and hence would guarantee a high return on investment. Not all experts agree, however. Some believe that the real return from public access will come from mobile workforce applications within governments, as internet access for citizens is mostly provided for free. The request for proposals by San Francisco, for instance, stated that the network was to be built, operated and maintained at no cost to the city, that the basic level of service should be free and that the entire city should be covered (Hudson, 2010). Investments for the projects being studied vary substantially, from approximately US$15 per inhabitant and US$64,000 per square km in Philadelphia to US$135 per inhabitant and US$130,000 per square km in St Cloud.[18] Contributing factors to the variety can safely be assumed to be the character of the terrain, the data transfer rate, the quality of service, whether the coverage is indoor or outdoor, etc.

The number of access points per square kilometre influences the performance of the network and is a major factor in the costs of the network. In the early projects the number of access points was typically six to eight per square kilometre, which increased to ten to fourteen in 2006.[19] To reach a 5 Mbit/s service rate, Toronto Hydro installed more than thirty-eight access points per square kilometre (Weiss and Huang, 2007).

The deployment of municipal wireless networks shows that infrastructure provision is directly linked to broader city policies related to the digital divide, city renewal, improving internal operations, etc. These goals influence the coverage (e.g. outdoor versus indoor) and topology of the networks (hub and spoke versus mesh), the choice of technology (in some projects WiMAX is considered as backhaul, to connect the Wi-Fi network to the fixed infrastructure, or as an upgrade from Wi-Fi), the price and the service modalities. The differences in the context between the United States and Europe explain to a large extent the trajectories being taken. These studies illustrate that Wi-Fi has evolved from its intended use in wireless corporate networking, with a market breakthrough in wireless home networking, to a wide variety of private entities and public–private partnerships that explore and exploit its potential. The cases show that Wi-Fi-based broadband access should not be considered a substitute for wired broadband access but, rather, as complementary access, reaching out to places and users that other networks cannot reach.

6.4   Summary of the Wi-Fi journey: WNANs, 2001–2007

The open standard upon which Wi-Fi equipment is based and the low prices resulting from large-scale adoption made Wi-Fi attractive for techno-enthusiasts to explore its technical features and pursue the creation of Wi-Fi-based community networks. The building of networks was facilitated by the two operational variants that the IEEE 802.11 standards support: access and point-to-point.

Creating Wi-Fi-based networks implied the introduction of TCP/IP on the network and transport layers to provide the routing function on top of the Wi-Fi protocol stack. The ability to access the equipment at the level of the drivers allowed for integration and optimisation using open source software.

Wireless neighbourhood area networks evolved from networks that were created by techno-enthusiasts in the early 2000s to networks that were initiated and deployed by municipalities from 2003 onwards.

6.5   Interpretation of the Wi-Fi case in the context of theory

In this section, as before, we interpret this lap of the innovation journey following the perspectives introduced in Chapter 1 – namely the innovation landscape, the innovation process and the institutional environment. In this chapter we have added the political/regulatory dimensions of Wi-Fi deployment.

Innovation landscape   In the development towards WNANs, Wi-Fi has evolved from being predominantly an access technology to a technology deployed for both access to and the backbone of a wireless network. The data transfer in the network is based on TCP/IP and, hence, the two innovation avenues of Wi-Fi and the Internet recombine, this time in the software area – in using the TCP/IP protocol stack – and in the use of open source routing software (see also Figure 6.1). Within the WNAN application, open standards and open source software are combined.

In the move from public access to public networking the reach of Wi-Fi expands again, to include Wi-Fi zones and Wi-Fi municipalities; allowing the end user to become semi-mobile.

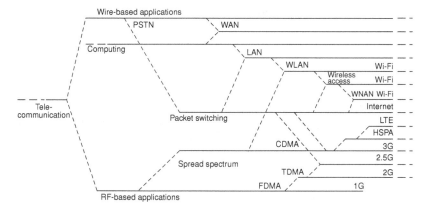

Figure 6.1 Wi-Fi and internet innovation avenues recombine

Innovation diffusion   Wireless neighbourhood area networks represent an additional trajectory for the diffusion of Wi-Fi technology. Through networking, the geographical coverage of Wi-Fi expands and, hence, its overall utility increases. Taking the eighty-eight WNANs identified in the Netherlands in the spring of 2006 as representative, we may expect the global deployment to be in the range of 5,000 to – potentially – 50,000.

Innovation process   As the case of Wireless Leiden illustrates, the linkage with open source software, as used in routing, and the fundamental principles of adding and sharing within the open source community allow others to benefit from the experience obtained by the Wireless Leiden group. The information is shared through a dedicated website, a 'wiki', and the use of a public licence for the enhancements that are made.

Sources of innovation   The emergence of Wi-Fi networking illustrates a new Wi-Fi deployment option that results from the interaction of the end users with the technology. The fact that Wi-Fi is a low-threshold technology, based on an open standard, allows the (professional) end user to become the locus of innovation in extending its use. This is an illustration of what von Hippel (2005) denotes as 'democratizing innovation' (for an elaboration of the user or community as the source of innovation, see Chapter 9).

6.5.1   Institutional environment and industry evolution

The use of Wi-Fi is governed by the regulations pertaining to the use of the radio frequency spectrum. This is not affected by the use of Wi-Fi as part of wireless community or municipal initiatives. In these applications, a wider reach and deeper penetration of the signal into homes and offices would be beneficial, however.

In the transition towards communication service provisioning, the rules and regulations pertaining to telecommunication operators and internet service providers may become applicable.

In the case of municipalities engaging in the deployment of Wi-Fi-based networks, the economic and political justification of local government involvement is an issue, in particular in those countries where the telecom reform process has introduced market forces so as to improve the provisioning of communication services. As Lehr, Sirbu and Gillett (2006) suggest,

According to the 'market failure' rationale, government intervention may be justified if private alternatives are perceived to be inadequate. The costs of deploying infrastructure and operating services may be too high relative to the revenue that can be expected so that an insufficient number of private sector providers enter the market. In the most extreme cases, it may be uneconomic for any private carrier to offer service. Or, it may be a natural monopoly/oligopoly that results in inadequate service provisioning.

Under these conditions municipal initiatives are likely to emerge, and they can provide justification for the municipal ownership of Wi-Fi-based networks. As van Audenhove *et al.* (2007) have shown, the role of the municipality can range from taking the initiative in stimulating network deployment to full network ownership and operation, the latter being more of an exception than the rule.

The firm or organisational entity   With the introduction of WNANs, a network operations role emerges that starts to resemble aspects of roles performed by telecommunication operators. Their networks are typically exploited for a profit and investment decisions are made centrally – i.e. on a 'top-down' basis. In community networks the investments are made by the participants, and so they are 'bottom-up'. The community network is typically 'open' and grows 'organically'.

In a municipal Wi-Fi initiative the local government takes the initiative, and/or arranges the implementation and/or takes an active part in the operations. For municipal governments the objective is not the exploitation of network for a profit but, rather, overseeing the implementation of an alternative network infrastructure that will benefit the community economically and socially.

As a community of volunteers, the case of Wireless Leiden shows the challenges an organisation faces when it does not have the incentive structure associated with firms or public organisations. The participation of the volunteers and their contribution to the work are not financially motivated, being more akin to the principles upon which the open source communities operate. The rules that Ostrom identified characterising the successful operation of the 'commons' appear to have a bearing on open source communities (Wendel de Joode, 2005), and, given the similarities, may be applicable to wireless community initiatives as well (Ostrom, 1990; Ostrom, Gardner and Walker, 1994).

Industry evolution   With the emergence of Wi-Fi community initiatives and, even more so, with the introduction of municipal Wi-Fi networks, the emphasis shifts from the provision of products to the provision of services. In the case of Wireless Leiden, the emphasis is on using Wi-Fi technology to provide internet access and free interconnection within the community. The Wireless Leiden Foundation deliberately avoided becoming a service provider.

Municipalities are involved in Wi-Fi network deployments as a way of improving communication service provisioning to the public and/or improving the access to and use of governmental services. Wi-Fi initiatives are thereby complementary to wired and other wireless infrastructures.

The success of Wi-Fi-based WNANs, combined with the use of open source computing and a growing interest in new types of mesh and ad hoc, or multi-hop, networking technologies, is helping to fuel interest in alternative industry structures (Lehr, Sirbu and Gillett, 2006; Sirbu, Lehr and Gillett, 2006). In a much-simplified and stylised form, the debate may be framed as a battle between the traditional service provider business model for providing network services versus one based on end user equipment. In the words of Sirbu, Lehr and Gillett (2006):

In the former, a service provider owns a large, fixed/sunk cost network that is used to provide shared access services to a large number of end-user nodes in return for usage-fees. In the latter, the edge-nodes are both end-users and relay points that may be interconnected into a mesh to provide wide-area connectivity. In the most extreme version, there is no centralised network coordination. Instead, the network grows 'virally' as end-users add equipment to the network.

Notes

1 The role of wireless community initiatives and neighbourhood area networks has been reported also from an 'inverse infrastructures' perspective (see Egyedi, Mehos and Vree, 2009).

2 From the community came the founders of many computer companies, including Bob Marsh, George Morrow, Adam Osborne and Lee Felsenstein, and Apple founders Steve Jobs and Steve Wozniak (Freiberger and Swaine, 1984).

3 The investigation was carried out by WiFisoft for the first Wireless Communications Camp. The count includes only those projects that have at least got a website and, as a minimum, one node operational. The count was sixty-eight in Spain, twenty-seven in the United Kingdom, fifteen in Germany and twelve in Greece.

4 Other early wireless community initiatives or neighbourhood area networks include, in the United States, NYC Wireless, Seattle Wireless and NoCatNet (see, for instance, Rao and Parikh, 2003) and, in Europe, Freifunk Berlin.

5 Personal communication from Schuurmans, 2007; see also van Drunen *et al.* (2003).

6 The gateway provided by ISP Demon provided high data rates but was deliberately limited in functionality, supporting http and https traffic only (i.e. port 80 support only).

7 Church service coverage used to be provided by the incumbent operator for many decades, but had then been discontinued.

8 The first board of the foundation consisted of Jasper Koolhaas, as chair, Marten Vijn, as secretary, and Huub Schuurmans, as treasurer (Vijn, Mourits and van 't Hart, 2007).

9 At the end of 2005 the network included 100 nodes with 45,000 digital images from the site surveys (Vijn, Mourits and van 't Hart, 2007).

10 In the Netherlands, the costs of monitoring facilities are, by law, borne by the operator.

11 For instance, volunteer Dirk-Willem van Gulik has worked on Apache (a web server software platform) since the early days of the National Center for Supercomputing Applications in the United States, and in 2007 he was the president of the Apache Software Foundation.

12 BSD licences represent a family of permissive free software licences. The original was used for the Berkeley Software Distribution (BSD), a UNIX-like operating system after which the licence is named (see the 'BSD license' entry on Wikipedia). The GNU (Gnu's Not UNIX) General Public License (or simply GPL) is a widely used free software licence. The GPL is the most popular and well-known example of the type of strong copyleft licence that requires derived works to be available under the same copyleft. Under this philosophy, the GPL grants the recipients of a computer programme the rights of the free software definition and uses copyleft to ensure that the freedoms are preserved, even when the work is changed or added to. This is in distinction to permissive free software licences, of which the BSD licences are the standard examples (see the 'General Public License' entry on Wikipedia).

13 The 'vrijwilligersverklaring' was a contentious issue. A few 'volunteers of the early hour' decided to leave the organisation of Wireless Leiden as a result, while some others remained active but did not sign the agreement.

14 The municipality of Leiden, recognising the importance of Wireless Leiden, has provided the foundation with funding for a strategic evaluation by an external consultancy organisation (Sikkema, 2007).

15 Weiss and Huang investigated twenty-eight municipal Wi-Fi projects in the United States.

16 The study includes the European cities of Bologna, Bristol, Cardiff, Düsseldorf, Leiden, London, Paris, Stockholm and Turku (Finland).

17 The projects in Westminster and Düsseldorf are not included as these do not provide citizens with access to the Internet. In the Westminster project the emphasis is on CCTV surveillance, and in Düsseldorf on city navigation and the monitoring of fire brigades in action.

18 These are rough estimates based on scarce material. Most cities do not disclose financial information on their initiatives.
19 In a study on behalf of SURFnet to assess the deployment of Wi-Fi as an extension of its fibre-based services for educational and research institutes, Stratix calculates on the basis of twenty-five access points per square kilometre for the city of Utrecht (Stratix, 2006).

References

Ballon, P., L. van Audenhove, M. Poel and T. Staelens (2007). 'Business models for wireless city networks in the EU and the US: public inputs and returns'. Paper presented at eighteenth European regional International Telecommunications Society conference. Istanbul, 4 September.
Bar, F., and N. Park (2006). 'Municipal Wi-Fi networks: the goals, practices, and policy implications of the US case'. *Communications and Strategies.* **1** (1), 107–26.
De Leeuw, G.-J. (2009). *Wi-Fi Community Initiatives: Update 2009.* Delft: Delft University of Technology.
Egyedi, T., D. C. Mehos and W. G. Vree (2009). 'New perspectives on inverse infrastructures'. Paper presented at the second international conference on 'Developing 21st century infrastructure networks'. Chennai, India, 10 December.
Freiberger, P., and M. Swaine (1984). *Fire in the Valley: The Making of the Personal Computer.* Berkeley, CA: Osborne/McGraw-Hill.
Hudson, H. E. (2010). 'Municipal wireless broadband: lessons from San Francisco and Silicon Valley'. *Telematics and Informatics.* **27** (1), 1–9.
Kharif, O. (2006). 'Microsoft's municipal Wi-Fi push'. New York: BusinessWeek.com. Available at www.businessweek.com/technology/content/nov2006/tc20061117_311713.htm?campaign_id=bier_tcv.g3a.rss1117c.
Lehr, W., M. Sirbu and S. E. Gillett (2006). 'Wireless is changing the policy calculus for municipal broadband'. *Government Information Quarterly.* **23** (3–4), 435–53.
Lemstra, W. (2003). *Verslag Bijeenkomst Wireless Leiden.* Delft: Department of Technology, Policy and Management, Delft University of Technology.
Living Labs (2007). 'European network of living labs: a first step towards a new innovation system'. Living Labs; www.cdt.ltu.se/main.php/ENoLL_Description%2020070316.pdf?fileitem=3238020 (accessed October 2008).
Ostrom, E. (1990). *Governing the Commons: The Evolution of Institutions for Collective Action.* Cambridge: Cambridge University Press.
Ostrom, E., Gardner, R. and Walker, J. (1994). *Rules, Games, and Common-pool Resources.* Ann Arbor: University of Michigan Press.
Rao, B., and M. A. Parikh (2003). 'Wireless broadband drivers and their social implications'. *Technology in Society.* **25** (4), 477–89.
Schreurs, M. (2006). *Wi-Fi Netwerk Initiatieven in Nederland.* Delft: Delft University of Technology.
Sikkema, K. (2007). 'Toekomstvisie voor Wireless Leiden'. Leiden: Bureau Blaauwberg.
Sirbu, M., W. Lehr and S. E. Gillett (2006). 'Evolving wireless access technologies for municipal broadband'. *Government Information Quarterly.* **23** (3–4), 480–502.

Stratix (2006). *Building Municipal Wireless Infrastructures: Feasibility Study for SURFnet.* Hilversum, Netherlands: Stratix.

Tapia, A., M. Stone and C. F. Maitland (2005). 'Public–private partnerships and the role of state and federal legislation in wireless municipal networks'. Paper presented at the thirty-third telecommunications policy research conference. Arlington, VA, 24 September.

Van Audenhove, L., P. Ballon, M. Poel and T. Staelens (2007). 'Government policy and wireless city networks: a comparative analysis of motivations, goals, services and their relation to network structure'. *Southern African Journal of Information and Communication.* **8**, 1008–135.

Van Drunen, R., D.-W. van Gulik, J. Koolhaas, H. Schuurmans and M. Vijn (2003). 'Building a wireless community network in the Netherlands'. In USENIX. *Proceedings of the FREENIX Track: 2003 USENIX Annual Technical Conference.* Berkeley, CA: USENIX, 219–30.

Vijn, M., and G. Mourits (2005). 'Wireless netwerk dekt Leiden'. *Informatie.* October.

Vijn, M., G. Mourits and H. van 't Hart (2007). 'Wireless netwerk dekt Leiden: de begin jaren van een draadloos netwerk'. Internal report.

Von Hippel, E. (2005). *Democratizing Innovation.* Cambridge, MA: MIT Press.

Weiss, M. B. H., and K. C. Huang (2007). 'To be or not to be: a comparative study of city-wide municipal Wi-Fi in the US'. Paper presented at thirty-third telecommunications policy research conference. Arlington, VA, 29 September.

Wendel de Joode, R. (2005). 'Understanding open source communities: an organisational perspective'. Dissertation. Department of Technology, Policy and Management, Delft University of Technology, Delft.

Part 2

The Wi-Fi Journey in Perspective

7 Wi-Fi in developing countries: catalyst for network extension and telecom reform

William Melody

7.1   Introduction

The revolution in telecommunication in the last generation has resulted from the ongoing dynamic interactions between new technologies, new market opportunities and new policies and regulations. One can find examples when the early development of a new technology, such as satellites, provided such obvious evidence of benefit in potential new services and markets that policies and regulations were changed in order to facilitate its application and further its development. There have been occasions when new market demands provided pressure for policy and regulation changes that opened new opportunities for technological development – such as spectrum allocation for wireless services. There have also been times when policy and regulation changes have led the way in creating a foundation for new technological and market development – such as the network unbundling to foster computer communication that facilitated the growth of the Internet. The basic interrelationships are illustrated in Figure 7.1.

If one looks beyond the main events, though, there is evidence that in almost all cases, including those cited above, there have been a series of ongoing dynamic interactions between technology, market and policy developments that gradually opened opportunities wider and wider. Established policies and regulation are unlikely to change unless there is some evidence of potential technological, market and/or social benefit. New services and markets will not be cultivated if technological capabilities and accommodating policies do not exist. New technologies are unlikely to be developed if they cannot be accommodated in policies and markets. Small changes in one factor lead to small changes in another, and, through a series of interactive feedback effects, the small changes provide a foundation for larger ones, and eventually what

The author thanks Wolter Lemstra for providing draft material on several case studies, based on input from Bjarke Nielsen, Mahabir Pun, Yahel Ben David, Ermanno Pietrosemoli, Dillo Lehlokoe, Pietro Bigi and Vic Hayes. Thanks also go to Richard Dowling, Bruce Girard, Divakar Goswami, Heather Hudson, Kas Kalba, Kammy Naidoo, Edwin Parker and Robert Walp for helpful comments and suggestions on an earlier draft.

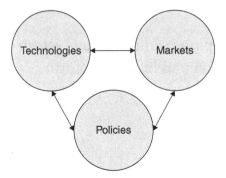

Figure 7.1 Basic interrelationships between technologies, markets and policies

is then sometimes seen as a revolutionary breakthrough. Although there are barriers to overcome and limiting conditions in all three areas, at any point in time the major limiting condition on the next stage of development may be a technological, economic or policy/regulatory barrier.

Wi-Fi technology and its associated markets and policies are still in the formative stages of development. The technology is young and remains on a path of steady innovation and improvement. New business models are being tested for different Wi-Fi environments. In most developing countries, however, policies and regulations – particularly those relating to spectrum allocation, licensing, interconnection and universal service funding – have not yet been adapted to reflect the opportunities provided by Wi-Fi. Services are being introduced in a variety of niche markets, testing their viability for further development through network expansion.

Until recently the early development of Wi-Fi was seen primarily as a technology enabling improved services at the customer end of networks in developed countries by providing 'hotspot' mobility in homes, offices, coffeehouses, airports and neighbourhoods. Experimentation is under way in the downtown areas of some cities for wider coverage.[1] For most users, these applications provide an enhancement of services they can access already, by providing improved flexibility, especially for those on the move.

Increasing attention is now being paid to Wi-Fi as an appropriate technology with distinct advantages for extending internet and broadband network links to rural and remote areas considered too costly to serve by established telecom operators using more established technologies. In developing countries, this opens opportunities to use Wi-Fi to extend networks to local areas where people have never had telecom services. This chapter examines the potential for Wi-Fi applications to extend the reach of telecom networks and services to the bottom of the pyramid (BOP) – i.e. to poor people in geographical regions of developing countries that have been considered unreachable. It pays particular attention to the interactions between technologies, markets and policies in fostering and/or restricting Wi-Fi network extensions, as a basis for pointing to the market arrangements and policies that are likely to be most supportive in extending networks to the BOP.

7.2   The challenge of universal access

The idea of universal access to telephone service has been part of telecom industry mythology for the better part of a century, and is written into the policies of many countries. It has been honoured more in the breach than in actual implementation, however. Most developed countries did not make serious attempts to achieve a universal telephone service until the more recent era of telecom reform and the challenge of competition to incumbent national monopolies.[2]

Until the mobile phone explosion of recent years, most developing countries had fixed network penetration rates of less than 10 per cent of the population, with geographical coverage for only a small part of the country. Prepaid mobile has dramatically improved coverage for voice services to more than half the world's population. The challenge of universal access today is extending network coverage to 'the other 2 to 3 billion', not only for voice but also for internet services.

During the telephone era the network extension policy objective in developed countries was to provide the public voice service to as many households as possible. The term 'universal service' was adopted first in the United States and then in other countries.[3] The standard measurement for universal service achievement in different countries, still reported in the statistical publications of the ITU, the Organisation for Economic Co-operation and Development (OECD) and other organisations, has been the percentage of households that are connected for public voice service by fixed network lines. With the development of the Internet, additional indicators for the penetration of internet access and household broadband connections are reported now as well.

The relevance and significance of 'household' indicators for measuring universal access is being undermined by the growth of mobile services, however, which are services to people, not households. Fixed-line household connections are increasingly being given up for mobile connections in many countries. Today a more appropriate indicator for the universality of network services measures the take-up per 100 population, an indicator of the access of people to services rather than services delivered to households (see also Sutherland, 2009).

For developing countries, the term 'universal access' has traditionally referred to access to a payphone within reasonable proximity (e.g. an hour's walk), and this is still used as a relevant indicator of network development for some countries. As the geographical coverage and user penetration by mobile networks in developing countries now greatly exceeds the inadequate fixed-network coverage by incumbent national operators, however, a more relevant universal access indicator is mobile phone users per 100 population.[4]

For internet services, the debate over the universality of access focuses on the 'digital divide' between those with and without access to internet services of a specified standard, with national indicators in the developed countries measuring the bandwidth capacity accessible by households. In most developing countries, served primarily by mobile networks designed for voice communication, access to internet services cannot be readily obtained outside major cities and towns. The opportunities for network enhancements to accommodate internet access come from technological upgrades of existing wireless transmission networks, linked where possible to innovative, low-cost, local networks, most commonly centred in community centres, schools, government offices or local businesses. Wi-Fi is a relatively new technology for providing these local networks. Unfortunately, telecom policy in many countries still designates the incumbent national fixed-network operator as the only 'universal service' provider and does not support – and, indeed, often restricts – innovative solutions by others.

Although technological capabilities have always been a necessary condition for extending telecom networks to serve the rural poor, they have never been sufficient. Attempts at 'technology injections' have always failed. Programmes must at one and the same time address the issues of the economic resources needed for the initial investment and the economic resources needed for continuing sustainable operation. The viable economic structures that are necessary are very different for universal access network extensions to the rural poor at the end of the line from what they are for profitable development at the centre of national networks. In addition, the best policy and regulation to support universal access extensions are different from those that support network enhancements at the centre.

Before examining the potential of Wi-Fi applications for extending networks to the rural poor at the BOP, it is important to be guided by the lessons learned about the enabling conditions for successful network extension from previous experience in the voice telephony era.

7.2.1   The traditional model for implementing universal access subsidies

The terms 'universal service', 'universal access' and 'digital divide' are used in government policies and regulations, and in the literature, in reference to the matter of extending telecom networks of sufficient capacity to provide universal access to designated services. In this chapter, the term 'universal access' is adopted as the generic term unless circumstances require that one of the others be used. The common objective is to extend networks everywhere to provide universal affordable access to a specified set of services.[5]

The traditional models used in attempting to implement universal access policies have involved subsidies intended to cover the higher costs of serving rural areas and to enable poor people to afford the basic public voice service. Historically, the most common approach has been the internal cross-subsidy model, in which the incumbent national operator is expected to extend its network to provide universal access to basic services, and to cover the costs by charging uniform prices to all users regardless of location. In most countries, attempts to implement this model have failed dramatically.

The incumbent national operators have had (and many still have) a virtual monopoly over fixed networks, with little incentive to operate efficiently or extend networks beyond profitable market segments. When networks have been extended marginally into unprofitable areas, costs have been high and little has been achieved. In the United States, the passage of the Communications Act of 1934 established a clear policy objective of providing a basic telephone service to everyone 'to the extent feasible'. During the Great Depression years of the 1930s, however, telephone penetration declined. By 1940 only 25 per cent of farms were connected, and AT&T resisted unprofitable network extensions (see also Mueller, 1993, 1997). A different implementation model, discussed below, was adopted.

In many countries, especially developing countries, telecom services were (and are) considered much less important than other social services, such as postal services, education, health and welfare (including the welfare of the government).[6] Funds for investment raised from telecom services were (and are) allocated not for universal service network extensions but for other government services and activities. In many developing countries, extremely high prices were set for international services, so as to raise hard currency for the Treasury from the shared revenues of inbound calls from developed countries – not for extending networks and services to the domestic population (see also Samarajiva, 2007).

The licensing of additional operators (primarily mobile) and the development of a degree of competition in many countries, and more intensive competition internationally, have eroded the foundations of the incumbent-based internal cross-subsidy model, which is premised upon monopoly provision. In the more open environment created by telecom reforms, not only is it more difficult to implement but the resistance of incumbent operators is increased. Nevertheless, the internal cross-subsidy model remains as a major factor in the policies and policy debates about universal access in many developing countries, often in attempts to justify restrictions on any competition. It is argued that constraints must be placed on competitors that do not have universal access responsibilities, or that competitors be required to contribute to a universal access fund that will be expended by the incumbent national operator to extend its fixed network.

In this environment, in which the principles of telecom reform have not yet been applied to universal access policies, it is very clear that there will be little progress made in extending networks towards universal access objectives no matter how great the potential benefits of a new technology such as Wi-Fi may be. The limiting factor for next-stage network development towards universal access may well be an inherited policy/regulation barrier.

7.2.2   Direct subsidy funds

In recent years there has been increasing use of direct subsidy funds to support universal access network extensions. The funds are provided primarily by a small universal access surcharge or tax on telecom service prices, and occasionally by government grant or donor contributions for limited time periods. To date, the results of this approach have been mixed. Some governments have allocated these funds uneconomically to politically motivated unsustainable projects. Others have not allocated the funds at all, seeming reluctant to invest in universal access network extensions.

There have been success stories, however, from countries where there is a credible commitment to implementing universal access policies. These typically specify the particular areas and services that the funds will support as a part of a coherent network development plan. They invite competitive bids based on specific licence conditions and include provisions for transparency, accountability and the monitoring of performance. When the funds have been allocated in this manner, the subsidy amounts needed for network development are typically a fraction of those forecast, which have usually been based on incumbent operator costs. Incumbents rarely win these bids (see also OECD, 2004).

The experience of Chile has been widely published (Wellenius, 2002). The minimum subsidy bids for about one-third of the universal access regions to be served were zero. The competitive bidders wanted only a licence to provide service. In another third of the regions, the minimum subsidy bids were significantly less than anticipated. In the final third of the regions, the subsidy needs were significant, but still less than expected. Other countries that have employed the model of direct subsidy allocations by transparent competitive bidding for specified network development have had positive results (see www.itu.int for case studies).

This is a universal access network development model in which the policy barrier of the internal cross-subsidy model and the market barrier of incumbent monopoly power have been overcome. A different policy model demonstrating a much stronger government policy commitment has prepared the ground for major network extensions that can take advantage of innovative ways of providing service, and innovative applications of technologies that are responsive to the specific conditions in the regions to be served. This is a policy environment in which Wi-Fi could play a major role in facilitating network extensions to unserved areas at the BOP.

7.2.3   Universal access and local participation

A common element found in the cases of successful programmes targeting universal access network extensions is a significant role for local participation. It has been the initiative and commitment of those living and working in unserved areas that, with various kinds of external support, have played a decisive role in extending the network to their localities and ensuring sustainable operations.

In the United States, when it became clear in the 1930s that the monopoly operators were not going to provide universal telephone access, an alternative programme was established in response to the political demands, which came primarily from farmers in the unserved rural areas. The Rural Electrification Administration (REA) was established by the federal government in the 1940s to provide low-cost loans, technical support and training for the development of local electricity and telephone distribution networks in unserved rural areas. Many thousands of rural co-operatives, local municipal operators and small private companies were established. Farmer lines[7] were employed, allowing local residents to provide a significant portion of the labour themselves so as to reduce costs.

This process of focusing directly on the specific conditions in the rural areas provided opportunities for new initiatives and innovations. It helped pioneer adaptations to technologies and services to serve rural areas at much-reduced cost with a service that met the local needs. By the more rigid and more costly standards and operating methods of the monopoly operators, these were commonly viewed as inferior technological, management and service adaptations. Back-up power supplies were below standard; local connections were often shared among several farms (called party lines); some of the work was carried out by volunteers without the formal professional certification required by the monopoly operators. It provided a basic service, though, which could then be upgraded as needs and circumstances changed; and it has been.

The REA programme was instrumental in extending universal access to Alaska in the 1970s, for which innovations in satellite applications[8] and small earth station development made backbone connections to local village distribution networks possible. Today there are still several thousand of these small local operators throughout the United States, active in getting internet connections extended to local schools, hospitals, community centres and homes in rural areas (Parker, 2000).

The experience in Canada has been similar. Universal telephone access was developed through programmes of government support for local initiatives, ranging from a province-wide co-operative in the most rural and sparsely settled province, Saskatchewan, to local co-operatives and farmers stringing telephone wire along their fences. Following this approach, Canada achieved one of the highest universal access penetration rates in the world in a country with one of the lowest population densities.

The Nordic countries historically have had, and currently have, the highest levels of universal access coverage in Europe, despite the fact that they are the countries with the thinnest population densities and most difficult geographic conditions. For the most part, the local networks were developed by local initiative, sometimes but not always with central government support. Finland still has more than sixty local telephone operators.

With the broadband information infrastructure now being developed throughout the United States, Canada and the Nordic countries, history is being repeated. Local participation is once again playing a significant role in driving the development of universal access to the Internet and to broadband, employing a variety of innovative applications of technologies and low-cost business models within a framework of flexible and supportive policy and regulation.

Parallel developments in developing countries have been rare, for a variety of reasons. In addition to the barriers of extreme poverty, formidable government bureaucracy and (sometimes) corruption that have characterised some developing countries, national policies reserving all telecom development to the national monopoly have made the possibility of local development virtually zero. The absence of a national backbone network to which local operators could connect has produced a second insurmountable barrier.

As a result of telecom reforms, the spread of wireless networks and the expansion of national fixed-backbone networks, however, opportunities have begun to open up in many developing countries in recent years. A number of initiatives developing local networks in previously unserved areas have been successful, including co-operatives, new private operators and public–private partnerships (Mahan and Melody, 2007; Siochru and Girard, 2005). The Grameen Telecom cellphone development in Bangladesh has been an outstanding success, but attributable in significant part to the failures of both fixed network development and government policy and regulation (Samarajiva and Zainudeen, 2008). Unfortunately, in most countries the limiting condition on network development is not local interest, innovative applications of technologies or new business models; it is obsolete restrictive policies and regulations.

7.3   Universal access in the information age

7.3.1   Internet economy and information society development

There is increasing evidence that access to telecom services and electronic information is becoming more central to economic and social activities. For more than a decade the literature has been flooded with research and discussion about the development of internet economies and information societies. Many national governments have issued policy statements directed at facilitating the transformation to future information societies.[9] In a high-profile initiative, the European Union, in its Lisbon Strategy 2000 policy, agreed to a set of 'eEurope action plans' to make Europe 'the most competitive and dynamic knowledge-based economy in the world by the year 2010' (EC, 2000). More recently, in June 2005, the European Union launched its Lisbon agenda i2010 'Information Society' initiative as a renewed commitment to the Lisbon reform agenda. This requires upgraded telecom networks across the European Union that can provide the broadband capacity needed for information societies (EC, 2005).

The adoption of information society policies is by no means limited to the developed countries (see www.itu.int for case studies). Whereas the developed countries have long recognised a need for enhancing the capacity of their telecom networks to promote their future information economies and societies, developing countries are only just beginning to acknowledge future information economy activity as strengthening the potential benefits, and therefore the economic and social justification, of extending telecom networks towards universal access. In both developed and developing countries, upgraded telecom networks are needed to provide the information infrastructure via which electronic services and information content will be supplied in future information societies. Enhanced telecom network connections will be needed in the workplace, schools, health and community centres and, where possible, residences, in the same way that the telephone has been essential for the development of industrial society.

7.3.2   Towards universal access to information infrastructure

The interpretation of the concept of universal access has changed as the telecom network has developed and become increasingly integrated into the economic, social, political and cultural lives of people in different countries and regions. The earliest conception of universal service was simply access to a telephone for emergencies – a concept that still applies in some parts of almost every country and large regions in developing countries today. As the telephone became more pervasive and integrated into economic activity, universal service was conceived as a connection first for businesses and then for residences, initially a party line shared with others and later a private connection.

In more recent times, with increased household penetration by personal computers in developed countries, the idea of universal access to a digital connection to permit internet access has been accepted. For example, following the European Commission's 1992 review of the telecom sector, the EC redefined the scope of universal service as basic voice telephony plus network access supporting voice, fax and low-speed data access.[10] With each review the services capacity of network access has been expanded; the current policy objective is to achieve universal broadband access, but the definition and scope for achieving that objective is left to the member states.

At national and international level alike there is a growing concern about a 'digital divide' in access to enhanced information services, both within countries (including the United States, European Union and other wealthy states) and between the rich and poor countries. It is apparent that, based on current trends, the problem of information infrastructure access will deny the majority of the world's population access to the internet economy and information society opportunities. Overcoming the digital divide will require a major global policy commitment to extend the advanced telecom network dramatically to the inadequately served poor in many rich countries and the unserved billions in the poorer countries. Following the World Summit on the Information Society in December 2003, a UN committee was established to review financing options for overcoming the digital divide. Despite strong policy commitments to network enhancements to create universal broadband access at home, there has been a noticeable absence of commitment from the rich countries to provide funding to overcome the international divide.

At the national level, many developed and developing countries have adopted programmes that provide subsidies for implementing a universal broadband access policy. Implementing the provisions of the Telecommunications Act of 1996, the United States' FCC introduced a new subsidy programme focused on universal access to internet services for rural schools, hospitals, libraries and community centres (Hudson, 2009). The subsidy is financed by an industry tax on revenue from specified services. This subsidy programme has been expanded to support higher-capacity broadband network extensions, and it is being expanded further as a major infrastructure priority of the administration of President Barack Obama.[11] Wireless operators are eligible to compete for projects extending universal access under these programmes and local authorities play the major role in the selection of the service provider.

In the United Kingdom, the communications minister released his interim report *Digital Britain* in January 2009, which calls for all homes to have access to 2 Mbit/s broadband services by 2012. Industry estimates that it could require some £2 billion to achieve this universal access. Wireless operators are expected to play a major role in implementing the new policy, as modifications of spectrum policy are being considered to encourage investment. Mobile operators may be allowed to keep their twenty-year 3G licences indefinitely if they commit themselves to network investment plans put forward by the minister, and conditions in existing 2G and 3G licences that restrict the services that can be provided may be removed.

Such an approach to broadband universal access development would be expedient in disguising the subsidy requirements and removing them from the government's budget. As the analysis above has demonstrated, however, a government policy asking incumbent operators to undertake internal cross-subsidies to provide universal service against their financial self-interest in a programme without transparency and accountability is likely to be costly and far less effective than planned. The UK approach under consideration is neither an efficient method of allocating subsidy funds nor an effective approach to managing spectrum policy. The long-run consequences are likely to be far more costly than a transparent, competitive subsidy allocation programme, and future spectrum policy options may be seriously constrained.

India's Department of Telecommunications has recently signed a memorandum of understanding with state-owned incumbent operator Bharat Sanchar Nigam Ltd (BSNL) to bring wireless broadband services to rural regions by 2011. A subsidy grant of Rs 18 billion from the Universal Service Obligation Fund for BSNL projects is part of a programme to increase broadband access to more than 20 million connections. BSNL will upgrade 29,000 exchanges for wireless broadband services. Each exchange will provide a single kiosk for public use and allow for thirty-one connections. Although this programme can be considered a step in the right direction, it fails to incorporate India's private operators, which have much broader wireless coverage in rural areas than BSNL, where, in a country with a population of a billion, there remains an enormous universal access challenge (Malik, 2007).

Most developing countries, like India, have programmes to upgrade and extend their national telecom networks. These programmes are relatively small, however, compared to what is needed to provide universal access, and in many cases priority is being given to upgrading the existing network for broadband access rather than to extending network coverage to unserved areas. These programmes offer little hope of network access for those at the BOP.

7.4   Towards universal access in developing countries

7.4.1   Cellular mobile for voice services

In developing countries, as in many developed ones, the incumbent national fixed-line operators have failed to develop universally accessible networks. In most developing countries, they have generally failed to develop national networks at all. In recent years the spread of cellular mobile phones has extended voice network coverage so substantially that, in most countries, mobile penetration exceeds fixed network penetration by a very large and ever-increasing margin.

The success of the mobile explosion in developing countries can be attributed to several key factors. Despite the rural poverty, the market environment was very favourable to development. Fixed networks were underdeveloped, reflecting a long-standing lack of investment. Significant pent-up demand was evidenced by long waiting lists for service. Most people who were ready, willing and able to pay for service were denied it because it was not available. Moreover, in most countries, multiple licences were awarded, eventually if not immediately; mobile operators were therefore subject to a degree of competition in rolling out their networks (see, for instance, Kalba, 2008a, 2008b, Mahan and Melody, 2009, and Samarajiva, 2006).

Thus the policy and regulatory environment made mobile development possible by reducing the barriers to market development and licensing new operators. Although this was often done initially to increase government revenue from licence fees, and with a view that mobile services would be a specialised niche market and not a threat to fixed network services, it nevertheless opened the market entry door to full-scale mobile market development.

In addition, technological advances were also favourable to these developments. The introduction of global standards allowed cost reductions from the large-scale production of equipment, improved quality of service and increased flexibility in use. Although priced higher than fixed network service, mobile networks offered a major qualitative improvement – mobility – and an alternative to those people on fixed network waiting lists. Moreover, the technology was subject to continuing improvements from the ongoing process of innovation.

The key factor in extending mobile networks and services to the poor in rural areas, however, has been the adoption of a new business model around prepaid rather than subscription services (see, for instance, Mahan, 2005). Mobile networks were extended to provide coverage in many poor rural areas because subscribers in the cities travelled to and through these areas and wanted access. The prepaid option made access possible for the poor who could not qualify for subscription service. With handset technology improving rapidly, second-hand handsets became affordable. Although prepaid prices have been significantly higher than subscription prices, with prepaid cards costs and usage can be directly controlled by the user. Receiving calls in most countries costs nothing. Usage can be shared with family and friends. Access minutes can be sold to others in the community.

Local villagers were able to create small businesses by managing a prepaid mobile phone. The real innovation that has stimulated the extension of mobile voice access to previously unserved areas has been the innovation at the BOP by the rural poor in controlling their costs and managing local demand. This was a business model not contemplated until the rural poor were given the opportunity to shape local voice service connections to their own unique circumstances (see, for example, Mahan and Melody, 2007, sect. 2). Today prepaid services account for more than 40 per cent of the mobile market in the OECD area and 80 per cent or more in virtually all developing countries.

It is noteworthy that the success of prepaid mobile in extending voice access to the rural poor was not the result of universal service policies or subsidies. In fact, in many countries they constituted policy and regulatory barriers that had to be overcome. The policies that made network expansion possible were those relating to spectrum allocation, the licensing of new operators, competition and rate regulation, not universal access. The successful business model was not developed by the mobile operators but, rather, by the rural poor users when they were given the opportunity. The mobile technology that contributed to the success was not that initially designed for subscribers in wealthier urban markets, but instead a more flexible design for prepaid use, sharing minutes for resale. Policies, business models and the technology employed all had to be adapted to the local circumstances, and the successful adaptation was done almost entirely by local participation. The essential conditions for network development towards universal access were demonstrated once again.

7.4.2   Towards internet and broadband access

Both the policy debate and policy development about broadband access are being driven by the leading developed countries and the conditions that prevail there. They have achieved universal access for voice and basic internet services. The next step is more bandwidth (broadband) to enable more advanced services that involve video and other higher-capacity communication requirements. For people at the BOP without access to any services, however, the challenge is the same as it has always been: to get connected. For those with access only to mobile voice, the challenge is to get access to an internet connection. Then they too can begin working their way up to a platform from which demands for more advanced services make bandwidth limitation a priority to be addressed.

One major barrier to network access in the poor rural areas of developing countries has been the absence of a nationwide backbone network to which a local network can connect. That deficiency is being addressed in many developing countries with the installation of new fibre cable, wireless and/or satellite backbone links, now making it possible for local networks to connect if they can overcome the other formidable difficulties of establishing a local network. The primary problem is that it is not economical for operators to develop local networks. Costs would be high, the ability to pay for service very low and usage highly uncertain. Subsidy requirements would be very large. In addition, typically there is an absence of electrical power. Clearly, extending operator networks down to the rural poor at the BOP is not a viable option, and it is not being undertaken. A token presence in each of the regions and areas of developed countries is the general target.

This story is not new, though. These circumstances have characterised network development from the earliest days of telephony. They have been overcome only by breaking the mould of centralised top-down network development on the basis of uniform policies, standardised technologies and conventional business models. A new set of policies, technologies and business models is required here, just as they were required to achieve universal access in the past. The policies, technologies and business models have to be adapted to local circumstances by supporting ultra-low-cost solutions involving significant local participation. The challenge is to devise workable solutions for providing some form of access. Once that has been obtained, the less difficult task of pursuing network improvements to provide additional services can be undertaken.

7.5   The Wi-Fi opportunity

7.5.1   Assessing technology options

Experimentation with a variety of different approaches to establishing local networks in poor rural areas of developing countries has always been a part of telecom development. A common theme has been the injection of subsidy funds from donors (governments, non-governmental organisations [NGOs], corporates and even universal service funds) to invest in new technologies as part of externally or centrally driven demonstration programmes. The focus of attention has been on technological capabilities and initial investment costs, with little or no attention to the necessary conditions for ongoing financial, technical and managerial sustainability at the local level. The programmes have usually terminated, therefore, as soon as the demonstration funding stops, as they are financially unsustainable. This is continuing today.

Current experimentation is under way using several different technologies to extend networks to the BOP. As cable technology options are both costly and time-consuming to develop, virtually all the experimentation involves wireless technologies and the use of solar power. Satellite service from small earth stations overcomes the problem of inadequate backbone links to the local area, but provides for only one local point of presence for a very large area. It also requires external technical and managerial support and shows no sign of financial sustainability once the external demonstration funding stops.

Cellular mobile networks are being extended further into rural areas with prepaid voice services, and many successes have been achieved. For example, the famous Grameen Telecom in Bangladesh has extended service to many thousands of previously unserved villages. Some 15,000 villages have not been reached, however. Moreover, prepaid voice over 2G networks cannot provide internet access.

New 3G services can include internet access on cellular phones; but the 3G cost model is much more expensive than the 2G prepaid voice model, and is clearly unsustainable at the BOP. WiMAX is making a major contribution to overcoming the backbone capacity problem in developing countries by extending backbone links further into poor rural areas, but it is not really an option for local networks at the BOP.

An essential characteristic of the application of all these technology applications is that they are centralised, top-down-driven approaches, extending the standard ways of providing national and international services over larger and larger national networks. These are all good developments, extending the geographical and service coverage of telecom networks, but they cannot be expected to reach the BOP in the poorest, more remote rural areas.

7.5.2   Wi-Fi characteristics

The first step in getting network access at the BOP is establishing a minimum-cost local connection that can be expanded later in quantity and quality as demand grows. This requires a wireless connection to a fixed location, but not mobility. The mobility capabilities of cellular mobile are significantly more technically complex and costly than Wi-Fi in terms of equipment, spectrum and power requirements. Fixed locations allow the use of multi-hop and mesh networks linking villages, and use lower frequencies that can reduce cost and increase signal performance. This allows Wi-Fi to use a larger bandwidth and communicate at much higher data rates than 3G technologies, making it far superior for internet access.

A key element of all wireless networks relates to the essential spectrum resource. Spectrum licensing requires formal applications to central government authorities containing a variety of technical, legal and financial information, and often representation and lobbying in capital cities, and then the payment of fees or bidding in auctions to obtain rights to the use of radio frequencies. This is an insurmountable barrier to any community at the BOP. In many countries, however, there are so-called 'Wi-Fi'-frequencies (2.4 GHz and 5 GHz in most countries) that have been classified as unlicensed and are used for research and experimentation. The ability to use this unlicensed spectrum opens a substantial opportunity for low-cost connections at the BOP.

The flexibility allowed for research and experimentation creates an environment supportive of continuous enhancements in capabilities, quality and cost, as has been demonstrated already in the 802.11 alphabet of technology improvements. Wi-Fi networks at the BOP can benefit significantly from the global market in Wi-Fi equipment, which is stimulating continuous improvements and driving down costs. For example, Wi-Fi capacity, quality and distance covered are all improving continuously. VoIP development is enabling voice services to be added to data services. In addition, a number of firms are testing improved solar and wind power for Wi-Fi. There are such a large number of rural and remote locations in the world without network access that there is now a dynamic global market developing Wi-Fi equipment adaptations to the circumstances at the BOP.

Wi-Fi networks are much less complex than those employing other technologies. Being separated from large national networks, they enable community networks to develop without large centralised organisations. They are relatively inexpensive and simple in design and can be deployed rapidly. Wi-Fi networks can be installed and supported by personnel with only basic knowledge and skills in networking. As the equipment is portable, the coordination of activities is not limited to a specific location. Moreover, the scalability of Wi-Fi networks allows for incremental growth in the size and complexity of a network in response to the needs of the community using it and the growing skills of the people supporting it. Community Wi-Fi networks can therefore benefit significantly from local participation in almost all phases of the operation, reducing costs, building constituencies of local participation and cultivating local demand.

The first Wi-Fi applications have shown that the initial demands for services are community demands relating to medical/health concerns, education/training and information relating to local and regional markets, particularly in agriculture, and simple e-commerce, such as receiving remittances. There is a synergy between supply and demand built around community participation under community conditions. The Wi-Fi model provides a unique opportunity to break the barrier of high-cost centralised network extension by a top-down delivery of standardised technologies, business models and policies.

7.6   Wi-Fi: early experience

Experimentation with Wi-Fi applications to provide internet access in rural and remote areas has been under way for some time. Surprisingly, it has taken place in the most developed as well as the least developed countries, as the Wi-Fi opportunity has exposed the fact that, even in the most developed countries with successful universal access policies for voice services, there are regions without access to the internet. Thus a community-driven Wi-Fi network in the rural Djursland region of Denmark – the country ranked first in the world in terms of broadband penetration – provides some 9,000 households, institutions and firms with internet access at a much lower cost than users in the urban centres of Denmark are charged.

7.6.1   DjurslandS.net, Denmark

Bjarke Nielsen, promoter of the community of volunteers, tells the story (Nielsen, 2007):

My vision of a broadband rural network came to life when the first wireless LAN devices with attractive data rates became available in 1991. However, it took until May 2003 for the first subscribers to be connected.

The project originated with the establishment of the Computer Boevl-Miljoe (Computer Support Community, or Boevl for short) in 1993. At monthly gatherings, people carried their computer in and volunteers worked together to repair the problems. In 1996 the Boevl managed to create a regional internet portal with much higher data rates than obtainable through the public switched telephone network in our rural community. Enjoying broadband internet access using the portal, the dream was that every rural citizen should be able to surf the internet from home with the same data rates through a shared high-speed access!

In 2000, encouraged by the increased data rate capabilities and the price erosion of Wi-Fi equipment, the Boevl formed a project group for the establishment of a broadband wireless network. In a small part of Djursland, the municipality of Noerre Djurs, the group campaigned for interest and quickly received 1,000 signatures for support; leading to the establishment of DjurslandS.net. In autumn 2001 the organisation created a board with two representatives of each of the eight municipalities covering the whole of Djursland, an area of 1,491 km^2 and a population of 82,420 living in about 36,000 households. The first task was to search for 'fiery souls' interested in information technology for the implementation of the plans.

The board continued to do research on rural broadband networking and discussed with some thirty internet service providers to provide internet access. Although, in the end, they were all eager to help, they all concluded that the investments required would be too high. The local incumbent telecom provider, TDC [Tele-Danmark Corporation], was also requested to provide broadband service over its existing telephone infrastructure. The problem was that the technology to provide broadband is digital subscriber loop, whereby the data rate decreases with the length of the telephone line. With most distances above 3 to 5 km from the telephone exchange the data rate would drop below the required level. The alternative, of adding telephone exchanges to reach the remote parts of the community with DSL, would be prohibitive.

In 2002 DjurslandS.net spelled out an experimental wireless 'landscapenet' project to supply the municipality of Noerre Djurs with wireless broadband access, with a calculated budget of €350,000, the most expensive item being the radio towers. In prospect was a 50 per cent grant from the European Union Regional Funds Objective 2 programme. By May 2002 the local association in Noerre Djurs submitted its request for support for the pilot project under the EU's regional funds. The decision was given in August 2002 and was positive. Unfortunately, it took till December 2002 for the group to receive the signed approval, and the amount allocated was €130,000. Moreover, the fine print revealed that payment was to be received in two instalments, each against proof of expenses being made. However, for the group to start the work, funds were needed up front. In January 2003, as the banks were not willing to furnish a loan, the group requested the municipality of Noerre Djurs for a cash credit of €35,000 as security, with the EU grant as a back-up. However, Noerre Djurs required approval by the government of Denmark, which turned down the request in order 'to avoid practices that distort competition'. Fortunately, the project was able to start as early as May 2003, on the basis of a €57,000 loan from private citizens.

Just over a year later thirty-eight areas were covered, which was ahead of the plan. Following the deployment in the first municipality, volunteers from the seven other municipalities were trained quickly, and they started building their networks within

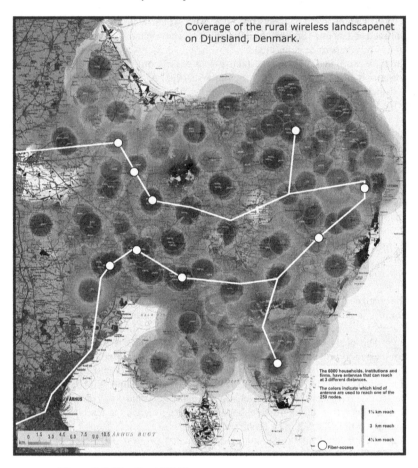

Figure 7.2 Djursland Wi-Fi coverage

one month of the start of the pilot project. The price erosion of Wi-Fi products and the development of home-built antennas enabled the EU funds to be applied to a much larger area. By February 2007 250 areas were covered and 5,000 households and businesses were connected, while the numbers of connections is still growing. See Figure 7.2 for a coverage map of Djursland at that time.

Today, with full coverage of the Djursland landscape through more than 400 antenna-amplified wireless gateways and more than 9,000 connections, one-third of the 82,000 citizens on the rural peninsula have broadband access to the internet through this voluntarily built, cheap wireless infrastructure. It has become normal for the users in the network to experience 10 Mbit/s internet both down- and upstream, and at a price that is only about one-third of the average market price in the cities for comparable services.

Similar Wi-Fi networks have been developed in Sweden, Finland, the United States, Canada and other developed countries, where Wi-Fi is gradually becoming the vehicle for achieving universal internet access in the most rural and remote areas. In nearly all the cases these developments are being driven by local initiative, in some cases by the same organisations that brought local telephony and electric power to these areas more than half a century earlier (for example, local co-operatives in the United States).

7.6.2   Nepal Wireless Networking Project

In the developing world, there are Wi-Fi networks in almost all countries that permit them and many that do not. At this juncture, however, most are at an experimental or early development stage, although there are many success stories. There are large established networks, such as that set up by the state government of the Indian state of Kerala primarily as a health and education network. Most are closer to the Nepal Wireless Networking Project of Himanchal High School, however, which was established to bring electronic communication to a difficult mountainous region that has never been connected. Mahabir Pun, who conceived and initiated the scheme, tells the story (Pun *et al.*, 2006):

Soon after I had learned to use email and Internet for the first time in 1996, I dreamed to connect Himanchal High School of Nangi, Nepal to the Internet. This was no small task then because the school had no electricity, no phone line, and no computers. The only way to access the Internet for me was a full day's travel by walking five hours downhill and a four-hour bus ride to the nearest city, called Pokhara. To make a long story short, I worked step by step with the villagers and a team of international volunteers to achieve this goal. We built a micro-hydrogenerator in the village. I learned how to assemble computers from donated parts received in wooden boxes. We received funding for the first phase of the project from the Donald Strauss Foundation through the University of California and subsidised equipment for a total of approximately US$6,000. By 2003, we had set up a limited Internet connection using Wi-Fi technology.

The project was formally started in 2003 as Nepal Wireless Networking Project to continue expanding the network throughout the area. By September 2006, we had connected fourteen villages to the network – ranging from 95 to 2,485 people and from 888 to 3,650 metres in altitude, using 28 IEEE 802.11b radios in the 2.4 GHz band and 5 radios in the 5.7 GHz band. Power for the remote stations is provided by solar panels, wind generators and a bicycle generator. We expanded services to include telemedicine – from Om Hospital in Pokhara – distance education, and telephone service – using VoIP connecting to the Nepal Telecom public network. Funding for the second phase of the project came from a World Bank grant through the Poverty Alleviation Funds of the government of Nepal supplemented by a grant from the George Mason University School of Public Policy in the USA, a total of approximately US$24,000. The total capital expenditure represents an investment of US$1.82 per inhabitant of the fourteen villages being served.

The Nepal Wireless Networking Project is a public enterprise because it is owned and run by the community high school, with an organisational structure that includes local schools, local governments and businesses. The services to the villagers are provided through independent communication centres in each village. Common caretaker organisations include mothers' groups, fathers' groups, school management committees, and communication centre management committees formed by the villagers.

Communication centres use the services offered by the Nepal Wireless Networking Project in various ways. First, the centre operates a cybercafé, charging users a small hourly fee (from US$0.21–0.43). On major trekking routes, tourists are charged a higher rate (US$1.36 per hour) to increase revenue. For phone calls the centres bill the user at a rate slightly above that charged by the Nepal Wireless Networking Project, including the charges paid to Nepal Telecom. This surplus is the major source of income for the communication centres. Some centres have started classes in basic computer literacy, which raises revenues and develops computer skills for people of all ages in the community. So far the project has created some part-time and full-time jobs, however not yet fully paid. The project has created volunteer and internship opportunities for software developers and college students from, e.g., the College of Information Technology in Kathmandu.

Following hard lobbying the Nepal government de-licensed the 2.4 GHz and 5.8 GHz bands in September 2006. We have come a long way since 1996, but we still have to go much further. We hope it will continue to prosper due to the improving political situation in Nepal.

Many thanks go to our international volunteers, who helped to bring donated equipment, set up the network, and taught villagers how to expand and maintain it by themselves. The project would have been just an unfulfilled dream of Himanchal Higher Secondary School had the international volunteers not devoted their time and skills to the project. More recently, a team of local experts from Nepal has given a great deal of time and energy to the project, which has helped us to expand our network, gather research data, and offer new services.

7.6.3   Dharamsala Community Wireless Network, India

Another example of Wi-Fi network building in the Indian Himalayas is the Dharamsala Community Wireless Network. The development is similar to the Nepalese wireless initiative, and with the AirJaldi organisation (a social enterprise with the goal of developing affordable broadband connectivity for rural communities in developing countries) supervising the operation of the network it has a strong emphasis on the role of volunteers and on capacity building. This account is derived from the project documentation aimed at sharing the AirJaldi experience through a 'wiki', and is supplemented with information obtained by Vic Hayes at the World Summit for Free Information Infrastructure held in Dharamsala in 2006 (Ben-David, 2007, and a personal communication with Yahel Ben-David, also in 2007):

Early in 2005, soon after the Indian government made the use of the Wi-Fi radio frequencies licence-exempt, the project began with 3 nodes within a radius of 10 km as an initiative of Yahel Ben-David, an IT expert who, together with the Tibetan Technology Center and other Dharamsala-based organisations, sought to interconnect and provide the Internet on an affordable, viable and sustainable basis.

Following the initial success they decided to scale up the operation to reach many more communities in the rural region. This expansion plan included capacity building of network operators and users to assure [*sic*] the independent operation after the initial support by volunteers from Western countries and from the free and open source software (FOSS) development groups would end.

In mid-2007 the network covered a radius of some 70 kilometres around Dharamsala and was a mix of point-to-point, point-to-multipoint and mesh topologies. The 'network' is a social enterprise that has a core team of paid employees, who are supported by volunteers and interns from India and elsewhere. It connects several villages, the Tibetan Children's Village and many institutions of the Tibetan community to each other and to the Internet and the telephone network.

The Dharamsala network is based on Wi-Fi equipment that is in part modified to provide long-range uninterruptible operation, is able to withstand extreme weather conditions, and can handle the required traffic control regimes. The routers include firewall functionality, encryption, quality-of-service policy enforcement, and environmental monitoring of power levels and temperature to allow remote operations from a Network Operations Center, using locally tailored field-proven open source software products.

A major challenge has been operation in one of the world's stormiest regions. It is not uncommon to see more than one lightning strike per second, with storms lasting for many hours over the course of the night. This affects the way antennae are to be placed in masts and the protection of the electronics. Another issue is the supply of power for units out in the wilderness, such as relay nodes with a router and two directional antennae in a mast. The power is obtained from solar cells, and accumulated in lead-acid batteries for operation during nights or overcast periods. The Low Voltage Disconnect circuits had to be modified to withstand power surges of 1,000 V and long periods of very low voltage. Moreover, the team designed and fabricated low-cost outdoor enclosures suitable for the local climate with the many lightning storms, and safe from inspection by monkeys.

Some of the most prominent changes resulting from the Dharamsala network are as follows. (1) Ease of communication (and thereby ongoing communication) with friends and relatives elsewhere (many of the customers are Tibetan refugees whose families are scattered all over India, in Tibet and in the West). This allows for parents to stay in touch with their children and vice versa, and for communication between siblings. (2) Use of web resources – many students and staff of the institutions connected to the Dharamsala network are now regularly using resources on the Internet for their homework and research projects. (3) Reaching out to the world – many of our customers had websites even before they became clients of the Dharamsala Network. Having fast and reliable connectivity available throughout campuses and offices has, however, contributed to having these tools used in a much more vibrant and dynamic manner – as website updates and responses to emails and queries can be handled by a number of people and with great ease, whereby the Dharamsala network offers free web-hosting services to all our clients.

Ben-David provides the following important guidelines, which are relevant for individuals or organisations pursuing similar initiatives.

Technologies should be relevant to the needs and realities of places where networks are built. This oft-mentioned point cannot be overemphasised. We have set up to create a state-of-the-art network that is technologically superior, reliable, affordable and easy to manage. Developing this network requires much more than simply putting together existing off-the-shelf products. The fact that the Dharamsala network was literally built on-site gave us a unique opportunity to witness and understand problems first-hand, and develop solutions that could be tested, integrated and successfully deployed within a relatively short time.

Human resources are crucial. There is no replacement for a capable team of network operators. While it will often be hard to find highly trained and experienced people to operate networks in rural areas, our experience taught us that local people, if given appropriate responsibility and training, can become superb and highly committed operators. We are currently in the process of developing special training programmes for such people.

Work together with your community. Let demand and local realities decide the pace and topology of your network. From our experiences, although the expansion patterns will rarely be in line with your own predictions, the growth rate will often be a positive surprise.

Be reliable; set your own (high) standards and live by them. Providing a service that is 'better than existing alternatives' is a tempting, but wrong, way of going about providing internet connectivity. One should define high standards from the early stages and live by them (one of our own slogans, for example, is 'When the network is down, we are up'). What might pass as good service today will surely not be regarded as such with time, and a disappointed captive customer who uses a service for lack of alternatives will be more than happy to dump such a provider as soon as he/she has a chance.

7.6.4   Mérida, Venezuela

Bridging large distances in the Andes using (modified) Wi-Fi equipment was trialled and applied at the Universidad de los Andes in Mérida, Venezuela, under the leadership of Professor Ermanno Pietrosemoli. He provides his personal account of the developments (Pietrosemoli, 2006, and a personal communication from Professor Pietrosemoli, 2007):[12]

From the early 1990s we recognised that data communications in our region had to rely on a wireless solution due to the lack of wired infrastructure. We focused our efforts on packet radio, using the radio amateur bands in VHF and UHF. In the latter, we were able to achieve data rates of 56 kbit/s, but this soon proved insufficient to meet the needs stimulated by the emergence of the World Wide Web. Therefore, we turned our attention to WLAN products that had recently been introduced in the 900 MHz ISM band, which were approved by the local regulator in 1993. We purchased a couple of full-length cards for US$750 each that came with small patch antennae meant for local communications. Our goal was to span a distance of 10 km, to La Aguada, our favourite repeater site perched on a 3,450 m mountain that commanded the city and much of the surrounding area. There were commercial antennae available for this purpose, but they sold for $2,400 apiece, so we decided to build a couple of Yagi [unidirectional] antennae for 915 MHz using the same technique that we had applied for 450 MHz. We were concerned that the Yagi would not accommodate the spread spectrum signal, but they worked well and we grew confident that we could rely on this technology for extending internet access from the communications lab at the Universidad de los Andes to some remote sites, including my residence, that lies 11 km from the repeater site and lacks a telephone line to this day. This worked very well, at a whopping 1 Mbit/s, when the internet access for the whole university was a meagre 128 kbit/s provided by a satellite dish on the top of our lab.

Encouraged by this result, we established several repeater sites to provide internet access in remote villages. In parallel, another network in the unlicensed 2.4 GHz band was also established using ORiNOCO COR with one of the links spanning 70 km, from Pico Espejo, at 4,765 m above sea level, to a remote village at 2,000 m.a.s.l.

On 13 April 2006, using off-the-shelf Linksys WRT54G routers with modified firmware and repurposed satellite antennae, we established a link on a 279 km path, with only 100 mW transmitting power; although the data rate was dismal. On 27 April 2007 we repeated the experiment on the same path using commercial 30 dBi (dB isotropic) antennae at each end, and achieved 65 kbit/s with the same Wi-Fi Linksys boxes – enough to support video transmission. We also tested on the same 279 km link a couple of Wi-Fi routers with a modified MAC layer developed by the TIER [Technology and Infrastructure for Emerging Regions] group led by Dr Eric Brewer at Berkeley University, and achieved a solid 3 Mbit/s throughput in each direction.

The next day we moved to another path, spanning 382 km, and again we were able to establish communication, both with the Linksys and the TIER boxes, thanks to an unencumbered line of sight with a minimum clearance of 2.6 Fl (first Fresnel zone). A video link was activated and the TIER boxes achieved a maximum data rate of 2 Mbit/s, but there was considerable fading and we would occasionally lose the signal.

Further experiments are planned on this path, but we can conclude that Wi-Fi has a significant role to play in long-distance communications in rural areas, at an unbeatable price.

7.6.5   Knysna network, South Africa

An example of Wi-Fi network building in South Africa is the public-private initiative at Knysna in the Western Cape province. The account is provided by Dillo Lehlokoe as part of a research project executed in the context of the executive masters programme on e-governance at the Ecole Polytechnique Fédérale de Lausanne, Switzerland (Lehlokoe, 2009), supplemented with data from an MSc thesis project executed by Pietro Bigi at the Department of Technology, Policy and Management of the Technical University of Delft (Bigi, 2009).

'Knysna UniFi' is an IP-based network, providing internet, voice (VoIP) and data services to the public and premium services to subscribers in the Knysna municipality area. According to the Knysna authorities, the initiative came about as a result of an amalgamation of various municipalities in the area into a single one, that of Knysna. The decision was then taken to establish a Wi-Fi-based network, with the intention of connecting sixty-four municipal offices which were geographically dispersed over 1,000 km². Prior to the establishment of the network, it was established that there was very little access to connectivity and communications between government departments was very poor. There were no interconnections between different systems and geographically isolated offices were connected via 64 kbit/s leased lines from incumbent operator Telkom. The deployment of wireless infrastructure was therefore expected to achieve the following objectives. (1) To provide faster, cheaper and 'always-on' connectivity to the staff at the Knysna municipal offices for remote data logging and access. (2) To offer emergency call services and toll-free municipal services to the underprivileged population of the municipality in 'underserved' areas, using VoIP telephony. (3) To offer low-cost internet services to residential/commercial subscribers, thereby extending the citizen reach. Six companies responded to the RFP issued by the municipality; the contract was awarded to UniNet. The Wi-Fi service was launched in July 2005.

In the establishment of the Knysna wireless zone, there were some major regulatory hurdles to be taken related to the old Telecommunications Act. Under this law, UniNet as a value added network service provider was not allowed to extend its own infrastructure across public roads but was forced to use Telkom's (the then national monopoly carrier) facilities. With the enactment of the Electronic Communications Act of 2006 the telecommunications sector became more liberalised, and it removed some restrictive provisions that were in place, thereby overcoming the roadblock that UniNet and Knysna had initially experienced.

The funding arrangements for the UniFi project showed the municipality's commitment to developing the ICT infrastructure for the region. The municipality allocated a percentage of its telecommunication budget towards funding of the project, which, according to the UniNet report, involved the payment of an initial lump sum (70 per cent of the total project cost), and the remaining amount was paid in phases or by milestones achieved. UniNet was responsible for the installation, management, maintenance, repairs and upgrading of the UniFi network for a monthly contract fee as governed by management contract.

In this project, low adoption rates with regard to internet and VoIP services in the residential, commercial and underserved areas were reported. For residential segments specifically, the reasons for the slow uptake were limited exposure to technology by citizens in the underserved areas and technological complexity; an older population make-up; prohibitive cost to many of Knysna's communities of access devices such as laptops, VoIP phones, palmtops, PCs with wireless cards; and a lack of digital skills on the part of citizens. These factors demonstrated a need for community training.

7.6.6   Mpumalanga network, South Africa

Another example of Wi-Fi-based networks in South Africa is the Mpumalanga Mesh Network in White River, the capital of the Mpumalanga province, in the Masoi Tribal land located in the north-east of White River, along the road that leads to the Kruger National Park's Numbi gate. This example of Wi-Fi-based networking initiatives addresses communication needs among hospitals in the rural area. Pietro Bigi provides the account (Bigi, 2009):

In South Africa 60 per cent of clinics are located in rural areas, with half of them without a communication system. The main purpose for tele-health is to extend the reach of health-care services to those rural areas where there are limited health resources. The First Mile First Inch project was initiated with the objective of identifying and developing models that would 'bypass' governmental and incumbent operator inefficiencies. The added value of this project is the creation of an open source Wi-Fi network development, allowing connection and services previously impossible for the entire population of the area. The main objective of the Mpumalanga Mesh Network project was to connect the clinics to the community hospital through a mesh wireless network.

In a mesh network each Wi-Fi station acts as a node, and communication is established by routing traffic through intermediate nodes to the destination node or to the backbone. In a mesh network it is necessary that each node sees at least one other node; in that way there is at least one link that connects one node to the next one, creating a network path. The availability of multiple network paths increases the capacity of the network and the reliability.

The network makes use of low-cost Wi-Fi routers, with 'Freifunk' routing software – an open source software using optimised link state routing as its routing protocol, which is very well known and successfully applied in many other projects around the world. The network is made up of Wi-Fi client stations that connect to a wireless backbone, expanding the reach of the signal, thereby creating a wider area being covered. For the connection with the 'outside world' the network is dependent on a very small aperture terminal (VSAT) connection provided by the incumbent operator Telkom, at a download data rate of 256 kbit/s and an upload rate of 64 kbit/s.

In addition, the Department of Science and Technology in South Africa, through the Innovation Fund project, has participated in the development and implementation of alternative communications infrastructures in a deep rural environment, independent of the national telecommunications operator, in support of local economic development. An example is the Tsilitwa Telehealth project in the Eastern Cape province (Morris and Makan, 2003; see also van Gorp and Morris, 2007, for a general overview).

7.7   Sharing the Wi-Fi field experience

The very practical lessons learned from these projects are shared through internet-based wikis and are passed on through local/regional training and educational programmes. For example, the Wireless Leiden community initiative has led to the organisation of Open Community Camps, starting in 2006 and aimed at disseminating the experience obtained in the context of the Wireless Leiden initiative and providing for hands-on training. Topics that have been covered include Wi-Fi networking, antenna making, open source (Linux and BSD), open hardware, network servers and network services. The camps have drawn participation from afar, including Tanzania, Nigeria, Papua New Guinea, Austria, the United Kingdom, France, Germany, Belgium and the Netherlands (for more information, see http//wifisoft.org).

The Boevl in Djursland is also involved in sharing knowledge and expertise. From 1999 to 2000 the Boevl collected recycled computers and set up five internet workshops in Kazakhstan and ten more in Lithuania. The experience obtained with the establishment of the Djursland network has been documented, and courses are available through the Djursland International Institute of Rural Wireless Broadband. The courses extend well beyond technical information, and include topics such as organising, campaigning, administration, equipment and tools, net planning and net building, web portal building and maintenance, user support and sustainability of the network, and handling of routers and servers (Nielsen, 2007).

The AirJaldi Network Academy, in Dharamsala and Dehra Dun, now provides courses as part of the Cisco Network Academy, including IT essentials and Cisco-certified network engineers.[13] At the Universidad de los Andes, in Mérida, experiences obtained with wireless techniques for internet access have been disseminated in international training events since 1992, leading to the creation of the Fundación Escuela Latinoamericana de Redes (EsLaRed), a not-for-profit organisation that has support from the Internet Society, the Latin American and Caribbean Internet Addresses Registry (LACNIC), the Abdus Salam International Centre for Theoretical Physics and the International Development Research Centre.[14]

At the international level, experience in building and operating Wi-Fi networks is shared through conferences and meetings, such as the 2006 World Summit for Free Information Infrastructures, held in Dharamsala. This conference and workshop were aimed at disseminating knowledge and skills on how to set up community networks in order to provide internet access in developing countries at very low costs.[15]

7.8   The role of policy and regulation

Although there are several thousand Wi-Fi initiatives throughout the developing countries, there is still no widespread general acceptance and support from government policy and regulation to help Wi-Fi become a major vehicle for providing access to unserved rural and remote areas at the BOP.

Although Wi-Fi technology provides a unique opportunity for extending internet access to the BOP, and local participation allows for business models appropriate to local circumstances, in many developing countries government policies provide formidable barriers to development and sustainability. This is no more evident than in spectrum licensing policy, in which, among developing countries, only about a half have provided unlicensed spectrum – in contrast to the developed countries, virtually all of which have. In many countries licence fees, taxes and other payments ensure there are no opportunities for the development of viable Wi-Fi networks in poor rural areas. This problem is

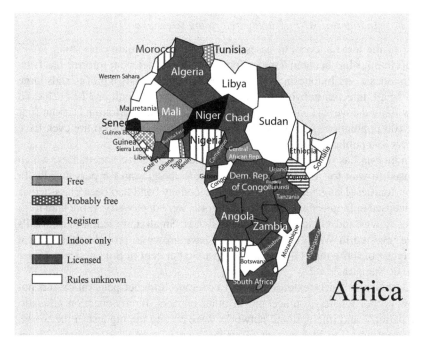

Figure 7.3 Licensing of Wi-Fi in Africa
Source: Based on information from www.openspectrum.info, 2007.

greatest in Africa, where relatively few countries provide unlicensed spectrum, and in some countries the relevant frequencies have been assigned for other uses. See Figure 7.3 for an illustration of the situation in Africa.

In many developing countries import duties, taxes and other fees increase the cost of equipment significantly. Local Wi-Fi initiatives do not have access to universal service subsidy funds, which are reserved for incumbents and large operators. Ironically, the small amount of revenues collected from Wi-Fi services in impoverished rural areas may actually be taxed, so as to contribute to universal service subsidy funds that are given to incumbent operators. Weak regulation often fails to ensure reasonable interconnection between Wi-Fi initiatives and national network operators. In some cases, incumbent operators have refused to interconnect at all.

Surprisingly, many local entrepreneurs have pursued Wi-Fi initiatives even in the face of these seemingly insurmountable barriers, smuggling in equipment and establishing 'un-legal'[16] Wi-Fi networks. Once established they become agents for telecom reforms that will remove the artificial policy barriers, if not get supportive policies adopted.

7.8.1   Indonesia: Wi-Fi practice reforming telecom policy[17]

One of the most successful cases in which a local initiative pursuing Wi-Fi opportunities has become a major force stimulating telecom reforms has been in Indonesia. As Indonesia is an enormous country consisting of islands large and small, telecom network development has been difficult and has achieved very limited coverage and penetration. Fixed network penetration is about four per 100 population. About half Indonesia's 70,000 villages do not even have access to a public phone.

Indonesia has developed an active internet community nonetheless, which refused to wait for telecom reform to prepare the ground for pursuing Wi-Fi opportunities. Long before the 2.4 GHz frequency band had been classified as unlicensed in Indonesia, local Wi-Fi networks were deployed in more than forty cities, towns and villages on different islands. Small and medium-sized ISPs have invested in Wi-Fi networks, which have grown to provide geographical coverage of more than 60 per cent of Java, 30 per cent of Sulawesi and 35 per cent of Sumatra.

Despite this fairly extensive Wi-Fi coverage, internet penetration did not grow proportionately, on account of other barriers. Interconnection prices to the national and international networks were among the highest in the world, representing 60 to 80 per cent of an ISP's costs, compared to about 25 per cent in other countries. For a long time the incumbent, PT Telkom, refused to make leased lines available to ISPs. As a result, they started using Wi-Fi links as a substitute for leased lines, even though it was not legal and there was a risk of closure or confiscation. Business customers subscribing to a leased line from the incumbent to provide dedicated internet access had to pay such high prices that some became unlicensed ISPs and provided internet services to the local area. In one case, 129 customers were being served, including five schools and twenty internet cafés, and neighbourhood networks connecting 104 homes.

The growth and development of 'un-legal' Wi-Fi in Indonesia has reached a level at which it can no longer be denied by obsolete policy restrictions, incumbent monopoly power or political resistance. The government was embarrassed into legally sanctioning unlicensed Wi-Fi and introducing some policy reforms. Leased line interconnection prices were reduced significantly, the incumbent has increased national backbone capacity, and alternative mobile operators have been licensed. There is a telecom regulator, but it is weak and a servant of the ministry.

Telecom reform in Indonesia is proceeding at a grudging pace, and only when pressures from international and domestic institutions require it. A major domestic force driving reform is the Wi-Fi/ISP community, which continues to grow in both urban and rural areas. It is a catalyst for extending networks to the BOP and a force of increasing influence in pushing the frontier of telecom reform.

7.9   Conclusion

Wi-Fi opens unique opportunities to achieve universal access in rural and remote areas at the BOP. The technological development is being driven by a very large global equipment market spanning a wide range of Wi-Fi applications in both developed and developing countries. Continuous improvements can be expected in its capacity and capabilities, together with reduced costs from economies of scale and scope in global equipment production. Service capabilities began with narrowband internet data services; but bandwidth capabilities are expanding, and VoIP makes voice services possible. Quality and security are lower than that provided on traditional telecom networks, but continually improving.

Although the distances over which Wi-Fi can be transmitted are significant, Wi-Fi's comparative advantage is as a local network technology. When it is extended to provide backbone links into national networks, it is either because of an inadequate national backbone network or so as to avoid an incumbent's monopoly prices for leased lines. Such Wi-Fi extensions may be necessary to force leased line price reductions, however.

Wi-Fi allows for low levels of investment, simple business models, significant local participation, training on the job and incremental growth in response to demand. Funding is conducive to minimum-risk micro-financing. Local entrepreneurship can come from anywhere, but it is a natural step for ISPs to take. In unserved areas, the establishment of a local ISP and a Wi-Fi network are interdependent, providing mutual benefits to one another and the community.

Policy and regulation in developing countries generally have provided a series of formidable barriers to Wi-Fi applications. More countries can be expected to designate unlicensed Wi-Fi spectrum as the evidence of successful applications spreads around the world. Import duties and taxes on Wi-Fi equipment are unlikely to be removed as they are a part of more general national trade policy that would need to be modified. Leased line interconnection to national backbone and international gateway networks is likely to remain a significant barrier in most countries, as most national incumbent operators have retained significant monopoly power, and telecom regulation is weak. In most countries it will be a while yet before effective competition forces prices down to more reasonable levels.

There is no sign so far that Wi-Fi networks in unserved areas will be eligible to receive subsidies from universal service funds, which have been fenced off for use by incumbent operators or large network operators implementing top-down strategies of network rollout from the centre. It is pretty clear that, in most countries, the most effective use of universal service funds would be to support Wi-Fi applications at the BOP through a micro-finance programme. The funding needs per village would be small and many initiatives would become self-sustaining after a few years.

If policy and regulation could be transformed and provide a fully supportive programme for providing universal access – through responsive spectrum management, import policies, telecom regulation and universal subsidy allocations – then the Wi-Fi opportunity could stimulate an era of universal access growth even more significant than the prepaid mobile voice revolution by building network links out from the BOP, rather than attempting to extend much higher-cost centralised national networks down to it. For the foreseeable future the limiting factor constraining future Wi-Fi applications in developing countries will be government policy and regulation. The pace of development in Wi-Fi applications will be constrained by the effectiveness of reformed government policy and regulation, not the capabilities of the Wi-Fi technology or of the business models of local Wi-Fi operators.

Notes

1 Wireless Leiden provides a good example; see Chapter 6 for more examples.
2 Australia, Canada, the United States and the Scandinavian countries have been the leaders in telecom network development, and achieved near-universal telephone service some time ago. The comment relates to the rest of the world. For the other European countries, network development has been driven primarily by EU policies and directives.
3 The term was coined by Theodore Vail, chairman of AT&T during the early twentieth century. His solution to the lack of interconnection between competing telephone companies was to create a single interconnected system – i.e. a universal service. There was no intention to connect people in outlying rural or unprofitable areas. Universal service policies extending networks towards universal access were adopted later by some US states and the federal government in the Communications Act of 1934 (see Mueller, 1997).
4 This indicator can be extremely difficult to measure, though, as the vast majority of connections are prepaid rather than by subscription, and counting the number of mobile phones in use and those who have access to them is far from a straightforward exercise (see Sutherland, 2009).
5 'Universal access' is also a more precise term these days, as the terminals needed to use telecom services, which can be very expensive for the rural poor, are not included. The original conception of 'universal service' was inclusive: it included the supply of the telephone that was the property of the monopoly provider.
6 There was a general failure, both in policy and in the literature, to recognise telecom services as an essential input to the universality, efficiency and quality of the perceived higher-order services.
7 Farmers installed the last mile (or several miles) of connection to the farm typically by running it along their fences.

8 Most notably, demand assignment multiple access (DAMA) systems allowed thin route locations to be served efficiently.

9 For early examples, see National Computer Board (1992), NTIA (1993), EC (1994a, 1994b, 1995), Industry Canada (1994), Ministry of Research (1995) and OECD (1996).

10 The terminals necessary to make use of these services were not part of this universal service/access policy, however.

11 Under the American Recovery and Reinvestment Act of 2009, US$7.2 billion in subsidies are allocated to help extend broadband internet services to underserved areas.

12 For an overview of Wi-Fi developments in Latin America, there are a number of articles that can be consulted, most with a contribution by Hernán Galperin, associate professor at the Universidad de San Andrés, Buenos Aires. See Bar and Galperin (2004, 2006), Bar and Riis (2000), Galperin (2005) and Galperin and Girard (2007).

13 Personal communication from Ben-David, 2007.

14 Personal communication from Pietrosemoli, 2007.

15 The event brought together 125 participants from seventeen countries for the four-day conference and forty people for hands-on training in a ten-day workshop.

16 This term was adopted by the ISPs to reflect the fact that the law was not sufficiently precise to be clear on the matter and the toleration extended to the widespread flouting of the rules governing Wi-Fi frequencies. See Goswami (2008) and Goswami and Purbo (2006).

17 This section is adapted from Goswami (2008).

References

Bar, F., and H. Galperin (2004). 'Building the wireless internet infrastructure: from cordless Ethernet archipelagos to wireless grids'. *Communications and Strategies.* **54** (2), 45–68.

(2006). 'The Microtelco opportunity: evidence from Latin America'. *Information Technologies and International Development.* **3** (2), 73–86.

Bar, F., and A. M. Riis (2000). 'Tapping user-driven innovation: a new rationale for universal service'. *The Information Society.* **16** (2), 99–108.

Ben-David, Y. (2007). 'Keeping the network alive'. Dharamsala: Tibetan Technology Center.

Bigi, P. (2009). 'WiMAX: the ultimate solution for rural areas or the next idle wireless technology?'. MSc thesis. Department of Technology, Policy and Management, Technical University of Delft.

EC (1994a). *Europe and the Global Information Society: Recommendations to the European Council* [Bangemann Report]. Brussels: EC.

(1994b). *Europe's Way to the Information Society: An Action Plan.* Brussels: EC.

(1995). *Conclusions of the G-7 Information Society Conference.* Brussels: EC.

(2000). *The Lisbon Council: An Agenda of Economic and Social Renewal for Europe.* DOC/00/7. Brussels: EC.

(2005). *i2010: A European Information Society for Growth and Employment.* COM (2005) 229. Brussels: EC.

Galperin, H. (2005). 'Wireless networks and rural development: opportunities for Latin America'. *Information Technologies and International Development.* **2** (3), 47–56.

Galperin, H., and B. Girard (2007). 'Microtelcos in Latin America and the Caribbean'. In H. Galperin and J. Mariscal (eds.). *Digital Poverty: Latin American and Caribbean Perspectives.* Rugby: Practical Action, 95–118.

Goswami, D. (2008). 'Wi-Fi: the network fix'. In R. Samarajiva and A. Zainudeen (eds.). *ICT Infrastructure in Emerging Asia: Policy and Regulatory Roadblocks.* New Delhi/Ottawa: Sage/IDRC, 131–56.

Goswami, D., and O. Purbo (2006). 'WiFi "Innovation" in Indonesia: working around hostile market and regulatory conditions'. Discussion Paper no. 0611. Kongens Lyngby, Denmark: World Dialogue on Regulation [WDR].

Hudson, H. (2009). 'The future of the E-Rate: US Universal Service Fund support for public access and social services'. In A. Schejter (ed.). *. . . And Communications for All: An Agenda for a New Administration.* Lanham, MD: Lexington Books, 239–60.

Industry Canada (1994). *The Canadian Information Highway.* Ottawa: Industry Canada.

Kalba, K. (2008a). 'The adoption of mobile phones in emerging markets'. *International Journal of Communication.* **2**, 631–61.

(2008b). *The Global Adoption and Diffusion of Mobile Phones.* Cambridge, MA: Center for Information Policy Research, Harvard University.

Lehlokoe, D. (2009). 'Adopting m-government as a complementary option for implementing e-government in South Africa'. Executive masters thesis. Ecole Polytechnique Fédérale de Lausanne, Switzerland.

Mahan, A. K. (2005). 'Prepaid mobile and network extension'. In A. K. Mahan and W. H. Melody (eds.). *Stimulating Investment in Network Development: Roles for Regulators.* Kongens Lyngby, Denmark: WDR, 63–76.

Mahan, A. K., and W. H. Melody (eds.) (2007). *Diversifying Participation in Network Development.* Montevideo: LIRNE.NET.

(2009). 'Network development: wireless applications for the next billion users'. *Info.* **11** (2), 2–5.

Malik, P. (2007). 'India's Universal Service Obligation for rural telecommunications: issues of design and implementation'. Telecommunications Policy Research Conference Paper no. 2007/687. Ann Arbor: University of Michigan. Available at http://web.si.umich.edu/tprc/papers/2007/687/TPRCPayalMalik.pdf (accessed 21 September 2009).

Ministry of Research (1995). *Info-Society 2000.* Copenhagen: Ministry of Research.

Morris, C., and A. Makan. (2003). *Tele-health: A Case Study in Tsilitwa, Eastern Cape.* Pretoria: Council for Scientific and Industrial Research.

Mueller, M. L. (1993). 'Universal service in telephone history: a reconstruction'. *Telecommunications Policy.* **17** (5), 352–69.

(1997). *Universal Service: Competition, Interconnection, and Monopoly in the Making of the American Telephone System.* Cambridge, MA/Washington, DC: MIT Press/AEI Press.

National Computer Board (1992). *A Vision of an Intelligent Island: The IT 2000 Report.* Singapore: National Computer Board.

Nielsen, B. (2007). 'Broadband in rural areas through self-organising'. Paper presented at IEEE Steinmetz Award seminar. Delft, 6 March.

NTIA (1993). *The National Information Infrastructure: Agenda for Action*. Washington, DC: NTIA.

OECD (1996). *The Knowledge-based Economy*. Paris: OECD.

(2004). *Leveraging Telecommunications Policies for Pro-poor Growth: Universal Access Funds with Minimum Subsidy Auctions*. Paris: OECD.

Parker, E. (2000). 'Closing the digital divide in rural America'. *Telecommunications Policy*. **24** (4), 281–90.

Pietrosemoli, E. (2006). 'Wireless networking in Mérida, Venezuela'. Paper presented at World Summit on Free Information Infrastructures conference. Dharamsala, 22 October.

Pun, M., R. Shields, R. Poudel and P. Mucci (2006). *Nepal Wireless Networking Project: Case Study and Evaluation Report*. Incheon, South Korea: UN Asia and Pacific Training Centre for Information and Communication Technology for Development.

Samarajiva, R. (2006). 'Preconditions for effective deployment of wireless technologies for development in the Asia-Pacific'. *Information Technologies and International Development*. **3** (2), 57–71.

(2007). 'Perverse universal service'. Kongens Lyngby, Denmark: World Dialogue on Regulation. Available at www.regulateonline.org/content/view/1061/77/1/8./<τπ/> (accessed 21 September 2009).

Samarajiva, R., and A. Zainudeen (eds.) (2008). *ICT Infrastructure in Emerging Asia: Policy and Regulatory Roadblocks*. New Delhi/Ottawa: Sage/IDRC.

Siochru, S., and B. Girard (2005). *Community-based Networks and Innovative Technologies: New Models to Serve and Empower the Poor*. New York: United Nations Development Programme.

Sutherland, E. (2009). 'Counting customers, subscribers and mobile phone numbers'. *Info*. **11** (2), 6–23.

Van Gorp, A., and C. Morris (2007). 'Rural connectivity through Wi-Fi: regulatory challenges and opportunities in Southern Africa'. Paper presented at the fifty-seventh annual conference of the International Communication Association. San Francisco, 23 May.

Wellenius, B. (2002). 'Closing the gap in access to rural communications: Chile 1995–2002'. Discussion Paper no. 430. Washington, DC: World Bank.

8   The Dutch connection to US-based NCR, AT&T, Lucent Technologies and Agere Systems

Wolter Lemstra and Marianne van der Steen,
with contributions from Ronald Brockmann,
Jaap Haartsen, Cees Links, Richard van Nee,
Bruce Tuch and Allert van Zelst

8.1   Introduction

In Chapters 2 to 6 the innovation journey of Wi-Fi has been explored and explained as a longitudinal case study, from its genesis in 1985 and subsequent developments until 2008. In Chapters 7 to 11 we take the Wi-Fi journey as a given, and investigate five dimensions of the journey that are of particular interest. In this chapter we look at the 'Dutch connection'. In acknowledgement of the fact that the Systems Engineering Centre in Utrecht has played such an important role in the development of Wi-Fi, we survey the relationship between the Wi-Fi journey and the Dutch national innovation system (NIS).

From the innovation journey we learned that the development of Wi-Fi was triggered by a policy change towards radio spectrum usage by the US Federal Communications Commission. This new opportunity to use RF spectrum without the need for a licence was taken up by a number of companies, including NCR, to start the development of wireless LANs. The account of the Wi-Fi journey also revealed that NCR's decision to allocate the feasibility study, and later product development, to the Utrecht Systems Engineering Centre was driven by the availability there of the knowledge required to create a wireless LAN. The Dutch connection we explore in this chapter concerns the role played by the Dutch national innovation system in the development of Wi-Fi. In order to do this, we first provide an overview of the Dutch innovation system in terms of its main institutions, and a historical account of RF technology and its applications in the Netherlands. Subsequently we look into the role of the various economic actors and their knowledge interactions that were instrumental in the development of Wi-Fi, and assess how the knowledge that had been acquired in the process migrated to other firms when the Utrecht Engineering Centre was closed.

8.2 Context: the Dutch national innovation system[1]

The concept of an NIS was developed in the late 1980s and early 1990s by a number of leading authors, such as Freeman (1987, 1988), Lundvall (1988, 1992), Nelson (1988, 1993), Nelson and Nelson (2002) and Patel and Pavitt (1994). A national innovation system involves institutions (public and private) and economic agents, which interact in the production, diffusion and use of new economic knowledge. Some authors have emphasised the national dimension of innovation systems, while others have placed more emphasis on (sub-)regions, such as Silicon Valley and Route 128 in Boston (Saxenian, 1994), and ICT clusters in the Netherlands (Bouwman and Hulsink, 2000). These studies illustrate the importance of proximity for knowledge flows between firms and the complementarities of firms in these clusters, thereby illustrating a trend from closed to more open models of innovation. The central idea behind 'open innovation' as expressed by Chesbrough (2003), is that, in a world of widely distributed knowledge, companies cannot afford to rely entirely on their own research efforts and should also buy or license processes or inventions from other companies.

In this section, therefore, we aim to describe the (open) innovation system of ICT and radio technology in the Netherlands from a historical perspective so as to position our Wi-Fi case. Based on the innovation system literature, we include the main institutions (i.e. framework conditions) from an historical perspective, the technological development (radio technology) and the main economic actors involved in the genesis of Wi-Fi (the knowledge network and their interactions). In order to do so in a structured way, we use a three-level model based on earlier work by van der Steen (1999) and of Groenewegen and van der Steen (2006); see Figure 8.1.

The first level represents the prevailing model of political economy, the role of the state in economic development and, in particular, innovation-related policies. The second level includes the structure and governance of the industrial sector. The third level, or actor level, reflects – in this case – interactions in the Wi-Fi-related knowledge network, as well as its technological competitors and, at times, alternative knowledge networks. The economic actors involved can be members of firms, of universities, entrepreneurs, policy makers, or members of other public sector entities.[2] In the following sections we discuss the three levels in greater detail.

8.2.1 The model of political economy and the role of the state

With respect to the first level – the political economy – we find at one end of the spectrum the (pure) market economies, based on the idea that it is through market forces that the maximisation of individual interest best promotes the

First level

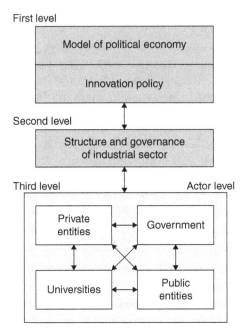

Figure 8.1 Institutional model: innovation
Source: Adapted from van der Steen (1999).

'public interest'. At the other end of the spectrum we find the centrally coordinated or planned economies, in which private interests are considered to be served best through the public domain. Today, with the prevalence of capitalistic market economies, the difference is more gradual, whereby a distinction can be made between the regulatory state and the developmental state. In both, the market is the central node: in the regulatory model the government is focused on the proper functioning of the market process, while in the developmental model the outcome of the process is also important. In the developmental model the government develops explicit targets and plans for economic development in general, and articulates the desirable developments at sector level (Groenewegen, 1989).

The Dutch-model can be considered a hybrid form, to be characterised as a social-market economy based on tripartite consultation between government, employers and employees. This dominant negotiation structure is the reason the Dutch model is often referred to as a 'consultation model of political economy'. The emergence of this model is often related to the period after the Second World War, when the rebuilding of the economy came to be viewed as a collective need and a collective experience.

Over the years the strongly institutionalised consultation structure led to an increase in rigidity (CPB [Centraal Planbureau: Netherlands Bureau for Economic Policy Analysis], 1997). In fact, the economy had effectively become subordinated to the social purposes of the state. Consequently, competitiveness decreased, in part as a result of the expansion of (semi-)governmental activities. The country came to resemble a social market economy (McKinsey, 1997); in certain circles the Dutch economy was now referred to as a 'cartel state' (OECD, 1987, 1993; van Rooy, 1992). The vulnerability of a cost-focused economic structure in combination with an expanding public sector and a lack of competitive pressure resulted in what Porter views as the 'diseases' of a welfare state (Porter, 1990). The OECD at this time referred to this situation as the 'Dutch disease' (OECD, 1993; van Rooy, 1992).

In the 1970s the Dutch economic system was hit by a serious economic setback. The oil crisis and the economic stagflation in world markets revealed the vulnerability of the economic structure. The market sector found it very difficult to cope with the increasing competitive pressures. The state was confronted with enormous costs – to pay the increasing number of unemployed – without having the ability to adjust its institutional structure to the new 'global' environment. The crisis, in combination with trends towards individualisation and secularisation, gradually changed the common view of the purpose of the economy. These strong pressures provided the incentive for a transformation of the economic system. As a consultation economy is characterised by a relatively high level of trust and cooperation between government, employers and employees, once the decision to change the system had been made everyone was committed. Hence, by the end of the 1980s and the early 1990s, the necessary wage reductions, expenditure cuts and institutional adjustments had been realised. In the 1990s this led to strong employment growth and the restoration of a healthy state budgetary situation.

These changes in the political economy thereby created an environment and new framework conditions that were more conducive for industry to generate a competitive advantage.

8.2.2   From industrial policy to innovation policy

In the 1980s technology innovation policies started to replace the (protective) industrial policies of the previous decades. The 'Innovation' paper issued by the Ministry of Economic Affairs marked this new policy orientation, acknowledging a new perspective on the innovation process, which already had become commonplace in business practice and needed to be incorporated into official policy formation (Groenewegen and van der Steen, 2007).

Historically, innovation policy had been based on the concept of a linear model, the 'innovation chain'. The first link in this chain was represented by fundamental research, usually performed at universities and research institutes. The relevant public policy was a science-focused policy, which was – and remains – the responsibility of the Ministry of Science and Education. The next link was represented by applied research, whereby the research and development efforts led to the application of knowledge into new products and services. Technology policy and industry policy are most relevant to this link in the chain, and are the responsibility of the Ministry of Economic Affairs. The final link in the chain was the diffusion of the knowledge through products and services in the various markets served by the companies involved. In this linear model, it was the science-related policies that constituted the most important lever for government.

The 'Innovation' paper marked a new perspective on innovation: 'Innovation as the engine of economic growth'. Innovations were recognised as the result of complex, non-linear interactive processes involving all elements of the innovation chain. The Paper also identified a mismatch between the demand side for knowledge – firms – and the supply side – the knowledge institutes. The paper provided guidance on what should be considered important in terms of technology policy, the constraints and opportunities, and the instruments available to improve economic competitiveness. The Ministry of Economic Affairs was called upon to provide the necessary integration between the ministries involved, resulting in the establishment of a Directorate for Technology Policy in 1983.

In 1984 the Zegveld Committee published its influential report *Towards a Market-oriented Technology Policy*, recognising the need to participate and compete in the global 'technology race' (Roobeek, 1990). In 1987 the Dekker Committee proposed improvements for the mismatch between the demand and supply of knowledge, of which several proposals were adopted by the government. Based on the recognition that small and medium-sized enterprises accounted for a major part of employment, the ministry tried to create a better institutional environment for innovative high-tech firms.

The 1980s became characterised by unprecedented flows of foreign direct investments, mergers, acquisitions and strategic alliances, as well as by ever-intensifying competition from Japanese and south-east Asian firms (Thurow, 1996). The so-called 'globalisation thesis' claimed that a new era had begun in international business, stretching beyond the recognised national borders. In such a context, national industrial policy would become obsolete. In the words of Reich (1991): 'There will be no national products or technologies, no national corporations, no national industries.'

The 1990 policy paper 'Economy with open borders' produced by the Ministry of Economic Affairs reflects the increasing importance of globalisation for the performance of the Dutch economy and introduces the 'industrial cluster' approach, which emphasises that, for a nation or region to gain a competitive advantage, it is necessary for the national (regional) part of an industry to be embedded in a dense network of relationships not just with other firms in the industry internationally (nationally), but also with universities and other innovative actors and users (Porter, 1990). The implication is that knowledge is recognised as the main production factor, and learning as the main process involved. This awareness resulted in subsequent policy papers, namely 'Competing with knowledge' in 1993, and 'Knowledge in action' in 1995, emphasising, on the one hand, the combination of a sound macroeconomic climate, a well-functioning market and the continuous development and application of new technologies and, on the other hand, the relevance of high-quality research by strengthening the existing knowledge infrastructures and their interactions with firms.

In this policy context, therefore, policy makers have come to acknowledge that (1) innovations, which occur when innovative actors interact, and (2) attracting innovative high-tech firms both constitute important pillars of national competitiveness. The resulting Promotion of Research and Development Act (Wet Bevordering Speur- en Ontwikkelingswerk (WBSO) Act) is an important policy instrument for stimulating the R&D activities of firms, which has in turn stimulated the innovation performance of the Netherlands, thereby playing a significant role in the innovation journey of Wi-Fi.

8.2.3   The WBSO Act

The government policy that has had a tangible impact on the Wi-Fi journey is the WBSO. The WBSO is a tax facility for firms with employees, self-employed people and knowledge institutes. These organisations have to pay reduced amounts of statutory payroll tax and social security contributions in respect of their own R&D staff. The WBSO is a generic instrument deployed by the national government to stimulate firms to execute research and development activities in the Netherlands, and it was introduced in 1994 (Brouwer et al., 2002). The WBSO is granted on the basis of the projects submitted in advance by users of the facility, and organisations are credited on the basis of actual R&D hours. According to the 2001–5 evaluation, for each €1.00 spent by the WBSO user population on R&D the facility provides on average for the equivalent of €1.72 worth of R&D efforts, the so-called 'bang for the buck', which includes the tax incentive and the extra R&D being spent from the user's own resources. Feedback from users suggests that, as a result of the WBSO, more than a half of them dare to tackle more risky R&D projects, perform the R&D in a shorter time frame, plan R&D activities better, tend to keep R&D out of harm's way in the event of spending cuts and perform more R&D internally and contract less work out (de Jong and Verhoeven, 2007).

The Wi-Fi case suggests that the WBSO played a role in the decision-making process regarding the R&D activities at the Utrecht Engineering Centre, particularly in the period when the Wi-Fi activities were part of AT&T and Lucent Technologies, as the Utrecht centre had to compete then with alternative R&D resources in the United States. In the related internal discussions, the fact that the hourly rate in the Netherlands was in effect lower than in the United States meant that, *ceteris paribus*, the R&D work should be allocated to the Dutch centre. Moreover, in the early period, when revenues were low, the WBSO allowed the development team to balance income and cost, thereby satisfying senior management's main evaluation criterion for the continuation of the project.[3]

This observation from the management involved in the Wi-Fi project is to some degree at variance with the observation in the EIM evaluation report, which suggests that the WBSO is less attractive for large firms (those with 250 or more employees) – a point that is noted in the report as an item for further scrutiny (de Jong and Verhoeven, 2007).

The EIM report refers to the earlier evaluation studies, which showed that the social efficiency of the WBSO is greater than the private efficiency resulting from the effects of knowledge spillovers.

8.3   Structure and governance of the sector

The second level within the model (Figure 8.1) entails the institutions related to the industrial sector, whereby the governance of an industrial sector involves the broad subset of economic, political, technical and socio-economic rules, incentives and constraints pertaining to the actors active in a particular industry.

For our goal of placing Wi-Fi development in the context of the Dutch industrial environment, we now review the changing innovation environment in which Wi-Fi was developed, followed by a short summary on the early application of RF technology in the Netherlands.

8.3.1   From closed to open innovation in the sector

Wi-Fi was part of a change in the socio-economic rules in the sector. In other words, the innovation model changed slowly from a closed model of innovation to an open model of innovation. We can illustrate this with the case of the large industrial laboratories, such as AT&T Bell Labs, which were typical examples of 'closed innovation', characterised by Chesbrough (2003, somewhat abridged) as: '(1) the smart people in the field work for us; (2) to profit from R&D, we must discover it, develop it and ship it ourselves; (3) if we discover it ourselves, we will get it to market first; (4) the company that gets an innovation to the market first will win; (5) if we create the most and the best ideas in the industry, we will win; (6) we should control our intellectual property, so that our competitors do not profit from our ideas'.

The invention of the transistor at AT&T Bell Labs in 1947 is a case in point, following on from William Shockley bringing together a team of expert physicists, chemists and engineers. The story continues, however, with Shockley leaving Bell Labs in 1957 to establish his own firm in Palo Alto, California. He attracted other experts, of whom eight left within a short space of time, because they were unhappy with his management style, and subsequently founded Fairchild Semiconductor in 1957, which would become the third company in what is now called Silicon Valley. Having made Fairchild Semiconductor a very successful company, but not satisfied with the priorities set by the owner, Fairchild Camera and Instrument Corporation, Robert Noyce, as general manager, and Gordon Moore, as head of R&D, left to form Intel Corporation in 1968 (Riordan and Hoddison, 1998). This account illustrates the 'embodied' knowledge flow as part of the 'closed innovation' model.

On the other hand, Philips, as it did not undertake significant R&D activities in the early years, obtained a licence from General Electric for the production of incandescent lamps. Later, as part of the objectives of the Natuurkundig Laboratorium (the Physics Laboratory, or NatLab), Philips created a strong patent portfolio, providing the company with an important position in the exchange of patents with other firms, including AT&T Bell Labs (Blanken, 1992).

While the genesis and early development of Wi-Fi can be placed within the environment of the 'closed innovation' model at NCR, and even more notably later within the industrial laboratories of AT&T/Lucent Technologies, its development already exhibits attributes that are related to the 'open innovation' model, which Chesbrough (2003, somewhat abridged) describes as: '(1) not all the smart people in the field work for us; we need to work with smart people inside and outside the company; (2) external R&D can create significant value; internal R&D is needed to claim some portion of that value; (3) we do not have to originate the research to profit from it; (4) building a better business model is better than getting to the market first; (5) if we make the best use of internal and external ideas, we will win; (6) we should profit from others using our intellectual property, and we should buy IP from others whenever it advances our business model'.

The decision by NCR to pursue an 'open standard' illustrates the point. In the development of the IEEE 802.11 standard, contributions from a wide range of organisations were leveraged (see Chapter 3 for the details). As the use of Wi-Fi evolved it became part of other business models: of telecommunication operators, of 'hotspot' operators, of municipalities. As part of these business models it allowed other innovations to take place, for example, in network access, in mesh networking and in closing the 'digital divide'.

It is important to acknowledge that, in both the 'closed innovation' and 'open innovation' models, the creation of knowledge is emphasised.

8.3.2   Early applications of RF technology in the Netherlands

The involvement of the Dutch in radio technology dates back to the early days of its application, although to start with it was mainly equipment from abroad that was used. A few facts can serve to illustrate this early involvement. In 1902 radio-telegraphy communication was established between the port of Hoek van Holland and the lightship *Maas*. In 1906 a general radio service with ships was established through the coastal station 'Scheveningen Haven', operated by the Radio Division of the government's Post and Telegraphy Department, using Telefunken equipment. Regular weather services were being provided by 1914. In that same year a law was enacted allowing the general public to use radio receiving stations without the need to apply for a licence. In 1916 'Radio Holland' was established through a collaboration of the major shipping companies in order to secure services during the period of the First World War, in which the Dutch remained neutral. In 1917 the consortium took steps to establish the Nederlandse Seintoestellen Fabriek (NSF), to engage in the manufacture of radio telegraph and radio telephone equipment. The same year the government allocated 5 million guilders (the equivalent of €2.2 million) to establish a radio service with the Netherlands East Indies (Nederlands-Indië), then a colony and now Indonesia. In 1918, though, NSF lost the government contract to the more experienced Telefunken of Germany. Using long-wave equipment, experimental transmissions from the Netherlands East Indies were received as early as 1919, and a regular service was established in 1923.[4] In 1929 the service was opened to the general public. In 1922, meanwhile, the first KLM passenger aeroplane was equipped with radio equipment on a trial basis (Blanken, 1992; Corver, 1928; Koomans, 1926; Vles, 2008).

The first experimental radio broadcasting service was provided by a radio amateur, Hanso Schotanus à Steringa Idzerda, in The Hague in 1919.[5] He had started his entrepreneurial activities in 1914, and his company became known as the Nederlandsche Radio Industrie; the Dutch army became his major client. In 1918 he started the sale of vacuum tubes made by Philips Electronics under the name 'Philips-Ideezet'. Idzerda and Philips jointly demonstrated radio-telephony for the first time at the Jaarbeurs (Annual Fair) in Utrecht in February 1919.[6] In August that year Idzerda and Philips obtained a licence from the government for the testing of radio-telegraphy and radio-telephony communication. In September Idzerda started to use this licence for radio broadcasts in the form of a 'Radio soirée-musicale', targeted at radio amateurs with the aim of boosting sales of his radio equipment. These broadcasts were announced in advance in the newspapers.[7] To finance his broadcasts he used commercials, and he also received sponsoring from the British newspaper the *Daily Mail*, as his broadcasts could be received across the English Channel (Blanken, 1992; de Boer, 1969).[8]

In 1923 the Nederlandse Seintoestellen Fabriek also started broadcasting services in Hilversum, using a licence for manufacturing and testing. The content of the broadcasts was provided by the Hollandse Draadlooze Omroep, the precursor of the Dutch broadcasting companies (AVRO, NCRV, KRO and VPRO). Philips became a major sponsor of these broadcasts, and also provided two 60 metre masts to replace the earlier 12 metre Marconi masts, to improve the signal quality. In 1927, to cater for the increasing demand for airtime by the young broadcasting organisations, a second transmitter was erected in Huizen, near Hilversum. NSF operated both transmitters to provide services to the broadcasters (Vogt, 1958).

In 1927 Philips brought into service its own short-wave transmitter in Eindhoven, using high-power water-cooled transmitting valves developed at the Philips NatLab.[9] The transmissions were successfully received in the Netherlands East Indies, making the achievement a world first. This transmitter was used by Queen Wilhelmina to address the people in the West Indies (Suriname and the Caribbean) for the first time as well as the East Indies. The Philips transmitter was also used to relay broadcasts on behalf of the BBC to the British colonies. These successes triggered an initiative to provide broadcasting services aimed at listeners in the East Indies. With the support of Dutch companies operating there a new entity was established: N.V. Philips' Omroep Holland-Indië (PHOHI). In 1928 trial operations started using a new transmitter and tower built in Huizen. In 1935 the Dutch government consolidated all broadcast transmitters through a new entity, NOZEMA, which undertook the renewal of the transmitters at a new location, with NSF supplying the equipment (de Boer, 1969; Vles, 2008; Vogt, 1958). The accumulated know-how on radio engineering in general and at Philips and the technical universities in particular contributed to the knowledge base of the NCR Engineering Centre, facilitating the innovation journey of Wi-Fi.

Following this overview of the institutional and technical framework conditions in the Netherlands, we now move on to the actor level.

8.4   The actor level: knowledge interactions

At the third level of the model (Figure 8.1), the actor level, we find private sector firms, universities, public entities and the government as they pertain to a specific industrial sector. The knowledge function and knowledge output of these four types of actors is depicted in Table 8.1.

Table 8.1 *Knowledge function and output of the four types of actors*

Types of agents	Knowledge function	Knowledge output
Government	• Public agents – e.g. Ministries of Education, Industry and Economic Affairs • Related agencies • Government administration • Political parties	• Institutions related to knowledge creation
Universities and scientific councils	• Education and training • Basic research • Research cooperation	• Embodied knowledge • Codified knowledge
Public entities	• Public R&D laboratories • Mission-oriented bodies – e.g. technical support agencies • Publicly owned companies – e.g. utilities • Technology transfer units	• Embodied knowledge • Codified knowledge
Private entities, firms	• Routine activity enterprises • R&D laboratories • R&D cooperation	• Embodied knowledge • Codified knowledge

Source: Based on van der Steen (1999).

Government   The public agents involved in the process of making technology policy in the Netherlands relevant to the ICT industry included the Ministry of Economic Affairs, the Ministry of Education, Culture and Science, the Ministry of Finance, the Supervisory Board on Science and Technology and the political parties. More recently, the 'Innovation Platform' and 'ICT-Regie' have been added as organisational entities to support the government by facilitating interaction within the sector.[10]

The Ministry of Economic Affairs is the main technology policy maker, focusing chiefly on the private business sector. This is the ministry that is charged with the coordination of technology policy with the other ministries. The Ministry of Education, Culture and Science is primarily responsible for science policies, which includes the universities, as well as for the coordination of science-related policies among the various ministries. The Supervisory Board on Science and Technology provides general advice to the government in the various areas of science and technology policies. Based on their expenditures on science and technology policies, these two ministries account for almost two-thirds of all spending (van der Steen, 1999). Other ministries spend significant amounts on science and technology in their specific fields of health care, agriculture, transport and water regulation.

Universities and scientific councils   There are thirteen universities in the Netherlands, including three universities of technology, located in Delft,

Eindhoven and Enschede (the University of Twente), which added other dis-
ciplines. The universities receive most of their funding from the Ministry of
Education, Culture and Science. This is known as 'first-stream funding', and
in 1994 it represented approximately 60 per cent of total funding (van der
Steen, 1999). The universities are also able to apply for project-based funding
through the Dutch Scientific Research Council (Nederlandse organisatie voor
Wetenschappelijk Onderzoek – NWO) and through the European Commission.
This is called 'second-stream funding', representing some 30 per cent of the
funding in 1994. Finally, there is the 'third-stream funding', which comes from
other sources, including the private sector. The Royal Netherlands Academy of
Arts and Sciences (Koninklijke Nederlandse Academie van Wetenschappen –
KNAW), the second scientific council, acts as an advisory board to the Ministry
of Education, Culture and Science. The KNAW also provides grants for young
researchers and funds several research institutes.

Public sector entities Public sector entities encompass publicly
financed R&D laboratories, including the TNO (the Netherlands Organisation for Applied Scientific Research), five large sector-specific technological
institutes and many smaller specialised institutes.

Private sector entities Private sector entities include the innovation
activities carried out within the various firms, either independently or in cooperation with others in a variety of forms.

Knowledge flows At the actor level we recognise the creation and
diffusion of knowledge.

In the following sections we illustrate these knowledge flows as they relate
to the Wi-Fi case: from Philips to NCR; the knowledge interactions with the
universities of technology; the connected but also competing innovation journey
related to Bluetooth; and the knowledge flow to other entrepreneurial activities
connected to the Wi-Fi innovation journey. These entrepreneurial activities
illustrate the 'embodiment' of the knowledge flows involved.

8.4.1 *The NCR Systems Engineering Centre and its knowledge network*

Multiple knowledge flows can be identified at the personal level that connect
to the NCR Systems Engineering Centre in Utrecht. There is (1) an industrial
linkage to Philips Electronics, through Bruce Tuch. There are (2) multiple linkages to universities, for example to the Eindhoven University of Technology,
through Tuch's MSc thesis work, and to the Delft University of Technology,
through the PhD research on SAW filters by Jaap Haartsen, who later became
the inventor/innovator of Bluetooth. There is (3) the entrepreneurial activity at
the University of Twente, which led to the early adoption of Wi-Fi technology
and the start-up called No Wires Needed (NWN). Other connections relate to

(4) intra-industry flows of knowledge: examples include Haartsen, who worked at Ericsson on the Bluetooth developments; Cees Links, who once he had concluded his Wi-Fi development work at Agere Systems created the start-up now called GreenPeak Technologies, to work on ultra-short-range devices also known as Zigbee; Richard van Nee, who moved to Airgo (a company recently acquired by Qualcomm) to become technology architect for the development of high-data-rate devices using multiple input/multiple output (MIMO) technology; Tuch, who, after having dissolved the Wi-Fi-related activities at Agere Systems, became the vice-president of the Business Development and Strategic Ventures Division at Motorola; and Vic Hayes, who joined the Delft University of Technology as a senior research fellow in order to contribute to this book. In the following sections we touch upon these examples of 'embodied' knowledge flows and describe the RF developments in which they are engaged.

8.4.2   NCR/AT&T/Lucent Technologies: being part of a multinational corporation

The Utrecht Systems Engineering Centre at the start of the Wi-Fi journey was part of NCR, which had its headquarters in Dayton, Ohio. Within NCR, its R&D activities were an integral part of the various business divisions, which were relatively independent. A comparatively small corporate centre coordinated the R&D activities between the divisions and took on the role of ensuring that R&D-related synergies were achieved across the corporation. During this period the expertise of the Utrecht Systems Engineering Centre was fairly self-contained. The flow of knowledge between the divisions was small-scale, and most knowledge was brought in through the hiring of new staff and the use of scientific literature and other sources, or was obtained through the company's own R&D efforts.

When AT&T acquired NCR in 1991, the Utrecht centre transitioned from the Financial Systems Division to the Network Products Division. As it became clear that the technology had an application scope beyond the NCR/AT&T product range, the group was transferred to the NCR Microelectronics Division, which was used to supply technology to the competition. When NCR considered selling its semiconductor activities, the WLAN group lobbied for a move to AT&T Network Systems. This request was accepted, and the group became part of the Wireless Business Unit.[11]

Within AT&T, and later within Lucent Technologies, R&D was carried out both centrally, as part of headquarters' activities, and in a distributed form, as part of the various product divisions, all the research groups together comprising the world-famous Bell Labs. In the central labs the more fundamental research was carried out, whereas within the divisions the R&D was very much product- or service-related. Within these corporations the sum spent on R&D would typically amount to 10 to 14 per cent of turnover, with the basic research – the 'R' component – receiving funding at the level of approximately 2 per cent of turnover. The strong emphasis within these corporations on the role of R&D provided the Engineering Centre, in principle, with access to a very large knowledge base. For AT&T and for Lucent Technologies alike, however, the most important customers were the Bell operating companies and AT&T itself, the major telecommunications operators in the United States. The product portfolio was centred around (large) switching and transmission systems, although, within the corporation, there were also products aimed at the enterprise market. In fact, NCR went on to become the core of the new Global Information Systems Division within AT&T.[12] Telecommunication systems aimed at the enterprise market were provided by the Information Systems Division and included a wide range of PABXs and key systems, while in the Consumer Products Division the emphasis was on payphones, telephone sets, cordless phones and related products.

Within this portfolio Wi-Fi was rather special. In its development, therefore, it did not benefit significantly from the mainstream activities within the corporation. In fact, it became the object of internal rivalry when the AT&T Consumer Products Division suggested 'blast[ing] WaveLAN out of the band' to create space for a new digital cordless phone (see the account by Cees Links in Chapter 4). Within Lucent Technologies, Wi-Fi development at one point became part of the Wireless Division – a unit that was primarily concerned with mobile systems such as CDMA and GSM. From the point of view of divisional management, the emerging opportunities for fixed wireless access systems were more attractive than the outlook for Wi-Fi, a product that would not be marketed to telecom operators, and so, for a period of time, funding was directed away from Wi-Fi, as were the R&D staff involved. As we have seen in Chapter 4, the call from Steve Jobs to Rich McGinn changed the entire course of events.

The direct benefit that AT&T (and later Lucent Technologies) brought to the Wi-Fi development team was the in-house Microelectronics Division, which had its own IC design and production facilities. This allowed the team in Utrecht to benefit from large-scale integration, in-house design support and quick turnaround times for sample production. These capabilities were vital factors in meeting the challenge that the contract with Apple had set in terms of cost reduction.

A tangible example of benefit being derived from the association with Bell Labs is in the development of the 'turbo version', when Tuch engaged the support of Bell Labs scientist and mathematician Israel bar-David, who spent his sabbatical year in Utrecht supporting the design of an 8 Mbit/s WLAN version, based on the new PPM technique.

In the end the Wi-Fi-related activities became part of Agere Systems, the former Microelectronics Division of Lucent Technologies that was made an independent company through a spin-off in 2001. After the acquisition by

Proxim of the infrastructure-related business in 2002, the focus of the development team was purely on chips and chipsets.

In hindsight, and according to the staff involved, Wi-Fi development benefited from the relatively large distance between the Utrecht Engineering Centre and Lucent Technologies' corporate headquarters in Murray Hill, New Jersey. With the R&D expenses involved being relatively moderate and the cost of closing down the activities being perceived as high, the Engineering Centre survived the close scrutiny by headquarters staff. In that way it was able to survive during the long gestation time, until the first profits were generated in 1996 and the business finally broke even in 2000.

8.4.3   Philips and Co.

Philips Electronics has a long history going back to 1891, when the company was founded as Philips and Co. by Frederik Philips and his son Gerard to manufacture incandescent lamps and other electrical articles, as well as the trading thereof (Heerding, 1980). The technology deployed for the manufacturing of incandescent lamps provided the company with a good starting point to produce vacuum or electron tubes as well, also called (thermionic) valves, used in radios to detect and amplify the RF signal. This applied in particular to the materials technology, the evacuation of the tubes, the behaviour of electrons in gases, and the sealing between glass and metal (Blanken, 1992).

In 1918 the first radio valves of 'type A' were manufactured by Philips, initiated by an order placed by à Steringa Idzerda to produce receiving triodes in modest volume, and also to produce transmitting triodes to build a transmitting station. In 1921 around 300 triodes of 'type D' were produced and an additional 100 transmitting valves in a workshop that was part of the NatLab, involving around four skilled production staff. The NatLab research was at the time aimed at improving incandescent lamps, which involved research into the properties of wolfram and the study of gas discharges, for which the German physicist Gustav Hertz was brought to Eindhoven.[13]

The NatLab had been established in 1913, and Gilles Holst and Ekko Oosterhuis were the first two scientists who were employed there. Both had previously worked at the Kamerlingh Onnes Laboratory of the University of Leiden, which had become world-famous for its low-temperature physics research.[14] To strengthen the NatLab's relationships with universities and to make it easier to attract scientists to work in an industrial laboratory, Holst, as the lab's director, organised research colloquia on a regular basis. The Austrian physicist Paul Ehrenfeld, who was working at the University of Leiden, would regularly attend these colloquia. Other participants were, for instance, Walther Kossel, James Franck, Wolfgang Pauli, Otto Stern, Albert Einstein, Hendrik Kramers and Arnold Sommerfeld (Blanken, 1992; de Vries, 2005).

From 1922 onwards the NatLab also focused on electronic valves, following a sharp increase in demand that had been initiated by a major order for 5,000 triodes placed by the Belgium government, followed in August by a contract for the delivery of 5,000 valves per month to Société Indépendente de Télégraphie sans Fil (SIF) of France. From then on demand for valves would not be determined any more by radio-telephony but by the needs arising from radio broadcasting. In 1925 Philips decided to engage in the manufacturing of radio sets. In 1926, to obtain the necessary manufacturing capacity, Philips took over the shares of NSF, which had run into financial distress. The following year the first two radio types aimed at the general public were demonstrated at the Jaarbeurs in Utrecht. In the first year demand was much greater than supply, but this situation had been reversed by the end of 1928, with total sales of 51,000 sets that year. Manufacturing capacity had to be expanded dramatically, in Eindhoven and in Hilversum. By 1930 the floor space in Eindhoven was doubled, and the total complement of staff had grown from 7,000 in 1925 to 23,000. The production of valves peaked at 11 million in 1929, falling back to 8.6 million in 1932 then climbing again to 11 million in 1934. In the same period, despite the Great Depression, the volume of radio sets being sold grew steadily from 200,000 to 670,000 (Blanken, 1992; Vogt, 1958).

The NatLab contributed to the development of the radio through, for instance, the development of the pentode, an amplifier tube designed by Bernhard Tellegen in 1926, resulting in one of the most important patents for Philips prior to the Second World War. Dr Balthasar van der Pol analysed the behaviour of feedback in amplifying circuits, and his team worked on the concept of the superheterodyne, which replaced the tuned radio frequency type, having a broader tuning range from 20 to 150 MHz.[15] In 1923 Holst and L. E. J. Brouwer introduced the chromium-iron melting technique for connecting metal to glass. This process enabled the production of water-cooled transmitter tubes of more than 20 kW (de Vries, 2005).

In 1935 the NatLab started to conduct research related to television. A TV transmitter for trial purposes was completed in Eindhoven in that year, mainly in response to activities taking place in Britain, which led to regular TV broadcasts by the BBC from Alexandra Palace in 1936. In 1938 Philips decided to start the development of a TV set for the general public and to give priority to the creation of a portfolio of patents in this field. The project was interrupted by the Second World War just before it reached the production phase (Blanken, 1992).

After the war NSF was transformed into N.V. Philips Telecommunicatie Industrie (PTI), with an expanded range of products, including TV transmitters, FM radio transmitters, cable multiplexing systems, teletype over radio (TOR), radar, telegraph switching and automatic telephone switching systems (PTI, 1955; Vogt, 1958). In this period close relationships developed with the Delft

University of Technology, through Professor Bähler, Professor Unk and, later, Professor de Kroes in the field of telephony, and Professor von Weiler in the field of radar technology. Professors Unk and de Kroes combined their senior management responsibilities within PTI with their academic engagements.

Between 1914 and 1960 the NatLab grew from an organisation with two scientists and a few laboratory assistants to one of 2,200 employees. In the period from 1946 to 1972 the majority of the scientists were recruited from the Delft University of Technology (about 300), and later some (100) were also recruited from the Eindhoven University of Technology, established in 1956. Other universities that supplied scientists included the University of Amsterdam (60), Utrecht (60), Leiden (50), the Free University of Amsterdam (25) and the University of Groningen (20) (de Vries, 2005). In parallel, the R&D activities within the product divisions expanded significantly, including the Elcoma Division and Philips Telecommunicatie Industrie.[16]

8.4.4   Knowledge flow: Philips to NCR

In Chapter 2 Bruce Tuch provided an account of his involvement in RF technology, combining his work at Philips with his studies at the Eindhoven University of Technology, which is repeated here in an abridged form:

I had already been working for four years in the Netherlands, in one of the largest consumer electronic companies, Philips, and one of the few left outside Japan that actually was doing R&D for large-volume consumer electronics markets. Philips was a great place, as I wanted to apply my background to 'real electrical engineering' with communications and radio waves – a forgotten field, since in the 1980s all electrical engineers gravitated towards the digital revolution. I wanted to learn more. I combined my work with getting my Dutch engineering degree at the Eindhoven University of Technology, which had to do with simulating RF IC behaviour with 'non-linearity' (in other words, predicting difficult circuit behaviour). I really learned the most from the lifetime experience of my Philips RF colleagues; some of whom had been working in the field for many years and had gained their RF 'wisdom' by experience. They could really 'feel' what a circuit would do. Yes, it could almost seem mystical: that 'black magician', who would lightly wave his hand over a circuit section, look at some display and determine how to fix things. I was at the crossover of this 'older art' and the new engineering generation, who tried to apply the rigour of analytic prediction as well, but still loved to keep some of that feeling.

Just before leaving from Philips to work for NCR at the Utrecht Engineering Centre, I finished working on the second RF/analogue design with my Philips colleagues, an RF tuner IC that would replace most of the components in a television tuner; this was a real breakthrough-type product at the time, going up to the UHF (800 MHz) frequency channels.

Through this transition, vital expertise in RF design moved from Philips Electronics 'in person' to NCR.

8.5 University to industry linkages: the Eindhoven, Delft and Twente Universities of Technology

While at NCR, Tuch found himself engaged again with the university world, this time with the Delft University of Technology, to obtain expertise on the implementation of surface acoustic wave filters. Tuch relates the story (see Chapter 4 for the broader context):

The challenge we were facing was to find the best approach to achieve the receiver function for spread spectrum. One option was to use ICs with digital signal processing techniques totally or to augment this with a component called a surface acoustic wave filter to take on the 'heavy lifting' of doing the spread-spectrum processing. At the time SAW filters for this type of function were military components costing US$100 or more each! I knew that this could be done by normal silicon-processing techniques that NCR had available in the Microelectronics Division; we just did not understand the design aspects. I contacted Professor Venema at Delft University of Technology, who was an expert in SAW devices, and started a research programme (NCR sponsored a PhD student from Delft, Jaap Haartsen) to design a 'SAW spread-spectrum demodulator' at different code lengths. This resulted in a working design (which we actually used in a wireless LAN demo unit) with a projected cost of less than US$5.

The 'PhD student from Delft', Haartsen, later worked in the field of data communications and became the inventor of the Bluetooth technology at Ericsson (see subsection 8.6.1 on Bluetooth below).

Another example of university knowledge being leveraged in the development of Wi-Fi relates to the beginning of the feasibility study period, as Hayes indicated that there was not much information available at the Engineering Centre on the propagation characteristics of indoor radio in the 900 MHz band. This information gap was (at least in part) filled by using the PhD research of Theodore Rappaport on indoor propagation, a dissertation research project executed at Purdue University, in Indiana, and concluded in 1987.[17]

Not only knowledge was being exchanged, but students at Twente University who were engaged in RF research recognised the potential of the new technology and founded a new company.

8.5.1 No Wires Needed: jumping on the bandwagon

Ronald Brockmann, one of the founders and former chief technology officer of this Netherlands-based start-up company, recounts the story of its creation and development.

In 1992 the students behind the magazine *HackTic* launched the first Dutch internet-based e-mail provider, which would lead to the first Dutch public ISP, called XS4ALL. This led to our vision that internet traffic could best be carried without wires. Accordingly, we started an investigation into wireless connectivity options and standards in that field. In 1993 this led to the founding of No Wires Needed BV, with its offices at the University of Twente campus. The nine-person team that founded the company consisted of students at the university with protocol expertise, a group of technology experts from Amsterdam with processing hardware expertise, and a management consultant to help our young team in business matters. From the outset the decision was made to actively follow the IEEE 802.11 standardisation process, which was at that time in the early phase of its development, but already appeared very promising.

Being on a shoestring budget but with high ambitions, several trade-offs had to be made. Clearly, there was no budget to custom-design ICs. Hence, the radio was purchased from GEC Plessey, which was offering a 2.4 GHz transceiver. We decided that the MAC was to be based on the ARM610, a 32 bit microprocessor core that was based on a reduced instruction set computing (RISC) design, which was available as a stand-alone IC, supported by field-programmable gate arrays for peripheral support. Our concept to use a standard 32 bit RISC core and write all MAC firmware in C code using standard tools – as opposed to applying semi-hard-wired ICs – was revolutionary at the time and very powerful, but also expensive. Fortunately, as IC technology progressed, the use of a RISC core became lower in cost, while the MAC implementations remained much more powerful than traditional approaches, giving us a clear competitive advantage.

NWN positioned itself as a supplier of value-added IEEE-802.11-compliant WLAN and bridge technology, as well as products with the 'most flexible' MAC through its software implementation. For instance, NWN appreciated the weaknesses of WEP security very early on, and launched AirLock (based on an enhanced cipher and public key cryptography) as a better alternative in 1998.[18]

NWN was one of the few successful Dutch technology start-ups of the early internet era. The company attracted angel funding in 1996, then venture capital funding in 1998, from Gilde IT and PARNIB (totalling approximately US$4 million). NWN successfully concluded a second round of funding through Kennet Capital and 3Com in 1999. In the period from 1993 to 1999 the number of staff grew to around sixty-five, with offices in California and New Jersey in the United States, as well as Coventry in the United Kingdom. The second round of funding allowed NWN to design its own MAC ICs. By this time NWN had become the only independent provider of IEEE 802.11 MAC technology in the world, allowing it to partner with several baseband/radio IC providers. We became, for instance, an OEM supplier to Compaq.

As the market matured it became clear that digital MAC and PHY chipsets would start to integrate. As a result, Intersil, the market leader in physical layer chipsets, actively started to try and acquire No Wires Needed, which at that time had a turnover of around US$2 million. Intersil was the former semiconductor unit of US-based Harris Corporation, which had become an independent entity through an initial public offering (IPO) in early 2000. The acquisition of NWN was concluded in the spring of that year, for the sum of US$115 million, in shares.

After the acquisition by Intersil the team continued to operate from its Bilthoven office, and, based on its strong market position and MAC expertise, made fundamental contributions to a more mature Wi-Fi standard, including the key MAC mechanisms of 802.11g (the coexistence of OFDM and CCK modulation), improved security (TKIP and AES-CCM) in 802.11i and the fundamentals of QoS operation in 802.11e to support VoIP and video. At Intersil we also produced the first single-chip Linux-based access point.

As the market became more competitive, with many new entrants, Intersil sold its WLAN unit to GlobespanVirata in 2003, which merged with Conexant in 2004. As part of a large-scale cost reduction effort the Bilthoven site was shut down in 2005, the activities being transferred to a company division in India. In the same year Brockmann founded Avinity to pursue internet-TV-related opportunities.

8.5.2   MIMO: multiple data flows

Another early university-related link involved a student from the Eindhoven University of Technology, Allert van Zelst, who joined the NCR Engineering Centre in order to execute his Masters graduation project in early 1994. This project was aimed at increasing the data rate of WLANs by exploiting space division multiplexing using multiple-antenna techniques, a principle known as multiple input/multiple output. He graduated in the autumn of 1994 and resumed his research on the topic of MIMO in 1999, as part of pursuing his PhD at Eindhoven. This research project was executed at and sponsored by Lucent Technologies, and later Agere Systems.[19] The research carried out at the Utrecht Engineering Centre, resulted in a test system demonstrating the feasibility of MIMO at data rates up to 162 Mbit/s. This was a first in the industry, and it drew considerable attention from the press (see, for example, Walko, 2002).

During his research van Zelst coached two more Masters students from the Eindhoven University of Technology at the Utrecht Engineering Centre: Tim Schenk, who started his MSc project early in the summer of 2001, on the 'Synchronisation of multiple-input multiple-output OFDM', and continued the research later, resulting in his PhD thesis 'RF impairment in multiple-antenna OFDM: influence and mitigation',[20] at Eindhoven in November 2006; and Robert van Poppel, who started his MSc project in the late summer of 2002, on the 'Analysis and measurement of wideband MIMO radio channels in indoor environments at 5.2 GHz'.[21]

In 2004, on the completion of his dissertation under the title of 'MIMO OFDM for wireless LANs' (van Zelst, 2004), van Zelst joined Airgo, a start-up company founded by people from Cisco and Lucent Technologies in 2001, with offices in Palo Alto and Breukelen, the Netherlands. There he joined his former thesis coach and one of the founders of Airgo, Dr Richard van Nee, who had left Lucent Technologies early in 2001 so as to be able to speed up the commercialisation of MIMO OFDM.

While working at Airgo they contributed extensively to the IEEE 802.11n working group, aimed at providing data rates of at least 100 Mbit/s with options of up to 600 Mbit/s – a significant increase compared to the then current IEEE 802.11g products with a maximum data rate of 54 Mbit/s, which would permit genuine competition with the 100 Mbit/s and 1 Gbit/s data rates of wired Ethernet.

Although the principle of MIMO looks quite straightforward, namely using multiple transmitters and receivers at the same carrier frequency to send multiple data streams to increase the data rate, the challenge is to recover these streams at the receiver. Van Zelst provides the background to this novel technique:

Research in information theory performed in the early 1990s had shown that important improvements in spectral efficiency can be achieved when multiple antennae are used at both the transmitter and the receiver sides, especially in rich-scattering environments (see, for example, Telatar, 1999). This resulted in a lot of research activity to develop practical communication schemes.[22] Two major schemes emerged: space-time coding (STC) and space division multiplexing (SDM). In STC the performance of the system is increased using different representations of the same data stream at each transmitter through encoding. In SDM a higher throughput is achieved by transmitting independent data streams at the different transmitters using the same carrier frequency. In the case of STC, advanced signal-processing algorithms at the receiver combine the signals to enhance the performance. In the case of SDM, advanced signal-processing algorithms recover the parallel streams of data, which are 'mixed up' in the air, using multiple receiving antennae.

The highest spectral efficiency gains are achieved when the individual channels, from every transmitting antenna to every receiving antenna, can be regarded as being independent. In practice this is the case in rich-scattering environments with, preferably, no direct communication path – i.e. no line of sight path being present between the transmitter and the receiver. This makes MIMO a very attractive technique for wireless LANs, as they are used primarily in indoor environments. It should be noted that this finding is counter-intuitive for most radio engineers, as, in free space, line of sight connections provide the better transmission performance.

Applying MIMO to WLANs would mean building upon the IEEE 802.11a/g standards, which use orthogonal frequency division multiplexing. The main reason that OFDM was selected as the transmission protocol for these standards is its capability to deal with the strong multi-path propagation effects present in indoor communication environments. In these environments the signals combine and lead to fading, whereby the received signal varies as a function of frequency, location and time. OFDM is an example of a multi-carrier technique that operates with specific orthogonality constraints between the sub-carriers to achieve high transmission quality. Although the OFDM principle has been around for many years, the state of the art of technology in the early 1990s finally made implementation feasible in practical terms. The robustness of OFDM against frequency selective fading and the favourable properties of indoor radio channels for SDM techniques made the combination a very attractive candidate for the high data rate extensions pursued by task group 'n' of the IEEE 802.11 working group. It is also the basis for the IEEE 802.16 standard that is known as WiMAX.[23]

Next to the transmission challenges described above, the introduction of MIMO was accompanied by the use of a wider transmission channel, from 20 to 40 MHz, and packet aggregation to reduce the transmission overhead.

Furthermore, coexistence issues had to be resolved, as legacy IEEE 802.11b/g devices cannot detect IEEE 802.11n transmissions, but do suffer from significant interference by IEEE 802.11n equipment. The additional benefit of having multiple antennae is the possibility of beam forming, which allows the range of transmission to be extended, for which multiple contending techniques were being proposed in the standards arena (see van Nee, 2006, 2007). The state of the art in this area is described in several recent books, such as the one by Boelcskei et al. (2006).

Airgo became the first company to provide MIMO-based consumer products with a 108 Mbit/s PC card, in 2003, to be followed by a 240 Mbit/s mini-card in 2007, the latter integrated in products by companies such as Linksys. In December 2006 Airgo was acquired by Qualcomm. This can be seen as a metaphorical 'closing of the circle', as Qualcomm was founded in 1985 in the United States to exploit spread-spectrum technologies, only to become the leader in CDMA technology (Lemstra and Hayes, 2009; Mock, 2005).

This account concludes the series of examples of knowledge flow involving universities. In the following section two examples are provided of developments of (in part) competing technologies and knowledge networks; both linked to the development of Wi-Fi.

8.6   Competing technologies and knowledge networks

8.6.1   Bluetooth: the need for ad hoc connectivity

Another university-related link involves Jaap Haartsen, who graduated at the Department of Electrical Engineering at the Delft University of Technology in 1986. Subsequently he started his PhD research, and became the 'PhD student from Delft' who provided the knowledge input on SAW filters and developed a product prototype for NCR as part of the feasibility study, which ran from 1986 to 1988. He concluded his PhD research in 1990 cum laude under the title 'Programmable SAW detection for on-chip programmable RF filters'. He then started work in the field of data communications with Ericsson in the United States and Sweden, and since 1999 he has been with Ericsson Radio Systems in Emmen, the Netherlands. In 2000 Haartsen was appointed as a (part-time) professor at the University of Twente in the field of mobile communications systems, with a focus on ad-hoc networking. From 1994 onwards, while at Ericsson, he was instrumental in the development of Bluetooth.

This positions the start of the Bluetooth innovation journey almost a decade after the start of the Wi-Fi journey. What follows is Haartsen's account of the genesis of Bluetooth:[24]

Channel-oriented   Device-oriented

Figure 8.2 Channel-oriented versus device-oriented approaches

Wi-Fi IEEE 802.11 can be considered as the success story for the wireless local area network. Likewise, Bluetooth™ can be considered as the success story for the wireless personal area network (WPAN). Back in 1994 the original motivation for developing the Bluetooth technology was to increase the sales of mobile phones by adding a wireless interface for local connectivity. This allowed the phone to connect to a myriad of local accessories. A new radio technology was required, optimised for establishing ad hoc connections, with the emphasis on low power consumption and low cost implementation. The applications of Bluetooth did not end at the mobile telephone, and small radios quickly found their way into all kinds of PC and consumer products, ranging from mice and keyboards to audio-streaming headsets and car kits.

The development of Bluetooth should be regarded as a development that was one of a kind. It shares the 2.4 GHz ISM band with Wi-Fi, but that is where the commonalities end. Wi-Fi is an access technology optimised for accessing a fixed network. In contrast, Bluetooth is an ad hoc technology optimised for making spontaneous connections between two units when in radio range. There is a major difference in the way connections are established. In Wi-Fi, radio nodes try to connect to a channel (either established centrally by an access point or distributed by stations). Only after accessing the channel are logical connections made to other nodes connected to that channel. In contrast, a Bluetooth radio node connects directly to another radio node. Therefore, only those nodes that really communicate with each other share a single channel. Figure 8.2 illustrates the general concepts of the channel-oriented WiFi approach and the device-oriented Bluetooth approach. Bluetooth applications are really personal applications, in which small ad hoc networks, piconets, are created among radio nodes for personal use.

For WPAN applications, the use of many different piconets, each belonging to the personal bubble of a user, is essential.

The birth of a new technology

A Bluetooth link can be regarded as a general cable replacement. Unlike a cable, though, a radio poses extra challenges, such as interference from other radios, finding other nodes to connect to, allowing multiple simultaneous connections, and low power consumption. In addition, the need for the ad hoc connectivity leads to new design requirements.

For the PHY layer, the selection of the RF band is essential. Because no infrastructure is present that would tie the radio operation to a restricted geographical area, an unlicensed radio band had to be found that is globally available. The 2.4 GHz ISM band appeared to be such a band, but it is not free from interference (although, back in 1994, its usage was still marginal; microwave ovens were regarded as the biggest menace). In addition, spectrum regulations demanded the use of spread-spectrum technology. Frequency hopping rather than direct sequence spread spectrum was selected for a number of reasons. (1) FH radios spread their signals over the entire 80 MHz ISM band but, at any one time, only a narrow channel of 1 MHz is occupied, offering better resilience to interference and near–far problems (in which the stronger signal of nearby stations makes the reception of weaker stations further away difficult). (2) It was felt, given the state of the art of technology in 1994, that FH radios would cost less to realise than DS radios. (3) Although FH radio did not have the potential for high data rates, this was not considered important since the channel would be shared only between a few personal devices. (4) Robustness in an interference-prone environment was the major driving point behind the choice of FH radios.

The motto became 'Filter and survive', meaning that most of the signals in the ISM spectrum were rejected by out-of-band filtering. This has proven to be a good strategy, especially considering the increased usage of the 2.4 GHz ISM band. The initial FH characteristics of Bluetooth closely followed the FH mode of the original IEEE 802.11 standard, which in itself was set by the FCC part 15 rules. GFSK modulation and hopping over seventy-nine carriers became the key radio parameters for Bluetooth. For a certain period, from 1995 to 1996, the use of a FH radio front-end serving a dual-mode Wi-Fi/Bluetooth transceiver was considered. Over time, however, it became clear that the non-hopping Wi-Fi variants had become dominant in the marketplace, and thus the dual-mode idea was eventually abandoned. Bluetooth applies a rather fast hopping rate – 1,600 hops per second. For each new packet transmitted, a new hop carrier is used.

Establishing a connection for two FH radios is a challenge. FH synchronisation requires the radio to align both in time and in frequency. Because of robustness (and, initially, regulatory) requirements, the initial uncertainty in frequency is large: each Bluetooth radio uses a thirty-two-hop sequence to establish a connection. Because of power consumption constraints (the receiver scans the frequencies only at a low duty cycle to save power), the initial uncertainty in time is also large. It was recognised that the units in an ad hoc technology are in stand-by mode most of the time. Therefore, all the effort to solve the initial time frequency uncertainty should be placed at the unit that tries to make a connection, which happens only occasionally. A Bluetooth unit in stand-by scans the thirty-two set-up carriers with a low duty cycle of about 1 per cent. The unit trying to make contact transmits control messages sequentially on all thirty-two set-up carriers at a hopping rate of 3,200 hops per second.

The Bluetooth technology provides true peer connectivity. There is no notion of uplink or downlink: time division duplex (TDD) is used to define two directions on the radio link. The absence of duplexers further reduces cost and power consumption. There is no central arbiter that controls the traffic in the air. Interference is minimised by applying different hop sequences for different piconets. From the start, it has been envisaged that Bluetooth will carry voice. In order to obtain QoS within the piconet, master and slave roles are defined. One unit on the piconet channel is assigned the master role whereas the rest are slaves. A master-controlled polling scheme is applied to prevent collisions on the piconet channel. Although FH provides robustness in an interference-prone and multi-path fading environment, the occasional loss of a packet cannot be prevented. Therefore, at the MAC layer, a fast retransmission protocol is used. Packets are sent back and forth between the units and piggyback acknowledged/not acknowledged information in their headers. Within 1.25 milliseconds the success or failure of a packet reception is notified and a retransmission can be applied if necessary.

Around 2000 it was recognised that Bluetooth serving the WPAN applications and Wi-Fi serving the WLAN applications would be the two winning technologies in the consumer electronics and personal computer environments. They share the same 2.4 GHz ISM band, however, and would probably be embedded in the same device (first a laptop/PC, later a mobile phone). To allow undisturbed communications in environments in which Wi-Fi and Bluetooth radios coexist, adaptive frequency hopping was specified in version 1.2 of the Bluetooth standard in 2004. Bluetooth units can now identify the frequencies used by near-by Wi-Fi radios and hop around those frequencies. In addition, schemes have been invented to control the traffic in the Bluetooth and Wi-Fi radios when implemented in the same product, avoiding simultaneous transmission and reception on the part of both radios; packet traffic arbitration (PTA) is the best-known technique.

From idea to market

Introducing a new technology for new uses and getting general market acceptance is not an easy task. The first concepts around Bluetooth were developed late in 1994, within the research facilities of Ericsson Mobile Phones in Lund, Sweden. Two research targets were defined: (1) developing a wireless technology for local connectivity around the mobile phone supporting both voice and data applications; and (2) developing a radio technology that allowed full complementary metal oxide semiconductor (CMOS) chip implementation. The latter target resulted in an iterative development process between CMOS circuit design and radio protocol design.

Early in 1997 Ericsson decided to share the technology with other parties. The main reason was that an ecosystem needed to be developed incorporating products that were not being produced by Ericsson, such as laptop computers. It was Intel that first recognised the full potential of the Bluetooth concept. It was decided to approach more parties to represent the mobile industry (Ericsson and Nokia) and the PC industry (IBM, Toshiba and Intel) better. These five companies became the first promoters of the Bluetooth Special Interest Group (SIG), which was established in February 1998. The first task of the SIG was to make the technology known to the entire industry. The first Bluetooth developers' conference was held in Atlanta, Georgia, in October 1998. By the end of that year more than 400 companies had already signed up as adopters of the technology. To accelerate the pace of adoption, the SIG has decided to use a zero-RAND IPR policy. Once ready, the specification would be free for everybody to download. IPR rights would be invoked only on specific implementations of the technology (see Chapter 3, section 10.1, for a discussion of intellectual property rights in relation to standards). Rapid acceptance was also envisaged by the cost target of a complete transceiver solution, which should be as low as US$5 for large volumes. Any additional royalties would compromise this low cost target.

It was in May 1999 that Bluetooth technology was launched commercially, in London. During the course of 1998 and 1999 the initial radio concept developed by Ericsson had been further refined, and protocol layers had been added by the five promoter companies. The first Bluetooth specification (version 1.0) was released in July 1999 and the first commercial products (among which were headsets, PC cards and dongles) followed during 2000.

In the years directly following the launch, expectations regarding Bluetooth technology were set very high. The technology was envisaged as being correct for virtually every new user in the local connectivity area. Like any new technology, though, producing stable solutions and guaranteeing full interoperability takes time. The financial crisis between 2001 and 2003, which disrupted the entire telecom industry, further delayed the mass proliferation foreseen for Bluetooth radios. From 2004, however, the mass production of Bluetooth chipsets really took off, boosted by the increase of mobile phone sales. In October 2006 the milestone of 1 billion Bluetooth radios installed was reached, with a weekly shipment of 12 million radios. By that time, the number of adopter companies had exceeded 7,500 and the cost of a Bluetooth solution had fallen to US$2.

Ericsson AB is the leading company behind the Bluetooth technology, and as early as 1998 it had dedicated an entire site at Emmen for the development of Bluetooth technology and products. In 2002 this location became a Sony Ericsson development site for Bluetooth accessories such as headsets and hands-free car kits. Moreover, at the science park near the University of Twente, Ericsson established a research centre dedicated to wireless technology. During the last decade of the twentieth century the R&D activities of Ericsson in Enschede were focused on DECT – digital cordless – solutions. The R&D site also played a role in the development of UMTS base stations for the Ericsson Group, based on W-CDMA radio access technology. Due to restructuring in the aftermath of the internet/telecom bubble, this entity was closed down. Some of the staff continued the wireless-related research through a new company, however: Twente Institute for Wireless and Mobile Communication.

Philips Semiconductor NV (nowadays known as NXP) has produced millions of Bluetooth chips, which are incorporated in numerous consumer products. Professor Haartsen now works at Sony Ericsson.

8.6.2   ZigBee: ultra short range

Chapter 4 includes a number of contributions by Cees Links in his capacity as the product line manager of WLANs at NCR and its corporate successors. Links stayed with the NCR Engineering Centre until 2002, the same year the WLAN infrastructure business was sold to Proxim. The remaining silicon-related activities were closed down in 2004. That year he started his own company, Xanadu Wireless, based in Utrecht, to focus on technology related to IEEE 802.15.4 and ZigBee standards for short-range devices (SRDs). Frans Frielink, a former colleague at Agere Systems, also joined Xanadu Wireless. In 2007 the company announced the acquisition of Ubiwave, a Belgium-based firm focusing on ZigBee protocols, and the transformation of the company into

GreenPeak Technologies, a full-system fabless semiconductor company with an emphasis on wireless sense and control networks in combination with ultra-low-power technology. The main institutional investors in GreenPeak are Gimv (Antwerp) and DFJ Esprit (London), and others include Motorola Ventures, the global investment arm of Motorola, and SenterNovem, an agency of the Dutch Ministry of Economic Affairs.

ZigBee refers to the specifications for a suite of communication protocols using small, low-power digital radios based on the IEEE 802.15.4 standard for low-data-rate WPANs, which was completed in 2003.[25] ZigBee is targeted at RF applications that require a low data rate, a long battery life and secure self-organising mesh networking. ZigBee operates in different sub-1 GHz ISM bands in Europe, the United States, Japan and China, and in the 2.4 GHz band globally. The over-the-air data rate is 250 kbit/s per channel in the 2.4 GHz band. ZigBee chips typically integrate radios, microcontrollers and flash memory, and the chip vendors usually also provide the ZigBee software stack and application profiles. Applications in the home include smart lighting, advance temperature control devices and all kinds of sensors for safety and security. In a mobile context ZigBee is used for m-payments, m-monitoring and control. In building environments it is used for security and access control, as well as energy monitoring. In industrial plants the application is related to process control, asset management and environmental management. The members of the ZigBee Alliance create public application profiles to provide a global standard for product interoperability regardless of manufacturer. The alliance certifies ZigBee products.

8.7   Other salient RF activities

The descriptions of GreenPeak and Zigbee conclude a series of illustrations of the knowledge flow that was once directed at the NCR Engineering Centre in Utrecht and later became directed away from the centre, to fan out to a number of start-up companies covering a wide range of wireless standards, from very low bit rates to very high bit rates.[26] Moreover, as Agere Systems terminated its WLAN activities, the accumulated expertise moved 'in person' to the larger companies as well, such as Motorola.

Of course, many more entrepreneurial initiatives of Dutch origin related to RF applications can be mentioned. These include PicoPoint, which provides 'hotspots' and roaming services; Ambient Systems (a spin-off from the University of Twente), which is active in the field of meshed sensor networks; Hopling Networks, a manufacturer of wireless networking systems; and Kogero (a spin-off of Wireless Leiden), which builds Wi-Fi networks. A major RF-sensing-related project that should be mentioned in this context is LOFAR

(LOw Frequency ARray), a novel software-based radio telescope (ASTRON, 2004):

LOFAR started as a new and innovative effort to force a breakthrough in sensitivity for astronomical observations at radio frequencies below 250 MHz. The basic technology of radio telescopes had not changed since the 1960s: large mechanical dish antennae collect signals before a receiver detects and analyses them. Half the cost of these telescopes lies in the steel and moving structure. A telescope 100 times larger than existing instruments would therefore be unaffordable. New technology was required to make the next step in sensitivity needed to unravel the secrets of the early universe and the physical processes in the centres of active galactic nuclei.

LOFAR is the first telescope of this new sort, using an array of simple omnidirectional antennae instead of mechanical signal processing with a dish antenna. The electronic signals from the antennae are digitised, transported to a central digital processor, and combined in software to emulate a conventional antenna. The cost is dominated by the cost of electronics and will follow Moore's law, becoming cheaper with time and allowing increasingly large telescopes to be built. So LOFAR is an IT telescope. The antennae are simple enough but there are a lot of them – 25,000 in the full LOFAR design. To make radio pictures of the sky with adequate sharpness, these antennae are to be arranged in clusters that are spread out over an area of ultimately 350 km in diameter. (In phase 1, which is currently funded, 15,000 antennae and maximum baselines of 100 km will be built.) Data transport requirements are in the range of many terabit/sec and the processing power needed is tens of teraflops.

It was soon realised that LOFAR could be turned into a more generic wide area sensor network. Sensors for geophysical research and studies in precision agriculture have been incorporated in LOFAR already. Several more applications are being considered, given the increasing interest in sensor networks that 'bring the environment on-line'.

The LOFAR project is being implemented through a consortium of eighteen organisations, including universities, and it is financially supported through provincial, national and European funding.

8.8   Conclusions

In reviewing the Wi-Fi case, and making allowance for the fact that the innovation 'trigger' for Wi-Fi was exogenous to the Netherlands, a number of conclusions can be drawn with respect to the role of the Dutch innovation system.

- The Dutch 'knowledge infrastructure' played a crucial role in creating the success of Wi-Fi.
- The acquired knowledge base of the Utrecht Engineering Centre played a crucial role in the assignment of the WLAN feasibility study and the subsequent R&D for Wi-Fi products to the centre.
- In the development of Wi-Fi, the universities of technology played a major role in providing important knowledge for the project, in particular those

at Delft and Eindhoven. On the other hand, NCR/AT&T/Lucent Technologies also provided ample opportunities for knowledge extension at these universities, in coming forward with MSc and PhD projects.

- Cutting-edge RF research is still being executed at all three universities of technology in the Netherlands.[27]
- Philips Electronics was, and still is, an important 'institution' in terms of creating and maintaining RF-related knowledge; this applies in particular to the Elcoma Division (Philips Semiconductors), and now NXP, as an independent entity.
- While the development of Wi-Fi may be perceived as incidental, it can also be regarded as an outcome of the vibrant knowledge infrastructure related to RF engineering in the Netherlands.
- Although the original Wi-Fi development team has been dissolved, the acquired knowledge is retained and transferred, often 'in person', to a range of other firms, which continue to pursue RF technology developments.
- Wi-Fi emerged in the relatively 'open' innovation environment of NCR, and then became part of the more 'closed' innovation environment of AT&T and Lucent Technologies. Nonetheless, the team was successful in pursuing an 'open standard' and collaborated closely with complementors and competitors in the industry.
- The Utrecht Engineering Centre, being part of a large (foreign) multinational firm, has been both a curse and a blessing for the development of Wi-Fi.
- The WBSO – a tax facility to stimulate R&D activities – provided the Utrecht Engineering Centre with a competitive edge, or, perhaps more accurately, softened the competitive disadvantage of the relatively high tax levels in the Netherlands compared to the United States.

Notes

1 This section draws upon the PhD research of Marianne van der Steen, published in 1999.
2 Note that a comprehensive treatise of the model as it applies to the Dutch context and the ICT sector in particular falls outside the scope of this chapter. For a general discussion of the innovation systems perspective, see van der Steen (1999), and, for a discussion of developments in the telecommunication sector, see Lemstra (2006).
3 Personal communication with Paul de Wit, 2008.
4 In Malabar near Bandoeng, on the island of Java, the world's largest long-wave antenna was constructed in order to bridge the immense 11,500 kilometre distance from the East Indies to the Netherlands. Independence from relay points owned and operated by either the Germans or the British was important during the First World War (Vles, 2008).
5 He received his licence under the call sign PCGG, using a wavelength of 670 metres. At the same time Philips received a licence with the call sign PCJJ, which

the company started to use in 1927 for short-wave transmission to the Netherlands East Indies (de Boer, 1969).

6 The equipment operated at a wavelength of 700 metres.

7 A claim can be made that Idzerda was the first provider of radio broadcasts, at least in Europe, where these services started in Germany in 1922 and the BBC started in 1924 in the United Kingdom (de Boer, 1969). The start of radio broadcasting in the United States is linked to Westinghouse providing a direct account of the presidential election on 2 November 1920 (Blanken, 1992).

8 In 1924 Idzerda ceased his broadcasting activities as his company went bankrupt (de Boer, 1969).

9 This was a result of the efforts of Johannes Jacques Numans, an enthusiast amateur radio operator, who, as a student at the Technical University of Delft, applied with Philips for a trainee position, for which he proposed building a short-wave radio transmitter to reach the Dutch East Indies. He managed to convince Anton Philips of his qualifications, and under the leadership of Dr Balthasar van der Pol the project was realised (Vles, 2008).

10 Other entities, such as Kennisland and ECP.nl, are supported by the government in order to stimulate innovation and encourage the adoption and use of ICT.

11 Although a merging of the microelectronics activities of NCR and AT&T was considered, the product lines they supported were too different, as were the design processes and foundries.

12 Upon the acquisition of NCR, the AT&T Computer Systems Division and NCR were merged into AT&T Global Information Systems, the idea being that the successful computer company NCR would fix the ailing AT&T computer division.

13 Hertz worked from 1920 to 1925 at the NatLab. Thereafter he became the director of the Physics Institute of the University of Halle. In 1925 he received the Nobel Prize in physics.

14 The period from 1870 to 1914 has been called the 'second golden age' of Dutch science, with van 't Hoff winning the first Nobel Prize in chemistry in 1901, Lorentz and Zeeman winning the physics prize in 1902, van der Waals physics in 1910 and Kamerlingh Onnes physics in 1913 (de Vries, 2005; Kox and Chamalaun, 1980).

15 In a 'tuned radio' receiver the radio signal is first amplified and then led through a detector to retrieve the audio frequency signal, which is subsequently amplified. In a 'superheterodyne' receiver the incoming signal is mixed with a signal from a local oscillator at an intermediate frequency, and the difference signal thus obtained is then led through a detector to retrieve the audio frequency signal, which is subsequently amplified (de Vries, 2005).

16 The international expansion of Philips resulted in the NatLab obtaining R&D entities abroad: Mullard in the United Kingdom, LEP in France, Briarcliff Manor in the United States, a laboratory in Brussels and two entities in Germany, at Aachen and Hamburg (de Vries, 2005).

17 University representatives were also involved in the IEEE 802.11 working group meetings and submitted proposals for consideration in the development of the standards. Universities that participated were: University of Aveiro (Portugal); University of California, Davis; Delft University of Technology; University of Las Palmas (Spain); University of Madrid; Stevens Institute of Technology (United States); University of Tel Aviv; Victoria University (Australia); Virginia Polytechnic Institute

and State University (United States); and Worcester Polytechnic Institute (United States).

18 A Diffie-Hellman session key with a 128 bit RC5 was used. As NWN was a Netherlands-based company, US export restrictions were not applicable.
19 The research was part of a broader project that involved the province of Brabant, KPN (the incumbent operator) and the TNO.
20 See www.timschenk.com.
21 See http://w3.ele.tue.nl/en/ecr/people/msc_graduates.
22 One example is the diagonally layered space-time architecture proposed by researchers at Bell Labs, known as BLAST (van Zelst, 2004).
23 OFDM is also applied in digital video broadcasting (DVB) and digital audio broadcasting (DAB).
24 Bluetooth was the name given to the development project by a collaborator at Intel. In 1999 it became the name of the technology, after the Danish Viking king Harald Blåtand (probably meaning 'dark-skinned great man'), who united Denmark and Norway around 960.
25 An urban myth perpetuated by the ZigBee Alliance is that the term 'ZigBee' derives from the silent, but powerful, method of communication used by honeybees to report information about food sources. Bob Metcalfe revealed in an interview in 2004, however, that the name was initially meaningless and had been chosen from a long list on the basis that it had no trademark liabilities (see http://en.wikipedia.org/wiki/ZigBee; accessed 3 December 2008).
26 A knowledge flow that remains to be discussed is directed at Taiwan, where the Wi-Fi chipsets were assembled into products for Lucent Technologies and later Agere Systems. In early 2000 close cooperation was required between the Engineering Centre and the manufacturer in order to achieve a significant increase in manufacturing volumes.
27 Currently, RF research at the three universities of technology covers four main research areas: (1) ultra-low-power sensor networks; (2) software-defined radio/cognitive radio; (3) ultra-high-speed data rates of 1 to 100 Gbit/s, mainly short range in the 60 GHz band and beyond; and (4) radar/imaging in the 10 to 400 GHz bands (personal communication from Mark Bentum, 2008).

References

ASTRON (2004). 'LOFAR'. Dwingeloo, Netherlands: ASTRON. Available at www.lofar.org/p/geninfo.htm (accessed 4 December 2008).

Blanken, I. J. (1992). *Geschiedenis van Philips Electronics N.V. Deel III*. Leiden: Martinus Nijhoff.

Boelcskei, H., D. Gesbert, C. Papadias and A. J. van der Veen (eds.) (2006). *Space-Time Wireless Systems: From Array Processing to MIMO Communications*. Cambridge: Cambridge University Press.

Bouwman, H., and W. Hulsink (2000). *Silicon Valley in de Polder: ICT-clusters in de Lage Landen*. Utrecht: Lemma.

Brouwer, E., P. den Hertog, T. Poot and J. Segers (2002). 'WBSO nader beschouwd: onderzoek naar de effectiviteit van de WBSO'. The Hague: Directorate of Innovation, Ministry of Economic Affairs.

Chesbrough, H. W. (2003). *Open Innovation: The New Imperative for Creating and Profiting from Technology*. Boston: Harvard Business School Press.

Corver, J. (1928). 'Het draadloos amateurstation'. Rotterdam: luna.nl; http://home.luna.nl/-arjan-muil/radio/nederlands/corver1.html (accessed 8 August 2008).

CPB (1997). *Challenging Neighbours: Rethinking German and Dutch Economic Institutions*. Berlin: Springer.

De Boer, P. A. (1969). *à Steringa Idzerda: De Pionier van de Radio-Omroep*. Bussum, Netherlands: de Muiderkring.

De Jong, J. P. J., and W. H. J. Verhoeven (2007). *WBSO Evaluation 2001–2005: Impacts, Target Group Reach and Implementation*. Zoetermeer, Netherlands: EIM.

De Vries, M. J. (2005). *80 Years of Research at the Philips Natuurkundig Laboratorium 1914–1994*. Amsterdam: Pallas.

Freeman, C. (1987). *Technology Policy and Economic Performance: Lessons from Japan*. London: Pinter.

  (1988). 'Japan: a new national system of innovation'. In G. Dosi, C. Freeman, R. R. Nelson, D. Silverberg and L. Soete (eds.). *Technical Change and Economic Theory*. London: Pinter, 330–48.

Groenewegen, J. P. M. (1989). *Planning in een Markteconomie*. Delft: Eburon.

Groenewegen, J. P. M., and M. van der Steen (2006). 'The evolution of national systems of innovation'. *Journal of Economic Issues*. **40** (2), 277–85.

  (2007). 'The evolutionary policy maker'. *Journal of Economic Issues*. **41** (2), 351–8.

Heerding, A. (1980). *Het Ontstaan van de Neerlandse Gloeilampenindustrie*. The Hague: Martinus Nijhoff.

Koomans, N. (1926). 'Geschiedkundig overzicht van het radiobedrijf van den rijksdienst der posterijen en telegrafie'. Rotterdam: luna.nl; http://home.luna.nl/-arjan-muil/radio/nederlands/corver1.html (accessed 8 August 2008).

Kox, A. J., and M. Chamalaun (1980). *Van Stevin tot Lorentz: Portretten van Nederlandse Natuurwetenschappers*. Amsterdam: Intermediair.

Lemstra, W. (2006). 'The Internet bubble and the impact on the development path of the telecommunication sector'. PhD dissertation. Department of Technology, Policy and Management, Delft University of Technology, Delft.

Lemstra, W., and V. Hayes (2009). 'License exempt: Wi-Fi complement to 3G'. *Telematics and Informatics*. **26 (3)**, 227–39.

Lundvall, B.-A. (1988). 'Innovation as an integrative process: from user–producer interaction to the national system of innovation'. In G. Dosi, C. Freeman, R. R. Nelson, D. Silverberg and L. Soete (eds.). *Technical Change and Economic Theory*. London: Pinter, 349–69.

  (1992). *National Systems of Innovation: Towards a Theory of Innovation and Interactive Learning*. London: Pinter.

McKinsey (1997). *Een Stimulans voor de Nederlandse Economie*. Amsterdam: McKinsey and Co.

Mock, D. (2005). *The Qualcomm Equation: How a Fledgling Telecom Company Forged a New Path to Big Profits and Market Dominance*. New York: AMACOM.

Nelson, R. R. (1988). 'Institutions supporting technical change in the United States'. In G. Dosi, C. Freeman, R. R. Nelson, D. Silverberg and L. Soete (eds.). *Technical Change and Economic Theory*. London: Pinter, 312–29.

  (ed.) (1993). *National Innovation Systems: A Comparative Analysis*. Oxford: Oxford University Press.

Nelson, R. R., and K. Nelson (2002). 'Technology, institutions, and innovation systems'. *Research Policy*. **31** (2), 265–72.

OECD (1987). *Structural Adjustment and Economic Performance*. Paris: OECD.

(1993). *Economic Survey of the Netherlands*. Paris: OECD.

Patel, N. V., and K. Pavitt (1994). 'The nature and economic importance of national innovation systems'. *STI Review*. **14**, 9–32.

Porter, M. E. (1990). *The Competitive Advantage of Nations*. New York: Free Press.

PTI (1955). *Een Bloem in het Veld der Techniek*. Hilversum: PTI.

Reich, R. (1991). *The Work of Nations: Preparing Ourselves for 21st-century Capitalism*. New York: Alfred Knopf.

Riordan, M., and L. Hoddison (1998). *Crystal Fire: The Invention of the Transistor and the Birth of the Information Age*. New York: Norton.

Roobeek, A. (1990). *Beyond the Technology Race: An Analysis of Technology Policy in Seven Industrial Countries*. Amsterdam: Elsevier Science.

Saxenian, A. (1994). *Regional Advantage: Culture and Competition in Silicon Valley and Route 128*. Cambridge, MA: Harvard University Press.

Telatar, E. (1999). 'Capacity of multi-antenna Gaussian channels'. *European Transactions on Telecommunications*. **10** (6), 585–95.

Thurow, L. C. (1996). *The Future of Capitalism: How Today's Economic Forces Shape Tomorrow's World*. London: Brealey.

Van der Steen, M. (1999). *Evolutionary Systems of Innovation: A Veblian-oriented Study into the Role of the Government Factor*. Assen, Netherlands: van Gorcum.

Van Nee, R. (2006). 'Current status of Wi-Fi standardization'. Paper presented at ninth annual international conference 'Economics of infrastructures'. Delft, 16 June.

(2007). '802.11n: continuing the Dutch legacy'. Paper presented at IEEE Steinmetz Award seminar. Delft, 6 March.

Van Rooy, Y. M. C. T. (1992). 'Het einde van het Kartelparadijs'. *ESB*. (September), 908–12.

Van Zelst, A. (2004). 'MIMO OFDM for wireless LANs'. Dissertation. Eindhoven University of Technology, Eindhoven.

Vles, H. (2008). *Hallo Bandoeng: Nederlandse Radiopioniers 1900–1945*. Zutphen, Netherlands: Walburg Pers.

Vogt, W. (1958). *Spanne en Spanning*. Hilversum: PTI.

Walko, J. (2002). 'Agere demos 162-Mbit/s wireless LAN'. Manhasset, NY: CommsDesign. Available at www.commsdesign.com/story/OEG20021118S0040 (accessed 3 December 2008).

9   Wi-Fi as community-based innovation

Ellen van Oost, Stefan Verhaegh and Nelly Oudshoorn,
with contributions from Wolter Lemstra

9.1   Introduction

In this third chapter on the broader perspectives of the Wi-Fi innovation journey, the role of the user in community-based innovation is studied in detail.

The domain of information and communication technologies has become one in which the boundaries between producers and users have become increasingly fuzzy. The availability of free and open source software is a clear example of how communities of computer users develop many varieties of software.[1] In a similar vein, many popular web services build on the efforts of – often experienced and skilful – users. Examples include the many blogs, podcasts and videocasts; customer-written product reviews on Amazon; and the free encyclopaedia Wikipedia. *Time* magazine even put 'You' (the internet user) on its cover as Person of the Year 2006.[2] At the physical layer of telecommunication infrastructures, however, user-initiated products and innovations are quite rare. This level is dominated by commercial telecom and cable operators, which finance, produce, install, maintain and innovate the expensive and often large-scale ICT infrastructures. Free access to radio frequency spectrum, originally intended for indoor use with Wi-Fi as a successful implementation of wireless local area networking, has inspired users to develop local wireless infrastructures themselves, however, challenging this organisational dominance.

As described in Chapter 6, in the Dutch city of Leiden a small group of residents managed to develop a city-wide wireless infrastructure offering local residents possibilities for free communication, under the name Wireless Leiden.[3] Although there are other major Wi-Fi initiatives, such as Freifunk in Berlin and DjurslandS.net in Denmark,[4] the completely wireless 'backbone' of the Leiden infrastructure was technically unique. In 2005 Wireless Leiden started to expand regionally, promoting its activities in other cities. Moreover, members of the Wireless Leiden community started to organise so-called 'boot camps' to share their expertise on an international basis, thus stimulating the potential

This chapter is an update of van Oost, Verhaegh and Oudshoorn (2009). It is included with permission from Sage.

diffusion of freely accessible wireless communication infrastructures.[5] Members of the community even built two Wi-Fi networks in Turkey.[6]

In this chapter we apply the conceptual vocabularies of innovation studies and actor network theory, which are appropriate for describing and understanding the development of this type of user-initiated innovation – one in which the concepts of 'community' and 'innovation' are closely intertwined. Although these theoretical approaches are useful in our case, we argue that the concept of 'community innovation' should be added to these vocabularies in order to capture the full dynamics of innovations initiated and shaped by user collectives. We aim to capture the dynamics of innovation processes that are initiated and shaped by a community of users such as Wireless Leiden. We build our theories on the strands of user-oriented research within the two academic disciplines of innovation studies and science and technology studies (STS).

Together with his collaborators, von Hippel has initiated and developed an impressive line of research addressing the active role of users in innovation processes (see Franke and Shah, 2003, Lüthje, Herstatt and von Hippel, 2005, Shah, 2006, von Hippel, 1976, 1986, 2005, and von Hippel and von Krogh, 2003). Core concepts in this strand of research are those of *lead users* and the *innovation community*. The second concept is especially fruitful in our case, because the community aspect is central to the development of Wireless Leiden. In the academic discipline of science and technology studies, the innovative agency of users in the dynamics of technological developments has increasingly drawn attention over the last decade as well (see, for instance, Oudshoorn and Pinch, 2003, and Rohracher, 2005). These studies often focus on user–producer interaction during the various stages of technological development. As is true of innovation studies, science and technology studies have paid less attention to understanding the innovative agency of *communities* of users.

Our argument is laid out as follows. In the next section we position our research theoretically within the current concerns of both innovation studies and science and technology studies. Next we offer a two-part description of the rise and development of Wireless Leiden. The first part describes the sociocultural negotiations that shaped Wi-Fi in the period when Wireless Leiden was being initiated. During this phase lead users, their innovative agency and information exchange were centre stage. The second part addresses the processes of growth and stabilisation of the wireless infrastructure as a collective action of an innovation community. We explore the roles of ideology, technical competences and managerial competences within the community and their impact on the actual shaping of Wireless Leiden as a city-wide, free wireless infrastructure. Finally, we evaluate our empirical findings in relation to current conceptual vocabularies from innovation studies and science and technology studies and discuss how these vocabularies can enrich each other.

9.2   Theoretical framework and methodology

For the construction of our theoretical framework we have drawn from two fields of research that look at the various roles and influences that users have in realising innovative products and services: innovation studies and science and technology studies; both elaborate the active role of users theoretically and empirically. So far, however, these two fields have taken only limited advantage of each other's insights. In their core literature only a few mutual references can be found.[7] Clearly, the two domains pursue divergent objectives, as reflected in their divergent research agendas. The work of von Hippel and his colleagues is primarily business-oriented and aims to enhance the quality of a company's innovation processes by making companies aware of users as a potentially rich source of innovative ideas for product development. Specifically, von Hippel has developed methods and toolkits for finding and tapping this source. In the field of STS, by contrast, the focus on users is often inspired by a sociopolitical (sometimes also a normative) agenda aimed at involving more social groups in technological development and empowering specific user groups. Moreover, the two fields use quite different methodologies: whereas innovation studies rely primarily on quantitative methods, the STS tradition mainly capitalises on the strategy of 'thick description' by carrying out qualitative case studies.

More recently, however, the mutual interest between these two fields has seemed to be growing, and it is possible to observe cautious shifts in agendas and methods. Von Hippel has recently broadened the scope of his work by repositioning the role of users as more central and essential in innovation processes (2005). Instead of depending on what producers offer them, users are increasingly able to develop what they want themselves. This trend towards 'democratising innovation', as von Hippel calls it, is enhanced substantially by the widespread use of ICT. According to von Hippel, this trend is relevant not only for industries and companies but also for policy makers and various social groups. The topic of democratising technology has been at the forefront of the research agenda in STS circles for a long time, but in recent years an interest in innovation processes has started to grow, to the extent that today the term 'science, technology and innovation studies' has become common.[8] Although there are still fundamental differences in styles of research between STS approaches and innovation studies, increasing levels of interest in understanding the growing role of users in innovation are evident in both fields.

This chapter aims to develop further the dialogue between the two fields by explicitly drawing together theoretical concepts from both strands in the analysis of Wireless Leiden as a case study. In the next two sections we discuss how the two fields have conceptualised (1) the innovative agency of users and (2) the innovation dynamics of communities of users.

9.2.1   The innovative agency of users

Von Hippel's long-term and sustained study of the active role of users in innovation has put the innovative agency of users firmly on the agenda of innovation studies. Based on earlier work in the 1970s, he introduced the key concept of 'lead user' in 1986 (von Hippel, 1976, 1986). Lead users are users who, first, 'face needs that will be general in a marketplace – but face them months or years before the bulk of that marketplace encounters them' and, second, are positioned 'to benefit significantly by obtaining a solution to those needs'. Lead users can – but need not – invent, design and build their own solutions to suit their needs. Since lead users are aware of future market needs, they have the potential to serve as an excellent 'need-forecasting laboratory for marketing research' (von Hippel, 1986). By emphasising lead users as a rich resource for corporate innovation, von Hippel has elaborated a methodology for marketing departments to identify lead users as representing the needs of the future market. As such, it is possible for them to play a major part in the design of prototypes of new products (von Hippel, 1988). See Chapter 4 section 2.7 for the role of Professor Hills at Carnegie Mellon University and section 4.1 for the role of Steve Jobs at Apple as lead users for the development of WLAN for AT&T and Lucent Technologies, respectively.

In his later work, von Hippel has proposed an institutional forum in which users and producers meet (von Hippel and Katz, 2002). Various STS scholars have also stressed the relevance of an institutional locus of this type – referred to as a 'nexus' (Schot, 2002) or a 'mediation junction' (Schot and Albert de la Bruheze, 2003) – to enhance the interrelationship of design and use. These loci are considered important places for social learning processes in which alignments in articulation processes between various actors from both contexts can be established (Rip, Misa and Schot, 1995; Stewart and Williams, 2005). In this area the concerns of innovation studies and STS appear to intersect, but there are differences as well. Whereas von Hippel has focused mainly on interactions with lead users, as those who represent future market needs, user-oriented STS scholars have emphasised the need to be sensitive to the diversity of users, who potentially have quite different needs and agendas (see, for example, Oudshoorn, Brouns and van Oost, 2005). In the latter domain, diversity is articulated along demographic lines (age/gender/class) or different positions (management/end users/non-users). Although von Hippel has paid less attention to this type of user diversity, one can credit his work for highlighting lead users as a specific group of users – one that did not arise from the general heuristic of diversity applied in STS. In this chapter we argue that *combining lead user analysis with attention to user diversity* – among lead users as well as other types of users – is fruitful when it comes to analysing the innovative agency of users.

A second concept from the STS terminology that is valuable for analysing user innovations is 'script'. This concept explicitly relates artefacts and their usage by suggesting that all designers base their products on envisaged users and specific use situations (Akrich, 1992). Accordingly, products contain a script, which is the materialised presentation of envisaged use. The use of a product is described in semiotic terms as the 'reading' of its script. In this analysis – which, essentially, involves adapting the new product to user environments – the meanings and uses of products, or even the products themselves, can be changed and adapted. Users may very well 'read' scripts in ways that differ from those intended by the designer. Lead users, in this conceptualisation, constitute a specific group of users who adopt specific, informed ways of not just reading but also introducing new scripts, by inscribing the characteristics of their specific use situation into the product (which in many cases even applies to its materiality as well).

Moreover, central in the script approach is the *symmetrical analysis* of interaction between user and artefact. Users and artefacts alike can be analysed as being attributed with (inscribed) agency and meaning that enable and constrain user practices and users' agency. Users and artefacts both shape, and at the same time are shaped by, the practice of usage. From an STS perspective, lead users' agency and meanings are analysed in direct relation to the inscribed agency and meanings (scripts) in the artefacts they use and produce. In our case study, then, we take the agency of artefact itself as a category of analysis – a focus that is absent in innovation studies – and argue its relevance for understanding the dynamics of where and how lead users and their activities come into being.

As our argument underlines, the conceptual vocabularies developed in STS and innovation studies may very well enrich each other. Linking the concept of lead user with user diversity and the symmetrical analysis of user–technology relations offers us an analytical framework for studying the innovative agency of users.

9.2.2   The innovative agency of communities

More recently, the rise of the Internet in general and open source communities in particular have boosted interest among scholars in innovation studies for innovations by user collectives, especially the phenomenon of non-profit collectives producing innovations.[9] To capture the dynamics of open source communities, various concepts have been developed: private–collective innovation (von Hippel and von Krogh, 2003), commons-based peer production (Benkler, 2002) and community-based innovation (Franke and Shah, 2003; Shah, 2005). Next to open source, the practices of extreme or specific types of sports – for example, kitesurfing, mountain biking, rodeo kayaking and handicapped sport – also provide a rich source of user communities producing innovations in sporting equipment (see Franke and Shah, 2003, Hienerth, 2006, Lüthje, Herstatt and von Hippel, 2005, and Shah, 2000).

In 2005 von Hippel made reference to this fast-growing cluster of publications in *Democratizing Innovation*. This is where he introduced the overarching concept of 'innovation community', defined as organised cooperation in the development, testing and diffusion of user-initiated innovations. Users as well as manufacturers can be members; the innovation community can be purely functional, but it may also fulfil the role of a social (virtual) community providing sociability, support, a sense of belonging and social identity (von Hippel, 2005). Although von Hippel defines innovation community broadly, he has mainly addressed and analysed it as a locus or setting for *exchanging* innovative ideas and information among involved individual community members. Based on work in STS, we have reason to expect that activities of innovation communities also involve collective work aimed at creating and sustaining stable networks.

Recent user innovation studies have explored the diversity and dynamics of the roles that participants can take on in innovation communities. In this regard, von Krogh, Spaeth and Lakhani (2003) have studied how newcomers' identities in an open source community evolve into those of accepted members; Shah and Tripsas (2004) explore user entrepreneurship by focusing on user-innovators starting their own firms; and Hienerth (2006) describes the dynamics of user innovation communities evolving into commercial and manufacturing communities following the commercialisation process of user innovations through the pioneering activities of user manufacturers. If the user-oriented strand of innovation studies has certainly produced a wealth of concepts and data on community driven innovation, these studies, too, are limited, notably in two ways. First, most studies on innovation communities either address one aspect (e.g. the role of knowledge exchange, the recruitment into an existing community, etc.) or focus on more complex processes at a specific time (e.g. the recruitment dynamics of new members into an existing community). An understanding of the life cycle dynamics of innovation communities (initiation, growth, stabilisation, etc.) is lacking. Second, these studies do not offer conceptual tools for understanding the work involved in aligning the technical and social elements of community-driven innovations.

To address the latter, we use the concept of 'heterogeneous engineering' (Callon, 1987; Law, 1991). Not only do engineers create and align technological elements but, equally importantly, they also bring various types of social, political, economic and cultural elements that are 'inextricably bound up into an organic whole' into line with scientific and technological elements (Callon, 1987). Heterogeneous engineers continuously perform various types of work to align both technical *and* social elements into an actor network so as to build the stable coalitions that are necessary for the successful development and implementation of an innovation. Similarly, innovative users are likely to perform these types of heterogeneous activities when bringing the various elements into line that are necessary for the development and stabilisation of both an innovation community *and* the innovations themselves (which also constitute the community). This is why we rely on the perspective of heterogeneous engineering to analyse innovative agency of communities by addressing the *heterogeneity of alignment work* in innovation communities.[10] Sensitised by STS research on invisible work (Shapin, 1989; Star and Strauss, 1999), we also seek to move beyond an exclusive focus on core actors and activities in the innovation community by rendering visible the role of community members who perform non-entrepreneurial activities, such as maintenance work and 'infrastructures of support'.

Given our theoretical concerns, we distinguish two main research questions that we address in the analysis of our case study of Wireless Leiden as an innovation community. First, which types of work are involved in initiating and developing a community-driven innovation? Second, which collective efforts are involved and how are they distributed across the network to ensure the growth and stabilisation of a community-driven innovation?

9.2.3   Methodology

Our specific theoretical framework and concerns have led us to embrace an explorative qualitative approach based on an in-depth case study. This research tactic, we believe, is most likely to be productive. For our data collection, we relied on three strategies. First, we explored all the information provided on the Wireless Leiden website and a 'wiki' (www.wirelessleiden.nl). This site proved to be a tremendously rich source, because – fully in the tradition of open source communities – maximal transparency is strived for regarding both material and organisational aspects. Minutes of meetings, discussions and debates were made available online, as well as many technical descriptions, guidelines and images of the various stages of the technological developments involved. Second, we held a series of in-depth interviews, seventeen in all, with ten core actors of Wireless Leiden. Third, we attended seven meetings organised by the Wireless Leiden board between January 2005 and April 2006. At these meetings we observed discussions, presentations and workshops, and we also interviewed additional participants. Subsequently our insights were updated in preparing the manuscript as part of this book.

9.3   The rise of Wireless Leiden as a user innovation

In this section we analyse the dynamics of the rise of a user community that created an innovative wireless network infrastructure built on Wi-Fi technology.

In describing these dynamics, we focus on the identification of lead users of Wi-Fi technology and the types of work they performed to align various actors – human actors as well as non-human artefacts – into a new network that would form the basis of the Wireless Leiden community. To understand the character and the type of work that lead users had to perform in order to align the Wi-Fi technology with their aims, we need insight into the script – the materialised prescribed use – of Wi-Fi itself. We begin, therefore, with a brief historical detour to explore how the Wi-Fi technology itself was constructed with a specific use in mind – thus both enabling and constraining the actual practices of the Wireless Leiden lead users.

9.3.1   The shaping of Wi-Fi as indoor local area technology

The WLAN – or, for that matter, the Wi-Fi – script evolved over a long period of time. Through the 1985 Rule and Order of the FCC some important elements were filled in. The use of spread-spectrum technology was prescribed, leaving open two options: direct sequence and frequency hopping. Moreover, the power levels were limited. The intended application was communication in general; the FCC envisaged both indoor and outdoor use of this wireless technology (for details, see Chapter 2).[11] The main parts of the script were subsequently filled in by engineers; the first intended applications were WLANs in industrial and business environments. Harmonisation and refinement of the script occurred primarily through the standardisation efforts within the IEEE 802.11 working group, resulting in the publication of the first standard in 1997. Alternative scripts were introduced, such as HomeRF and HIPERLAN, but they did not become successful (for details, see Chapter 3).

The use of WLANs in homes became inscribed through the agreement between Apple and Lucent Technologies, resulting in the introduction of the Apple AirPort in 1999. The script became firmly embedded in the computing arena through the cooperation of Lucent Technologies with Microsoft to include WLAN support in the XP operating system. Consumers wishing to control their wireless equipment from within open source operating systems such as Linux or FreeBSD were (as yet) not served. Through industry cooperation in the Wi-Fi Alliance, DS-type products emerged as the predominant model and the script became firm through interoperability testing and the issuance of the Wi-Fi label for compatibility (see also Chapter 4). The script was extended to public access through the introduction of 'hotspot' services, popularised through Starbucks, from 2001 onwards (see Chapter 5).

Evidently, the standardised Wi-Fi equipment had a clear indoor and localised use application script that imposed restrictions on the conditions in which these devices could be used. Wi-Fi devices not only constrained use practices, however, but also invited and enabled new ones. Some groups of users saw the potential of the Wi-Fi technology for solving practical problems such as providing rural areas and remote villages with broadband internet access. Other, ideologically driven groups of users saw opportunities for Wi-Fi technology to create so-called wireless Freenets – community wireless networks free of governmental or corporate restraints. Wireless Leiden is one such initiative. The type of work that had to be performed by these users to align the Wi-Fi technology with their vision of establishing free wireless communication networks was influenced by the existing indoor-use and access-only script. The main work the Leiden initiators had to perform in the beginning involved the *re-engineering* of the existing Wi-Fi script.

9.3.2   *Reshaping Wi-Fi as outdoor longer-distance technology*[12]

As introduced in Chapter 6, the first ideas about a wireless community network in Leiden can be traced back to 2001, when a Leiden resident, Jasper Koolhaas, discovered Wi-Fi technology. Koolhaas, trained as an electrotechnical engineer and fascinated by computers, networks and the Internet, saw the potential of Wi-Fi technology for creating a free wireless infrastructure. Later, when we interviewed him (25 October 2005), he recounted his 'Eureka' insight into the use of Wi-Fi as a network:

When thinking about this some more, at one point I thought: 'Holy smoke, this is not just interesting– this is earth-shaking. For the first time in history people like you and me can build an infrastructure themselves.' Until then [this had been] something only possible for governments or big companies . . . Admittedly, radio amateurs [had been] doing the same for some time, but that infrastructure was accessible for licensed ham[13] operators only; and this is an unlicensed band, free to use for all.

Clearly, the script of the standardised Wi-Fi devices had both enabling and constraining features for users. It made it possible for them to think of a new, cheap and free infrastructure, yet its users' connections were constrained by distance. What type of work was needed to re-engineer the inscribed script?

By using a local network of computer hobbyists, Koolhaas managed to bring in a few additional motivated participants, among them Marten Vijn, a Linux user. In the autumn of 2001 they started to experiment with Wi-Fi devices so as to achieve long distance connections. In doing so, they performed various types of work to deconstruct the inscribed script in regular Wi-Fi devices. They had to find a solution for increasing the range of the radio waves without increasing the output power; they experimented with different types of antennae; and they had to make the devices weatherproof for outdoor use. It turned out to be a difficult task to get the weak radio waves working in the Wi-Fi assemblage they envisaged. The initiators of Wireless Leiden tried to find solutions in using other types of antennae. Increasing the output power was not an option, as this would break the formal regulations and would imply an illegal wireless network, risking fines and the confiscation of their devices by Agentschap Telecom, the organisation that supervises the use of the radio spectrum in the Netherlands. Despite all their efforts and knowledge of computers and computer networks, they failed to get the Wi-Fi radio waves to connect two distant nodes.

It took the experiences and knowledge of two Leiden radio amateurs to 'manage' the radio waves. These radio hobbyists brought in a good-working and cheap antenna that had been developed in radio amateur circles, the so-called 'quad' antenna.[14] The version specifically modified for Wi-Fi use, called a bi-quad, improved the amplification of the radio waves significantly. Constructed out of just a few parts, it was easy to build and cheap as well. In 'line of sight' situations this antenna could bridge distances of several kilometres.[15]

Now that re-engineering of the range had succeeded, the indoor part of the script still had to be re-engineered into a design that allowed outdoor use. The bi-quad antenna was weatherproof, but the electronics of the Wi-Fi equipment were not. In principle, one could connect an outdoor antenna to the indoor electronic parts by using a cable, but this would significantly attenuate the signal. Therefore, the Wireless Leiden initiators chose to develop a new 'integrated' outdoor device, and thus they had to find ways to protect the delicate electronics against rain and wind. Simple and cheap objects such as drainpipes and plastic lunchboxes were used to house the electronics. The work involved patching firmware, as well as writing and adapting device drivers for Linux. Using home-built outdoor Wi-Fi nodes, the first data packet of the Wireless Leiden group was successfully transmitted in January 2002.

9.3.3   Reshaping Wi-Fi as a wide area network

The next challenge the group faced in building a network is that Wi-Fi is designed as a network access solution and not to function as a network node. In home applications, Wi-Fi access points are typically connected via ADSL or a cable modem to provide connectivity with the 'public' network, in particular the Internet. Through the functionality of an in-built router an AP can support multiple computers.[16] In this way, therefore, family members can share the access provided. Depending on how the AP is configured, any Wi-Fi-compatible computer within the coverage range of the AP may use the AP to access the Internet. This may include house guests, neighbours or passers-by.[17] This is the so-called 'infrastructure' or 'managed' mode of the IEEE 802.11 standard. Wi-Fi stations can also communicate directly with each other, however (i.e. without an AP), in the so-called 'peer-to-peer' or 'ad hoc' mode.[18] In this mode, each Wi-Fi-equipped PC can be considered a Wi-Fi island, also called a Wi-Fi cell. If more than two of these islands can be connected, a Wi-Fi-based neighbourhood area network can be created. The 802.11 standard does not provide an automatic means to communicate through intermediary stations, however. An alternative approach is using the so-called 'repeater' mode, whereby APs are interconnected using radio links rather than cables. This mode appeared suitable for the purpose, and it was chosen by the Wireless Leiden initiators. Each network node is therefore equipped with three APs, one using an omnidirectional antenna to serve nearby Wi-Fi stations, and two with unidirectional antennae to provide a link to two neighbouring nodes (Wireless Leiden, 2006).

The network node is a PC equipped with special software to provide the network function, which includes the issuance of IP addresses (the Dynamic Host Configuration Protocol (DHCP) function), the directory function of relating the name to IP address (the domain name system (DNS) function), the routing function (based on the Open Shortest Path First (OSPF) protocol) and the remote maintenance functionality (based on the Secure SHell (SSH) protocol). Recognising that the reliability of the network depends on the proper functioning of the nodes, which are often located at places that are difficult to access, such as rooftops and church towers, the procedure to create a node would be standardised in the form of a 'NodeFactory'. The 'master' machine of the 'NodeFactory' runs on the FreeBSD 5.0 operating system. The version management is based on Subversion, an open source application that runs over the Web and that allows for 'anonymous' users. On this platform, specific Wireless Leiden functionality (Webweaving) has been added, as well as a configuration database (Genesis) (Wireless Leiden, 2006).

One of the first applications on the network became a major challenge, the live video broadcasting of the Rapenburg Concert in September 2002. The main issue appeared to be the drivers under Linux, which is why a transition was made to the use of FreeBSD (Vijn, Mourits and van 't Hart, 2007).

As Wireless Leiden became more well known, several Leiden residents volunteered to help expand the network with new nodes. Creating a new node implied considerable alignment work in terms of various actors and artefacts. The introduction of a new node starts with the application of the 'hexagonal grid', a theoretical node plan with links of 800 metres. The following step is to find an appropriate location as close as possible to the ideal location. Having identified the location, a site survey is performed, including field strength measurements (van Drunen et al., 2003).[19] The next step is obtaining the cooperation of the location owner; here the embedding of the volunteers in the local community becomes essential. The actual installation is based on standardised usage of the hardware, and the use of tools such as the Netstumbler. Figure 9.1 reflects the extent of the Wireless Leiden network in September 2004.

As the network grew new issues emerged. The OSPF-based routing software of Zebra and Quagga appeared to break at around forty nodes. This issue was

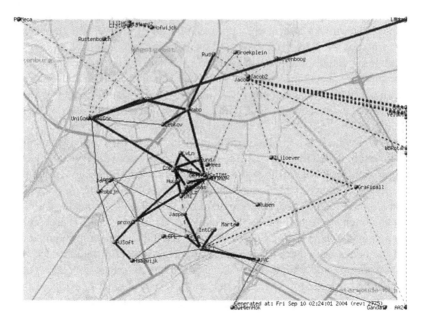

Figure 9.1 Wireless Leiden network, September 2004
Notes: Solid line: connection; dotted line: no connection; thickness of line: denotes traffic intensity

first tackled by using static routing, but in parallel Lodewijk Vöge developed a new dynamic routing software package. The package, Lvrouted, grew with the network and has proved itself to be reliable. As the network grew and as more users started to rely on its services (for example, in August 2005 some 2,500 users were active on the network: Vijn, Mourits and van 't Hart, 2007), network management became important. Jorg Bosman created a network monitoring tool based on Nagios, which displays in a 'NodeMap' the real-time status of the nodes and links. Operational data on the nodes is now collected automatically and logged. Interference levels have also increased with the growth of the network, which is why channels are now automatically selected out of the thirteen channels available within the band.[20]

Leiden's group of Wi-Fi initiators and volunteers successfully re-engineered the existing Wi-Fi devices from short-range indoor devices into long-distance outdoor devices, and complemented the Wi-Fi access with network node functionality. The vision of a free infrastructure for Leiden residents that Koolhaas had articulated some months beforehand had become so realistic by August 2002 with the successful re-engineering activities that the initiators decided to establish the formal association called Wireless Leiden. Its main purpose was to further the development of the wireless infrastructure so that Leiden residents could use it to communicate freely with each other.

9.3.4   User-initiated innovation as a collective activity of re-engineering

The application of Wi-Fi devices in a network configuration can be characterised as a lead users' innovation. The users involved envisaged a new type of use/need that had not been anticipated by the producers of the Wi-Fi device, and they were to benefit from the solutions to that need as well. The dynamics of this lead users' innovation can be characterised in two ways. First, these users actively resisted an explicit inscribed script of an existing device. This script itself defined the type of work that needed to be done before the re-engineering of this script was successful. Second, this re-engineering was a *collective* activity. Not only was the exchange of information and knowledge essential in realising this lead users' innovation, but so was the alignment of different types of knowledge. In this case, combining the knowledge of three different domains – computer networks, open source software and radio waves – proved crucial. These different types of knowledge were distributed over more than one person.

The actors in the Wireless Leiden project had very different backgrounds. Pooling their diverse interests, expertise, resources and contacts enabled them collectively to engineer a wireless network configuration that worked. Although the literature on users as sources of innovation conveys the image of the 'professional amateur' (Leadbeater and Miller, 2004), most of those who were engaged in the project were professionally involved in careers related to issues that needed to be solved. For instance, professional network infrastructure builders both in the field of wired and wireless topologies were involved, as well as actors with experience relating to organisation structures, the programming of embedded devices, open source software development consultancy or writing complex algorithmic software.

In a user-initiated innovation in which the necessary expertise and knowledge are distributed across various actors, it is likely that one of them fulfils an explicit coordinating role. In the case of Wireless Leiden, it was the initiator, Koolhaas, who in the process took on the role of lead user; he aligned and coordinated both the actors and the artefacts required for realising a re-engineered Wi-Fi device.

A second finding from this case is that lead user innovations can be understood as the result of a social process in which the actual shape is negotiated between the actors and the envisaged user and the use situation is configured (Woolgar, 1991). Koolhaas translated his ideal of a Freenet – a free and cheap wireless network available for everybody – into requirements that had to fit the needs of ordinary residents of Leiden as end users. This led to (re-)design choices that were in line with legality, low costs, reliability, constructability and usability. Interestingly, the two radio amateurs who joined this project after some months had already established in 1999 a long-distance wireless connection of 9 kilometres between their respective homes for sharing broadband internet with HomeRF, an alternative WLAN standard that failed to generate wide industry support. For their connection, though, the two bought an expensive professional hi-gain antenna. Because they acted on their purely personal needs, the radio amateurs had no incentive to share their solution. Only through active efforts on the part of Koolhaas, who had serendipitously found out about their home-built wireless connection, did they become involved in the Wireless Leiden initiative. This is a nice example of what von Hippel (1994) calls 'sticky information', which is available only locally, if not individually. Because the ideals of the Wireless Leiden initiators were public-oriented, from the outset the initiative relied on the openness and accessibility of their information and knowledge as a central organising principle. Translating the ideology of sharing knowledge into technology, they installed a wiki – a website accessible for reading *and* writing by anyone – as a way of collecting and communicating all the information about their project and actively involving new participants.[21]

9.4   The growth of Wireless Leiden as a community-driven innovation

When the collective re-engineering of the existing Wi-Fi technology was realised, the newly established association faced the challenge of putting this wireless network into use, as well as expanding it and increasing its user base. Building a freely accessible wireless network for general public use and organising both the growth and stabilisation of a city-wide structure with only volunteers as human resources seemed a daunting task. Sustaining a large-scale system involved a great deal of maintenance activities, but hiring employees for routine tasks was no option for this volunteer initiative.

This challenge was energetically taken up by the project's initiators and a growing circle of volunteering Leiden residents. Whereas in the middle of 2002 the newly established Wireless Leiden Foundation had a rudimentary wireless network in place consisting of four nodes and a dozen involved users, by the end of 2004 the network had been extended to over fifty wireless nodes (broadly covering the downtown area), while around eighty volunteers performed various kinds of tasks and some 2,000 local residents were connected to the wireless network for activities such as web browsing, file sharing, chatting, gaming and making VoIP phone calls.

In this section we unravel the types of work and activities required to establish, extend and stabilise such a wireless network. If the earlier development can be understood as a collective process of re-engineering an existing technology by a group of lead users, we analyse the further development of Wireless Leiden as a *community driven* innovation. We elaborate the concept of innovation community put forward by von Hippel – who actually focuses on the role of information exchange – by addressing the variety and heterogeneity of activities performed in such a community.

9.4.1   Aligning new actors, shaping heterogeneous user roles

In order to realise the project's growth, both the wireless infrastructure and its user base were developed simultaneously; one could not evolve without the other. Managing this complex coevolution of the material infrastructure together with the organisational community structure required very *different types of work*. In this process of aligning, coordinating, managing and regulating the various materials and actors, *different types of user roles* were constructed and various kinds of work and responsibilities were distributed across these various user roles.

9.4.2   The organisational user as sponsor

One of the first issues to be tackled by the initiators – most of whom joined the board of the Wireless Leiden Foundation – involved the cost of the new wireless nodes. Until then they had paid for the technology they needed to purchase, but this was not possible any more now that their goal was to realise an extended, free public infrastructure.[22] Meanwhile, a new Wi-Fi enthusiast, Huub Schuurmans, had joined the initiative, and he brought with him new knowledge and expertise, which played a central role in organising and coordinating the further growth of the network. Schuurmans (a former scientific attaché for the Ministry of Economic Affairs who founded the Netherlands Office for Science and Technology in Silicon Valley, and who had been involved in the management of innovation and development at oil company Royal Dutch Shell) was an expert on, as he put it, 'open innovations, managing public relations and creating a footprint'.[23]

Schuurmans proved to be the driving force behind a continuous, intensive publicity campaign, resulting in widespread publicity for Wireless Leiden, and he arranged contacts with various Leiden organisations that might want to support the network. For instance, he asked various organisations to sponsor a node. The first official node sponsor was the local software company Cope, which decided to sponsor two new nodes. In return, Cope used the Wireless Leiden infrastructure as its own virtual private network, allowing employees safe and free access to the company network from their homes. In fact, this new *sponsor-user* role approach provided the model for integrating local companies and other donor organisations into the project's infrastructure. Sponsors would pay for new nodes, which in turn were given the sponsors' names, and, more importantly still, they became *users* of the Wireless Leiden infrastructure as well. Wireless Leiden could offer them a VPN with a better performance than any commercially available system. As Koolhaas explained in his interview:

> This company, Cope, paid for two nodes, and . . . in an organisational sense this was the first building block of Wireless Leiden. Earlier, the focus was on technical issues, but now it grew more into an organisation because the basic idea itself became clearer: a company would fund the building of new nodes because it would serve their own needs, yet it would be helpful to other people as well. Thus this model reinforced the network's inner dynamic.

After the first companies had started to pay for new nodes the Wireless Leiden Foundation managed to convince public organisations such as local schools and libraries to join the project as well. At one point the enthusiasm for participating in Wireless Leiden was so great that the volunteers in charge of constructing and programming the nodes could not even keep up with the new requests.

9.4.3   The volunteer-user

In 2002 the influx of Wireless Leiden enthusiasts increased sharply, while the small group of Wi-Fi initiators meanwhile evolved into a much larger group consisting of dozens of volunteers. To manage all these people, the notion of 'official Wireless Leiden volunteer' was invented. In practice, this was just a way of making the existing situation explicit, whereby only registered members had access to e-mail correspondence. There was another new element: in order to become an official volunteer, one had to sign a contract. This contract was meant to protect volunteers against liability claims pertaining to, for instance, accidents that might occur during the building of a new network node, such as people or objects falling off a rooftop. At the same time, a volunteer also officially waived his/her rights to any intellectual property claims. For this purpose, two Wireless Leiden members employed as lawyers developed a specially crafted 'Wireless Leiden licence'. The contract was meant to prevent people from patenting novelties invented by using the Wireless Leiden network.

To coordinate all those new volunteers effectively, various subgroups were formed in which volunteers could specialise in issues tied to the Wireless Leiden project that had their particular interest, such as building nodes, maintaining the website or writing software code. In addition, another Wireless Leiden participant, Dirk-Willem van Gulik, former president of the Apache software foundation, introduced the 'who builds decides' rule, in order to prevent the possibility of endless debates without anything being achieved. Over time, several formalised procedures came into being as the organising principles of the Wireless Leiden community, while the Wireless Leiden board held control over the 'interface' used towards the 'outside' world.

9.4.4   The residential end user

In January 2003 internet service provider Demon started to sponsor Wireless Leiden with access to three of its ADSL internet lines. This allowed Wireless Leiden to offer free internet access (at least to the WWW part of the Internet) to local residents. This new option attracted many new users, and in this way Wireless Leiden configured a new type of user: the residential end user who wanted to associate him-/herself with Wireless Leiden to surf the web or send e-mail through a free web mail account, but who was not interested in additional services.

Wireless Leiden was able to accommodate end users who lived in the parts of Leiden that were covered. Users living outside the reach of existing Wi-Fi nodes initiated the construction of new nodes so as to link their neighbourhood to the Wireless Leiden backbone themselves. To realise new nodes, they performed various heterogeneous activities: finding a sponsor, asking volunteers to assemble and programme the node, locating suitable positions to place nodes and getting permission and access to electricity from homeowners. The board of the Wireless Leiden Foundation organised open meetings for interested residents in order to work on creating new nodes.

This new type of end user no longer needed to have either the knowledge about installing outdoor Wi-Fi or the motivation to let the overall project succeed, however. One of the radio amateurs, Wireless Leiden member Johan de Stigter, sold ready-made Wi-Fi aerials, a product with commercial potential. To make it easier for end users to connect to the 'free Internet', he developed a black box end user solution. This made it no longer necessary to tinker with and disassemble commercial routers and solder one's own bi-quad antenna to produce a 'drainpipe client hack'. His company, Gandalf, released a €250 plug-and-play device called Wandy (a contraction of 'WAN' and 'handy'). In this way de Stigter developed 'drainpipe clients' into a mature consumer product.[24] The Wandy kit contained everything users needed, provided they were able to receive the Wi-Fi waves in their neighbourhood. His kit was available at a Leiden electronics shop that also offered additional installation assistance if it was needed.

9.4.5   The maintenance user

With the increasing number of nodes, volunteers and end users, the maintenance of the network became a topic of discussion. The growing group of residential end users implied higher expectations about the reliability of the Wireless Leiden network and its services. The number of nodes increased sharply, requiring routine maintenance work. Although there were many volunteers by now, most of them were willing only to try out new and 'exciting' things, and they were much more reluctant to perform 'routine' jobs. To solve this problem, in April 2004 the Wireless Leiden board constructed a new user role: the node adoption volunteer (NAV). These special volunteers were prominent users of a specific network node, and if 'their' node was functioning erratically they were usually among the first to notice. Alternatively, if a local user of a certain node complained a few times when it did not function properly he/she would be asked to become responsible for keeping an eye on a local network node. In the case of a malfunction, the NAV was supposed to check the situation, press the reset button and test if the connection came 'up' again. If not, the whole node was disconnected and brought to one of the more experienced volunteers and exchanged for a working one. To assist the node adoption volunteers, more technically experienced Wireless Leiden users produced special standardised checklist forms to assist them with on-site node failure debugging. By constructing the role of the NAV, the Wireless Leiden network builders delegated some aspects of the maintenance work to local users.

9.5   The Wireless Leiden community as a sociotechnical network

In our Wireless Leiden case study we have encountered phenomena that cannot be described adequately by the theoretical framework offered by von Hippel (2005). In particular, his concepts of 'innovation community' and 'lead user' fall short. Whereas in the innovation community concept it is information exchange between (lead) users that is central, our empirical findings illustrate that the innovation community members perform many more activities. More central than the exchange of information is the continuous coordination of the heterogeneous resources that make up Wireless Leiden.

Furthermore, our analysis reveals that the shaping of this wireless infrastructure should take into account a wide variety of different types of users, rather than be understood in terms of lead users only. The Wireless Leiden case comprises an array of different user roles, each one of them contributing to a specific and vital element of the growth and stabilisation of Wireless Leiden. Both the wireless infrastructure (the innovation) and the organisation structure (the community) developed in mutually interconnected ways. In the same way that Hughes (1983) describes all the work that had to be done by Edison to build up the 'networks of power' to bring electrical lighting into the homes of US citizens, the Wireless Leiden co-operative had to create a supportive network as well in order to make the 'free wireless' a configuration that 'works'. The entanglement of the Wireless Leiden infrastructure and community is visible in the way a wireless network node functions. We understand it as a hybrid entity of technical elements – antennae, cables, PCs, software, Wi-Fi devices, the roof – as well as human elements, including the sponsor, the builder, the node adoption volunteer and the roof owner. Without any of these elements, a Wireless Leiden node would not function properly, or even exist in the first place.

For realising the growth and stabilisation of Wireless Leiden, the diversity of available skills and competences proved crucial. In the early period the necessary skills were primarily of a technical nature, and geared towards the use of radio waves, but, aside from technical and programming skills, in the phase of growth and stabilisation it was managerial, organisational, public relations and legal skills that helped to solve many problems. The growth and stabilisation of the wireless infrastructure was based on constructing, aligning, tuning and supervising the heterogeneous user groups. Skilfully organised and properly timed PR activities contributed to the numerous successful alignments between various social groups and Wireless Leiden. It is in particular the heterogeneity of all these activities that contrasts with von Hippel's focus on the circulation of information.

9.6   Understanding Wireless Leiden as 'community innovation'

Von Hippel and his collaborators have focused on how technical innovations often have their origins in a social community of experienced users. Although this approach has been productive, this conceptualisation of innovation community does not allow for describing user-initiated innovation processes in which the community is *part of the innovation itself*. Formulated alternatively, it is inadequate to assume an a priori distinction between the 'technical' innovation and the 'social' community, let alone a causal relationship. Our case study of Wireless Leiden shows that its development can be understood as a process of *coevolution* of both the technical infrastructure and the social community.

For this reason, we have proposed the concept of *community innovation* as a way to conceptualise the type of user-initiated innovations whereby the community itself is an essential element of the innovation. This concept makes it possible to understand the specific dynamics of these types of user-initiated innovations, and we would like to single out three of its advantages in particular. First, the concept facilitates analysis of the growth and stabilisation of the innovation as the result of the activities of a community of actors who are users and producers simultaneously. For many of the actors involved it is precisely the expertise originating in this 'double' role of creating as well as using an innovation that fuels their active involvement. Von Hippel (2005) also addresses this phenomenon for explaining lead users' activities. In contrast, the concept of community innovation draws attention to the diverse competences and expertise of multiple users that are necessary to deal with the dynamics of the growth and stabilisation of the innovation.

Second, the concept of community innovation brings to the fore the work required for innovation by heterogeneous collectives, most notably the coordination of the alignment and management of the various actors. In the case of Wireless Leiden, this coordination was performed predominantly by a core group of approximately eight to ten community members, who, as it happens, also constituted the board of the Wireless Leiden Foundation. In order to reach an understanding of the dynamics of the growth and stabilisation, and the actual shape, of the Wireless Leiden community innovation, the characteristics of this core group, most notably their skills in engineering the technical and social simultaneously, seem central. The composition, the shared ideology, the range of competences and the knowledge distributed across the core group – all these factors have greatly influenced the actual shape Wireless Leiden has taken as a free-to-use wireless infrastructure with a wireless backbone that, in terms of its size, is unique in the world.

The third benefit of the community innovation concept is that it portrays innovation as an evolving sociotechnical network in which humans and artefacts alike are active and become aligned. Innovations such as Wireless Leiden can be studied as a sociotechnical chimera, built from a variety of different elements: all kinds of different people, e-mail clients, websites, ideals about freedom, dreams about large-scale free infrastructure networks, unlicensed radio bands, cheap consumer-grade Wi-Fi devices, computers, antennae, laws and regulations about Wi-Fi use and international standards. The social and ideological characteristics of the innovation community and the type of knowledge and expertise available in the network have shaped the technological, material aspect.

Clearly, the community innovation concept requires further study and elaboration. A qualitative analysis of other types of innovations by user communities, such as Wikipedia and Second Life, may reveal other dynamics of growth and stabilisation. In addition, comparing Wireless Leiden with other Wi-Fi innovation communities, such as DjurslandS.net (Denmark) and Dharamsala (India), as described in Chapter 7, will yield more insights into the circumstances and conditions of distinct patterns in the various stages of community-driven innovations.

As our argument has demonstrated, the notion of community innovation can develop into a relevant conceptual tool that helps to increase our understanding of current and future tendencies in an emerging civil society in which ordinary citizens become more and more actively involved in shaping their technical and social environment. These same tendencies are identified by innovation expert Leadbeater as well (Leadbeater, 2005; Leadbeater and Miller, 2004) and, last but not least, by von Hippel, who suggests that innovations by users will be key to twenty-first-century innovation (von Hippel, 2005).

Notes

1 A non-comprehensive overview of academic studies on free and open source software is available from http://opensource.mit.edu. Although numerous articles on FOSS have appeared, Lin (2005) states in her assessment of the current literature that 'research done from the sociological perspective' is still missing.
2 *Time*, 2006, volume 168, issue 26.
3 At the end of 2005 Wireless Leiden covered most of the Leiden area and registered thousands of different IP addresses.
4 For Freifunk-Berlin, see http://start.freifunk.net; for Djursland, see Chapter 7 and http://diirwb.net.
5 For details, see http://opencommunitycamp.org/trac.
6 A press release is available at www.wirelessleiden.nl/pers/persberichten/persbericht_karaman_reis.shtml.
7 This finding is based on the analysis of the three core book publications, two on user studies in science and technology studies (Oudshoorn and Pinch, 2003; Rohracher, 2005) and one from innovation studies (von Hippel, 2005).
8 The current European network of excellence PRIME (Policies and Research on Innovation in the Move towards a European Research Area) is exemplary in this respect. Whereas Oudshoorn and Pinch only footnote von Hippel in their overview of the role of users in technology development (2003), they explicitly discuss the user-oriented innovation studies in a more recently published review of user–technology relations (2008).
9 Community informatics is another strand of literature that deals with questions about ICT innovations by, for and in communities. For recent overviews, see Day and Schuler (2004), Gurstein (2000), Keeble and Loader (2001) and Schuler and Day (2004).
10 Truffer and Dürrenberger (1997), for example, address the relevance of heterogeneity by emphasising the role of 'outsiders' in creating 'innovation milieus'.
11 Although some publications explore Wi-Fi community initiatives (Rheingold, 2002: chap. 6; Sandvig, 2004), only Sandvig focuses explicitly on community Wi-Fi as a locus for diffusion, experimentation, innovation, popularisation and the provision of new features and services. No study appears to be available on the dynamics of emerging Wi-Fi community initiatives.
12 See Chapter 7 and the case of Mérida for the achievement of much longer distances with Wi-Fi equipment.
13 The term 'ham' as a nickname for amateur radio operators originated in a pejorative usage by operators in commercial and professional radio communities. The word was subsequently welcomed by amateur radio operators, and it stuck; see http://en.wikipedia.org/wiki/Etymology_of_ham_radio.
14 Radio amateur Clarence Moore invented the quad antenna, and in 1951 he received a US patent for it (US2537191); see www.pentodepress.com/receiving/patents/2537191.pdf.

15 Interview with Evert Verduin, 27 March 2006.
16 In the original business application environment for WLANs, APs would be connected to the wired Ethernet, which would form the distribution system in the 802.11 terminology.
17 The sharing of internet access is considered by (most) operators to be an unintended use of the fixed network access facilities. Many operators have adjusted their supply contracts to make access sharing illegal. Enforcement is a totally different matter, however; see, for instance, Camponovo and Cerutti (2005) for the legal implications, and on 'intent to connect' Verma *et al.* (2002).
18 For details of the IEEE 802.11 architecture descriptions, see, for example, Orhtman and Roeder (2003).
19 The planning approach is based on radio planning in cellular networks. As most of the commercially available radio planning tools require large computing infrastructure, subscriptions to maps and other geographic information system data, it is not feasible for a volunteer organisation to run these simulations. A sponsor had been found who was capable and willing to provide these services to Wireless Leiden, however (van Drunen *et al.*, 2003).
20 Within the IEEE 802.11 standard, the use of the channels varies slightly between Europe, the United States and Asia.
21 Because of increasing amounts of 'link spam', the wiki was closed off and a Subversion server took over the role of document and code repository (interview with Koolhaas, 25 October 2005).
22 The costs of a robust node, consisting of two interlinks for backbone communication and one access point for local access, are between €1,000 and €1,500 (interview with Koolhaas, 25 October 2005).
23 Interview with Schuurmans, 9 October 2005.
24 The Wandy kit was not targeted exclusively at Leiden residents but to a wider market for broadband internet access solutions in remote places, such as camping sites. More information is available at www.wandy.nl.

References

Akrich, M. (1992). 'The de-scription of technological objects'. In W. Bijker and J. Law (eds.). *Shaping Technology, Building Society: Studies in Sociotechnical Change.* Cambridge, MA: MIT Press, 205–24.

Benkler, Y. (2002). 'Coase's penguin, or, Linux and the nature of the firm'. *Yale Law Journal.* **112** (3), 369–446.

Callon, M. (1987). 'Society in the making: the study of technology as a tool for sociological analysis'. In W. E. Bijker, T. Hughes and T. Pinch (eds.). *The Social Construction of Technological Systems: New Directions in the Sociology and History of Technology.* Cambridge, MA: MIT Press, 83–103.

Camponovo, G., and D. Cerutti (2005). 'WLAN communities and internet access sharing: a regulatory overview'. In IEEE. *2005 International Conference on Mobile Business.* New York: IEEE Press, 281–7.

Day, P., and D. Schuler (2004). 'Community practice: an alternative vision of the network society'. In P. Day and D. Schuler (eds.). *Community Practice in the Network Society: Local Action/Global Interaction.* London: Routledge, 3–20.

Franke, N., and S. Shah (2003). 'How communities support innovative activities: an exploration of assistance and sharing among end-users'. *Research Policy*. **31** (1), 157–78.

Gurstein, M. (ed.) (2000). *Community Informatics: Enabling Communities with Information and Communication Technologies*. Hershey, PA: IGI Global.

Hienerth, C. (2006). 'The commercialization of user innovations: the development of the rodeo kayak industry'. *R&D Management*. **36** (3), 273–94.

Hughes, T. P. (1983). *Networks of Power: Electrification in Western Society 1880–1930*. Baltimore: Johns Hopkins University Press.

Keeble, L., and B. D. Loader (eds.) (2001). *Community Informatics: Shaping Computer-mediated Social Relations*. London: Routledge.

Law, J. (ed.) (1991). *A Sociology of Monsters: Essays on Power, Technology and Domination*. London: Routledge.

Leadbeater, C. (2005). 'Swarms and innovation'. Presentation at the 'Creative capital' conference. Amsterdam, 17 March. Available at http://connectmedia.waag.org/media/ccc/050317leadbeater.mov (accessed 12 May 2007).

Leadbeater, C., and P. Miller (2004). *The Pro-Am Revolution: How Enthusiasts Are Changing Our Economy and Society*. London: Demos.

Lin, Y. (2005). 'The future of sociology of FLOSS'. *First Monday*. Special Issue 2; http://firstmonday.org/htbin/cgiwrap/bin/ojs/index.php/fm/rt/printerfriendly/1467/1382.

Lüthje, C., C. Herstatt and E. von Hippel (2005). 'User-innovators and "local" information: the case of mountain biking'. *Research Policy*. **34** (6), 951–65.

Ohrtman, F., and K. Roeder (2003). *Wi-Fi Handbook: Building 802.11b Wireless Networks*. New York: McGraw-Hill.

Oost, E. van, S. Verhaegh and N. Oudshoorn (2009). 'From innovation community to community innovation: user-initiated innovation in Wireless Leiden'. *Science, Technology and Human Values*. **34** (2), 182–205.

Oudshoorn, N., M. Brouns and E. van Oost (2005). 'Diversity and distributed agency in the design and use of medical video-communication technologies'. In H. Harbers (ed.). *Inside the Politics of Technology: Agency and Normativity in the Co-production of Technology and Society*. Amsterdam: Amsterdam University Press, 85–105.

Oudshoorn, N., and T. Pinch (eds.) (2003). *How Users Matter: The Co-construction of Users and Technologies*. Cambridge, MA: MIT Press.

(eds.) (2008). *User–Technology Relationships: Some Recent Developments*. Cambridge, MA: MIT Press.

Rheingold, H. (2002). *Smart Mobs: The Next Social Revolution*. Cambridge, MA: Perseus.

Rip, A., T. J. Misa and J. Schot (eds.) (1995). *Managing Technology in Society. The Approach of Constructive Technology Assessment*. London: Pinter.

Rohracher, H. (ed.) (2005). *User Involvement in Innovation Processes: Strategies and Limitations from a Sociotechnical Perspective*. Munich: Profil Verlag.

Sandvig, C. (2004). 'An initial assessment of cooperative action in Wi-Fi networking'. *Telecommunications Policy*. **28** (7–8), 597–602.

Schot, J. (2002). 'Constructive technology assessment and technology dynamics: the case of clean technologies'. *Science, Technology and Human Values*. **14** (1), 36–56.

Schot, J., and A. Albert de la Bruheze (2003). 'The mediated design of products, consumption, and consumers in the twentieth century'. In N. Oudshoorn and T. Pinch (eds.). *How Users Matter: The Co-construction of Users and Technologies*. Cambridge, MA: MIT Press, 229–46.

Schuler, D., and P. Day (eds.) (2004). *Shaping the Network Society: The New Role of Civic Society in Cyberspace*. Cambridge, MA: MIT Press.

Shah, S. (2000). 'Sources and patterns of innovation in a consumer products field: innovations in sporting equipment'. Sloan Working Paper no. 4105. Cambridge, MA: MIT.

(2005). 'Open beyond software'. In D. Cooper, C. DiBona and M. Stone (eds.). *Open Sources 2.0*. Sebastopol, CA: O'Reilly, 339–60.

(2006). 'Motivation, governance, and the viability of hybrid forms in open source software development'. *Management Science*. **52** (7), 1000–14.

Shah, S., and M. Tripsas (2004). 'When do user-innovators start firms? Towards a theory of user entrepreneurship'. Working Paper no. 04-0106. Chicago: University of Illinois. Available at http://userinnovation.nit.edu (accessed 25 October 2007).

Shapin, S. (1989). 'The invisible technician'. *American Scientist*. **77** (6), 554–63.

Star, S. L., and A. Strauss (1999). 'Layers of silence, arenas of voice: the ecology of visible and invisible work'. *Computer Supported Cooperative Work*. **8** (1), 9–30.

Stewart, J., and R. Williams (2005). 'The wrong trousers? Beyond the design fallacy: social learning and the user'. In H. Rohracher (ed.). *User Involvement in Innovation Processes*. Munich: Profil Verlag, 39–72.

Truffer, B., and G. Dürrenberger (1997). 'Outsider initiatives in the reconstruction of the car: the case of lightweight vehicle milieus in Switzerland'. *Science, Technology, and Human Values*. **22** (2), 207–34.

Van Drunen, R., D.-W. van Gulik, J. Koolhaas, H. Schuurmans and M. Vijn (2003). 'Building a wireless community network in the Netherlands'. In USENIX. *Proceedings of the FREENIX Track: 2003 USENIX Annual Technical Conference*. Berkeley, CA: USENIX, 219–30.

Verma, S., P. Beckman and R. C. Nickerson (2002). 'Identification of issues and business models for wireless internet service providers and neighborhood area networks'. In J. R. Beer, R. C. Nickerson and S. Veran (eds.). *Proceedings of the Workshop on Wireless Strategy in the Enterprise: An International Research Perspective*. Berkeley: University of California Press, 53–62.

Vijn, M., G. Mourits and H. van 't Hart (2007). 'Wireless network dekt Leiden: de begin jaren van een draadloos netwerk'. *Informatie*. October.

Von Hippel, E. (1976). 'The dominant role of users in the scientific instrument innovation process'. *Research Policy*. **5** (3), 212–39.

(1986). 'Lead users: a source of novel product concepts'. *Management Science*. **32** (7), 791–805.

(1988). *The Sources of Innovation*. Oxford: Oxford University Press.

(1994). 'Sticky information and the locus of problem solving: implications for innovation'. *Management Science*. **40** (4), 429–39.

(2005). *Democratizing Innovation*. Cambridge, MA: MIT Press.

Von Hippel, E., and R. Katz (2002). 'Shifting innovation to users via toolkits'. *Management Science*. **48** (7), 821–33.

Von Hippel, E., and G. von Krogh (2003). 'Open source software and the "private-collective" innovation model: issues for organization science'. *Organization Science*. **14** (2), 209–23.

Von Krogh, G., S. Spaeth and K. R. Lakhani (2003). 'Community, joining, and specialization in open source software innovation: a case study'. *Research Policy*. **32** (7), 1217–41.

Wireless Leiden (2006). 'Techniek'. Leiden: Wireless Leiden; www.wirelessleiden.nl/techniek (accessed June 2006).

Woolgar, S. (1991). 'Configuring the user: the case of usability trials'. In J. Law (ed.). *A Sociology of Monsters: Essays on Power, Technology and Domination*. London: Routledge, 57–99.

10 The governance of radio spectrum: licence-exempt devices

Peter Anker and Wolter Lemstra,
with contributions from Vic Hayes

10.1 Introduction

From the innovation journey of Wi-Fi, to the extent that it has been unfolded, we may conclude that Wi-Fi has become a prime example of a global success story in the shared use of radio frequency spectrum. This success is special, as the common use of a natural resource is often associated with the phenomenon of the 'tragedy of the commons', when the appropriation of a resource exceeds its ability to be provisioned or replenished. This is typically the case if access to the resource is unrestricted or open. The success of Wi-Fi stems from the fact that access to the resource (the propagation of electromagnetic waves in free space)[1] is open, but highly regulated. In the regulation of access, use is made of a combination of technological and institutional arrangements, the origins of which can be traced back to the early days of radio; this includes regulation of the power level, the use of protocols, the modulation technique and the definition of the rights to use the RF spectrum.

What distinguishes success from failure is also strongly linked to the way the resource is exploited – i.e. the business model deployed by the entrepreneurs involved and, in particular, the magnitude of the investments incurred and the time required for these investments to be recovered. Here, for instance, lies an important difference between two principal forms of wireless access – unlicensed and licensed – of which Wi-Fi and cellular, respectively, are the prime examples.

The history of radio communication also shows the importance of coopera-tion between governmental and industrial actors in achieving successful shared use of the RF spectrum; Wi-Fi is a case in point. Hence, in this chapter we look at the historical regulatory context for the present-day success of Wi-Fi and explore what is required to continue the success of the common use of the spectrum. The context is set by a summary of historical developments in the use and governance of radio spectrum. This is followed by an investigation of the governance of licence-exempt devices in the United States and Europe, and in summary form in China, Japan and South Korea. This includes a discussion of the transition to the 2.4 GHz band and the allocation of the 5 GHz band. The

288

chapter closes with a discussion of the role of the ITU in short-range devices, and an exploration of the developments towards more frequency-agile devices and dynamic spectrum access.

10.2   The theoretical framing of 'common use'

For the emergence of the concept of the 'common use' of a natural resource (and the radio frequency spectrum is often compared to a natural resource), we have to go back in the history of humanity, to the transition from the hunter-gatherer period to that of domestication and farming. This transition is regarded as having been triggered by a depletion of the natural resources necessary to sustain our hunter-gatherer mode of living, and resulted in a need to settle and secure adequate food supply through farming. This transition increased considerably the need for 'coordination' among the people in the use of a natural resource, in this case the land. Since this transition, many forms of 'common use' have evolved and survived over the centuries. Examples are the 'commons', pastures that are in common use by farmers, and alpine meadows, but they also include forests, fishery grounds and the common use of irrigation systems and underground water reservoirs. Early forms of coordination pre-date the emergence of governments and their role in governing economic and social activity. These forms of coordination were, typically, small-scale in terms of the geography covered and the numbers of people involved. Moreover, the people who were involved in the shared use were usually part of the same culture, and shared a set of norms and values that allowed effective coordination mechanisms to emerge and develop, in step with the technological means available to exploit a particular natural resource.

Not all coordination mechanisms have been successful over extended periods of time, however. In 1968 Hardin reported in *Science* about the link between the 'tragedy of the commons', as he termed it, and population growth (Hardin, 1968). The general message was that the common use of a natural resource is at risk through excessive use – that is, when the appropriation of the resource is greater than the rate at which it can be provided or replenished. This is typically the case if access to the resource is unrestricted or open. Ostrom and others have carried out extensive studies into the emergence and sustainability of successful governance mechanisms for the common use of natural resources (Ostrom, 1990; Ostrom, Gardner and Walker, 1994).[2]

10.3   Historical development in the use of radio spectrum

The radio frequency spectrum is a resource with the characteristics of a common pool. An important characteristic of RF waves is that the use of the same frequency by multiple transmitters at the same place and time will lead to interference, and hence to the distortion of the intended communication between the sender and receiver.[3] Interestingly, unlike many other forms of 'common pools', the RF 'resource' is non-depleting, in that after it is released from use the interference stops and the 'resource' is immediately available for reuse.

In the early days of radio communication – e.g. wireless telegraphy between ships and between ship and shore – the means of communication was simple, based on switching on or off the signal of the radio transmitter.[4] The information was transferred using short and long signals according to the Morse code, which employs a series of 'dots' and 'dashes' to represent each letter of the alphabet. The 'coordination' between the transmitting and receiving stations was manual – i.e. the radio operators listened to each other's transmissions and had to tune the signal power to be both audible and least disturbing to others. Moreover, they were responsible for the coding and decoding of the messages.

One of the first successful business models using radio-telegraphy, which can be regarded as the exploitation of a 'claimed private commons', resulted from the entrepreneurial initiatives by Marconi.[5] Following a period of manufacturing radio equipment only, the Marconi Wireless Telegraph Company started to build and exploit coastal radio stations and the operation of radios on board ships. This initiative also led to the first 'market failure' or 'coordination failure', when it appeared that Marconi had instructed his operators, trained and licensed to operate Marconi equipment, to refuse to relay messages received from competing operators, such as those using Telefunken equipment. In 1902 this became apparent to Heinrich von Hohenzollern, a Prussian prince, when travelling from the United States back to Germany, as he could not send a courtesy message to President Roosevelt. This contributed to the convening of the first governmental meeting on the governance of RF spectrum in 1903 in Berlin, at which it was decided that telegrams should be handled irrespective of the system of radio that was used. The subsequent meeting, in 1906, which brought together representatives of twenty-nine nations, can be considered the start of the international coordination of spectrum use with the signing of the first International Radiotelegraph Convention, modelled on the Convention of the International Telegraph Union of St Petersburg in 1875. Two wavelengths were allocated for public correspondence in the maritime services, at 500 and 1,000 kHz; frequencies below 188 kHz were reserved for long-distance communication by coastal stations. The frequency range between 188 and 500 kHz was reserved for military and naval usage. Moreover, all details of stations, their frequency use, their hours of operation, their call signs and the radio system they used, were to be sent to the Bureau of the ITU, in Bern, Switzerland. The radio stations would require a government licence and operators had to have a certificate as to their competences (ITU, 1965).

This interconnection between radio operators was considered to be in the public interest in terms of bolstering the safety of people at sea, and in order to ensure the continuous availability of the service at all times. This need for rules of engagement and international coordination was reinforced by the *Titanic* disaster in 1912.[6] Ever since then governments have assumed an active role in the coordination of the use of the RF spectrum. Henceforth, in maritime radio the 500 kHz channel for radio-telegraphy and the 2,182 kHz channel for radio-telephony have come to be used as a calling frequency and as an emergency signalling frequency, while other frequencies are used as working frequencies for follow-on communication. This facilitates efficient use of the available radio communication channels, and at the same time provides support for the monitoring of emergency transmissions, in the process offering a public service using a commercial incentive scheme (ITU, 1965; Jackson, 2005).

In 1906 the first radio broadcast, or demonstration of radio-telephony, took place near New York, organised by Fessenden and Alexanderson. This led on to radio broadcasting in the 1920s and 1930s, and to radio receivers appearing in most homes.[7] In 1933 Armstrong received a patent on the invention of frequency modulation (FM), which affords a much better transmission quality than amplitude modulation (AM).[8]

As radio broadcasting provides an attractive means of influencing public opinion, RF spectrum regulation around this time took on a new, political, dimension in relation to 'free speech'. The use of the RF spectrum was extended to the shortwave bands (3 MHz and above) mainly as a result of work by radio amateurs. Eighty countries were represented at the radio conference held in Washington, DC, in 1927 and sixty-four private broadcasting organisations participated on a non-voting basis. During the conference, protocols for charging and international accounting were decided upon.[9] Moreover, the use of spark sets was strongly discouraged so as to cope with the increasing demand for bandwidth. The Radio Consultative Committee was established, one of its tasks being the drawing up of the first frequency allocation table; the useful RF spectrum was considered to lie in the range from 10 kHz to 60 MHz. In the 1932 Madrid conference the frequency tolerances and the acceptable frequency bandwidths were drawn up for the first time. An extension of the frequency table to 300 MHz was proposed. Moreover, regional broadcasting conferences were established to address conflicting interests better. During the 1938 Cairo conference the decision was taken to allocate radio channels for intercontinental air routes (ITU, 1965).

The precursor of the television appeared in the 1920s, with the first experimental but regular broadcast services occurring in the mid-1930s, only to be interrupted by the Second World War. Three different systems emerged: the US (using 525 lines to build up the image), the French (819 lines) and the UK (405 lines). In 1935 the development of radar was undertaken by Watson-Watt at the British National Physical Laboratory, and it became a major RF application during the war (ITU, 1965).

In 1946 a mobile telephony service was introduced when AT&T, with the permission of the FCC, provided the first commercial car-borne service in St Louis, Missouri, which quickly expanded to cover the major cities in the United States (Manninen, 2002; Meurling and Jeans, 1994). In 1947 Bell Labs introduced the concept of cellular communications in order to resolve the capacity constraints of these systems through the geographical reuse of frequencies. To make the concept work, however, the principle of 'switchover' between cells had to be realised – a functionality for which the technology would not be available until the 1970s. It was also in 1947 that plans for a public mobile phone service were developed in the Netherlands, which led to the introduction of mobile services in 1949 – a first in Europe; connections were put in place by an operator. The service proved its value during the major flooding in 1953, when the wireline infrastructure was out of action (Schuilenga *et al.*, 1981).

Personal radio services began in 1945 when the FCC allowed short-distance radio services in the 460 to 470 MHz band. Gross, the inventor of the walkie-talkie, started to market class B hand-held terminals for the general public in the late 1940s. In 1958 the class D Citizens' Band service was opened in the 27 MHz band, initially providing for twenty-three channels, and it became very popular in the 1970s and early 1980s. Around 1960 the FCC permitted the use of a single, shared radio channel in land mobile communication. With hardware extensions, such as tone-coded squelch or the Listen Before Talk (LBT) protocol, and with the fact that most transmitted messages were short, shared channel communication became very efficient (Jackson, 2005).

Preceded by Sputnik 1, the world's first artificial satellite, launched by the Soviet Union in 1957, Echo 1, launched by the United States in 1960, became the first passive communications satellite, to be followed by Telstar 1, the first active satellite, in 1962. The first successful geostationary satellite, Syncom 2, was launched in 1963. In that same year, at the Geneva conference, frequency bands totalling 60 GHz would be allocated to the various kinds of space services, with 2.8 GHz reserved for communications satellites (ITU, 1965).

In 1970, in the context of pan-Nordic cooperation, the internal study commissioned by Televerket[10] on mobile communication formed the basis for a working party that subsequently recommended the construction of a new, pan-Nordic automatic mobile telephone system, to be based on the cellular concept. A trial was successfully concluded in 1978, and the world's first cellular system was inaugurated on 1 September 1981 in Saudi Arabia, based on the Nordic Mobile Telephone system (Manninen, 2002; Meurling and Jeans, 1994).

In 1968 the FCC initiated proceedings for the deployment of cellular communications in the United States; the first commercial licence was granted in

1983. The first analogue cellular service based on the AMPS (Advanced Mobile Phone System) specification by Bell Labs was introduced by Illinois Bell in Chicago in the same year (Botto, 2002; Manninen, 2002; Mock, 2005; Rey, 1983).

Preceded by initiatives of the French PTT pursuing the potential of pan-European mobile communications, the British and French incumbent operators having decided to cooperate in specifying a joint system and the Nordic administrations having initiated the NMT-2 Group to explore 'mobile communications for the future', the Dutch made a recommendation to CEPT to start procedures leading to 'the construction of a pan-European automatic telephone service on the 900 MHz band' in June 1982. This resulted in a working party being created, the Groupe de travail Spécial pour les services Mobiles (in short: GSM), to develop a specification aimed at resolving the capacity shortage of the analogue systems and resolving the incompatibility between the multiple standards being used in Europe. In 1986 the decision was taken to develop a digital system based on time division multiple access. In 1987 incumbent operators from thirteen countries signed an MoU to commit themselves to the network roll-out and cooperation on commercial and operational matters, such as tariff principles (e.g. the calling party pays) and accounting. In the autumn of 1992 GSM was launched in seven countries by thirteen operators (GSM Association, 2004; Manninen, 2002; Meurling and Jeans, 1994).

In 1988 the US Cellular Telecommunications Industry Association (CTIA) published a set of requirements for the industry with the objective of increasing the capacity of the analogue network tenfold, in addition to improving reliability and quality. Qualcomm used this opportunity to pitch for a new concept, code division multiple access, based on spread-spectrum techniques. CDMA was considered too complex and not a proven concept, however, and the Telecommunications Industry Association (TIA) voted for a TDMA specification to be called IS-54 or D-AMPS. The advantage was that TDMA could be positioned as an upgrade of AMPS using the existing base stations. In 1994 the FCC auctioned large blocks of spectrum in the 1,900 MHz band for personal communications services (PCS). By 1997 more than 50 per cent of the PCS licensees had implemented CDMA technology (Manninen, 2002; Meurling and Jeans, 1994; Mock, 2005).[11]

10.4   The radio spectrum governance paradigm

The coordination regime that has emerged and continues to prevail today is based on the (international) allocation of specific RF bands to particular applications and (groups of) users. At the highest level, the ITU Radiocommunication Sector provides coordination under the auspices of the United Nations.[12]

Refinements are made through assignments at the national level, including the number of operators licensed to exploit a certain type of service, the permitted signal power and, sometimes, a (type of) standard to be used. The use of a standard allows private parties to agree upon certain characteristics of RF use and obviates the need for governments to specify these characteristics as part of a licensing process. As radio waves do not stop at political or geographical borders, the assignment of frequency bands has always been subject to close coordination between neighbouring states.

Under this regime, the 'common use' of spectrum is controlled through the regulation of access to the RF spectrum and through RF use prescriptions.

For entrepreneurs in the wireless industry, the RF spectrum is an input to the production process. Depending on the frequency band (which determines the propagation characteristics) and the conditions associated with the RF spectrum assignment (e.g. the duration of licences, the bandwidth, the number of licensees), the RF spectrum is valued differently. The monetary value also depends on the way the RF spectrum is awarded to contending parties – e.g. through a 'beauty contest' or through an auction. The licensing regime provides entrepreneurs with a relatively high degree of certainty regarding the use of RF spectrum, and this facilitates the financing of the (deep) investments required for the infrastructure build-up. This form of 'common use' of RF spectrum for cellular or mobile communications may be summarised in the words of Hazlett (2006) as follows: 'The state has awarded exclusive spectrum usage rights to operators who effectively reassign use rights in negotiated agreements with select third-party vendors, such as handset makers, and reassign spectrum access rights on a national level and on a mass-market scale to subscribers.'

In their role of governing the RF spectrum, governments have also assigned RF spectrum to 'internal users', such as the military, the emergency services and air traffic control. A third category of allocations and assignments is concerned with the category of licence-exempt use of RF spectrum. These unlicensed devices, sometimes also called short-range devices, operate[13] on a variety of frequencies. That unlicensed devices are exempted from having an individual licence does not mean there are no regulations applying to these devices. The way in which they are regulated varies between the different regions of the world. In most cases these devices have to share the frequencies with licensed applications, and they are generally prohibited from causing harmful interference to those applications yet have to tolerate interference from them. Some national administrations have established regulations to give a certain degree of protection to unlicensed devices. This is mostly done for applications that are considered important to the general public. An example of this kind of application is the ultra-low-power active medical implant communication device (ITU, 2006).

10.5   Radio spectrum governance in the United States: unlicensed devices

In the United States, historically the unlicensed use of RF spectrum has been associated with two categories of devices that have become known by the sections of the FCC regulations that describe the conditions of their use: Part 15 and Part 18 devices.

10.5.1   Part 15 devices

In 1938 the FCC first permitted radio devices to be sold and operated without a licence. This was a result of what Carter (2009) calls a possible oversight of fundamental physical phenomena by the Communications Act of 1934, which was aimed at awarding rights to the use of the RF spectrum through licensing discrete organisational entities, namely that nearly all electrical devices leak or reradiate electromagnetic energy at very low power levels. This coincided with radio device manufacturers introducing short-range, low-duty-cycle communication devices. The FCC set out to regulate the use of these devices on the basis of the reasoning that, if the RF emissions of these devices were sufficiently weak and short range, they would not rise to the level of harmful interference, and thus there would be no engineering reason to suppress their use. The regulation of these devices became known as Part 15 of Title 47 of the Code of Federal Regulations, most of the time simply referred to as Part 15. Under these rules, (1) users have no vested right to continue using the frequency; (2) users have to accept any interference generated by all other users, including other unlicensed users; (3) users may not cause harmful interference; (4) users must cease operation if notified by the FCC that the device is causing harmful interference; and (5) equipment must be authorised (certified) to show compliance with FCC standards before it can be marketed or imported. The limit set to these devices regarding field strength was 15 μV/m at a distance equivalent to the wavelength of the operating frequency divided by 2π. The devices were expected to operate in the range of 0.3 to 30 MHz, and therefore also in bands in which licences had been granted (Carter, 2009; FCC, 1987).

Over the years the FCC adjusted the rules to permit the use of higher power in higher frequency bands, which have higher levels of attenuation. Many device-specific adjustments were made to the Part 15 rules to accommodate the use of, for example, wireless microphones, telemetry systems, garage door openers, field disturbance sensors, anti-pilferage systems in retail stores and cordless telephones. As a consequence, the rules became complex, restrictive and internally inconsistent, and so it was that the FCC initiated an omnibus revision procedure in 1985. The resultant 1989 revision distinguished three broad categories: (1) unintentional radiators, such as central processing unit

Table 10.1 *Bands designated for ISM applications*

Band	Bandwidth	Centre frequency	Exceptions
6,765–6,795 kHz	30 kHz	6,780 kHz	
13,553–13,567 kHz	14 kHz	13,560 kHz	
26,957–27,283 kHz	326 kHz	27,120 kHz	
40.66–40.70 MHz	0.4 MHz	40.68 MHz	
433.05–434.79 MHz	1.74 MHz	433.92 MHz	Only in Region 1, except in the countries mentioned in footnote no. S5.280.[14]
902–928 MHz	26 MHz	915 MHz	Only in Region 2.[15]
2,400–2,500 MHz	100 MHz	2,450 MHz	
5,725–5,875 MHz	150 MHz	5,800 MHz	
24–24.25 GHz	250 MHz	24.125 GHz	
61–61.5 GHz	500 MHz	61.25 GHz	
122–123 GHz	1000 MHz	122.5 GHz	
244–246 GHz	2000 MHz	245 GHz	

Source: ITU (1998).

boards and power supplies; (2) incidental radiators, such as electric motors; and (3) intentional radiators – i.e. radio transmitters. The latter are allowed to operate under general emission limits in any band, except certain sensitive or safety-related bands, or under provisions that allow higher emission levels in certain designated bands (Carter, 2009).

Before Part 15 devices can be placed on the market the equipment manufacturer or importer has to test the products to ensure that they comply with the rules by certification or by a declaration of conformity. Certification is issued on the basis of test data that the manufacturer or importer supplies to the FCC. These test data usually come from tests that are carried out by a laboratory that the FCC knows and trusts. A declaration of conformity is a somewhat simpler procedure, whereby the manufacturer or importer issues a formal statement to the FCC indicating that the device has been tested at an accredited laboratory and that it complies with the rules.[16]

10.5.2   Part 18 devices

For the application of equipment or appliances designed to generate and use locally generated RF energy for industrial, scientific, medical and domestic purposes – to produce physical, biological or chemical effects through heating, the ionisation of gases, mechanical vibrations and the acceleration of charged particles – a range of frequency bands have been allocated, internationally coordinated through the ITU (see Table 10.1). In the United States the regulation of these devices is documented under Part 18 of Title 47 of the Code of Federal Regulations.

In principle, applications in the field of telecommunications are excluded from these bands. In general the same rules apply as for Part 15 devices, except that in the allocated bands there is no field strength limit, though there are strict limitations set to the field strength outside the band.

10.5.3   The 1985 landmark decision by the FCC: WLANs

In 1985 the FCC, through its Report and Order of 9 May, allowed for the first time unlicensed RF communication devices based on spread-spectrum techniques – in essence, Part 15 devices – to use RF bands assigned to Part 18 devices (FCC, 1985). Although the MITRE Corporation report that investigated the potential benefits, costs and risks of spread-spectrum communications did not identify a strong need from the industry, the report did identify the ISM bands as bands 'in which spread spectrum techniques may be able to improve the utilization of the spectrum ... [as these bands] are relatively unsuitable for applications requiring guaranteed high levels of performance. Indeed, since users of the ISM bands are not nominally protected from interference, it can be argued that any productive use of these bands frees other spectrum resources that are needed by applications requiring protection from interference' (MITRE Corporation, 1980). See Chapter 2 for an elaboration on spread spectrum and the background to this rule change.

The FCC notice of inquiry, which would lead to the 1985 decision, proposed using spread spectrum as an 'underlay' within other bands – i.e. sharing the frequencies with other services. The notice triggered comments expressing fear of interference and the difficulty of tracing the source of interference. Based on the responses received, the FCC proposed two rule changes: one for the licensed use of spread spectrum in the police bands and one for unlicensed use. The unlicensed proposal called for an underlay on the spectrum above 70 MHz at very low power (below –41 dBm) and one for unspecified power limits in three bands designated for ISM applications: 915 MHz, 2.45 GHz and 5.8 GHz (personal communication from Marcus, 2007). The FCC's further notice triggered many comments favouring the proposed authorisation in the ISM bands. Subsequently the FCC dropped the proposal for an underlay and issued a ruling on the use of spread spectrum in the three bands designated for ISM applications: 26 MHz bandwidth around the centre frequency of 915 MHz, 100 MHz at 2.45 GHz, and 150 MHz at 5.8 GHz. The limitation on peak power was set at a level of 1 Watt, determined on the basis of an expected coverage area of one square mile. No limitations were specified for the antenna gain.[17]

Although no licence is required to use the RF equipment in these designated bands, strict rules have been set for the use, and manufacturers of equipment have to ensure compliance with these rules. In the ISM bands the access to the 'common use' of RF spectrum is unrestricted. The limitations set by governments to the emitted power are the primary means of limiting interference and avoiding a 'tragedy of the commons'.

Here, again, the RF spectrum can be regarded as a productive input for entrepreneurs, albeit primarily for equipment manufacturers. There is no exclusivity, however, and hence there is no certainty as to the number of actors now or in the future who may wish to use the 'RF spectrum commons'. Therefore, the risk associated with investment decisions to be made by entrepreneurs is much akin to investment decisions in product development in open competitive markets. These issues can be framed theoretically under the headings of strategic management (see, for example, de Wit and Meyer, 2004, Mahoney, 2005, and Porter, 1980) and innovation management (see, for instance, Fagerberg, Mowery and Nelson, 2005, Lundvall, 1992, Nelson and Winter, 1977, Tidd, Bessant and Pavitt, 2001, and von Hippel, 1988).

10.5.4   Obtaining additional spectrum: PCS

On 28 June 1990, just before the establishment of the IEEE 802.11 working group, the FCC released a notice of inquiry into the matter of amendment of the commission's rules to establish new personal communications services (FCC, 1990a). This notice provided a first opportunity to claim unlicensed RF spectrum outside the ISM bands for the use by RLANs. Accordingly, in July the IEEE 802.4 working group, the group led by Vic Hayes of NCR, provided comments to the FCC urging the commission to expand the scope of its inquiry so that the competing needs for spectrum for WLAN data communication services could be considered concurrently (IEEE, 1990a). In September the group submitted reply comments to the FCC referring to and supporting the comments from Apple and NCR regarding the need for spectrum in relation to the expected market size of wireless local area networks (IEEE, 1990b). In January 1991 Apple filed a petition for a separate allocation of spectrum for data personal communications services (Apple, 1991). The IEEE 802.11 working group filed its comments to support this allocation of a separate part of the RF spectrum for data communication (IEEE, 1991a).

In 1992 the FCC submitted a notice of proposed rulemaking in ET Docket no. 92–9 (emerging technologies spectrum), proposing to allocate 220 MHz of spectrum between 1,850 and 2,200 MHz, with reference to the 1992 world radiocommunication conference decision with respect to the mobile satellite services (MSS) allocations in the 1,930 to 2,025 MHz and 2,120 to 2,200 MHz bands, and the future public land mobile telecommunications service (FPLMTS) in the 1,885 to 2,025 MHz and 2,110 to 2,200 MHz bands

Table 10.2 *RF band allocations for PCS in the United States*

RF band	Application
901–902 MHz	PCS
929–930 MHz	Domestic public land mobile and private land mobile
930–931 MHz	PCS
931–932 MHz	Domestic public land mobile and private land mobile
940–941 MHz	PCS
1,850–1,910 MHz	PCS (private operational fixed microwave and RF devices)
1,910–1,920 MHz	Data communications equipment
1,920–1,930 MHz	Cordless phones etc.

(FCC, 1992b). In the notice of proposed rulemaking and tentative decision (FCC, 1992a), however, the rules allocated a mere 5 per cent, equivalent to 10 MHz of the total unlicensed allocation to unlicensed data personal communications services (see also Table 10.2).

For cordless phones to be used in the unlicensed PCS band, industry had to buy out the incumbent fixed point-to-point service users. It incorporated the activity under the 'unlicensed transition and management [UTAM] of the 1,910–1,930 MHz band' in order to deal with the finances and the permissions.

The IEEE 802 Committee, on behalf of the 802.11 working group, filed comments to the effect that 10 MHz was insufficient for RLAN systems, as the need was estimated to be 70 to 140 MHz (IEEE, 1992). This 10 MHz data PCS band was not taken up by industry; in fact, it was never used.[18]

10.5.5 Transition to 2.45 GHz in the United States

The FCC Report and Order had assigned three ISM bands for WLAN use, including the 2.45 GHz band. The 915 MHz lower-frequency range had initially been used, as this RF band had the advantage of a larger reach (about a factor of 2.5), as the attenuation of radio waves increases with frequency. In the 2.45 GHz band more spectrum had been assigned, however, 83.5 MHz versus 26 MHz, so more channels could be accommodated and used simultaneously, which would increase the overall data rate and, hence, systems performance. In the 915 MHz band only one channel could be accommodated but at 2.45 GHz thirteen channels could be made available at 5 MHz intervals. As the channel width is 20 MHz, however, only three channels are non-overlapping. The channels in between these non-overlapping channels can be used when other users are separated enough – e.g. by distance or through walls – such that the potentially interfering signals are sufficiently attenuated. The transition from 915 MHz to 2.45 GHz was driven by market forces and occurred in 1993 (see also Chapter 4 section 2.6).

In that year an opportunity arose to assign more spectrum to RLAN devices, as the US Congress passed a bill (Title VI of the Omnibus Budget Reconciliation Act of 1993) identifying 235 MHz of radio spectrum for transfer from federal government use to private sector use. The 2,402 to 2,417 MHz band was handed over through the NTIA, the body responsible for government use of RF spectrum, as a band open for auctioning (NTIA, 1994). The IEEE 802 Committee filed comments to the effect that this band needed to be designated for RLAN devices (IEEE, 1994a).

In the NPRM of the related FCC proceedings, Office of Engineering and Technology Docket no. 94–32, the FCC followed the NTIA proposal (FCC, 1994). Again the IEEE 802 working group filed comments (IEEE, 1994b). Eventually, the FCC decided to refrain from reallocating the band for licensed services in favour of the RLAN devices (FCC, 1995).

In 1997 another contender for the use of the 2.45 GHz band emerged, from an unexpected source: the lighting industry. Two companies requested the FCC for a rules change to support the use of RF energy to stimulate particular gases to excite visible light. General Electric requested the use of the 2.2 to 2.8 MHz band, while Fusion requested the use of the 2.4 GHz band. Fusion also requested permission for much higher line-conducted emissions than permitted in Part 15 of the regulations (25 to 35 dB above non-consumer limits). In addition, the Part 18 regulations did not specify radiated emission limits above 1 GHz. The FCC proposed to limit the radiation to 100 μV/m (microvolts per metre) for non-consumer equipment and 50 μV/m for consumer equipment (FCC, 1998).

In July 1998 the IEEE 802 Committee filed comments on the NPRM with a request to put limits on the out-of-band radiation, expecting that the in-band radiation would also be limited (IEEE, 1998a). In a second ex parte letter, the committee expressed concern that RF lighting could become a serious source of interference for RLAN devices and stated that more study was needed into the emission characteristics of microwave lighting, requesting that a joint study be undertaken before widespread introduction was permitted (IEEE, 1998b). In March 1999 the committee filed another ex parte letter proposing a 'spectrum mask', which defines the permitted emission levels over the frequency band being used, permitting 100 μV/m at 10 m in the upper 5 MHz of the 2,400 to 2,483.5 MHz band and 60 μV/m at 3 m in the remainder of the 2.4 GHz band (IEEE, 1999). In July of that year the committee filed yet another ex parte letter with a new spectrum mask: 1 μV/m at 3 m (average) in the band 2,400 to 2,460 MHz, 330 μV/m at 3 m (average) in the band 2,460 to 2,480 MHz and 1 μV/m at 3 m (average) in the band 2,480 to 2,500 MHz.

In May 2003 the FCC ordered the termination of the docket because Fusion, the only interested party, had ceased its development of RF lighting (FCC, 2003a). In November the FCC released a second order in response to petitions from XM Radio and Sirius Satellite Radio, requesting clarification of the order. The FCC confirmed that the proceeding was terminated (FCC, 2003b).

10.6   Radio spectrum governance in Europe

In Europe there is a long history of cooperation in the field of telecommunications regulations, which became formalised in 1959 with the establishment of the European Conference of Postal and Telecommunications Administrations by nineteen countries, which grew to twenty-six during the first ten years of its existence. The original members were the PTT administrations, the incumbent operators, mostly as state-run monopolies. The early activities of CEPT were concerned primarily with tariff principles and other relevant issues that needed to be settled among the PTTs. Later the activities expanded to include cooperation on commercial, operational, regulatory and technical standardisation issues.

In 1988, as a result of a lobby from the European Commission, CEPT decided to create the European Telecommunications Standards Institute. All telecommunication standardisation activities within CEPT were transferred to this newly formed institute. In most European countries in the late 1980s and early 1990s the national PTTs were split into a telecommunications operator and a postal services operator, and subsequently the new entities were privatised. The postal operators created their own European organisation, PostEurop, and the telecommunications operators created the European Telecommunications Network Operators' Association (ETNO). As a consequence, CEPT became a body for policy makers and regulators. Subsequently CEPT membership has expanded to include the central and eastern European countries; with forty-eight members the organisation now covers almost the entire geographical area of Europe (CEPT, 2008b; Ryan, 2005).

Within CEPT, the European Radiocommunications Committee (ERC) was set up to address all radio-communication-related matters. The prime objective of the ERC was to develop European harmonisation measures for the allocation and the use of radio frequencies. The ERC sought consensus between administrations for the development of decisions and recommendations. The implementation of these measures is on a voluntary basis.[19]

The involvement of CEPT in the European harmonisation effort was recognised in the European Union through Council Resolution 90/C 166/02 (EC, 1990). In this resolution the European Commission gave support to CEPT to set up the European Radiocommunications Office (ERO), as a permanent office to support the ERC. The ERO was formally opened on 6 May 1991 and is located in Copenhagen. The leading role of CEPT in the harmonisation of spectrum in the European Union was reiterated in 1992 in Council Resolution 92/C 318/01 (EC, 1992).

The only frequency bands that were harmonised throughout the European Union in the late 1980s and early 1990s through the involvement of the EC were frequency bands for the digital system for mobile communications (GSM),[20] a pan-European system for radio paging (ERMES)[21] and the DECT system for digital cordless telecommunications.[22] GSM and ERMES were subject to licensing, while DECT operated on a licence-exempt basis.

In the early 1990s there were a number of specific RF sub-bands designated for licence-exempt low-power applications through ERC recommendations. The most notable are the wide-band transmission systems in the 2.4 GHz band (CEPT, 1991) and the frequency bands for HIPERLANs in the 5 and 17 GHz range (CEPT, 1992). The regulations for short-range devices within the CEPT countries were based on different types of legislation and different frequency plans, however, and there were all kinds of national deviations from the ERC recommendations.

In the mid-1990s the ERC decided to combine all its recommendations on SRDs into a single recommendation, ERC/REC 70–03, which came into force in 1997. This recommendation was created to provide an overview of the spectrum available for the various types of low-power devices, together with the associated technical and regulatory parameters. The recommendation provides an outline of the common spectrum allocations for SRDs for countries within CEPT. Not all the allocations are available in all countries, however, and therefore the recommendation includes an appendix spelling out the national deviations. The recommendation classifies the SRDs into thirteen different categories. Wi-Fi equipment operating in the 2.4 and 5 GHz band falls into the category of 'wideband data transmission systems and wireless access systems, including radio local area networks'. This recommendation is updated on a regular basis to reflect current practice (CEPT, 2006; ERC, 2008).

In 1994 the ERC adopted a recommendation aimed at removing the requirement that all radio equipment that is placed on the market needs to be tested in each CEPT country individually. The recommendation still included the requirement to apply for conformity assessment in each country, however (ERC, 1994; ITU, 2006). To resolve this issue, the ERC adopted a decision on 'the mutual recognition of conformity assessment procedures including marking of radio equipment and radio terminal equipment' in 1997 (ERC, 1997). The aim of this decision was to accept the conformity assessment procedures carried out under the responsibility of one of the PTT administrations by another CEPT member country, without additional national procedures.

10.6.1   Involvement of the European Commission

Throughout the 1990s the European Commission gradually increased its involvement in spectrum issues, as the use of the RF spectrum started to affect the 'internal market'. The first intervention was related to the creation of a single European (internal) market for equipment. On 9 March 1999 the European Commission published the R&TTE Directive 1999/5/EC (EC, 1999). This directive, which came into force in April 2000, replaced the old system of type approval for radio equipment under the ERC rules for placing onto the European market and putting into service radio equipment and telecommunications terminal equipment, and made the rulings mandatory. The R&TTE Directive covers most products[23] that use the radio frequency spectrum, including unlicensed devices. The directive obviates the need for national approval regulations. All equipment that is placed on the market must comply with a set of essential requirements, covering the protection of health and safety, electromagnetic emissions and the immunity of the equipment and effective use of the radio spectrum so as to avoid harmful interference.

Equipment manufactured in accordance with a harmonised standard (HS)[24] may be placed on the market within the European Union. Certain restrictions may apply to the use of radio equipment if the frequencies are not harmonised in the European Union, however.[25] If an HS is used, the manufacturer has to perform some specific radio tests and can make its own declaration of conformity (self-declaration), stating that the product satisfies the essential requirements; there is no need for an external body to perform the testing. When an HS is not available or not appropriate, a manufacturer needs to demonstrate more extensively how the requirements of the directive are being met through testing, to be documented in a 'technical construction file'. This file has to be reviewed and approved by a notified body.

Another EU intervention in radio spectrum management came with the introduction of the new regulatory framework. This framework was aimed at furthering the liberalisation, harmonisation and simplification of the regulations in the telecommunications sector. The Framework Directive (2002/21/EC),[26] on a common regulatory framework for electronic communications networks and services, states that the allocation and assignment of radio frequencies by national regulatory authorities are to be based on objective, transparent, non-discriminatory and proportionate criteria. The related Authorisation Directive (2002/20/EC)[27] specifies the circumstances under which the granting of an individual licence is being allowed. The directive states that granting of an individual licence is allowed only to ensure an efficient use of radio frequencies. The directive also limits the conditions that may be attached to the rights of use for radio frequencies. The licensing and the formulation of the conditions under which the radio frequencies may be used are left to the member states.

Under this new regime, the harmonisation of the spectrum is still left to CEPT. The 2002 Radio Spectrum Decision by the European Commission (2002/676/EC) created the possibility of imposing technical harmonisation measures on the member states, however. This decision created a legal framework for 'the harmonised availability and efficient use of radio spectrum in the European Union for the establishment and functioning of the internal market in Community policy areas, such as electronic communications, broadcasting and transport'. In its implementation of the decision the European Commission is assisted by the newly formed Radio Spectrum Committee (RSC). The EC can issue mandates to CEPT to advise on technical harmonisation measures. The RSC approves CEPT reports and associated technical implementation measures prepared by the EC. The implementation of these measures is mandatory for the EU member states (EC, 2002).

In November 2006 a decision of the European Commission was published on the harmonisation of the radio spectrum for use by short-range devices. The annex of this decision contains a list of frequency bands and related technical parameters for six different types of SRD. All of the frequency bands had already been harmonised through the provisions of ERC Recommendation 70–03. The role of this decision is to provide additional legal certainty. The annex to the decision is updated annually (EC, 2006).

10.6.2   Europe allocating the 2.45 GHz band: WLANs

While in the United States the 915 MHz band is designated for ISM applications including WLANs, in Europe the 915 MHz band had been assigned for the use of GSM, the European digital cellular communication system. As the licences for GSM were granted to network operators on a semi-exclusive basis, this was considered to be incompatible with the licence-exempt regime of WLANs. In 1990, within CEPT, an ad hoc group was formed with the task of preparing recommendations for the use of the 2.45 GHz ISM band for wireless LANs in Europe. In 1991 this effort was supported by a letter from the IEEE 802.11 working group that was sent to all administrations, asking for their cooperation in assigning the same spectrum for unlicensed use (IEEE, 1991b). In 1991 CEPT allowed the use of the 2.45 GHz band in the European Union (CEPT, 1991), to be ratified by the European Commission in 1992, although the technical approval rules still had to be defined by ETSI; this was completed in 1993 (ETSI, 1993). The output power limit was set thereby at 100 mW, including antenna gain, and a power density requirement was set at a maximum of 10 mW/MHz (for the NCR perspective on the European developments, see Chapter 4).

In 1997 the radio frequency identification (RFID) industry approached the CEPT joint project team on 2.45 GHz SRDs with a request to permit a higher power level for (passive) RF-based identification devices. The original request was for twice the permitted power, but with each subsequent meeting the requested power level doubled until the 4 W level, which was permitted in the United States, was reached. During the process, therefore, the Wi-Fi industry had to watch the activities of the RFID industry constantly in order to protect its interests. The result was that the devices were permitted in mid-band for 8 MHz (2,446 to 2,454 MHz).

10.7   Unlicensed devices outside the United States and Europe

10.7.1   Unlicensed devices in China: WLANs

China has regulations in place for devices without the need for individual licences. The unlicensed devices are classified into twelve categories related to the maximum radiated power, between 750 μW and 1 Watt. China has assigned frequency bands that are generally not the same as in other regions, except for some ISM bands. The unlicensed devices have no protection against interference from other radio stations or ISM applications and may not produce harmful interference. If harmful interference is caused the device must cease operations, and be put into operation again only after measures have been taken to eliminate such interference.

Unlicensed devices will have to pass examinations and tests as required by the Ministry of Information Industry (MII), to ensure that the devices comply with the rules. In the absence of type approval by the ministry the devices may not be produced, sold or used within the country (ITU, 2006).

The first band that was opened for unlicensed use in China was the 2.4 GHz band. In 2001 the MII issued IDW [2001] 653 to this effect, the main purpose of the regulation being to open the 2.4 GHz band. Since this was China's first experiment with unlicensed devices it was decided to be conservative, with a low limit on transmit power of 10 mW (IEEE, 2002).

In November 2003 the General Administration of Quality Supervision, Inspection and Quarantine (GAQSIQ) and the Standardisation Administration of China (SAC) issued a decree that all WLAN equipment should be in line with the national standard GB 15629.11 as of 1 June 2004. GB 15629.11 was similar to IEEE 802.11b, including a transmit power limit of 100 mW. The only exception was a security protocol known as the WLAN Authentication and Privacy Infrastructure (WAPI), which is not compatible with the wired equivalent privacy security protocol used by 802.11 (TransAsia Lawyers, 2003). The US government and foreign suppliers protested against the mandatory implementation of WAPI. On 21 April 2004 the Chinese government and the US government reached an agreement to delay the implementation of WAPI indefinitely (TransAsia Lawyers, 2004).

The SAC decided to submit WAPI to the ISO standards organisation for recognition as an international standard. This submission occurred at about the same time as the IEEE 802.11i standard was being submitted for ratification. ISO decided to put both standards to a ballot, and the result, declared on 8 March 2006, was a rejection of WAPI in favour of 802.11i. Chinese officials declared afterwards that WAPI would still be promoted and used domestically nonetheless (*China Daily*, 2006).

10.7.2   Unlicensed devices in Japan: WLANs

In Japan, the establishment of a radio station requires in principle a licence from the Ministry of Internal Affairs and Communications (MIC). Radio stations emitting at low power can be established without obtaining an individual licence, however, provided that a certification of conformity with the required technical standards has been granted for the equipment used. Low-power stations are classified in fifteen different categories, including a category for low-power data communication systems and wireless LANs. For each designated frequency band the type of emission, the channel spacing, the occupied bandwidth, the antenna power, the antenna gain and the carrier sense are prescribed (ITU, 2006).

Unlicensed use of the 2.4 GHz band for wireless LAN was introduced in December 1993. In Japan the 2.4 GHz ISM band is somewhat extended from the international harmonised band, and ranges from 2,400 to 2,497 MHz. Frequency hopping with a high power of 10 mW/MHz is allowed only in the 2,471 to 2,497 MHz range. Frequency hopping is also allowed in the 2,427 to 2,470.75 MHz range with a reduced power level of 3 mW/MHz. Direct sequence and OFDM modulation techniques are allowed in the 2.4 GHz band with a maximum radiated power of 10 mW/MHz (IEEE, 2007; ITU, 2006; MIC, 2006).[28]

10.7.3   Unlicensed devices in South Korea: WLANs

Radio stations that may operate without an individual licence are listed in article 30 of the Presidential Decree of Radio Act. They are classified into nine categories, including a category of 'extremely low-power devices' (LPD class 1), a category of 'low-power devices' (LPD class 2) and a category of 'specified low-power devices'. Within the latter category there are twelve types of applications defined. One type of application is 'data communication', of which Wi-Fi in the 2.4 GHz band is an example. Another type of application concerns 'wireless access systems including RLAN' in the 5 GHz band.

The spectrum requirements and the technical criteria for these 'specified low-power' radio stations are established in the regulations produced by the Ministry of Information and Communication, which define the power levels for these SRDs between 3 mW and 10 mW, except those for RLANs and vehicle identification systems.

As a basic principle, South Korea's Radio Wave Act stipulates: 'Any person who intends to manufacture or import apparatus for wireless facilities and equipment shall undergo a type approval test conducted by the Minister of Information and Communication and file a type registration with the Minister of Information and Communication' (ITU, 2006).

The 2.4 GHz band has been licence-exempt in South Korea since January 2003. The antenna power of the RLAN equipment should be equal to or less than 10 mW/MHz for direct sequence and orthogonal frequency modulation and 3 mW peak power divided by hopping bandwidth (MHz) for frequency hopping. The absolute gain of the transmitting antenna shall be equal to or less than 6 dBi, or 20 dBi for fixed point-to-point applications.

10.7.4   Unlicensed devices in other countries: WLANs

All major industrial countries allow wireless LAN devices in the 2.4 GHz band. Those countries that have close relations with the United States tend to follow the rules defined by the FCC, such as a maximum 1 W transmitted power with a maximum antenna gain of factor 4 and a minimum 'processing gain' of 10 for direct sequence transmitters. Those countries that have stronger relations with Europe follow the rules set by the CEPT, such as a maximum of 100 mW output power, including antenna gain, and a maximum power density requirement of 10 mW/MHz, instead of a processing gain requirement.

Although the 2.4 GHz spectrum is available in virtually all countries around the world, in many countries in Africa and the Middle East, and in Russia, the use of WLANs requires a licence either in general or for outdoor use.

The IEEE 802.11 working group realised that there were various national restrictions to the use of the 2.4 GHz band. In order to simplify the worldwide usage of WLANs in the 2.4 GHz band, IEEE 802.11d was developed as an amendment to the standard, so as to facilitate deployment by allowing an access point to 'describe' the configurations that are permitted for the client stations to use. IEEE 802.11d was adopted in June 2001.

10.8   Towards a global allocation of the 5 GHz band for WLANs

10.8.1   Europe allocating the 5 GHz band: HIPERLANs

In 1992 CEPT identified higher frequency bands (non-ISM bands) for potential wireless LAN applications. CEPT identified the 5.15 to 5.25 GHz band and the 17.1 to 17.3 GHz band, with a potential extension, namely the 5.25 to 5.3 GHz band, on a national basis. This spectrum was designated for HIPERLANs on a non-interference and non-protection basis (CEPT, 1992). ETSI established a technical committee for the development of the HIPERLAN standard (see Chapter 3 for a discussion of the HIPERLAN standard).

The 5 GHz band did not remain uniquely identified with HIPERLANs, however. The operators of the MSS detected an oversight, in that they had forgotten to request an uplink frequency during the world radiocommunication conference of 1992. In their request they indicated that, in their assessment, the uplink could coexist with HIPERLANs operating in the 5.15 to 5.25 GHz band. Consequently, the 1995 world radiocommunication conference decided to allocate on a primary basis a band overlapping with the lower HIPERLAN band, as documented in ERC Decision no. 96/03 (CEPT, 1996). Shortly after this allocation, however, the satellite operators claimed that, if too many HIPERLANs were deployed in an particular area, they would receive harmful interference. As a result, CEPT was forced to lower the power limit of HIPERLANs from 1 W to 200 mW and to restrict them to indoor use (CEPT, 1999a, 1999b). This decision also included the assignment of an additional 255 MHz (5,470 to 5,725 MHz) for HIPERLANs to allow spreading of the signal power, the inclusion of transmit power control to minimise the aggregate transmitted power in the MSS band, and dynamic frequency selection to prevent the use of frequencies already used by the incumbent users and other HIPERLAN devices. In December 2000 Project IEEE 802.11h, 'Spectrum and transmit power management extensions in the 5 GHz band in Europe', was approved to cover these modifications. The extension of the standard was approved at the end of 2003.

To prevent similar surprises in the future, at the 2000 world radiocommunication conference the European regulators proposed an agenda item for the 2003 conference to allocate globally the HIPERLAN-related frequencies (a total of 455 MHz in the 5 GHz band) on a co-primary basis (for an explanation, see section 10.9). As a consequence, all (existing) users of services in this band were responsible for assessing their position and preparing the necessary paperwork, and when appropriate they would have to lobby the administrations to support their position. At the 2003 world radiocommunication conference, Resolution 229 responded positively to the agenda item and made the allocation for 445 MHz of spectrum to wireless access systems (WASs) including RLANs on a co-primary basis.

10.8.2   *The United States allocating the 5 GHz band*

In 1995, triggered by the European assignments of the 5 GHz HIPER-LAN bands, through petitions by the Wireless Information Networks Forum (WINForum), an association of radio manufacturing and computer companies formed to promote the development of wireless information networks, and by Apple, spectrum assignments in the 5 GHz band for WLANs were being pursued with the Federal Communications Commission (Apple, 1995; WINForum, 1995). On 6 May 1996 the FCC responded with a rulemaking procedure (FCC, 1996), and decided in a Report and Order on 9 January 1997 the assignment of

RF spectrum for the operation of so-called unlicensed – national information infrastructure (U-NII) devices in the 5,150 to 5,350 MHz and 5,725 to 5,825 MHz bands, a total of 300 MHz (FCC, 1997). The higher U-NII band coincided with part of the already assigned ISM band.

10.9   The public–private coordination of RF spectrum use

Because there are many more requests for assignments of frequencies than there are frequencies available within the RF spectrum, services that can share frequencies with other services receive an allocation by the world radiocommunication conference within the same frequency band. Before such allocations are made, the possibilities for sharing and the conditions for sharing are analysed and documented. In a sharing arrangement, the main service becomes the primary service and the other services receive a secondary status. The primary service is protected from interference from the other services in the band; the rules state: '[S]econdary services shall not cause harmful interference to primary services, and can not claim protection from harmful interference from primary services.' In turn, secondary services can claim protection from the same or other secondary services. As further requests for frequency spectrum were received, new subcategories were introduced within the primary and secondary category: co-primary and co-secondary services, each allocated with a hierarchy of rights.

It is worth noting that the Wi-Fi devices in the 2.45 GHz band were designated by national regulatory agencies on a non-protection, non-interference basis – i.e., at the lowest level of the pecking order. The HIPERLAN frequencies in the 5 GHz band were also originally assigned on a non-protection, non-interference basis. The case described above regarding the satellite uplink implied a case of shared use with HIPERLANs. The additional 455 MHz targeted in the 5 GHz band would lead to another more contentious case of shared use of RF spectrum.

Lucent Technologies, through Vic Hayes, recognised the importance of the European sharing proposal with HIPERLANs for the future of Wi-Fi, but also realised that it would take a significant effort to coalesce the industry to make this co-allocation to be applicable to Wi-Fi as a primary service. In this respect, telecommunications companies have a long tradition of fighting for their rights, and tend to allocate ample funding to defend their cases. Computer companies operate with much lower margins, however, and typically allocate lower budgets to standardisation efforts. Moreover, they lack the experience to act successfully in this forum.

When the agenda for the 2003 world radiocommunication conference appeared, the first activity involved the IEEE 802.11 working group. There the need for a study into the sharing proposal was acknowledged, along with the fact that it would have to involve a law firm to formulate the petitions to the FCC. This was considered an activity outside the charter of the IEEE, however. Thus it was that, at the start of 2001, Hayes began a rally in the one-year-old Wireless Ethernet Compatibility Alliance to establish a regulatory committee with sufficient decision power to be able to act quickly in response to the events that would develop at the regulatory agencies, and with sufficient funding to engage a law firm to assist in the generation and implementation of all required actions. Hayes, who had served the maximum term of ten years as chairperson of IEEE 802.11, was available, and he was assigned to the task. He relates the story:

The first order of business was to propose the establishment of new rules in the United States for an allocation of spectrum. These rules should be in accordance with the European proposal, which was on the agenda of the 2003 world radiocommunication conference, to ensure that the US representatives could support this proposal. Through the WECA Alliance[29] we made a petition to the FCC to start the rule-making process in line with the conference proposal (WECA, 2002a).[30] The next step for rule making is a notice to the public 'at large' requesting comments on the petition. The response from the NTIA, the agency responsible for the spectrum assigned for governmental use, was one of strong opposition to the allocation of a co-primary status, as between 5,470 and 5,725 MHz the frequency band was already allocated for use by the US government, linked to the Radio Location Service, involving radar technology. As a consequence, the US position at the 2003 conference would have been negative.

Removing this obstacle was a major task for the Regulatory Committee of the WECA. We first contracted a radar expert to perform a 'sharing' study for wireless LAN devices with a long list of radar devices. Based on the knowledge we obtained, members of the committee worked the issue at national, regional and international levels in close cooperation with our radar expert. This effort resulted in the WECA filing a notice with two documents, 'RLAN radar sharing study' and 'RLAN radar characterization model' (WECA, 2002b), and was concluded with a meeting between the NTIA, the FCC and the Regulatory Committee members, which resulted in an agreement on 31 January 2003 on how to share the band at co-primary level (NTIA, 2003). This result was obtained just in time for the conference, which was held in June. With this obstacle removed, the US position changed from 'violently against' into 'absolutely in favour' and the Wi-Fi Alliance received excellent support from the US delegation at the conference. Meanwhile, members of the Wi-Fi Alliance participated in the FCC preparatory meetings for the conference, in the CEPT task group for the 5 GHz allocation, as well as in meetings in the ITU-R of the task force on WASs.

Thanks to the European initiative and the strong support of the European member states at the conference, combined with the support from the United States, Resolution 229 allocated 'wireless access systems, including radio LANs', to the mobile service on a co-primary basis (World Radiocommunication Conference, 2003). The agreed sharing rules require that the WASs monitor frequencies before they transmit and use only channels that are not used by radar systems. Furthermore, during their operation, they have to monitor constantly the frequencies within the band, and if a conflict arises with a radar system they have to terminate the transfer of payload, find a new free channel and continue only with the transmission of so-called management frames to relocate the receiving station to the new channel.

In November 2003 the FCC released its Report and Order 03–122 to implement the world radiocommunication conference decision in Part 15, for unlicensed communication devices (FCC, 2003b). In November 2004 the CEPT decision ECC/DEC/(04)08 implemented the conference resolution, with the qualification 'for unlicensed devices' (CEPT, 2004).

10.10   The role of the ITU with respect to short-range devices

The radio frequency spectrum is governed globally by the International Telecommunications Union. The Radiocommunication Sector of the ITU develops and adopts the so-called Radio Regulations, a binding international treaty, which has developed into a voluminous set of rules. The Radio Regulations are aimed at the avoidance of radio interference through the division of the RF spectrum into bands, which are allocated to one or more services out of the forty different radio services that are defined.[31] A wide range of regulatory, operational and technical provisions ensure that radio services are compatible with each other and harmful interference between countries is avoided. The Radio Regulations are updated in response to changes in needs and demands at the successive world radiocommunication conferences, which are held every three to four years.

The Radio Regulations do not deal with the process of authorising frequency usage. Moreover, short-range devices are not regarded as a radio service in terms of the Radio Regulations. Consequently, SRD applications do not have a 'status' in the sense of a primary or a secondary service, and therefore they are not permitted to cause harmful interference to, nor claim protection from, radio services.

Nonetheless, as early as 1993 ITU-R Study Group 1 decided to study the spectrum governance aspects related to short-range communication by adopting Question ITU-R 201/1, 'Spectrum management aspects of short-range communication systems'. This question called for a study in order to generate a recommendation addressing: (1) technical questions related to the spectrum efficiency of short-range systems (e.g. modulation, access techniques and protocols); (2) sharing techniques to avoid harmful interference between short-range systems; and (3) identifying frequency ranges that are particularly suitable for short-range systems with various operational parameters in various environments (CEPT, 2006).

No contributions were made in response to this question, however. As a result the ITU-R Study Group 1 tried to make a fresh start by adopting a new enquiry, Question ITU-R 213/1, 'Technical and operating parameters and spectrum requirements for short-range devices'. This new question again aimed at studies on the technical and operating parameters for SRDs as well as identifying frequency bands and spectrum requirements to facilitate global access and applications with regard to SRDs. In taking up the drafting of the new recommendation, however, it soon became clear that there were big differences in the regulations for short-range devices between the three ITU regions. From this investigation it became obvious, therefore, that a global solution for frequency assignments and the related technical and operating parameters could not be found. Accordingly, it was decided to develop a recommendation that consisted of a common part describing the SRD applications and the commonly used frequency ranges (which are mainly the ISM bands) and a number of appendices in which the regulations for SRDs for various regions and countries are explained. This recommendation, ITU-R SM.1538, 'Technical and operating parameters and spectrum requirements for short-range radiocommunication devices', was first adopted in 2001, and remains subject to revisions on a regular basis as new information becomes available. Currently the recommendation includes the provisions stipulated for Europe, the United States, China, Japan and South Korea.

In 2007 the radiocommunication assembly[32] decided to undertake a new attempt and to go one step further, and adopted Resolution 54, 'Studies to achieve harmonisation for short-range radiocommunication devices (SRDs)'. This resolution calls for studies to enable the implementation of advanced technologies for SRDs, thereby focusing in particular on a strategy for the future. These studies should emphasise the collection of information on SRDs that use advanced spectrum access and frequency-tuning techniques in order to understand their capabilities, at the same time ensuring protection to radiocommunication services, and to advise on a mechanism that might ease the use of relevant frequency bands and/or frequency tuning ranges, preferably on a global or regional basis, that are suitable for SRDs.

At the 2007 world radiocommunication conference, which directly followed the radiocommunication assembly, the implications of short-range devices and the use of the ISM bands for radio services were discussed further. At the conference the decision was made to put this subject on the agenda of the next conference under agenda item 1.22, to 'examine the effect of emissions from short-range devices on radiocommunication services'. This agenda item addresses the problem of interference to the radio services through the use of short-range devices. The associated Resolution 953 'invites ITU-R to study emissions from SRDs, in particular RFIDs, inside and outside the frequency bands designated in the Radio Regulations for ISM applications to ensure adequate protection of radiocommunication service'. As can be seen, the ITU-R acknowledges the fact that the use of short-range devices is increasing, but continues to see them as devices that fall outside the scope of the international regulations regarding the allocation of radio spectrum. Other than the statement that SRDs may not claim any protection from the radio services as defined in the Radio Regulations, they are completely disregarded. The only exception in the Radio Regulations is formulated in footnote 5.116 to the table of frequency allocations; this footnote urges PTT administrations to authorise the use of the band 3,155 to 3,195 kHz for low-power wireless hearing aids, with a possible extension up to 3,400 kHz to cater for local needs.

The only way to get an allocation for SRDs is to include them under the definition of a radio service, as has been done for the RLAN systems in the 5 GHz band: at the 2003 world radiocommunication conference, when it was decided to allocate the 5,150 to 5,350 MHz and 5,470 to 5,725 MHz bands for 'Wireless Access Systems including RLAN'. Since RLAN systems are not a defined service in the Radio Regulations, this allocation was made possible only by making an allocation to the mobile service. The use of these bands by the mobile service is restricted to wireless access systems, including radio local area networks, through Resolution 229. The mobile service is restricted so as to avoid interference with the other primary services, mainly radar systems. The avoidance of interference is based on a mechanism to detect radar systems and as a result avoid use, or vacating a channel identified as being occupied by radar equipment. This mechanism is called dynamic frequency selection (DFS). Its purpose and performance criteria are defined in Recommendation ITU-R M.1652. This solution has been achieved as a result of the close cooperation between regulators and the industry, as is explained in the previous section.

10.11   Frequency agile devices and dynamic spectrum access[33]

The number of short-range devices and their applications has been growing significantly in recent years. Mott MacDonald estimated the European market for unlicensed devices and services to have been worth nearly €15 billion in 2006, and expected the figure to rise to more than €25 billion in 2009 (Mott MacDonald, 2006).

The growth in the number of devices and applications has increased the pressure on regulators to allow more co-allocation in existing bands and the opening up of new frequency bands. While co-allocation is often feasible, CEPT has concluded that the execution of the required compatibility studies can be a lengthy process, and that the overall process for identifying and allocating new spectrum for SRDs is time-consuming (CEPT, 2006). In the earlier generation of SRDs the potential for interference with other legitimate users was managed through the limitation of the radiated power and/or restrictions on the proportion of time during which the devices are allowed to operate (the duty cycle). Today, more advanced interference mitigation techniques are needed – and available – to ease sharing, such as spread-spectrum modulation and the use of LBT and other 'polite' protocols. In the same report, CEPT concludes that new and evolving technologies are needed to ease sharing, such as frequency agile and intelligent radio devices that can detect and avoid any existing use within a given radio channel. A good example of this kind of techniques is dynamic frequency selection, as applied in the 5 GHz RLAN systems (see section 10.9).

These frequency agile and intelligent technologies, such as cognitive radio (CR), not only have the potential to make more efficient use of spectrum but also offer more versatility and flexibility, with an increased ability to adapt their operations on the basis of external factors. The application of these technologies requires changes in the spectrum governance regime, however, to take advantage of their potential for more efficient use of spectrum. There is a need for dynamic spectrum access (DSA), and with it a paradigm shift from a static to a dynamic spectrum governance model. The following section explores the implications of DSA for spectrum management.

10.11.1 Towards dynamic spectrum access

In Gilder's article 'Auctioning the airwaves', published in *Forbes* on 11 April 1994, the author envisaged a future in which 'the wireless systems . . . will offer bandwidth on demand and send packets wherever there is space'. Dynamic spectrum access is based on the notion of the existence of 'space' or 'white spots' – i.e. frequencies assigned to a primary user that are at a particular time and at a particular geographic location not occupied by that user (Haykin, 2005).[34] The objective of DSA is to provide the means to make these white spots available for secondary users. In this context, 'secondary' means that the 'white spots' may be used by a secondary user as long as this usage does not interfere with the usage of the primary user – i.e. no (harmful) interference to the primary user is allowed, and a primary user has priority in access to the radio spectrum.

The basic approach of a DSA system is to access the radio spectrum based on the system's own judgement of the local use; it is also called opportunistic spectrum access (OSA). The system applying OSA identifies 'white spots' in the radio spectrum and then transmits over sections of the spectrum that are not in use. OSA has the additional complexity, however, that it needs to keep listening for other transmitters in order to vacate a 'white spot' when a primary user starts accessing it.

This opportunistic behaviour gives rise to a particular problem that is known as the 'hidden node' problem, whereby the DSA system is inadvertently not able to detect the primary usage of a frequency channel. There are different reasons for the occurrence of the 'hidden node' problem. One of the most eminent reasons is that a primary transmitter is not detected because of 'shadowing', for instance due to an obstruction (such as a building or a mountain) in between the primary user and the DSA system. The hidden node problem makes the detection of spectrum usage by no means an easy task. In general, the sensitivity of the DSA system will have to outperform primary user receivers by a wide margin (Ghasemi and Sousa, 2008; Pawelczak, 2008).

Next to the application of detectors that are much more sensitive than typical receivers,[35] there are at least three options to overcome this hidden node problem. One of the options is to share sensing information between the various DSA systems in an area. This is known as cooperative or collaborative detection. Cooperation can improve the probability of detection and reduce the detection time, and thus increase the overall agility. The drawback is the overhead needed to exchange sensing information. A second option is to obtain information about the local use of a frequency band from a database. In this case the DSA system must be aware of its geographical position – e.g. by incorporating radio navigation in the terminal; the DSA system will need to have access to the database on a regular basis, and the database will have to be kept up to date. This option is especially suitable in cases in which the spectrum usage of the primary user does not change frequently, for example in a broadcasting band. A third option is to use a local radio beacon that transmits information to DSA systems nearby. The beacon transmits information about the availability of spectrum, and possibly usage conditions, to the DSA systems in that area.

These solutions lead to a need for an information channel; either between DSA systems to share sensing information, or between a DSA system and a central entity to obtain information about usage possibilities. This information channel is called a cognition-supporting pilot channel or cognitive pilot channel (CPC). There are different possibilities for the implementation of a CPC. The CPC can use a new, dedicated (ideally worldwide-harmonised) frequency, a specific channel of existing access technology, or a combination thereof.

10.11.2 Implications of dynamic spectrum access for spectrum governance

There are no international treaties that prohibit the use of dynamic access to spectrum in general or cognitive radio in particular.[36] The current regulation regimes do put barriers in the way of the successful use of more dynamic forms of spectrum access, however. In most countries the radio spectrum governance regime is based on a static approach, whereby the radio spectrum is split into fixed blocks that are then assigned to a specific service or technology. For instance, there are bands designated for analogue radio broadcasting, air traffic control, emergency services, television broadcasting and mobile radio. The frequency blocks are assigned exclusively to licensees to offer these services. The introduction of DSA in these exclusively designated and assigned frequency bands is possible only if these bands are opened up for other services and technologies. Since the designation of bands to specific services and the rules under which they may be used have their origin in the international framework, the need arises to adapt both the international and national regulatory frameworks for the management of RF spectrum.

10.11.3 Adapting the international regulatory framework

There is a need to enhance the regulatory framework at an international level to allow for more flexibility in the use of RF spectrum and there is a need for harmonisation activities related to dynamic spectrum access, including cooperation between DSA systems or between DSA systems and a central entity.

Activities related to these tasks have already started within the ITU-R. At the 2007 world radiocommunication conference a decision was taken to put two items on the agenda for the 2011 conference.[37] Agenda item 1.2 concerns the allowing of more flexibility in the use of spectrum:

1.2 taking into account the ITU-R studies carried out in accordance with Resolution 951 . . . to take appropriate action with a view to enhancing the international regulatory framework.

The related Resolution 951 identifies the need for further studies in order to develop concepts and procedures for enhancing the Radio Regulations to meet the demands of current, emerging and future radio applications, while taking into account existing services and usage. The studies should take into consideration the fact that evolving and emerging radiocommunication technologies may enable sharing possibilities and may lead to more frequency-agile and interference-tolerant equipment, and consequently to more flexible use of spectrum, and that these evolving and emerging technologies may not require band segmentation within the traditional spectrum allocation framework.

The other agenda item (1.19) is specifically about software-defined radio (SDR) and CR:

1.19 to consider regulatory measures and their relevance, in order to enable the introduction of software-defined radio and cognitive radio systems, based on the results of ITU-R studies, in accordance with Resolution 956.

Study Group 1 (spectrum management) of the ITU-R is responsible for the relevant studies needed in preparation for the 2011 conference. Within working party 1B of Study Group 1, work has started to develop definitions of software-defined radio and cognitive radio systems, to facilitate the discussion of related concepts, such as the cognition-supporting pilot channel and a database, and to identify potential regulatory issues associated with SDR and CR systems. A so-called correspondence group has been set up to speed up the work.

It remains unclear what the potential changes to the Radio Regulations should be in addition to the need for more flexibility (which is tackled in agenda item 1.2). The only remaining issue that might have an impact on the Radio Regulations is the need for a globally harmonised CPC. Further studies are needed to prove the viability of DSA based on a local radio beacon, however.

There might also be a need for regulators to get involved in order to create a database with local information on spectrum usage, and to ensure standardisation of the protocols needed to access this database. This task has no implications for the Radio Regulations, however.

The radiocommunication assembly prior to the 2007 conference decided to place question ITU-R 241–1/5, 'Cognitive radio systems in the mobile service', on the agenda of Study Group 5 (terrestrial services) for the forthcoming study period. This question lists the following issues to be studied (ITU, 2007):

(1) What is the ITU definition of cognitive radio systems?
(2) What are the closely related radio technologies (e.g. smart radio, reconfigurable radio, policy-defined adaptive radio and their associated control mechanisms) and their functionalities that may be a part of cognitive radio systems?
(3) What key technical characteristics, requirements, performance and benefits are associated with the implementation of cognitive radio systems?
(4) What are the potential applications of cognitive radio systems and their impact on spectrum management?
(5) What are the operational implications (including privacy and authentication) of cognitive radio systems?
(6) What are the cognitive capabilities that could facilitate coexistence with existing systems in the mobile service and in other radiocommunication services, such as broadcast, mobile satellite or fixed?
(7) What spectrum-sharing techniques can be used to implement cognitive radio systems to ensure coexistence with other users?
(8) How can cognitive radio systems promote the efficient use of radio resources?

Study Group 5 is expected to deliver a response to this question in the form of a report, or possibly recommendations, by 2010. Study Group 5 is already working on a report on 'Cognitive radio systems in the land mobile service'.

Within the European Union there are a number of activities to introduce more flexibility into the use of spectrum (WAPECS)[38] and to introduce secondary trading.[39] Both issues are included in the European Commission's proposals for the ongoing EU telecoms review. The EC has also mandated the European Communications Committee to carry out a study into the introduction of cognitive radio in the television bands. The ensuing report indicates that the feasibility of the introduction of CR systems has not yet been conclusively demonstrated. Since the CR technology is at a very early stage, CEPT recommends looking more deeply into the requirements within the European environment for CR devices to be deployed in 'white space' spectrum in order to facilitate the further development of CR technology. The current CEPT view is that any new 'white space' applications should be used on a non-protected, non-interfering basis (CEPT, 2008a).

10.11.4 Adapting national regulatory frameworks

The various national spectrum management authorities will have to adapt the national regulatory frameworks in order to improve efficiency and flexibility in the use of spectrum. From a regulatory perspective, there are two different models that can be considered to improve efficiency and flexibility: a model based on tradable property rights and a model based on open access (Faulhaber, 2006). These models need to be linked to the new technological capabilities of CR and DSA.

10.11.5 Dynamic spectrum access in an open access regime

An open access regime is a regime in which a user can have access to spectrum without the need for a licence. In this case, a DSA system can have access to 'white spots' on a secondary basis without the need to have an individual licence. There are only general conditions imposed on the secondary use of the band. Access to 'white spots' can be facilitated in an open access regime if strict rules are defined to keep the interference to the primary users at an acceptable level. This level will have to be clearly defined by the regulator. The definition of an appropriate level is no easy task, however. If the level is too restrictive the potential gains of opportunistic spectrum access are marginal, while a level that is too permissive may affect the quality of service of the primary user. The regulator will have to cooperate with industry in order to set a realistic level that is based on the technological state of the art.

Irrespective of the interference level that is defined, the potential for interference will always remain, and there are no guarantees with an OSA system having access to spectrum. This sets limitations on the use of opportunistic spectrum access and on the types of applications that can be supported in an open access regime. Opportunistic spectrum access is typically expected to be restricted to low-end applications, involving low-power devices. The growth in demand for mobile spectrum is mainly for asymmetric intermittent access, however. OSA systems may therefore become used for mainstream services or supplementing mainstream services in conveying their asymmetric load.[40] OSA is also of interest to military users wishing to set up ad hoc networks without the need for central coordination. The bottom line is that OSA provides an opportunity to ease the sharing between existing, primary, users and

SRDs in bands in which sharing via conventional means is difficult, if not impossible.

Although both proposals addressed no technical issues and were mainly aiming at packet data communication, it was a sign for radio regulators that real steps in liberalising spectrum markets should be taken – i.e. it was clearly visible that it might be better to encourage licensed parties to share their non-utilised resources. Therefore, in 2002 the FCC issued Docket no. 98–153, permitting many users to transmit on a single channel, using low-power communication based on ultra-wideband (UWB) technology. The recently released FCC Docket no. 03–122 revisited Part 15, allowing wireless data users to share channels with radar systems on an LBT basis.

10.11.6 Dynamic spectrum access in a market-based approach

A market-based approach to RF spectrum management is based on the introduction of property rights. This approach is characterised by three interlinked elements (adapted from Baumol and Robyn, 2006):

(1) well-defined exclusive rights to the use of spectrum;
(2) a market-type mechanism, such as an auction, for an initial allocation of spectrum rights; and
(3) a secondary market in which these rights can be sold or leased.

In this case the regulator will have to assume the responsibility to set well-defined usage rights in the market, with as few usage restrictions as possible.

A number of countries have already introduced measures to permit secondary trading. In most cases, however, approval from the authorities is required before trading may take place. These kinds of barriers make instant trading impossible and, hence, will have to be removed if the full potential of DSA is to be exploited.

A market-based approach is expected to provide the potential for active coordination between the primary user and the secondary (cognitive) user about the likelihood of interference, and on guarantees about access to spectrum. If the barriers to instant trading are removed, the opportunity to buy and sell rights to access spectrum can be based on the actual demand for spectrum. This creates the opportunity to use DSA systems for higher-valued services, such as mobile telephony, and for a spot market to be introduced. A spot market is a perfect means to acquire and sell rights to spectrum access on the basis of the actual demand at any given moment in time.[41]

Information about the actual ownership of RF spectrum rights will have to be readily available to facilitate trading. The regulator is ideally positioned to perform the task of keeping the records of these ownership rights to the use of radio spectrum. The inclusion of monitoring information about the actual usage of spectrum by the primary users can further facilitate trading by providing more insights into the possibilities for secondary usage.

10.11.7 First dynamic spectrum access applications

The first implementation of spectrum sensing was probably in cordless telephony. A typical DECT cordless telephone selects a frequency channel based on its sensing of the channels available. Cordless telephones use an exclusively assigned frequency band, however; sensing is used only to find a vacant channel within the band. This was implemented so as to have an automatic mechanism for avoiding the use of channels from neighbouring cordless telephones.[42]

The first application that senses the available channels to detect and avoid other users is unlicensed wireless LAN in the 5 GHz band. The WLAN uses a subset of OSA, called dynamic frequency selection. DFS is used to prevent a device from accessing a specific frequency channel if it is in use by a primary user, notably radar systems (see also section 10.9). The difference between OSA and DFS is that DFS is not used to seek spectrum access but to prevent spectrum access if co-channel interference might occur. Close cooperation between regulators and industry was needed to define and standardise DFS in such a way that it can detect all different types of radar systems that are active in the bands involved.

The first application of cognitive radio is foreseen in the 'white spots' of the TV bands based on opportunistic spectrum access. The FCC has already published, in 2004, an NPRM to permit unlicensed opportunistic access to 'white spaces' in the TV bands (FCC, 2004). In response to this notice the IEEE has created a working group, IEEE 802.22, which aims to develop a standard based on opportunistic spectrum access of the television bands to provide fixed wireless broadband access in rural and remote areas.

On 4 November 2008 the FCC adopted rules to allow unlicensed radio transmitters to operate in the 'white spaces' of the broadcasting TV bands. Several safeguards are included to prevent harmful interference to the primary users, notably television reception and wireless microphones. The use of 'white spaces' is based on a combination of sensing technology and local information of spectrum usage. A database will have to be established to provide this information (FCC, 2008).[43]

10.11.8 Conclusions

Today's spectrum management is still based on the same principles that were set out at the time of crystal radio. This results in highly ineffective use of spectrum. The Wi-Fi case shows that successful use of RF spectrum is possible under a licence-exempt regime. New innovative technologies, such as cognitive radio systems, offer huge potential for a further increase in spectrum efficiency, thereby facilitating dynamic spectrum access. DSA is a 'return to basics' of RF spectrum management – i.e. the avoidance of harmful interference. To make

DSA possible, RF spectrum regulations will need to be adapted. An absolute prerequisite for DSA is the need for more flexibility in the use of the RF spectrum.

The spectrum management authorities and industry will have to work in close cooperation to realise the goal of dynamic spectrum access. One of the collaborative fields will involve defining the requirements for spectrum sensing and the associated interference limits to primary users.

A too narrow focus on an open access regime for realising DSA will limit the possibilities for new emerging technologies, such as cognitive radio. Adopting elements of a market-based approach in addition will be beneficial for reaching the goal of more efficient spectrum usage, in that access to spectrum will be based on actual demand.

Notes

1 Electromagnetic waves are not a natural resource; they are generated by natural phenomena, such as lightning, as well as artificially; a radio transmitter is a good example, but it is also the case that sparks lead to the generation of electromagnetic waves.

2 They have also studied cases of failures, and have derived a set of rules that appear to be important in the establishment of successful self-governance regimes for so-called common-pool resources (CPRs). The design rules derived from long-enduring CPR institutions are: (1) the common-pool resource has clearly defined boundaries; (2) there is congruence between the appropriation and provision rules and local conditions; (3) there exist collective choice arrangements; (4) the CPR is actively monitored; (5) when required, graduated sanctions are applied; (6) conflict resolution mechanisms are in place; and (7) there is a minimal recognition of rights to organise (Ostrom, 1990). An example of a more recent study of a common-pool resource, with an application of these rules, is the organisation of the 'open source' community by Wendel de Joode (2005).

3 Note that radio waves fade with distance. Moreover, fading increases with the frequency used. Antennae have a significant influence on the characteristics of both the receiver and the transmitter (personal communication with Michael Marcus, 2009).

4 In 1901 the first transatlantic radio telegraph message was sent, between Poldhu in Cornwall and St Johns in Newfoundland, a distance of some 3,500 km. The frequency used was approximately 328 kHz (ITU, 1965).

5 In 1897 Marconi received his first patent in radio telegraphy, building upon inventions by many other physicists, such as Branly, and following the scientific work of Hertz and Maxwell on electromagnetic waves (ITU, 1965).

6 In 1909 radio communication had been critical to the saving of some 1,700 people after a collision between two ships in dense fog near the American coast. In 1912 the *Titanic* struck an iceberg on its maiden voyage, with some 1,500 people on board. Although other ships were within radio reach, they did not know about the disaster as they had no radio equipment on board. Moreover, a radio message from another

ship intending to warn the *Titanic* had not come through as the operator on the *Titanic* had been busy on another conversation; as 'the spark sets used a very wide bandwidth, two chatting operators practically blanketed any other vessel within 100 kilometres that might have wanted to use the air' (ITU, 1965).

7 Critical to the development of radio communication and broadcasting was the invention and application of the vacuum tube by Fleming in 1904 and its amplification by De Forest in 1906 (ITU, 1965).

8 The deployment of FM is considered to have been set back for decades by an FCC decision in 1945 to move the FM radio spectrum from 42 to 50 MHz to 88 to 108 MHz, rendering all Armstrong-era FM receivers useless overnight, and extending the RCA AM radio stronghold (see Wikipedia entry for Edwin Howard Armstrong, at http://en.wikipedia.org/w/index.php?title=Edwin_Howard_Armstrong&printable=yes (accessed 24 December 2008).

9 These agreements were not signed by the United States and Canada, as their radio communications were in the hands of private companies (ITU, 1965).

10 Televerket, the Swedish telecommunication administration, was a state-run organisation that provided the country with telephone services. In 1993 it became a state-owned stock company called Telia AB.

11 For the first generation of cellular technology (1G), the FCC mandated the application of TDMA. In 1987 the FCC surprised the industry by deciding not to pick a 2G standard, only to prescribe that 2G technologies had to coexist with 1G and that 2G mobiles had to be able to operate in 1G mode to maintain interoperability – a decision that was inspired by the positive initial results of CDMA (personal communication from Marcus, 2009).

12 The International Telecommunications Union is a UN treaty organisation. The ITU-R convenes a world radiocommunication conference every three to four years, at which major agreements about the allocation and (international) use of radio frequencies are endorsed. The members of the ITU are the national states, which are represented through government officials.

13 In this context, the term 'unlicensed devices' is used to denote devices with low radiated power that are intended for mass-market applications. They communicate over a short range and have a low risk of causing interference, features that make individual licensing impractical.

14 Region 1 consists of Europe and Africa, including Armenia, Azerbaijan, Georgia, Kazakhstan, Kyrgyzstan, Mongolia, the Russian Federation, Tajikistan, Turkey, Turkmenistan, Ukraine and Uzbekistan.

15 Region 2 consists of North, Central and South America.

16 In general, the approvals are now issued by private sector telecommunications certification bodies (TCBs) authorised by the FCC (private communication from Marcus, 2009).

17 In 1990 the FCC changed the rules and specified a maximum antenna gain to prevent interference: directional antennae with up to 6 dBi directional gain would be allowed on the transmitting units without penalty (FCC, 1990b).

18 A check on the approvals database of the FCC performed on 8 November 2008 revealed that no equipment had been approved.

19 Following a reorganisation of CEPT in the autumn of 2001, all activities related to electronic communications, including radio communications, are addressed by the Electronic Communications Committee (ECC); see www.ero.dk/ecc.

20 Council Directive 87/372/EEC of 25 June 1987 on the frequency bands to be reserved for the coordinated introduction of public pan-European cellular digital land-based mobile communications in the European Community.

21 Council Directive 90/544/EEC of 9 October 1990 on the frequency bands designated for the coordinated introduction of pan-European land-based public radio paging in the European Community.

22 Council Directive 91/287/EEC of 3 June 1991 on the frequency band to be designated for the coordinated introduction of digital European cordless telecommunications into the European Community.

23 The directive does not cover radio equipment used by radio amateurs, maritime and aviation equipment and equipment used for public protection and defence purposes.

24 A harmonised standard is a particular form of European standard (EN) that can be produced only by a recognised European Standards Organisation (i.e. CEN, CENELEC and ETSI) under a mandate from the European Commission.

25 If the radio equipment uses frequencies that are not harmonised throughout the European Union, an alert sign has to be put on each piece of apparatus and it must be made clear to the user which restrictions apply.

26 Directive 2002/21/EC of the European Parliament and of the Council of 7 March 2002 on a common regulatory framework for electronic communications networks and services (Framework Directive).

27 Directive 2002/20/EC of the European Parliament and of the Council of 7 March 2002 on the authorisation of electronic communications networks and services (Authorisation Directive).

28 Due to the extension of the 2.4 GHz band Japan has designated one extra channel within the band (channel 14, with a central frequency of 2,484 MHz).

29 The Wireless Ethernet Compatibility Alliance later adopted the name Wi-Fi Alliance.

30 For further details on the FCC procedure of rule making, see Chapter 2.

31 These radio services include services such as fixed, mobile, satellite, amateur, radio navigation and radio astronomy. Most bands are shared between primary and secondary services. Primary services have priority in the event of conflicts resulting in harmful interference.

32 Radiocommunication assemblies are responsible for the structure, the work programme and the approval of radiocommunication studies and associated recommendations from the ITU-R. A radiocommunication assembly is convened every three to four years, normally prior to a world radiocommunication conference (see www. telecomabc.com/r/ra.html).

33 This section is based on Anker (2008).

34 Examples of white spots are the empty spaces (guard bands) between TV channels. The actual size and frequency range of the white spot will be different in different locations.

35 A technology for implementing very sensitive detectors is called 'feature detector' or 'cyclostationary detector', a by-product of military R&D (personal communication from Marcus, 2009).

36 A few countries, including the United States and Ireland, have already made provision to allow the introduction of cognitive radio (see also Akalu, 2008).

37 The 2011 world radiocommunication conference has now been rescheduled to take place in 2012.

38 WAPECS (Wireless Access Policy for Electronic Communications Services) is a framework for the provision of electronic communications services, within a set of frequency bands to be identified and agreed between European Union member states, in which a range of electronic communications networks and electronic communications services may be offered on a technology- and service-neutral basis, provided that certain technical requirements to avoid interference are met, to guarantee the effective and efficient use of the spectrum, and that the authorisation conditions do not distort competition.
39 EC communication COM(2005)400, 'A market-based approach to spectrum management in the European Union'.
40 Private communication from Marcus, 2009.
41 As early as 1995 Noam at Columbia University proposed an 'open spectrum access' paradigm in which interested parties would pay for bandwidth whenever demand occurs (Noam, 1995).
42 Dynamic frequency selection was introduced in the subsequent European standards for cordless telephony, the analogue CT.1 system and the digital CT.2 and DECT systems.
43 A variety of appeals are pending, and the new rules do not go into effect until both a database manager and a transmitter ID standard have been selected (Private communication from Marcus, 2009).

References

Akalu, R. (2008). 'Spectrum management and cognitive radio in Ireland'. Paper presented at the first annual conference of the multidisciplinary journal *Competition and Regulation in Network Industries*. Brussels, 28 November.
Anker, P. (2008). 'Does cognitive radio need policy innovation?'. Paper presented at the first annual conference of the multidisciplinary journal *Competition and Regulation in Network Industries*. Brussels, 28 November.
Apple (1991). 'Petition for rulemaking "Data-PCS" in the matter of: amendment of Section 2.106 of the Commission's rules to establish a new radio service for local area high speed data communications among personal computing devices'. Cupertino, CA: Apple.
  (1995). 'Petition for rulemaking "NII band" in the matter of: allocation of spectrum in the 5 GHz band to establish a wireless component in the national information infrastructure'. Cupertino, CA: Apple.
Baumol, W. J., and D. Robyn (2006). *Toward an Evolutionary Regime for Spectrum Governance : Licensing or Unrestricted Entry?* Washington, DC: Brookings Institution Press.
Botto, F. (2002). *Encyclopedia of Wireless Telecommunications*. New York: McGraw-Hill.
Carter, K. R. (2009). 'Unlicensed to kill: a brief history of the Part 15 rules'. *Info.* **11** (5), 8–18.
CEPT (1991). 'Wide band data transmission systems using spread-spectrum technology in the 2.5 GHz band', Recommendation T/R 10–01. Copenhagen: CEPT.
  (1992). 'Harmonised radio frequency bands for high performance radio local area networks (HIPERLANs) in the 5 GHz and 17 GHz frequency range', Recommendation T/R 22–06. Copenhagen: CEPT.

(1996). 'Decision of 7 March 1996 on the harmonised frequency band to be designated for the introduction of high performance radio local area networks (HIPERLANs)', Decision EC/(96)03. Copenhagen: CEPT.

(1999a). 'Study of the frequency sharing between HIPERLANs and MSS feeder links in the 5 GHz band', Report no. 67. Copenhagen: CEPT.

(1999b). 'Decision of 29 November 1999 on the harmonised frequency bands to be designated for the introduction of high performance radio local area networks (HIPERLANs)', Decision EC/(99)23. Copenhagen: CEPT.

(2004). 'Decision of 12 November on the harmonised use of the 5 GHz frequency bands for the implementation of wireless access systems including radio local area networks (WAS/RLANs)', Decision ECC/DEC/(04)08. Copenhagen: CEPT. Available at www.ero.dk/documentation/docs/doc98/official/pdf/REP067. PDF (accessed 5 November 2008).

(2006). 'Report from CEPT to the European Commission in response to the mandate to: develop a strategy to improve the effectiveness and flexibility of spectrum availability for short range devices (SRDs)', Report 014. Copenhagen: CEPT.

(2008a). 'Technical considerations regarding harmonisation options for the digital dividend: a preliminary assessment of the feasibility of fitting new/future applications/services into non-harmonised spectrum of the digital dividend (namely the so-called "white spaces" between allotments)'. Copenhagen: CEPT. Available at www.erodocdb.dk/doks/doccategoryECC.aspx?doccatid=16 (accessed 1 November 2008).

(2008b). What is CEPT?'. Copenhagen: CEPT. Available at www.cept.org (accessed 23 November 2008).

China Daily (2006). 'ISO votes down China encryption system'. *China Daily*. 14 March. Available at www.chinadaily.com.cn/english/doc/2006–03/14/content_535210.htm (accessed 23 November 2008).

De Wit, B., and R. Meyer (2004). *Strategy: Process, Content, Context – An International Perspective*. London: Thomson.

EC (1990). 'Council Resolution of 28 June 1990 on the strengthening of the Europe-wide cooperation on radio frequencies, in particular with regard to services with a pan-European dimension'. *Official Journal*. C 166, 4–6. Available at http://eurlex.europa.eu/LexUriServ/LexUriServ.do?uri=CELEX:31990Y0707(02):EN:HTML (accessed 23 November 2008).

(1992). 'Council Resolution of 19 November 1992 on the implementation in the Community of the European Radiocommunications Committee decisions'. *Official Journal*. C 318, 1. Available at http://eur-lex.europa.eu/LexUriServ/LexUriServ.do?uri=CELEX:31992Y1204(01):EN:HTML (accessed 23 November 2008).

(1999). 'Directive 1999/5/EC of the European Parliament and of the Council of 9 March 1999 on radio equipment and telecommunications terminal equipment and the mutual recognition of their conformity'. *Official Journal*. L 091, 10–28. Available at http://eur-lex.europa.eu/LexUriServ/LexUriServ.do?uri=CELEX:31999L0005:EN:HTML (accessed 23 November 2008).

(2002). 'Decision 676/2002/EC of the European Parliament and of the Council of 7 March 2002 on a regulatory framework for radio spectrum policy in the European Community (Radio Spectrum Decision)'. *Official Journal*. L 108, 1–6. Available at http://eur-lex.europa.eu/pri/en/oj/dat/2002/l_108/ l_10820020424en00010006.pdf (accessed 23 November 2008).

(2006). 'Decision 2006/771/EC of the Commission of 9 November 2006 on harmonisation of the radio spectrum for use by short-range devices'. *Official Journal.* L 312, 66–70. Available at http://eur-lex.europa.eu/LexUriServ/LexUriServ.do?uri= OJ:L:2006:312:0066:0070:EN:pdf (accessed 23 November 2008).

ERC (1994). 'Procedure for mutual recognition of type testing and type approval for radio equipment', Recommendation 01–06. Copenhagen: ERC.

(1997). 'Decision on the mutual recognition of conformity assessment procedures including marking of radio equipment and radio terminal equipment', Decision (97)10. Copenhagen: ERC.

(2008). 'Recommendation (Tromsø 1997 and subsequent amendments) relating to the use of short range devices (SRDs)', Recommendation 70–03. Copenhagen: ERC.

ETSI (1993). 'Radio equipment and systems (RES): wideband transmission systems; technical characteristics and test conditions for data transmission equipment operating in the 2.4 GHz ISM band and using spread spectrum modulation techniques', Recommendation ETS 300 328. Sophia-Antipolis: ETSI.

Fagerberg, J., D. C. Mowery and R. R. Nelson (eds.) (2005). *The Oxford Handbook of Innovation.* Oxford: Oxford University Press.

Faulhaber, G. R. (2006). 'The future of wireless telecommunications: spectrum as a critical resource'. *Information Economics and Policy.* **18** (3), 256–71.

FCC (1985). 'First Report and Order in the matter of authorization of spread spectrum and other wideband emissions not presently provided for in the FCC Rules and Regulations', General Docket no. 81–413. Washington, DC: FCC.

(1987). 'Revision of Part 15 of the rules regarding the operation of radio frequency devices without an individual license', General Docket no. 87–389. Washington, DC: FCC.

(1990a). 'Notice of inquiry in the matter of amendment of the Commission's rules to establish new personal communications services', General Docket no. 90–314. Washington, DC: FCC.

(1990b). 'Report and Order in the matter of amendment of Parts 2 and 15 of the rules with regard to the operation of spread spectrum systems', General Docket no. 89–354. Washington, DC: FCC.

(1992a). 'Notice of proposed rulemaking and tentative decision in the matter of the Commission's rules to establish new personal communications services', Engineering and Technology Docket no. 90–314. Washington, DC: FCC.

(1992b). 'Notice of proposed rulemaking in the matter of redevelopment of spectrum to encourage innovation in the use of new telecommunications technologies', Engineering and Technology Docket no. 92–9. Washington, DC: FCC.

(1994). 'Notice of proposed rulemaking in the matter of allocation of spectrum below 3 GHz transferred from government use', Engineering and Technology Docket no. 94–32. Washington, DC: FCC.

(1995). 'First Report and Order and second notice of proposed rulemaking in the matter of allocation of spectrum below 3 GHz transferred from government use', Engineering and Technology Docket no. 94–32. Washington, DC: FCC.

(1996). 'Notice of proposed rulemaking in the matter of amendment of the Commission's rules for unlicensed NII/Supernet operations in the 5 GHz frequency range', Engineering and Technology Docket no. 96–102. Washington, DC: FCC.

(1997). 'Report and Order in the matter of amendment of the Commission's rules to provide for operation of unlicensed NII devices in the 5 GHz frequency range', Engineering and Technology Docket no. 96–102. Washington, DC: FCC.

(1998). 'Notice of proposed rulemaking in the matter 1998 biennial regulatory review – amendment of Part 18 of the Commission's rules to update regulations for RF lighting devices', Engineering and Technology Docket no. 98–42. Washington, DC: FCC.

(2003a). 'Order in the matter 1998 biennial regulatory review – amendment of Part 18 of the Commission's rules to update regulations for RF lighting devices', Engineering and Technology Docket no. 98–42. Washington, DC: FCC.

(2003b). 'Report and Order in the matter revision of Parts 2 and 15 of the Commission's rules to permit unlicensed national information infrastructure devices in the 5 GHz band', Engineering and Technology Docket no. 03–122. Washington, DC: FCC.

(2004). 'Notice of proposed rulemaking in the matter of unlicensed operation in the TV broadcast bands (ET Docket no. 04–186) and additional spectrum for unlicensed devices below 900 MHz and in the 3 GHz band (ET Docket no. 02–380)', FCC 04–113. Washington, DC: FCC.

(2008). 'Second Report and Order and memorandum opinion and order', FCC 08–260. Washington, DC: FCC.

Ghasemi, A., and E. S. Sousa (2008). 'Spectrum sensing in cognitive radio networks: requirements, challenges and design trade-offs'. *IEEE Communications Magazine.* **46** (4), 32–9.

GSM Association (2004). 'History and statistics of GSM'. London: GSM Association. Available at www.gsmworld.com/about/history (accessed 15 October 2004).

Hardin, G. (1968). 'The tragedy of the commons'. *Science.* **162**, 1243–8.

Haykin, S. (2005). 'Cognitive radio: brain-empowered wireless communications'. *IEEE Journal on Selected Areas in Communications.* **23** (**2**), 201–20.

Hazlett, T. W. (2006). 'The spectrum-allocation debate: an analysis'. *IEEE Internet Computing.* **10** (5), 68–74.

IEEE (1990a). 'Response of IEEE 802 local area network standards to the NoI GEN Docket 90–314', Document IEEE P802.11/90–006. New York: IEEE.

(1990b). 'Reply comments of IEEE 802 local area network standards to the NoI GEN Docket 90–314', Document IEEE P802.11/90–021. New York: IEEE.

(1991a). 'Comment of IEEE 802 local area network standards to the Apple petition in the matter amendment of Section 2.106 RM No. 7618 of the Commission's rules to establish a new radio service for local area high speed data communications among personal computing devices', Document IEEE P802.11/91–059. New York: IEEE.

(1991b). 'IEEE P802 request for world-wide coordinated radio frequency spectrum for local area computer communications', Document IEEE P802.11/91–109. New York: IEEE.

(1992). 'Comments on NPRM 90–314/92–9, in the matter of redevelopment of spectrum to encourage innovation in the use of new telecoms technologies', Document IEEE P802.11–92/141. New York: IEEE.

(1994a). 'Comments on notice of inquiry by NTIA, on the "Preliminary spectrum reallocation report"', Document IEEE P802.11–94/165. New York: IEEE.

(1994b). 'Comments on NPRM 94–32, in the matter of allocation of spectrum below 3 GHz transferred from government use', Document IEEE P802.11–94/306. New York: IEEE.

(1998a). 'Comments of the IEEE 802 Standards Committee on NPRM 98–42, in the matter of 1998 biennial regulatory review – amendment of Part 18 of the Commission's rules to update regulations for RF lighting devices'. New York: IEEE.

(1998b). 'Ex parte letter from the IEEE 802 Standards Committee on NPRM 98–42, in the matter of 1998 biennial regulatory review – amendment of Part 18 of the Commission's rules to update regulations for RF lighting devices'. New York: IEEE.

(1999). 'Ex parte letter from the IEEE 802 Standards Committee on NPRM 98–42, in the matter of 1998 biennial regulatory review – amendment of Part 18 of the Commission's rules to update regulations for RF lighting devices'. New York: IEEE.

(2002). 'IEEE P802 radio regulations: summary of WECA meeting with Chinese MII regulatory officials, Beijing, China', Document IEEE 802.RR-02/032r0. New York: IEEE.

(2007). 'IEEE standard for information technology: telecommunications and information exchange between systems – local and metropolitan area networks – specific requirements Part 11: wireless LAN medium access control (MAC), and physical layer (PHY) specifications', IEEE Standard 802.11™-2007. New York: IEEE.

ITU (1965). *From Semaphore to Satellite: Celebrating the Centenary of the ITU*. Geneva: ITU.

(1998). *Radio Regulations*. Geneva: ITU.

(2006). 'Technical and operating parameters and spectrum requirements for short-range radiocommunication devices', Recommendation ITU-R SM.1538–2. Geneva: ITU.

(2007). 'Cognitive radio systems in the mobile service', Question ITU-R 241–1/5. Geneva: ITU. Available at www.itu.int/publ/R-QUE-SG05.241/en (accessed 1 November 2008).

Jackson, C. (2005). 'Dynamic sharing of radio spectrum: a brief history'. In IEEE. *New Frontiers in Dynamic Spectrum Access Networks, 2005*. New York: IEEE Press, 445–66.

Lundvall, B.-A. (1992). *National Systems of Innovation: Towards a Theory of Innovation and Interactive Learning*. London: Pinter.

Mahoney, J. T. (2005). *Economic Foundations of Strategy*. Thousand Oaks, CA: Sage.

Manninen, A. T. (2002). 'Elaboration of NMT and GSM standards: from idea to market'. Dissertation. Department of Humanities, University of Jyväskylä, Jyväskylä, Finland.

Meurling, J., and R. Jeans (1994). *The Mobile Phone Book: The Invention of the Mobile Telephone Industry*. London: CommunicationsWeek International.

MIC (2006). *MIC Communications News*. 17. Available at www.soumu.go.jp/joho_tsusin/eng/newsletter.html (accessed 1 November 2008).

MITRE Corporation (1980). *Potential Use of Spread Spectrum Techniques in Non-government Applications*. Springfield, VA: National Technical Information Service.

Mock, D. (2005). *The Qualcomm Equation: How a Fledgling Telecom Company Forged a New Path to Big Profits and Market Dominance*. New York: AMACOM.

Mott MacDonald (2006). *Study on Legal, Economic and Technical Aspects of 'Collective Use' of Spectrum in the European Community*. Croydon: Mott MacDonald.

Nelson, R. R., and S. G. Winter (1977). 'In search of a useful theory of innovation'. *Research Policy*. **6** (1), 36–76.

Noam, E. M. (1995). 'Taking the next step beyond spectrum auctions: open spectrum access'. *IEEE Communications Magazine*. **33** (12), 66–73.

NTIA (1994). 'Notice of inquiry re "Preliminary spectrum reallocation response to Title VI – Omnibus Reconciliation Act of 1993" released on February 10, 1994', Document 94–27. Washington, DC: NTIA.

(2003). 'Agreement reached regarding US position on 5 GHz wireless access devices'. Washington, DC: NTIA. Available at www.ntia.doc.gov/ntiahome/press/2003/5ghzagreement.htm (accessed 1 June 2006).

Ostrom, E. (1990). *Governing the Commons: The Evolution of Institutions for Collective Action*. Cambridge: Cambridge University Press.

Ostrom, E., R. Gardner and J. Walker (1994). *Rules, Games, and Common-Pool Resources*. Ann Arbor: University of Michigan Press.

Pawelczak, P. (2008). 'Technical challenges of cognitive radio-related systems'. Paper presented at the first annual conference of the multidisciplinary journal *Competition and Regulation in Network Industries*. Brussels, 28 November.

Porter, M. E. (1980). *Competitive Strategy: Techniques for Analyzing Industries and Competitors*. New York: Free Press.

Rey, R. F. (ed.) (1983). *Engineering and Operations in the Bell System*. Murray Hill, NJ: AT&T Bell Laboratories.

Ryan, P. S. (2005). 'European spectrum management principles'. *Journal of Computer and Information Law*. **23** (2), 277–85.

Schuilenga, J. H., J. D. Tours, J. G. Visser and J. Bruggeman (eds.) (1981). *Honderd Jaar Telefoon*. The Hague: Staatsbedrijf der Posterijen, Telegrafie en Telefonie.

Tidd, J., J. Bessant and K. Pavitt (2001). *Managing Innovation: Integrating Technological, Market and Organizational Change*. Chichester: John Wiley.

TransAsia Lawyers (2003). 'China's new WLAN/WAPI standards'. *PRC Telecoms, Media and Technology Law Newsletter*. 23 December.

(2004). 'Technical standards with Chinese characteristics: WAPI, RFID and mobile DTT'. *PRC Telecoms, Media and Technology Law Newsletter*. 30 April.

Von Hippel, E. (1988). *The Sources of Innovation*. Oxford: Oxford University Press.

WECA (2002a). 'Petition for rulemaking of the Wireless Ethernet Compatibility Alliance to permit unlicensed national information infrastructure devices to operate in the 5,470–5,725 GHz band'. Austin, TX: WECA.

(2002b). 'Supplement filing in the RM-10371, petition for rulemaking of the Wireless Ethernet Compatibility Alliance to permit unlicensed national information infrastructure devices to operate in the 5,470–5,725 GHz band'. Austin, TX: WECA.

Wendel de Joode, R. (2005). 'Understanding open source communities: an organisational perspective'. Dissertation. Department of Technology, Policy and Management, Delft University of Technology, Delft.

WINForum (1995). 'In the matter of: petition for rulemaking to allocate the 5.1–5.25 GHz band and adopt service rules for a shared unlicensed personal radio network'. Willowbrook, IL: WINForum.

World Radiocommunication Conference (2003). 'Use of the bands 5,150–5,250 MHz, 5,250–5,350 MHz and 5,470–5,725 MHz by the mobile service for the implementation of wireless access systems including radio local area networks', Resolution 229 (WRC-03). Geneva: World Radiocommunication Conference.

11 Exploring the future of Wi-Fi

Pierre Rossel and Matthias Finger

11.1 Introduction

Wi-Fi is beyond doubt an astonishing phenomenon, primarily because it involves the almost magical capacity to carry out actions at a distance, to exert control over machines and to process data and communicate with other human beings in a cordless, immaterial and yet quite reliable manner. In addition, Wi-Fi is not only growing in terms of numbers, but is also becoming pervasive in many respects. We are not concerned so much with the remarkable features and development patterns of Wi-Fi, however, as with the open-ended questions that Wi-Fi still raises and the uncertainties and complexities it carries with it.

In this chapter, we envisage the possible futures of Wi-Fi. In the second section, we acknowledge the historical build-up and successful characteristics of Wi-Fi. In this evolution we include quantitative and qualitative evidence, as well as a few material narratives that are strongly supportive of current Wi-Fi developments. In this context, we consider what to make of the various forecasts, and how to establish the kind of knowledge perspective that users and decision makers can work with, and therefore what kind of methodological pathways may help us reach our goal. In the third section, we discuss the question of whether the future of Wi-Fi can somehow be 'guessed' from existing innovation models, or how to use such models in an open and helpful manner. In the fourth section, we explore the Wi-Fi journey that still lies ahead of us, in terms of options, contexts and conditions, in particular through a micro-Delphi study – i.e. a specific enquiry among experts. We present the rough output of this exploratory study in the form of potential scenarios. In the fifth and concluding section, we examine what might be some weak signals of change or, on the contrary, might be reinforcements of trends that provide early indications as to the Wi-Fi to come in the next ten years or so. We argue that one of the aspects that will be a deciding factor between the various options is the dynamic tension between innovation and regulation.

11.2   Appraising the current Wi-Fi trend

11.2.1   Wi-Fi: an undeniable success story – likely to continue

Wi-Fi was born in the 1980s as a tentative solution, an idea based upon the prospect of combining successfully two technological fields: radio-wave-supported communication, on the one hand, and computer-relevant information processing, on the other. It took numerous efforts and attempts, with different possible orientations and support contexts, to achieve a workable and sustainable form of wireless data transmission. The basic strand known today as the IEEE 802.11 family of standards, which eventually passed all the tests thrown at it, and moreover made a respectable market debut (with over 300 million chipsets sold in 2006, according to the Wi-Fi Alliance) and in all cases became a reliable channel for remote computing, first took place in a corporate environment – i.e. NCR.[1] In one sense, it could be said that Wi-Fi, in the very pattern of how it was born and developed, nearly qualifies as an example of what von Hippel (1988, 2005) terms user innovation – in other words, innovation as the achievement of users who were dissatisfied with what the market was offering and who felt they could create their own solutions in a particular area of competence and needs to be addressed. The fact that in the case of Wi-Fi it all happened within a corporate environment makes it disputably a 'pure' user innovation process, but it remains the case that it was continuously improved upon by a dispersed community of enthusiastic users, within the IEEE standardisation process. This particular form of innovation undoubtedly contributed to its success, as it was not the sole proposal of one company wishing to sell a new product on the market but, rather, the combined effort of an increasingly vast community of actors, first within and then beyond – far beyond – the original IEEE and the Wi-Fi Alliance,[2] in parallel with growing communities of 'hotspots' (or Wi-Fi access points to the Internet), scattered all over the world, in particular in OECD countries. These different but nevertheless converging dynamics, starting with the resolution of the first technicalities in the 1980s, continuing with the development of the 802.11 standard in the 1990s, then finally maturing with the decisive emergence of a market, in different sectors, from 2000 on, constitute what we can now identify as a *trend* (see Schwarz, 2008).

Some features of this trend are measurable in a strictly quantifiable form, others in more qualitative terms, but they all give us indications on the strength, speed, geographical scope and diversity of the Wi-Fi expansion. If we are to consider its possible futures, we need first to be precise about these specific expressions of success. We have identified eight such Wi-Fi development indicators – a large number, arguably, but a trend is made of redundant signals. They are as follows.

(1) One of the most interesting indicators of the trend is undoubtedly the continuous improvement and power upgrade of the Wi-Fi standard, through successive rounds, proposals, disputes and closures on specific solutions, from 802.11a, b to g and now n (including the 'i' standard for security matters), with no boundaries in sight for the moment as to how far this continual upgrading movement can bring us. It means also, at each round, (a) increased performance in terms of outreach distance, number of walls that can be coped with and, of course, bandwidth; (b) at the same time, a growing number of technical disputes and of (different) actors involved in the settlement of the disputes, which for the 'n' standard completion, for instance, involved examining over 12,000 disputes,[3] with more and more corporate players both battling and constructing technologically reliable, as well as commercially viable, futures. Another parameter, namely the ease of installing and setting up Wi-Fi configurations, tends to follow that same quantitative evolution.[4] With the 'n' standard, however, beyond 100 Mbit/s bandwidth effectiveness and full triple play[5] are realistically within reach. In the history of Wi-Fi, and even if we can assume that progress will continue to be made, the 'n' standard constitutes a decisive threshold.[6]

(2) Another indicator is the number of users, institutional experts, scientific bodies and corporations involved in the Wi-Fi Alliance, as ongoing evidence of the rising interest it conveys. More refined statistics could even give us further clues as to what the sub-trends are in this case, either in geographical or socio-economic terms. At this level, diversity increase is the main constructive finding for our consideration.

(3) The number of access points to Wi-Fi services (the so-called 'hotspots') could also provide quite useful indications as to the Wi-Fi expansion, but there are no global statistics, only regional ones. Indeed, real statistics would imply the development of an aggregative community of actors of different kinds, from individual users to organisations, from the public and private sectors alike. Together, these social contributions to Wi-Fi show that (a) the number of internet access points continues to expand; and (b) the territorial penetration of Wi-Fi becomes increasingly more perceptible (the positive 'club' or 'externality capture' effect), not just locally but also in showing the overall Wi-Fi vitality in diverse areas of the world (the diffusion of innovation effect). These dynamics, in spite of ICTs being more and more global, stress the importance of Wi-Fi as a system supporting proximity and community services (see Hyman and Katz, 2001). This provides us with, if not an absolute view on Wi-Fi, at least a growing and tangible sense that the attempt to offer territorial coverage and a viable alternative to fixed-cable infrastructure is worth the effort. At the same time, though, this community preference is replicable almost everywhere, turning Wi-Fi diffusion into a 'fractal' success (i.e. the replication,

at each level – world, national, regional, municipal – of the same diffusion pattern).

(4) In support of this hypothesis, currently, one of the most entrepreneurial types of actors for Wi-Fi access point dissemination, after airports, train stations,[7] universities, libraries, hotels and cafés, public places, just to mention pioneering venues, is the city. Indeed, the world over, cities of all sizes, from very big to very small,[8] and with very different economic traditions and motivations, deploy a Wi-Fi infrastructure of some kind; sometimes they just encourage the setting up of a few 'hotspots', but often public policy is ambitious and subsidises coverage (many access points) or even meshing options (Wi-Fi users playing the role of overall communication relays), as in Paris, for instance, with the initiative of key competitors to the incumbent operator.[9]

(5) Although it is difficult to assess remote access to the Internet in real-time growth terms, this form of dissemination clearly claims that the spread of internet access to increasingly numerous faraway locations is an evidence of Wi-Fi penetration. As it spreads more and more to off-track (i.e. non urban) locations or places characterised by extreme physical or climate conditions (mountainous or peripheral regions, but also areas with communication problems, such as Greenland, Tibet or the Sahara Desert), this form of expansion may nowadays seem almost trivial; it is not, however, as it requires each time a specific set-up solution for mainstream communication or backbone access. According to the leveraging conditions for the costs involved in the targeted domains of application (e.g. research, oil exploration, peasant communities in regional health hubs, etc.), satellite connections will be preferred to fixed cable for global linkage, with Wi-Fi providing the demand aggregation function to allow cost sharing. In the absence of statistics, however, this particular segment of the Wi-Fi development can qualify for being essentially a qualitative indicator. In fact, the reporting of spectacular remote connections says more about the fact that accessing the Internet is feasible from such locations than about the actual dissemination of the technology.

(6) Another indicator, with both qualitative and quantitative dimensions (albeit not easy to establish in the latter case, however), is the dissemination of Wi-Fi capabilities to an increasing range of pieces of digital equipment, which may sometimes just fit into a 'computer-to-terminal' scheme but which, when connected (as a collection of dispersed functionalities), can also be configured into all sorts of digital ecosystems, either in the domestic 'infotainment' sphere or in the corporate contexts of service delivery (geolocation, security, production process, RIFD tracing and tracking designs, etc.).

(7) In a similar vein, it is important to stress that Wi-Fi is not the only wireless communication solution proposed today[10] but just one of several technological systems providing wireless services, all of them acting as a heavy trend (wireless communication). At the moment Wi-Fi is benefiting from this positive overall development effect, rather than suffering from a possible selective process in comparison with the others. Aside from Wi-Fi, we have infrared communication, Bluetooth, RFID, NMT, GSM and CDMA, and there are also other, more recent standards for mobile communication, such as UMTS, but even more so high speed packet access (HSPA) and Long Term Evolution (LTE), the next generation of cellular mobile communications also known as 4G.

(8) The most obvious indication of Wi-Fi progression, however, is probably linked to the fact that all new-build laptops and an increasingly large number of mobile phones (all of them in one or two years' time) have embedded Wi-Fi functionalities, following with a delay the general evolution of the 802.11 standard (meaning that the implementation of the 'n' version will be the next step). The only problem with these figures, and closely related to the numbers of such items sold, is that they say little about usage forms and usage intensity, making this indicator something of an indirect one. At some point in the future, however, it might become sufficiently standardised that it will (almost) correspond to the number of ICT items sold globally.

All these elements give us a flavour, though not an accurate figure, of the trend we are trying to depict. A number of forecasts (see, for instance, Techcast)[11] simply build upon these data and project them into the future, with the addition of some modifications in order to reflect either positive or negative factors and various scenarios. Provided our expectations about forecasts are realistic, and we do not look to them for firm predictions[12] but simply to provide indications, they can be reasonably useful.

One important player in the forecasting field is Gartner, which, for the last four years, has repeatedly revised its forecasts upwards, whether of predictions concerning the expansion of hotspots[13] or of various types of devices sold, such that its 2010 forecasts are that Bluetooth phone sales will hit 1 billion, Wi-Fi 362 million and WiMAX 27 million.[14] At the same time, the nature of what we mean by Wi-Fi is changing, with a rising incidence of embedded devices (in mobile sets in particular). According to ABI Research, the forecast is for Wi-Fi in non-traditional devices to surpass networking equipment in a few years. In 2012 1.2 billion Wi-Fi chipsets will ship, ABI Research estimates, and, of these, 500 million will be embedded in mobile handsets. The remaining 700 million will be split more or less evenly between other consumer electronics devices and traditional network computing equipment, the study finds.[15]

To summarise the situation, Wi-Fi is doing well and seems to be playing a full part in the development of the 'information society' in most of its aspects. Indeed, it is doing so well and fitting the trend towards more open and user-sensitive solutions that the above-mentioned forecast starts to appear plausible. Various problems may lie ahead, however, requiring a more critical analysis. (1) The future, including the evolution of the information society, is not determined by technological factors alone, even well-performing ones. (2) Even in terms of communications technologies, Wi-Fi is not the only option, and it is not difficult to envisage a variety of alternative scenarios for the expansion of communication. (3) Other, more drastic modifications to the trend growth forecast cannot be ruled out, such as various types of risks, even though they remain remote possibilities. The next two sections are devoted to the exploration and evaluation of these alternatives.

11.3   Converging with forecasts: technological innovation models as clues?

From the previous section, it would seem that Wi-Fi has the potential to take off dramatically and become a great commercial success. The issue is not that simple, however. One key question is related to the role of technology in societal dynamics – a relationship that no innovation models have convincingly explained so far. For some of these models, which are particularly useful for their forecasts, there is a reasonably good level of predictive ability; this is not the case for others, though, as their starting point is the assumption that the type of process we are dealing with here is one in which many strands are likely to combine with each other, producing an altogether more complex and open-ended series of futures in which several stakeholders will have a say. The danger with such an approach is that this diversity may not necessarily be cohesive, and may even incorporate conflicting interests, some of which eventually select specific technological options, towards outcomes that currently remain unpredictable. A more general question, therefore, is whether it is possible in innovation models to identify clues as to the future development of a specific technology – in our case, Wi-Fi. This question is worth looking into in more depth.

In order to do this, we first suggest a useful classification of approaches, then evaluate how a series of models may or may not provide indications about the future of Wi-Fi (e.g. related to the standard, the technology, the business model), and on what bases, and conclude by putting forward our own position, expressed both in market and societal dynamics terms.

11.3.1   Models, approaches, theories and schools

Thousands of articles and books have already been published on innovations and innovation theories. Any theoretical position attempting to account for this diversity is therefore inherently problematic, and will probably adopt a standpoint that implies that other approaches are considered inadequate. No consensus is currently in sight, and nor does it seem that there is any likelihood of a theory of theories emerging to settle the ongoing disputes. In this sense, we are in a knowledge dynamics resembling Lakatos's perspective (in which a series of research programmes can appear successively, and concurrent paradigms can unfold in parallel) rather than in a Kuhnian one (in which one paradigm emerges periodically as dominant over preceding ones, which are then disqualified).

There are models of all kinds, for general or sectoral usages, and either for the whole market or territorially bound. In this section, we scrutinise a number of them and evaluate their productive potential for delivering insights into the future of specific technological innovations.

To start with, one of the most fundamental criteria concerns the basic philosophical status of technology, in terms of visualising its role as a factor that might influence social and economic development. In this specific and narrower view, we can distinguish between three sets of theories and models. The first is deterministic by inclination, envisaging a relationship in which technology has a strong impact on society. The second, in contrast, considers that the type of context that is created when technology is produced is relatively open, with a variety of options remaining possible, in which it is the successive choices made by social actors, and not by technology itself, that ultimately define what kind of situation involving both technology and societal forms will prevail. In this latter approach, society impacts technology rather than the reverse; it is said to be constructivist, as sociotechnical artefacts and systems are constructed in stages shaped by multiple choices. In between these two positions, there are attempts to envisage both options as complementary valid explanations. At the end of this chapter, we examine the value of this third position, but only after having evaluated the other two as a 'future-oriented source', bearing in mind the particular focus on Wi-Fi.

11.3.2   Technologies as guidelines: the deterministic approaches

If we leave aside the broad deterministic perspectives associated with classical thinkers of science and technology,[16] which tend to be too general to be of any use in our case, the most common set of models to be examined consists of the diffusionist ones, which are especially relevant for Wi-Fi issues as most of the eight indicators presented in the second section show that the technology is spreading. Bass (1986) and Rogers (2003)[17] are the authorities in this domain, along with Davis and his technology acceptance model (TAM), on how technology is received and its patterns of uptake (1989). They have provided models and theories explaining how technologies diffuse in space and time (in a manner that is in some respects like the propagation of a disease), as well as their rate of adoption (Bass) and the critical moments of their life cycle (Rogers). All the modelling produced in this perspective suggests that Wi-Fi development is in its infancy, and likely to expand much more, before becoming less attractive later on – an outcome that, clearly, is not likely in the foreseeable future. This should be very reassuring for the promoters of Wi-Fi (if not for the limits of the diffusion theory), as the procedure is essentially monofactorial and linear, with little sensitivity to complex cross-factoring and disruptive influences.[18]

Another, closely related narrative is the famous sequence of 'early market', 'crossing the chasm', into the 'bowling alley' and 'main street' proposed by Moore (1991).

The diffusionist approach has its merits, of course, but it needs to be borne in mind that its forecasts only suggest some possible futures, rather than delivering actual predictions.[19] Other deterministic approaches are less obvious, and even non-explicit, but they should still be taken into account. We want to address all the models dealing with innovation dynamics, including those that are used not to report upon specific processes but to deliver predictive indications, based on the assumption that the model is sufficiently relevant that the future will continue to fit its shape and characteristics. This is typically the case when long-wave (Kondratiev) cycles are presumed to indicate what is likely to come next, rather than support an explanation of the past (see, for example, Marchetti, 1980, 1982, 1987, 1991); but it is also the case when a model that has been used to describe a series of developments (such as Sawhney's 'infrastructure development model', for instance) is considered to be valid to describe seemingly similar ongoing innovation processes (although the similarity can be somewhat difficult to establish in this case).

Sawhney (1992) analyses telephone infrastructure development, in particular in the United States and Canada, and the development of other networks, such as telegraph and railroad, and then (2003) benchmarks his own 'infrastructure development model' against current findings on Wi-Fi. He manages to identify the first three of the eight stages of his model, but somehow inconclusively, as he himself raises more questions than answers as to how it can continue. It is worth here contrasting the linear mindset underpinning the Sawhney model with the study by Vree (2000), which stresses the frequent indeterminacy of an invention in its early stages. If the most famous historical example of such indeterminacy is probably the initial usage of telephone to transmit not voice but music, let us think of how the mobile phone has now evolved into a multi-usage tool, rather than just being a phone that has become transportable, displaying an impressive range of new service features, all unheard of in the fixed-line phone realm: short message service, multimedia messaging service, games, photography and video, music and radio, mobile TV streaming, internet access, steadily increasingly computing power, Global Positioning System capability, e-payment and key capacities, and, soon, meshing possibilities and sensor-based capabilities. None of these features was even considered in earlier stages of mobile phone development. The whole trajectory is in fact typical of serendipitous dynamics, which also disqualifies monofactorial and substitution-minded approaches, as Rossel and Finger (2007) have demonstrated for the issue of how mobile telephony termination costs are most often modelled and defined.

We now come to the situation in which innovation specialists claim that models allow them to derive convincing clues as to what will come next, even in disruptive dynamics, as Christensen does (Christensen, Anthony and Roth, 2004; Christensen and Raynor, 2003). In his view, disruptiveness means, essentially, 'new products in new markets'. As we will see in the fourth section of this chapter, disruptiveness may encompass more than that, and convey processes that are considerably more difficult to incorporate in classical innovation models. To give one example: if wireless technologies develop to the point that they constitute convincing and robust alternatives to fixed-cable infrastructures, they are not only new, in the Christensen sense, but also fundamentally disruptive for telecom incumbents' core business. Section 4 looks at how to treat this particular problem.

All these theories are thought-provoking, and even relevant, in the sense that they can provide useful explanatory suggestions; they can even help consider challenging options for the future, but certainly not to the point of conclusively 'knowing', and thereby expressing a 'truth' as to what possibility is most likely to become reality, solely on the basis of their modelling support. Our attitude, therefore, should be open, but at the same time cautious. Wi-Fi is certainly part of the current Kondratiev cycle organised around the clustering force of ICTs, as described by Freeman and Perez (1988) – but probably not to the extent of allowing us to know exactly, within that paradigm, how diverse and specific technological trajectories will actually unfold.

11.3.3   Technologies as social constructions

The other and, as it were, opposite approach, the constructivist one (the term should, arguably, be put it in the plural form, as there are several schools active in this field), tells us no more about the future, because nearly all options can be envisaged. This is especially true in the case of those approaches supporting the idea that technology has no fate other than what a series of sequential decisions eventually make it – i.e. the future is made by socio-economic actors making choices. In this perspective (if an actor-oriented analysis can help make explicit the linkages and interplays taking place within a particular innovation process), the number of variables involved is often too important simply to allow an extrapolation from current known dimensions to what is most likely to happen.

Technology is shaped by human (and social) actors, but we do not know in advance how. The examination of trends of how such actors tend to use, consume and transform technology, communicate about it or build communities to modify its original impact may constitute a strong initial knowledge stock, but pushing it systematically into the future is a foresight exercise of its own (on the user-driven co-design of technologies, for example, or actor-based morphological exploration) (see, for instance, Sørensen and Williams, 2002). In the case of Wi-Fi, constructivism, in contrast to a strictly diffusionist approach, involves taking account not only of growth figures but also of behaviours and choices, made by different sorts of users (including intermediate and professional users), that are constantly helping the technology to change (new standards, more types of equipment, new usages, new business models, new regulatory stakes).

11.3.4   The case for a middle-of-the-road epistemological space in the interplay between technologies and society

Finally, some help may come from the third way. In this category, we have in particular all the arguments on the notion of convergence. While, in some policy statements, convergence is presented as an obvious process, understood by everybody in a similar manner and leading to the same future, if we consider the vast literature on that theme, it becomes possible to distinguish between various types or levels of convergence: (1) economic, with the exchange of similar products on telecom channels – i.e. bits and data in standard formats; (2) technological, with overlaps, redundancy and cross-fertilisation between devices and platforms; and finally (3) human-societal, with globally congruent tendencies in terms of knowledge, miniaturisation, computing power and forms of usages or impacts. It is even more important, in this domain, to observe the diversity of stakeholder attitudes, however: some use the notion of convergence to prove their point or to explain what is taking place, while others expect the convergence to be reinforced as a desirable future, which policy should help this happen (and to some extent make it self-fulfilling),[20] whereas, for yet others, it is still an open question.

The assumptions supporting the first two approaches are (1) that convergence is undoubtedly taking place and (2), in addition, it is desirable and we should encourage it. There is an element of wishful thinking here, though, and the stance is probably challenged insufficiently by adherents of other theories. The result of this misguided use of the convergence notion is a form of predictive framing for a wide technological landscape, Wi-Fi being quite clearly part of the trend. The more or less explicit assumption here is that there is room for everybody in the 'information society', increasingly empowering the users and citizens. We too acknowledge convergence processes of diverse kinds, but at the same time observe the existence of diverging dynamics, constantly making futures for alternative options (high-performance device diversification, combinations that convey new potential, community usages and business models, lifestyles that evolve at their own pace, social divides that grow, risks that do not disappear, etc.).

Another useful approach to consider from a middle-of-the-road perspective is the evolutionary economics one, considering the importance of cycles and driving forces in the economic game, but also emphasising selective factors and actors that always have the power to influence the fate of a given technological solution, not always necessarily rewarding the best-performing ones,[21] but instead mixing various types of dimensions in the selection process. In this sense, one of the most interesting correctives to the linear model of innovation that has been put forward is the famous so-called 'chain-linked' model of Kline and Rosenberg (1986), involving three kinds of improvements: (1) various possible feedbacks between subsequent and earlier stages of an innovation process; (2) the interplay between various types of stakeholder during the process to support the development of the knowledge base (necessary for the targeted innovation, but also contributing to the development of knowledge in general, a spillover being inevitable); and (3), most importantly, envisaging the possibility of a prospective market as the real starting point of any innovative and entrepreneurial activity (rather than the proposal of a new idea, as held by the linear model of innovation). The two main reasons behind this last point, which completely fit the Schumpeterian tradition, are that (1) there are always many new ideas to be coped with, and a selection process must take place to invest only in those that hold out the promise of returns; and (2) these returns will ultimately be measured in market terms and not in science and technology terms (even if these express a supposedly superior performance). There is also a third reason: that the development of the knowledge base, mentioned as a key contribution of the Kline and Rosenberg model, concerns just the same, not only technological improvements but a broader set of issues, such as change and competence management, market organisation, intellectual capital protection, regulatory constraints, style and goodwill, business models, etc.

In reality, the variety of reasons for which a linear innovation process may fail to succeed is much more important than just suggesting that there is a severe dropout along the technology-push line of sight – i.e. from idea to product. User-driven shaping influences, risks identified by citizens or their representatives, the raising of acceptance issues at any moment (even late in the innovation process), transaction costs (Williamson, 1981, 1996) and institutional readjustments (Perez, 2002), among other factors, may all interfere with the purely 'Rogerian' destiny of a given technology. In fact, the linear model of innovation is exceptionally rare in practice, and the initial sources of innovation, power struggles in the Porter sense or market and industry battlefields provide us more with indications of complexity than with clues as to the future of a particular technological concern. The only interesting information to stress, in this theoretical window, in which several types of factors intermingle, is that, for the moment, the linear spreading of specific technologies is hardly linear, because of the fact that telecom incumbents, in most OECD countries at least, are engaged in resisting the wireless solutions of the Wi-Fi and WiMAX standards and, given the power they have on the market, in maintaining what have been until now alternative infrastructural options in quite a low profile. This could change, however, especially if new technological solutions are tested and appear to work (we examine such 'UFOs' in the fourth section of this chapter), or if supranational pressures or competition end up undermining the convenient dominance of traditional telecom infrastructure.

11.3.5   Market views on modelling implications

Translated into market terms, one could make an approximation by saying that the deterministic approach is typically reflected in the 'push' view of how market forces tend to unfold for a given sector, industry or product, while constructivist views would better fit a 'pull' perspective. What we saw in section 2 was the expression of a concerted 'push'; indeed, a number of communities can be said to be continuously 'pushing' (see Rossel and Finger, 2005). What is more interesting, though, is to see how users of different kinds and at different levels are eager to play their part and demand more efficiency, more options, more continuity and more combinations of services. If we take the broad picture of not just Wi-Fi but also other technologies and telecom services and usages, however, we start perceiving a multiplicity of selective factors that bring socio-economic actors back in the centre of the process, which hint instead at 'pull' conditions to explain the relative evolution of each specific telecom channel. Again, here, we find both explanations complementary rather than conflictive, and 'push-pull' moves and strategies, including within the strategy of a single telecom or ICT actor, are far from rare.

We have seen how limited a model the linear approach to innovation is, with serendipity, hybridisation or opportunistically discovered 'butterfly' effects applying more often than planning. Bearing this in mind, one could say that, nevertheless, until now the Wi-Fi pathway has been remarkably linear and push-like. The most probable explanations are (1) 'internally', the obstinate endeavour of some of the promoters, overcoming several of the obstacles that are typical of radical innovation dynamics; and (2) 'externally', the fact that

Wi-Fi is an open standard, already going in the direction of emerging open worlds (another heavy trend), and increasingly attractive for users of ICTs in general. This diversity of factors, again, suggests a need to pay attention to several modelling perspectives, including their possible mutual influence.

It is worth emphasising that, even in a purely technological perspective, Wi-Fi is not alone in its league, namely the wireless ICT arena, and wireless technologies themselves have to be positioned within a wider scope of communication and processing options, bearing in mind in particular the performance and services offered by the next generation of fixed and mobile infrastructure. This incoming horizon will convey various combinations of technological solutions and fit diverse societal forms and pressures, which will eventually be shaped into markets, institutions, policies, culturally fashionable usages and citizen-sensitive acceptance schemes. Any reflection on the future of Wi-Fi must take into account that level of complexity. Anything else would run the risk of being too naïve, or at least failing to accept the complexity and multiplicity of dimensions that will shape the domain of wireless at large, and that of Wi-Fi in particular.

11.3.6   Conclusion: preparing for more difficult tasks

The interim conclusion of this section is that, although innovation models provide the analyst with thought-provoking clues, and are most useful when monitoring change processes or considering short-term investments, they do not really deliver knowledge about the future of a domain such as Wi-Fi, and, moreover, may even suggest contradictory outcomes. We cannot know the future, of course, but in order to visualise how to improve the level of preparedness for coping with still uncertain outcomes, not least concerning the domain of wireless, we advocate deriving additional clues from complementary methods that are more clearly oriented towards the exploration of futures. Although, when considering rough data growth and geographical diffusion, Wi-Fi appears to be a fairly typical 'Bass object', in reality numerous actors, factors and associated processes have tended to co-produce the actual Wi-Fi trend, and there is no reason to think that this will simplify in the future. Wi-Fi belongs to a societal landscape encompassing complex socio-economic and technological change dynamics, and therefore requires non-superficial inferences when it comes to considering stakes and options to come. In this quite open context, we must recognise that the amount of effort invested so far in the promotion of Wi-Fi by its inventor(s)[22] is so impressive that the capability to pursue some form of construction goal in the Wi-Fi area, continuing the original 802.11 rationale, epic narrative and success curve, is in the range of trajectories likely to influence the overall Wi-Fi future. In this case, we are more in a configuration in which some stakeholders can make, to some extent, their own future ('future building'),[23] rather than trying to find an absolute model or method for 'future guessing'. Having stressed this remarkable activity, however, it is also necessary to situate it in the broad picture of innovation dynamics taking place in the development of the information society as a whole (in which not all factors are always converging and automatically cumulative). This requires at least an enlarged modelling and methodological scope, which it is to be hoped will produce more open and diverse scenarios (in particular not biased by volition or specific stakeholders' interests). Even though Wi-Fi is currently expanding, its future is not yet guarantted, and it would be a wise move to consider and benchmark several futures rather than just the one.

In market terms, considering the models and approaches that could provide clues, we perceive the push-pull types of shaping processes as occurring relatively frequently, with middle-of-the-road interplay between deterministic- and constructivist-minded moves from the diverse stakeholders. This orientation seems quite relevant with regard to the typical indeterminacy of early development stages of network or systemic technologies (we are not in a substitution rationale), bearing in mind also that Wi-Fi development may still involve unexpected selective inflections (in an evolutionary economics perspective) and some institutional adjustments (of a regulatory kind, for instance).

11.4   A futures study approach to emerging wireless technologies[24]

In our study of the future we concur with Deterding, for many years the chairman of Shell, when he said: 'It is impossible to predict the future, but also dangerous not to try.'

11.4.1   Initial methodological choices

The first choice we made was to take advantage of heterogeneous sources and studies: first, the already substantial literature, often of a technical nature, and some evaluative studies as well; and, second, a series of interviews that formed part of a micro-Delphi study conducted for a reflection on Wi-Fi's future, which was itself part of a broader research project within the COST A22 action regarding the future of ICT. The methodology used here combines two types of approaches: one was inspired by the Delphi procedure,[25] but simplified and aimed at getting information from experts on certain key questions concerning the future of wireless technologies; the other one, of a morphological nature, consisted of reflecting on a series of options within the possible field of alternatives. Let us see first how the Delphi technique has been used.

Seeking to take advantage of the interactive expert group management procedure of the Delphi method, but without several of its shortcomings, Rossel et al. (1999), in their technology assessment of the Swiss maglev project Swissmetro,

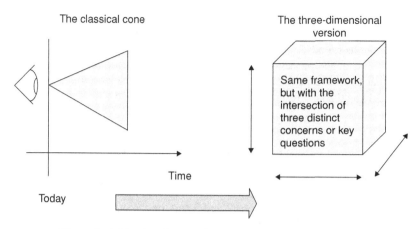

The classical cone

The three-dimensional version

Same framework, but with the intersection of three distinct concerns or key questions

Time

Today

Figure 11.1 Framing the questions in the Delphi method

developed a downsized version of the method that they called 'micro-Delphi'. The basic characteristics of a micro-Delphi study conform to the objective of harvesting opinions from experts through two or three rounds of questions, punctuated by a tentative synthesis of answers communicated back to the experts for the next round, but transformed in the case of micro-Delphi in the following way.

- As there is only limited time available, the topic has to be focused.
- There are fewer experts,[26] but they are all already professionally experienced in the topic's challenges, stakes and dilemmas.
- There are fewer questions (see below), but they home in, essentially, on the key problems to be considered, drawn from prior knowledge, including literature.
- The system functions best in emerging or even breakthrough situations, in which a significant level of indeterminacy continues to prevail (i.e. experts do not know; all they can do is make thought-provoking suggestions and produce facts associated with credible reasoning).
- The consensus-focused operation typically linked with the second Delphi round should leave enough room for highly qualitative perceptions and differences, the reformulation of questions therefore being of the utmost importance.

In order to focus more tightly and get more precise answers, the morphological procedure associated with the micro-Delphi exercise we carried out was altered from a two- into a three-dimensional perspective – i.e. from the 'cone of all possible options between two extremes' into a cross-cutting questioning of three independent and contrasting sets of variables (see Figure 11.1). Basically, each question takes the form: 'Do you see rather factor A becoming prevalent in the coming years or, instead, factor B?' As we are in a Delphi perspective, in each round a different set of variables can be used, according to the results of the previous rounds.

At the end of the process, we should have enough material to design scenarios that can have back-casting meaning (we come back to this aspect in section 5.1) on the near future of the topic we are concerned with – in this case, Wi-Fi.

11.4.2   An initial set of questions and then two rounds of interactions

To start with, we had a set of initial concerns or broad questions, arising from the issue of the future of Wi-Fi, reflecting, on the one hand, the questions and controversies mentioned in sections 2 and 3 and, on the other hand, stemming from an analysis of the literature.

- What is the role for Wi-Fi in the overall development of ICT and, more broadly, in the evolution of the information society, and what is likely to be the extent and pace of progression of this role, if any?
- What kind of dominance or, in contrast, complementarity will characterise Wi-Fi's future?
- What business models are most likely to prevail, including possible new ones that are yet to emerge?
- What kind of wild cards (possibly good, but more usually negative shocks) can we imagine, either ones that may have a limited impact, but also major ones, likely to have a global and irreversible effect?
- More profoundly (and this is a typical early detection problem), how can we take into account our possible wish to see Wi-Fi succeed in the way we appraise the various options as to its future?

All these concerns were envisaged for the 2015 time horizon. Further time targets are discussed in the conclusion.

These questions were rather unfit for the micro-Delphi exercise, and had to be 'translated'. For the first round of the procedure, we ended up with the three following questions.

(1) Do you consider it likely that there will be a growing dominance of a specific technology to cover communication needs (as the new prevailing substitute solution for traditional copper-cabling control schemes, among which Wi-Fi is then a possible candidate) or, instead, do you see several partially competing solutions developing?
(2) Do you see security issues as acting like a referee in selecting future solutions or combinations thereof, or is this problem likely to be solved more or less in parallel for all technologies?
(3) Will territory (urban setting dominant, size and distances, remoteness, physical conditions, roaming issues, incumbent control) play a role in selecting best solutions or combinations thereof or, on the contrary, will

we see different territorial situations and issues addressed by different solutions, which will continue to evolve and compete in the future?

The answers were a little surprising, although they were not conclusive, and they were either targeted towards the disambiguation of some issues or raised other, newer ones, and often they expressed preferences, allowing us to propose a first synthesis and formulate a second set of questions that made the best use of the first round's answers.

For the second round, the three questions were the following ones.

(1) Do you see as possible the emergence of 'best combinations of technologies' to support the most frequent territorial and business needs or, in contrast, that diverse tracks will continue to be developed through even harsher competition?

(2) Will the content industry or other non-technological factors play a major selecting/structuring role or do you see technological devices and standards pushing their way towards greater performance in all the current domains currently supported by ICT, more or less at the same pace?

(3) Will major strategic and territorial differentiations play a role in the way telecommunication structures itself in years to come (for instance, the South supporting specific non-cable-based solutions, China and other emerging markets imposing standards) or do you see open competition around post-incumbent and cable-based configurations continuing in a globally homogeneous way?

For each of the two rounds, we also asked an open question on possible wild cards, or unanticipated processes that can take place and change everything (major risks, proven concerns, either on health or environmental grounds, major political turmoil, etc.). At the end of the two rounds, we were able to produce a synthesis and suggest a limited number of tentative scenarios.

11.4.3 An intermediate synthesis

Our synthesis can be summarised into fifteen bullet points.

- Many competing solutions will continue to develop in parallel (with increased performance levels), with even tougher competitive schemes (some solutions, of course, being eliminated in the process) and yet more innovation and forms of outputs delivered.
- Functions and devices supporting wireless capabilities will continue to diversify and expand (the provision of internet access being less and less the crucial issue), for short-range and longer-range or even long-distance solutions (including specific point-to-point needs for all ranges), but not as universal solutions (again, due to the variety of competing communication technology combinations).
- Mobile telephony is not just a communication standard but also one of the carriers of next-generation network effectiveness, and given the enormous

amount of money invested will therefore develop as a vector for other standards, including Wi-Fi.

- Users will play an increasingly important role, either from lifestyle options (including fun fashion or selectively managing the tendency towards ultra-connectedness and 'ubiquity'), communities of practice, territorial communities or new business models, in defining reputation, ease of use, interfacing preferences, pricing benchmarks or content-processing schemes, all feeding corporate developments with critical information.

- Open standards and applications and, at the same time, closed standards and applications will continue to develop, on the one hand competing in and on the other hand tending to address different kinds of markets.

- More standards and radio frequency flexibility schemes will transform the role of regulatory bodies and international organisations towards arbitration rather than scarce public good licensing and specifications.

- New forms of convergence will emerge (based upon standard families, for instance), in particular when VoIP has improved in quality and security and when mobile internet security schemes have arrived at a point of maturity.

- The content industry will play a driving role in the immediate future in pushing some technological combinations more strongly than others, but, in the longer term, privacy and security issues will establish regulation concerns that we will have to learn how to formulate and use (for the various emerging stakes in terms of the regulation of ICT, see Rossel and Finger, 2007).

- In this context of proliferation, the current dominant standards (and Wi-Fi is one of them) will continue to prevail and expand, but in the medium term (beyond 2015) others are likely to emerge.

- The future of Wi-Fi will be embedded in the coming competition to find the best telecom and ICT combinations that address the most frequent needs (business, territorial coverage, long-distance options).

- The incumbent control schemes will resist and then collapse (this is likely to happen before 2015).

- Next-generation networking (NGN – whatever that actually means, and regardless of whether it will mean a specific level of achievements and coherent service packaging or just a trend) will broadly encompass all the options that we know today, cabling as well as wireless ones, continuously selecting some of them and making room for newer candidates.

- Developing countries and emerging markets, having a distinct past, may play an interfering role in pushing some technological options, and even achieving leapfrogging short cuts that may affect the whole world.

- A possible health issue concerning 'radio-smog' harming humans is not to be dismissed, although it is far from established for the moment.

- The environmental and carbon footprint of ICT, though still unclear for the moment, may become a big issue, increasingly leading to solution-selecting competitions.

On the basis of these points, we have worked out five distinct scenarios for the 2015 horizon, focused on wireless futures in general (i.e. not just on Wi-Fi).

11.4.4 Scenarios

There are, of course, many ways to produce scenarios. We should never forget that they do not come from any particular knowledge of the future that we could possibly have but, rather, from our percepts and constructs. Their design and presentation are therefore a matter of choice. Most common are reporting sets comprising three, four or five scenarios. Having four makes it possible to oppose them two by two and therefore position key criteria and critical dimensions on the basis of that matrix. The shortcoming with this format is that it tends to be more difficult to use in terms of decision making and strategic options, as the centre part of the matrix, drawing as it does upon existing knowledge, always seems to be more likely than its extremes. The option of having three or five scenarios, on the contrary, tends to result in a hierarchy, or at least a preferred ordering of the outcomes (it is difficult to design five equally attractive, robust and convincing scenarios). When there are more than five scenarios available, a downstream need for some form of shortlisting is most likely, while, with fewer scenarios (two or even one), the chances are high that some choice has probably already been made, at some stage upstream of the foresight process.

In our case, we have come up with five scenarios, which we evaluate in the fifth section. The order of the presentation of the scenarios below is of no intrinsic significance, of course. Their overall value resides mainly in their differences.

Scenario 1: ubiquitous, but with caution increasingly exercised   More technology and more productivity, greater bandwidth and higher risks constitute the expanding borders of an 'all-tech' trend, but some disruptive attitudes and policies are evident as well, based upon shared worries and risks of social catastrophes. The over-surveillance and over-connectedness typical of the ubiquitous information society make ever more space for priority activities, and the evaluation of new technologies becomes increasingly holistic (economic benefit and an underlying commitment to uphold Moore's law are no longer the ultimate values). All the same, in the broad sense, ICT innovations continue to act as the fuel of the current Kondratiev cycle and continue to maintain high expectations of all kinds regarding telecoms, and wireless solutions become more sophisticated and fit diverse specific situations. Balancing better performance and social risks is considered to be a new learning challenge for the

350 The Wi-Fi Journey in Perspective

generations to come, in the same way that others in the past had to do with their new technologies. Emerging countries tend to be torn between imitating OECD countries and experimenting with developments on their own terms, reflecting the contradictory messages coming from OECD countries. Wi-Fi, as a generally community-oriented solution, continues to expand (being pushed by users), but gradually comes to incorporate the group of technology solutions that will have to be evaluated and decided upon at some point in the future, with more holistic criteria.

Scenario 2: multiple choices   This scenario resembles what happened in 2008 but with all factors developing to higher levels of specific or combined performance and diversification. Productivity increases, but so do the risks, which tend to proliferate. The multiplicity of devices, both wireless and fixed, increases, in line with the extension of current Wi-Fi and WiMAX standards, to mobile telephony 3.5 or platforms that are still more advanced, as well as other wireless solutions (wireless local loop – unlicensed mobile access (WLL-UMA), for instance), especially in emerging markets, combined with specific point-to-point choices that continue to compete for the medium-range distance market, all partially packaged in attempts at new-generation network proposals, with the industrial and service sectors showing the way; political turmoil and competition between traditional OECD and emerging markets boost the number of accepted standards or variations. Business-wise, new models continue to emerge, with a variety of ways to service the market operating concurrently. This multiplicity makes for favourable conditions for developing countries to try out their own mix. In 2015 the situation is still unclear, but wireless solutions appear to be flourishing more and more, including the Wi-Fi legacy.

Scenario 3: new regulatory skills   There is a basic productive and dynamic tension between tendencies to innovate and the need to regulate, and, given the volume of new challenges generated by ICT (property rights, environmental issues, the supervision of radio frequency usage, financial loopholes, internet-based or other niches for criminal activities, etc.), many states develop an effective level of expertise in controlling most critical issues, while preserving open competition in most markets such that innovation continues to expand and generate economic activity. This amounts to an increase in performance linked not only with the new ICT solutions but also with the complexity of their governance and regulation. Security issues are well balanced with privacy and liberty concerns. A stable type of mastery over ICT usages seems to have been established, at least for the moment; suites of best-practice policies, which some wireless solutions already incorporate, are constantly being evaluated for possible adoption more widely, rather in the way that new technologies are assessed in the health care industry.

Scenario 4: a trade-off for new qualities   Ubiquity has been shown to have limits for privacy and security issues, in many domains (e-government, finance, learning), and so choices are increasingly being made for more qualitative selections of technologies, in a manner supportive of more fundamental societal goals and compatible both with sound environment management and local development particularities. The risks linked with wireless expansion are seriously taken into account and moderate usages prevail, while the possibility of disconnecting oneself, either temporarily or more permanently, is not considered to be either heretical or antisocial. Emerging countries, after an imitative period, start to develop their own configurations, taking into account not merely performance considerations but also local business initiatives, the question of social cohesion, health issues and the need for long-term precautions. Following an intense benchmarking and carbon footprint evaluation of critical technological solutions, wireless standards that fit this 'soft' evolution better start to prevail, and some countries decide to support them.

Scenario 5: all high-tech   In this scenario we are getting closer to high-definition TV standards (4,000 x 4,000) and ultra-broadband delivery capacity, at least for fibre to the home (FttH) systems, and reasonable alternatives for mobile viewing. Virtual worlds are improved to truly functional levels and the meshing up of various wireless standards constitutes good community substitutes for traditional infrastructures, but with acceptable roaming and long-distance schemes, all increasingly well packaged in next-generation network servicing. Meanwhile, more interface options allows for ambient environment interactions and industrial performance gets a boost from the integration of various cutting-edge technologies; economies benefit from such enabling toolsets and the social creativity associated with these usages, and business models follow. Higher performance levels are expected in the near future. The world is increasingly divided between 'haves' and 'have nots', and, in addition, these divides are themselves unstable: those who 'have' may still 'fall back' in the event of marginal conditions, as once someone has started along this course he/she has to keep track of technological evolution all his/her life (for the dynamic divide aspects, see Rossel and Glassey, 2005).

11.4.5   A need for narrowing down complexity and evaluating options

Having proposed this set of options as relevant for thinking about wireless futures at the 2015 horizon, we should now define the basis on which they are to be evaluated, and see how they give us indicative clues as to how to conclude our current reflection on the topic. This is the goal of the last section. For the moment, let us emphasise that the value of our scenarios is purposely uneven. Scenarios 4 and 5 are very unlikely for 2015, because they comprise features that have emerged only up to a point from our interviews; they nonetheless constitute useful options to reflect upon, as they increase the differentiating dimensions of the other three scenarios, for two of them are in some ways too realistic (scenarios 1 and 2), while scenario 3 is extremely idealistic. It is worth reminding ourselves that scenarios are not real states of the future; they are simply options for helping us think about the future so as to increase our level of preparedness. We now see how these diverse characterisations can help us.

11.5   Generating utility from our findings

There are a number of goals of this fifth section: to evaluate the tentative scenarios of the previous section; to situate our reflections on the dynamics of wireless development for various time horizons (and not just for 2015, which was only a reference point); and to examine various stakeholders' roles within the widespread paradigm of the tension between innovation and regulation. These objectives will be achieved partly in sequence and partly in a cross-referential form, as the issues are all interrelated.

11.5.1   How do we evaluate scenarios?

One easy answer to this question has been proposed by Morrison and Wilson (1996), who classify weak signals according to the level of (1) certainty and (2) the impact that they can be associated with. This on the face of it thought-provoking view is a two-by-two matrix of options. Our five scenarios could swiftly be filtered into relevant positioning. As has already been pointed out, however (Rossel, 2007, 2009), this approach completely overlooks the kind of implicit inferences that are used to decide what is certain or uncertain, as well as to define the levels of impact to come. The Morrison and Wilson matrix is typical of a non-reflexive epistemology (i.e. there is no reflection on the underpinning assumptions, boundaries and influence of the heterogeneity of causal explanations), in which the future is envisaged as knowledge 'already out there', just waiting for the analyst to discover and make sense of, for any further types of usage. It is fundamentally non-constructivist. It may work well for very short-term and narrow problems, with very little risk of disruptive outcomes. Any (more) complex issue with multiple time perspectives and a variety of stakeholder viewpoints simply cannot be analysed adequately this way, and will require a more demanding approach.

To keep it within limits, in our case, we basically show how, by varying the time perspective, the suggestions embedded in the various scenarios take on different meanings, and therefore different forms of usage and readiness, which will also vary according to the different stakeholders involved (public policy, science, wireless technology producers, end user communities, services and industries making heavy usage of ICTs, cities, regional development agencies, etc.). We do not describe the relations between the time horizon, the feature and the meaning for all these actors, instead simply pointing out a few key tracks as being broadly indicative of current trends, and possible futures, for three distinct time horizons. To that end, we distinguish the shaping and the impact of features for three such timelines: the short term, 2015 and the longer term (to reiterate, there is no particular significance attached to 2015, as it was no more than a reference horizon for the micro-Delphi exercise). Now, in just the same vein, we have a broader need: putting all our data into a more dynamic perspective. In order to do this, and generate a better analysis of deployments of wireless technologies and Wi-Fi in particular, we adopt here not a forecasting approach but, instead, a back-casting approach.

11.5.2   Beyond 2015: the longer term

As time passes, more convergence takes place – but also more divergence; differentiation may therefore also affect the construction of further standards. The most likely aspect of this is the awareness, beyond the push approach of every particular standards community, for the sake of its own legitimacy and interests, that overall framework standards are needed. The exploration by Tan and Bing (2003)[27] on the internetworking of wireless and cellular networks and the Gartner forecast of 2005 that by 2010 mobile telephony (based on generations 2, 2.5, 3 and 3.5) and other wireless standards (Wi-Fi, WiMAX and others) will converge[28] will become more and more of a challenge to achieve, and, if the first attempts do not prove entirely satisfactory, efforts will be redoubled. It remains to be seen, however, whether such attempts support an open or closed view of technological standardisation (scenario 1, 'ubiquitous, but with caution increasingly exercised'), or develop as parallel endeavours on both sides of the coin (scenario 2, 'multiple choices').

As time passes, more risks are likely to remind us of their possible unfolding. Health issues in particular will continue to trigger university research and public-interest-oriented NGOs (the World Health Organization, for instance) and may give more substance to the still rather faint voice of present-day whistleblowers. At some point, the increased use of radio waves and higher power levels that may lead to some microwave oven effect will undoubtedly remain on the radar of specific concern groups. The case histories of asbestos and Vioxx, both of which turned out to have serious side effects years after their appearance and the initial worldwide acclaim, are reminders of what can happen. The chief issue may well arise in the arena of environmental concerns, however. To date there has been no consistent and consensual carbon footprint evaluation of ICT. Here and there, weak signals of a major problem looming ahead have come up, but so far with no generally agreed-upon supporting methodology. The problem is twofold: the carbon emissions associated with the production and maintenance of ICT items in all their many forms, and the dispersion into the environment of hazardous materials and micro-objects, which are already said to be in the trillions. The development of RFID-driven solutions and sensor networks (which by extreme miniaturisation aim at the 'smart dust' paradigm) will provide us not only with ambient intelligent environments but also with an increase in micro-component scattering.

From the point of view of this latter risk, Wi-Fi may well be fine, much better than for the previous risk mentioned here, the health issue. This needs to be measured, documented and benchmarked, however. There is no reason for not thinking, in this case, that the environmental rating of wireless technologies will somehow decide their selection as good practices and solutions. To reach that level of holistic concern fully, there will have to be social movements, grass-roots and user-community-driven, that generate the pressure and, in parallel, a considerable increase in regulatory and policy-making solutions in order to have the vision to confront the kind of problems that the development of ICT is increasingly posing. At that point, the knowledge base to leverage this kind of follow-up (environmental analysis as a new knowledge industry) and the strategic issues linked to national or regional compliance schemes will also be part of the picture; this should take place sometime after 2015, and more acutely so somewhen between 2020 and 2040. This consideration paves the way for a return to our window of attention of scenario 3 ('new regulatory skills') and even scenario 4 ('a trade-off for new qualities').

As time passes, it may also be the case that the disruptive potential of major strategic security issues worldwide becomes heightened, to the extent of modifying the current appraisal grid (this would constitute a true wild card, in this case). There is no way to prepare oneself for eventualities of this type; all one can do is bear in mind that the shape of things as they are currently perceived may not always hold. Again, this advocates taking scenario 4 seriously, as it aims at proactively diminishing vulnerabilities and dependencies. To boost the weight of this scenario even more, let us also add that some of the psychological stress and privacy issues linked with the ubiquitous society (over-connectedness and over-surveillance) will start to be thoroughly examined and taken care of, as a legal issue as well as a public health issue.

The paradox of the 'beyond 2015' time horizon is that this is also the timescale necessary for the full deployment of the 'next-generation networking' paradigm, in which various, albeit not too numerous, solutions will be chosen for solving the technicalities and service demands of most basic communication and processing configurations (some current standards may then have to 'merge').[29] Although this vision resembles the 'all high-tech' scenario 5, in reality, for the various above-mentioned reasons, a strong demand for governance and sophisticated regulatory schemes will also emerge, at all political levels, including internationally, making room for key aspects of scenario 3.

11.5.3   Around 2015

Two paradoxical influences are likely to exert pressure on this time horizon. One comes from the future, so to speak, as several of the risk factors depicted in the previous section will already have been perceived, and will be partially enacted in attempts to contain them. The other influence comes from our present trend, evident for some time, of pushing successful solutions towards more widespread adoption, with more 'embarkable' and mobile, multifaceted and intercommunicating devices and applications, partially diverging but also phasing in parts of the NGN paradigm.

What is likely to take place, by 2015, is a clarification of business models linked with emerging technological solutions (mobile internet services, grid networks, Wi-Fi communities, Wi-Fi–WiMAX and other combinations, Web 2.0 dynamics, open standards and applications, virtual life usages, etc.). From what we know today, there is no reason to think that Wi-Fi and technological combinations involving wireless solutions will not play a favourable role in this clearing process. It should not be forgotten that one key issue is to support the alternatives to current or residual incumbent control over fixed-line infrastructures; any additional degree of freedom over what we have will give new roles to the best currently growing solutions (such as Wi-Fi). Scenarios 1 and 2 both comply with this observation.

In this process, the content industry will play an early role, as we can already see some evidence of such a trend occurring. At some point, however, in a very Schumpeterian manner ('creative destruction'), simply delivering more contents, more rapidly to more devices will not do, and other industries will enter the fray so as to secure the best return on investment for themselves (education, health, security and industrial databases are a few candidates). 2015 might be a little bit early for this shift, but some aspects of it may already be perceptible (we have also said that scenario 3, with extended governance and regulation capabilities to decide innovation pushes, will become increasingly important). As a matter of fact, for the less passive activities (content capture is a form of immediate consumption), variable radio spectrum implementation, multiple standard switching and 'platforming' devices and applications deployed in an open and context-relevant manner (prefiguring the NGN paradigm) will create complex situations in which an 'all high-tech' approach will not flourish, while enhanced governance and regulation will create the necessary guidelines, protection and arbitration framework. For Wi-Fi, this evolution may mean that the current multiple device orientation (Wi-Fi in nearly every ICT object, and not just PCs) may prevail over its capacity actually to provide local access to the

Internet, at least as a stand-alone solution; within technological combinations, but one that remains to be tested and benchmarked. Wi-Fi has every chance to be successful in this time horizon.

Finally, VoIP should improve in quality and security, to the point of being able to change the 'usual suspects' casting of the telecoms arena (but, again, within a clarification of the business processes involved, and also subject to some key regulatory provisions); under these conditions, at some point most probably before 2015, it should start playing the role of change accelerator (for the immediate difficulties of packaging VoIP in relevant business models, see the interesting study by Bubley, 2007).

11.5.4   The short term

In the next three to five years, two types of processes are explored. One concerns the interplay between Wi-Fi and WiMAX (will they compete or combine?),[30] as well as other technological and standard combinations for solving densely urbanised coverage needs, medium-distance demand for broadband continuity or point-to-point specific needs. The other is the extent to which proposals for mobile telephony of 3.5G standard and beyond actually bypass current established telecom configurations, including, possibly, Wi-Fi and WiMAX meshing up. As has already been said, the most probable result of this technological confrontation is that, as we get closer to 2015, the distinction will diminish. For the moment, however, we observe an explosion of proposals, either of stand-alone technologies to convey the essentials of telecommunication, or within combinations. This is the uncertainty confronting scenarios 1 and 2. Let us examine these two problems step by step.

Wi-Fi has a huge potential for expanding, diversifying the landscape of ICT local loops and constituting, in particular, urban settings – something that, among all the examined options, is the closest thing to an alternative. It is a universal solution (the same plug and play system functions everywhere), implemented in portable computers and mobile telephony, but also in a growing number of multimedia tools and functions, either in domestic or less domestic usages. It is an open standard and will be continuously improved upon, for quite a while, thanks to an expanding support development community. Through (1) the improvement of performance both in terms of power and quality (incoming IEEE 802.11n or beyond), (2) the increasing number of access points and (3) the meshing option (the ability of subscribers to play a relay role for larger-scale communication schemes), it can deliver an alternative solution to fixed-line constraints, and therefore holds out considerable promise. This probably means continuous expansion, provided that high-level cryptography is increasingly applied. Proximity services, following the work of Hyman and Katz (2001), are indeed promised to a high level of diversity, customisation and effectiveness. Communities of users will most probably keep proving to be very creative and dynamic in their proliferation, including in solutions that propose a choice between various technological channels, improving flexibility for the consumer (some new user innovation scheme associated with Wi-Fi may even appear). More and more cities will become flagships for what extensive Wi-Fi coverage integrated with other ICT offerings can really do (the emerging examples of Oklahoma City and Birmingham are interesting attempts in this direction).

All this may fall just short of providing a universal solution.[31] As a matter of fact, over and above some on-site implementation intricacies and functioning discontinuities, the main problems of Wi-Fi are (1) its dependence on the backbone level of telecommunication for larger-scale transit; (2) business models, which still vacillate between free urban offers, expensive local rents (hotels, airports), hardware dissemination value and proximity application benefits; (3) complex roaming issues, in the event that Wi-Fi was conceived at some point as a universal solution; and (4) security weakness as universal infrastructure (it would take another level of redundancy to solve this problem bottom-up and another level of investment to solve it top-down). One of the potential solutions, in the case of inclination towards adopting one main technological alternative to fixed lines, would seem to lie in the combination of Wi-Fi with WiMAX.

WiMAX presents several seductive features, such as diffusion outreach (several kilometres), high bandwidth (VDSL level) and no line-of-sight needs. It has some disadvantages too, however. It is for the moment a more costly alternative, not stabilised (it has several sub-standards, with configurations that are not very easy to implement), and it still lacks the level of experience that the Wi-Fi community has. All experiments also show that its territorial management and optimisation is not a trivial task. These initial shortcomings may rapidly disappear, of course, but the business model remains unclear (descending flow is one thing, 'unicasting' to the individual user another one, and interacting bottom-up or sideways yet another).[32] Just as in the case of Wi-Fi, numerous cities have started trials, and in so doing they constitute themselves (for diverse reasons that should be better understood) as infrastructure developers; but it is not so obvious, in the medium term (beyond the initial experimental stage), that they can do better (namely more cheaply and with a sufficiently high level of quality) than industry.[33] In fact, provided that WiMAX enhances its efficiency and affordability, it can represent a substitution option for rural access, niche markets (fairs, for instance) and, of course, a meso-level backbone (if it can be so termed) for developing countries (which are also experimenting with other solutions, such as WLL-UMA in north Africa, for example). Here again, however, it is mostly a question of time, as some services, such as high-definition TV, are probably too demanding to pass through WiMAX; this technology is also, in that sense, a bridge towards other technological generations that are yet to appear. In the specific cases described above, though, this timescale may be long enough to develop interesting business and societal options and a combination of technologies in which WiMAX may play a supportive role. For the next five to eight years, however, fixed-line and VDSL services will provide a competing alternative, maintaining WiMAX, and even Wi-Fi for local loops, in a preliminary stage of effectiveness.

In reality, the main issue with WiMAX, besides its 'performance limitation'[34] (it is powerful, but when it comes to competing with NGN it struggles), is the fact that it is a broadcasting means (one-to-many) with, as we have said, a seemingly complex and, for the moment, still unclear business models.[35] This is, at one and the same time, a handicap (in the case of a universal solution competing with NGN to come) and an advantage for niche markets or developing countries.[36] This is why we see it as at best a partial answer to the first question raised in this section, including the optimal case of a combination with Wi-Fi (although this is not going to be as easy as it may look, involving in particular some regulation issues, in interference arbitration, for instance, and some industrial risk taking in combining Wi-Fi and WiMAX tightly, as Intel, for one, is trying to do).

The second issue raised in this section is linked to the question of a possible upcoming convergence of Wi-Fi and WiMAX with mobile telephony standards, or, on the contrary, a rapid expansion of these latter systems, which could conceivably dispose of all the others (here the unequal research budgets involved also need to be taken into consideration, the advantage being clearly on the side of mobile telephony). In order to remain level-headed in this dilemma, one could take shelter in the impression that there is no problem, as every new mobile device now incorporates Wi-Fi, and soon WiMAX too. This could prove to be an illusion, though, as it is one of the many facilities that mobile handsets can be equipped with; within the transition towards higher performance levels, there is a greater diversity of services offered by mobile telephony. Already, in terms of sheer performance, such compromises as GPRS and Sprint-Nextel have provided an interesting internet access level (sheer performance, as has already been mentioned, is not the only measure of business success), and are soon to rise to higher levels of performance. Now there are also post-UMTS solutions, as, for example, high speed downlink packet access (HSDPA), high-speed space division multiple access (HSDMA) and high speed uplink packet access (HSUPA), or others, closer to 4G, such as high capacity space division multiple access (HC-SDMA) or 802.15 ultra-wideband (UWB) and HSPA/LTE,[37] which are likely to provide services that it would be almost impossible for Wi-Fi or WiMAX to approach. It is not just a matter of bandwidth but also of the diversity of services embedded, of cellular effectiveness and even of lifestyle. Further standards of mobile telephony will do even better. Competition is likely to increase, standards and technologies are to be tested at an even faster pace, with, of course, some systems dropping out along the way. Our view, nevertheless, especially taking into consideration the fact that several types of factors, not only technological ones, will play a role in future business models and territorial coverage for high-level service delivery, is that Wi-Fi and WiMAX will continue to grow and play a role, thereby fitting the spirit of our scenarios 1 and 2.[38]

The last open issue is the question of combinations: can mobile telephony standards for 3.5G and higher merge in the near term with Wi-Fi? The answer is clearly a 'No' for an absolute merger. It is 'Yes', however, if one considers the community of industries, researchers and service specialists involved in promoting several options concurrently to be part of a heavy trend in which most stakeholders may prefer betting on several tracks rather than just one. In this sense, further options are still open, to converge more, and even leave room for new bridging standards, as we have seen for more remote time horizons. There are sufficiently numerous and diverse telecom solution combinations, for the moment, for most of them to retain some momentum, Wi-Fi in particular, which, in this combinatorial game, plays in several different categories (the ultra-local loop of a wider internet access provision, community solutions, indoor solutions and multi-device interconnection, just to mention the main important ones). In both the current situation and the medium term (the next five to eight years), there is a clear divergence trend of multiple technological options, standards, philosophies, business models and markets. This argues for Wi-Fi remaining a reassuring reference in the turbulent years to come, stable as it is, continuously expanding, popular, inexpensive and supported by communities everywhere, as well as by new device producers and new wearable equipment providers – at least until bandwidth level requirements and interoperability issues enter the equation. The short- to medium-term outlook looks decidedly positive for Wi-Fi.

11.6   Conclusion: quite an open situation

The situation facing the current expansion of wireless technologies is extraordinarily open, and it would therefore be foolish to conclude with a closed form of comment (pretending to know what is going to take place) in such explorative circumstances. The answer will also vary according to the type of stakeholder. Accordingly, the best way to conclude is probably this: to suggest that, on the basis of all the preceding analyses, each stakeholder should look to its own needs when adopting a stance, develop a strategy and create a decision-making procedure if needed. Moreover, as we have presented our findings not only for a predetermined time horizon (2015) but also in a dynamic form, each stakeholder should be able to set up some follow-up activity, again, according to its needs and context. In all likelihood, policy makers and regulators can also derive clues for their work. Companies involved in the production of wireless technologies are invited to think beyond the very short term, typical of the real-time level of orders-linked perception that structures the life of enterprises.

For NGOs and civil society actors, there are undoubtedly a series of challenges ahead, in which they will be closely involved, and, clearly, our reflections may occasion a strategic review of possible actions in the wireless domain, as well as with regard to the future of the information society as a whole. For research communities, it seems that they are still engrossed with tough technological challenges to come up with reliable achievements, such as variable radio spectrum, mobile network management, various security and interoperability issues, as well as nano-sensor programming, just to mention a few. Increasingly, they should channel their energies into wider agendas, including health risk and environmental concern issues. Convincing business models also have a significant role in deciding the choice of contemporary topics for scientific research, not to mention the already strong influence that industrial R&D exerts.

Finally, at more strategic levels, it has to be acknowledged that new forms of ICT also constitute ammunition for nations, whether for their alliances or for their antagonisms, in their divisions and possible battles. These considerations, in our case, remain a wild card: capable of generating new policies, but also one that should always be present in the minds of decision makers when it comes to taking the medium term into account.

Notes

1 There were, of course, previous attempts, in particular in the United States, but they proved unsatisfactory in terms of effective service delivery and prospects for rapid growth. In contrast, even in its early stages, the value that Wi-Fi would bring was apparent, according to Vic Hayes, who recalls how the working group deployed its own technology to share documents and speed up communication across attendees at its six annual conferences (see www.cm.com/it-channel/50500272). During that initial stage, the community of promoters consisted essentially of engineers. They were indeed user-innovators.

2 See www.wi-fi.org.

3 To be precise: 435 voters produced 12,277 comments to be resolved.

4 Beyond increases in power and reliability, specific problems also have to be resolved, such as improving meshing and roaming effectiveness, for instance; these undoubtedly constitute key dimensions of the next frontier (IEEE 802.11 task groups for the 'r' and 's' standards).

5 Full triple play consists of a combined offer of internet access, telephony and radio and television distribution.

6 Full triple play (a full video bitstream for digital TV in particular) has a threshold at 11 Mbit/s, but 'true' effectiveness involves a bit flow some five times superior, in terms of potential rate, in order to guarantee such an operational regime. Hence

the importance of the 'n' standard, not only for PCs, portable or not, but also for screens, printers, high-definition TV screens and content players, digital cameras, mobile phones, etc. See www.commsdesign.com/design_corner/showArticle.jhtml? articleID=17200165 and www.xs4all.nl/~vichayes/Wi-Fi_Workshop_2006/Status_Standards_Work.pdf.

7 Gradually, high-performance trains are also incorporating Wi-Fi services. France's latest high-speed rail line, for example, TGV Est (Train à Grande Vitesse East), will be equipped by the end of 2010 with a variety of services on its fifty-six trains.

8 If we take the example of France, we have not just Paris but also Blanquefort, in the Bordeaux area.

9 These early meshing claims are still more experimental and subject to failure than real commercial leads, but they show a new way into telecom and internet access, and they constitute a weak signal of change.

10 We are not considering the failed proposals here. It is important all the same to bear in mind that quite a severe selection process has already taken place among the various wireless communications solutions that have been conceived and tested in the last two decades.

11 See www.techcast.org.

12 Forecasts represent a type of information, built upon particular hypotheses that make good use of past data; they are not equivalent to knowing the future. Constructed so as to reflect one or just a few factors, and often with an optimistic filter applied to data that tend to reinforce the trend rather than incorporating the totality of factors involved, forecasts need to be treated with caution. For instance, they are not generally sensitive to unexpected or disruptive events; in fact, quite the opposite.

13 See www.newswireless.net/index.cfm/article/994.

14 See www.gartner.com/DisplayDocument?id=500033. WiMAX is a telecommuncations technology that provides wireless transmission of data using a variety of transmission modes, from point-to-point links to portable and fully mobile internet access. The technology provides a data rate of up to 3 Mbit/s and is based on the IEEE 802.16 standard.

15 See http://telephonyonline.com/wireless/news/wifi_alliance_certified_112007.

16 This category embraces a large number, starting with Marx and the evolutionary anthropologists of the nineteenth century, to twentieth-century thinkers such as Mumford, Gille, Ellul and Simondon, to mention just a few, all of whom, in their own terms, developed the key concept of according the material form of technology the status of super-determinant, even when envisaged in a programmatic perspective. Some of them leant towards giving their super-explanatory factor a positive influence (e.g. Marx, Gille and Simondon), while others stressed the opposite: the rather negative influence of technology (e.g. Mumford and Ellul). For most of them it is hardly possible to speak of an innovation model as such, just an explanatory theory, with the possible exception of Gille (1978) and his concept of 'système technique' (technological system). This builds upon the series of technological jumps in performance, which relate to innovations in key domains such as energy, time and measurement, food and agriculture, and materials, or any more modern equivalent when we get closer to our time. Seen in this perspective, Wi-Fi would be one co-component of such a jump.

17 Rogers first presented his concept of the 'S curve' in 1962.

18 Indeed, diffusionism is strongly supportive of the linear model of innovation philosophy, which, to sum up a variety of innovation narratives, basically says that some people think, invent and propose new solutions, which are worked out to become functional and reliable, then produced and eventually sold as consumer goods or services.

19 The observation can be made here that most forecasts based on the 'observable' dynamics of the growth of Wi-Fi in reality filter mainly 'internal' or closely associated factors, and it is far rarer (understandably) for models to admit 'external' factors, such as non-Wi-Fi ones, or ones apparently not related, as this makes the procedure considerably more complex. We progressively explore the significance of these more indirect influences.

20 For the first two viewpoints on convergence in European technologies, see, for instance, Bernold (2004) and Nordmann (2004), as well as the more systematic assessment on fixed–mobile technology convergence by Shneyderman and Casati (2008). See also, for more recent works on the wireless–mobile convergence, the 2006 study by the Wi-Fi Alliance, which is available at www.wi-fi.org/files/wp_13_White_Paper_Wi-Fi_Mobile_Convergence.pdf.

21 It is worth recalling that the Macintosh did not dislodge the 'IBM' PCs, just as Betamax did not eradicate the lower-profile VHS. This problem, in which sheer performance sometimes does not reflect market needs perfectly, is a strong limitation to a predominantly 'push' approach to innovation (see below).

22 The use of the 'inventors' concept hints, in this case, at the broad Dutch scientific and industrial environment – the NCR Utrecht Systems Engineering Centre as a root post, along with the Philips Electronic linkage (see some of the earlier chapters).

23 In futures studies, this concept is attracting increasing attention, although it is somehow disruptive in the management arena: 'future making', which is typical, for instance, of entrepreneurship, among other behaviours, does not unfold on the basis of decision making as a result of perfect information acquisition, but, to the contrary, gives an a posteriori 'right' or 'wrong' status to upstream knowledge by acting and making one particular future take place, successfully, it is to be hoped (under the auspices of reasonably evaluated risks, momentum and committed determination, instead of perfect information and, only then, action).

24 It has been possible to carry out a broad methodological assignment regarding Wi-Fi as a result of learning steps (1) encompassed in past studies looking at ICT (with special expertise developed in the domains of e-working, e-learning and e-government), (2) taking into account the proliferation of other forward-looking studies conducted by agencies, non-European as well as European, on the future of information society technologies, (3) resulting from relevant 'domestic' developments, such as studies carried out by the management of network industries department of the Ecole Polytechnique Fédérale de Lausanne in emerging domains such as the intelligent stamp or mobile termination costs, or within its leading executive Masters programme in e-governance (exploring in a variety of ways the future of e-government) and (4) emerging as a positive co-effect of the EPFL's leading participation first in the COST A22 action on new foresight methods (chairing the working group on the seeds of change) and then in a specific Swiss-funded study on the future of ICT.

25 The Delphi method is one of the oldest forms of futures studies methodologies, created in the wake of the Second World War within the RAND Corporation, which

formalised it in the 1960s (see Dalkey and Helmer-Hirschberg, 1968, and Helmer-Hirschberg, 1967, by two of the official creators of the Delphi method, and Brown, 1968, and Sackman, 1974). It is convenient, productive and relatively easy to roll out. Its history is already substantial (see, in particular, the handbook approach by Linstone and Turoff, 1975), and criticisms have appeared only recently, addressing the limitations of Delphi exercises in general, but especially in large-scale operations (Heraud, 2002; Heraud, Munier and Nanopoulos, 1997); see also Shin (1998, 2001), among others.

26 In our case, out of thirty possible experts linked with our various researches, just fifteen were finally chosen for the micro-Delphi study, coming from both the private sector and the scientific research arena in eleven countries.

27 See also the more recent edited book by Bing (2008).

28 See http://blogs.zdnet.com/BTL/?p=1403. This is a convergence of markets, as multiple technologies are combined in one device.

29 What is meant by 'next-generation networking' is a combination of technologies offering a diversified yet supposedly consistent and cohesive set of options for delivering and accessing all IP solutions and a high bandwidth level for communications. It would involve both fixed-line solutions, mainly making use of optical fibre and supporting the chosen scheme, besides the backbone, of FttH, and mobile offerings. This set of technological solutions, which can be combined and configured for versatile service delivery, will allow for real-time multi-channel, multimedia-format interactive integration, not only for individuals (who would then have an excess of power available) but most probably for businesses and administrations as well. NGN involves issues of a technological nature, which have to converge gradually and be tested as full-package solutions at some point in the future, and also of knowledge management (the complex usage problem) and legal constraints (what is a 'communication session' from the point of view of a lawyer?).

30 In connection with WiMAX, it is interesting to see that, in spite of the often announced failure of this technology (see, for instance, www.thestandard.com/news/2008/03/25/airspan-blames-customer-poor-wimax-performance and web20. telecomtv.com/pages/?newsid=42882&id=e9381817–0593–417a-8639–c4c53e2a2a10) and the not so clear business model that still makes numerous telecom players hesitant about using it, major industry players are pushing strongly to make things happen, as one can see with the three big WiMAX conferences held in 2008, in Singapore, Amsterdam and Rio de Janeiro (see www.wimax-vision. com/newt/l/wimaxvision/magazine_view.html?section=5).

31 Techcast (www.techcast.org) considers Wi-Fi to have entered the mainstream communication technological domain (the early stage of maturity) in 2005. Compared with this optimistic vision, we would say, on the issue of Wi-Fi as a universal solution, 'Yes and no' – but probably 'No' if we had to decide.

32 WiMAX also has a very dynamic support community promoting the WiMAX standard (the WiMAX Forum, an industry-led organisation), and several chip manufacturers have already got involved in this upcoming business, such as Intel, Motorola, Samsung and Nokia, with WiMAX handsets being introduced in 2008.

33 On this question, we find again the old idea that the state has to deliver the service itself, and can actually do it better than the private sector, instead of regulating a

self-standing private market that develops this service. Public–private partnerships could rapidly become a best practice in this area.

34 We have been told, informally, that experiments in mobile WiMAX carried out in Trondheim, Norway, showed that all the performance claims of WiMAX are verified except for the outreach distance – and by a massive margin, as, rather than the 50 kilometres often claimed for the technology, we were told the actual outreach performance did not exceed 500 metres! If this result was to be confirmed in other contexts, WiMAX, although still ahead of the current 3G level, would have to face some tough competition from the next generation of mobile telephony, in particular considering such issues as price, of course, but also in terms of security and interference management.

35 In the 2008 Barcelona conference on 'Wireless and digital cities' (11–13 November; see www.wirelesscitiescongress.eu), most players insisted on the fact that, without associated services, there is virtually no business model to speak of.

36 This may represent a technological wild card, however, provided that all the limitations we have mentioned are resolved. It certainly represents a technology worth following up. For the moment, Swisscom, for example, has a licence that it does not really use (except for specific experiments).

37 For those mortals who, like most of us, find it difficult to follow this blizzard of acronyms, see the interesting article by CNET News (2006).

38 Given the complexity of the situation, it is no surprise that the 'Wireless broadband' conference, supported by the Wi-Fi Alliance, that took place in Moscow 16–17 April 2008 looked in detail at the very topic of 'Comparing WiMAX, EV-DO [Evolution – Data Optimized], HSPA, LTE: performance numbers and targets, recommendations, deployment scenarios, etc.'.

References

Bass, F. M. (1986). 'The adoption of a marketing model: comments and observations'. In V. Mahajan and Y. Wind (eds.). *Innovation Diffusion Models of New Product Acceptance*. Cambridge, MA: Ballinger, 203–32.

Bernold, T. (2004). *Converging Technologies for a Diverse Europe*. Brussels: European Commission.

Bing, B. (ed.) (2008). *Emerging Technologies in Wireless LANs: Theory, Design, and Deployment*. Cambridge: Cambridge University Press.

Brown, B. (1968). 'Delphi process: a methodology used for the elicitation of opinions of experts'. Paper no. P-3925. Santa Monica, CA: RAND Corporation.

Bubley, D. (2007). *Evolution of Mobile VoIP: VoIPo3G Business Models*. London: Disruptive Analysis. Available at www.disruptive-analysis.com/voipo3g.htm.

Christensen, C. M., S. D. Anthony and E. A. Roth (2004). *Seeing What's Next: Using Theories of Innovation to Predict Industry Change*. Cambridge, MA: Harvard Business School Press.

Christensen, C. M., and M. E. Raynor (2003). *The Innovator's Solution: Creating and Sustaining Successful Growth*. Cambridge, MA: Harvard Business School Press.

CNET News (2006). 'The wireless alphabet soup'. San Francisco: CNET News. Available at www.news.com/The-wireless-alphabet-soup/2100–1039_3–6038991.html.

Dalkey, N., and O. Helmer-Hirschberg (1968). 'An experimental application of the Delphi method in the use of experts'. *Management Science*. **9** (3), 458–67.

Davis, F. D. (1989). 'Perceived usefulness, perceived ease of use, and user acceptance of information technology'. *MIS Quarterly*. **13** (3), 319–40.

Freeman, C., and C. Perez (1988). 'Structural crises of adjustment, business cycles and investment behaviour'. In G. Dosi, C. Freeman, R. R. Nelson and L. Soete (eds.). *Technological Change and Economic Theory*. London: Pinter, 38–66.

Gille, B. (1978). *Histoire des techniques: Technique et civilisations, technique et sciences*. Paris: Gallimard.

Helmer-Hirschberg, O. (1967). 'Analysis of the future: the Delphi method'. Paper no. P-3558. Santa Monica, CA: RAND Corporation.

Heraud, J.-A. (2002). 'The comparison of a Delphi foresight survey on the environmental technologies of the future in Japan, Germany and France'. Beta Working Paper no. 9906. Strasbourg: University Louis Pasteur.

Heraud, J.-A., F. Munier, F. and K. Nanopoulos (1997). 'Potentialités et limites d'un exercice de prospective de type Delphi: application d'une méthode de segmentation à l'enquête sur les technologies du futur'. *Futuribles*. **218** (16), 33–53.

Hyman, M., and R. L. Katz (2001). 'Alternative industry futures in the global internet economy'. In L. W. McKnight, P. M. Vaaler and R. L. Katz (eds.). *Creative Destruction: Business Survival Strategies in the Global Internet Economy*. Cambridge, MA: MIT Press, 229–39.

Kline, S., and N. Rosenberg (1986). 'An overview of innovation'. In R. Landau and N. Rosenberg (eds.). *The Positive Sum Strategy: Harnessing Technology for Economic Growth*. Washington, DC: National Academy Press, 275–305.

Linstone, H., and M. Turoff (eds.) (1975). *The Delphi Method: Techniques and Applications*. Reading, MA: Addison Wesley.

Marchetti, C. (1980). 'Society as a learning system: discovery, invention, and innovation cycles revisited'. *Technological Forecasting and Social Change*. **18** (3), 267–82.

(1982). 'Invention et innovation: les cycles revisités'. *Futuribles*. **53** (1), 43–58.

(1987). 'The Kondratiev cycle: predicting for the next 25 years'. In Research and Development Society. *R+D for the 21st Century: An Analysis of Trends Affecting Strategies for Industrial Innovation*. Cranfield: Cranfield Press.

(1991). 'A forecasting model for research and innovation activities in selected areas: a support for strategic choices'. Paper presented at international course on research and innovation management. Venice, 13 September.

Moore, G. A. (1991). *Crossing the Chasm: Marketing and Selling High-tech Products to Mainstream Customers*. New York: HarperCollins.

Morrison, J., and I. Wilson (1996). 'The strategic management response to the challenge of global change'. Horizon, University of North Carolina, Chapel Hill. Available at http://horizon.unc.edu/courses/papers/Scenario_wksp.html (accessed 1 June 2008).

Nordmann, A. (2004). *Converging Technologies: Shaping the Future of European Societies*. Brussels: European Commission.

Perez, C. (2002). *Technological Revolutions and Financial Capital: The Dynamics of Bubbles and Golden Ages*. Cheltenham: Edward Elgar.

Rogers, E. M. (2003). *Diffusion of Innovations*. New York: Free Press.

Rossel, P. (2007). 'Meta-framing: the art of putting weak signals in perspective'. Paper presented at the conference 'From oracles to dialogue: exploring new ways to explore the future'. Athens, 10 July.

(2009). 'Weak signals as a flexible framing space for enhanced management and decision-making'. *Technology Analysis and Strategic Management.* **21** (3), 307–20.

Rossel, P., F. Bosset, O. Glassey and R. Mantilleri (1999). 'Les enjeux des transports à grande vitesse: des méthodes pour l'évaluation des innovations technologiques – l'exemple de Swissmetro'. Logistics, Economics and Management Report no. 1999-004. Lausanne: EPFL.

Rossel, P., and M. Finger (2005). 'Competing networks, competing rationales: the case of wireless communication emergence'. Paper presented at second international conference on economics and management of networks. Budapest, 17 September.

(2007). *Regulation and Termination Rates in Mobile Telephony: State of Affairs and Options.* Chichester: Praxis.

Rossel, P., and O. Glassey (2005). 'Bridging over the dynamic divide: when e-activities are e-learning reinforcement contexts'. Paper presented at the fourth World Scientific and Engineering Academy and Society international conference on e-activities. Miami, 19 November.

Sackman, H. (1974). 'Delphi assessment: expert opinion, forecasting, and group process'. Report no. R-1283-PR. Santa Monica, CA: RAND Corporation.

Sawhney, H. (1992). 'The public telephone network: stages in infrastructure development'. *Telecommunications Policy.* **16** (7), 538–52.

(2003). 'Wi-Fi and the rerun of the cycle'. *Info.* **5** (6), 25–33.

Schwarz, J.-O. (2008). 'Assessing the future of futures studies in management'. *Futures.* **40** (3), 237–46.

Shin, T. (1998). 'Using Delphi for a long-range technology forecasting, and assessing directions of future R&D activities: the Korean exercise'. *Technology Forecasting and Social Change.* **58** (1), 125–54.

(2001). 'Delphi study at the multi-country level: gains and limitations'. In National Institute of Science and Technology Policy [NISTEP]. *Proceedings of the International Conference on Technology Foresight.* Tokyo: NISTEP, 161–72.

Shneyderman, A., and A. Casati (2008). *Fixed Mobile Convergence: Voice over Wi-Fi, IMS, UMA/GAN, Femtocells, and Other Enablers.* New York: McGraw-Hill.

Sørensen, K., and R. Williams (eds.) (2002). *Shaping Technology, Guiding Policy: Concepts, Spaces and Tools.* Cheltenham: Edward Elgar.

Tan, T. K., and B. Bing (2003). *World Wide Wi-Fi: Technological Trends and Business Strategies.* New York: John Wiley.

Von Hippel, E. (1988). *The Sources of Innovation.* Oxford: Oxford University Press.

(2005). *Democratizing Innovation.* Cambridge, MA: MIT Press.

Vree, W. (2000). 'Inverse infrastructures: emergence by symbiosis and reuse'. Delft University of Technology, Delft.

Williamson, O. E. (1981). 'The economics of organization: the transaction cost approach'. *American Journal of Sociology.* **87** (3), 548–77.

(1996). *The Mechanisms of Governance.* Oxford: Oxford University Press.

12 Reflections and implications for policy and strategy formation

Wolter Lemstra and John Groenewegen

12.1 Summary[1]

The present-day success of Wi-Fi can be traced back to a change in US government policy intended to simplify the rules for the use of radio frequency spectrum and to the idea to allow the public use of spread-spectrum technology. The 1985 decision of the Federal Communications Commission to allow spread-spectrum-based radio communication in the three bands designated for industrial, scientific and medical applications encouraged communication firms to innovate and develop new short-range data communication products. NCR recognised the need to leverage existing standardised communication protocols and became the driving force in the development and adoption of an open wireless LAN standard, IEEE 802.11, as were its corporate successors AT&T, Lucent Technologies and Agere Systems.

Thanks to contractual agreements with Apple and subsequent cooperation with Microsoft, the product reached the mass market. In the process the product moved from its intended use, as a WLAN in the corporate environment, to application in the home. Subsequently the home and business use was extended further through the provision of internet access services at 'hotspots' and 'hotzones', and more recently through city-wide Wi-Fi networking. The low-threshold technology also resulted in networks being created by communities of volunteers, in developed as well as developing countries, to provide alternative network access, filling a void left by the incumbent telecommunications operators. The case history of Wi-Fi is an illustration of how innovation can be triggered by policy, developed by industry and shaped by its users.

12.2 Reflecting on innovation

The Wi-Fi case is a good example of an 'innovation journey' (van de Ven et al., 1999), and it illustrates how a new 'innovation avenue' (Sahal, 1981, 1985) emerges as a fusion of two existing avenues: wired LANs and radio technology (see also Figure 12.1). This fusion leads to new branching, whereby

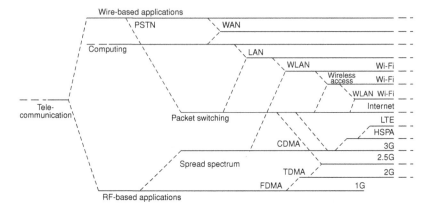

Figure 12.1 Wi-Fi and internet innovation avenues recombine

the application of Wi-Fi is shifting from wireless LAN to wireless access to wireless networking.

The case is also a good illustration of the different sources of innovation that play a role in the shaping of a product or service, as argued by von Hippel (1988, 2005). In our case, the emphasis has shifted from the more traditional role of the manufacturer to include the operator, as the supplier of a service, and the users building Wi-Fi-based community networks.

In the Wi-Fi case we can also recognise the notions of evolutionary theory – i.e. novelty generation, transmission and selection, as well as retention. The Wi-Fi development can be related to Nelson and Winter (1977, 1982), who argue that technical advance is an evolutionary process in which new technological alternatives compete with each other and with prevailing practice, whereby *ex post* selection determines the winners and losers, usually with considerable *ex ante* uncertainty regarding the outcome. In this we recognise the Lamarckian reading of economic evolution, which allows acquired characteristics based on learning to be passed on and which acknowledges purposeful intention with respect to changing behaviour. This is in contrast to the Darwinian reading, in which change can take place only through mutations at birth and which is considered to be random (van der Steen, 1999).

The development of Wi-Fi was triggered by a major shift in the radio spectrum regulations: the assignment by the FCC of unlicensed radio frequency spectrum for communication purposes. The technology to be applied had been developed in the military domain and was now prescribed for use in the private domain. This can be characterised as a change in the institutional selection environment. Although the FCC ruling prescribed a certain type of technology, firms generated a broad variety of initial products using proprietary protocols.

From a theoretical perspective, the FCC opened up the possibility of novelty generation. The incompatibility resulted in a fragmented product market, increasing the risk for the users with respect to future developments. Through NCR's assumption of a leadership role in establishing a coalition, the novelty generation in the product market moved to the selection mechanism of the standardisation process. This entailed a process of retention and learning on the part of the various firms involved in the development of Wi-Fi. A strong contribution to the development of the content of the standard, a high degree of participation and skilful negotiation and manoeuvring are the major ingredients determining the outcome of this process – a process facilitated through well-established formal procedures within the IEEE.[2]

Wi-Fi emerged as the winner of the battle with HomeRF and HIPERLAN. This connects to the economic literature describing how a dominant design emerges (Abernathy and Utterback, 1978). Once resources have come to be focused principally on the leading technology, further improvements may soon make it and its further developments the only economic way to proceed, because competing designs are left so far behind (Nelson and Winter, 1977, 1982). The case also shows the importance of compatibility with software platforms in forging the successful adoption of this hardware-oriented product (Gawer and Cusumano, 2002).[3] The involvement of the same 'cast of characters' over the full period of the standards development, product development and corporate transitions has undoubtedly contributed to the successful innovation journey.

The aspect of retention can best be illustrated by characterising the Wi-Fi-based ecosystem that has emerged and is continuing to evolve (de Leeuw, 2006, 2007 and personal communication, 2009; Kamp, 2005).

- In 2004 the Wi-Fi-related product market was estimated at US$3.5 billion. In the third quarter of 2007 over 43 million WLAN NICs were shipped from Taiwan, 37 per cent more than in the previous year.
- The portfolio included chips and chipsets, PC adapters (PCI, USB, CF/SDIO), networking devices (access points, bridges, gateways and routers) and antennae and boosters.
- A market scan carried out in 2007 identified 180 end product vendors, providing 3,289 different products.
- Client devices that include Wi-Fi functionality include notebooks, PDAs, mobile phones, streaming music and video players, digital cameras, printers, video beamers, gaming devices and home audio-systems.
- As of April 2009 the Wi-Fi directory of Jiwire listed a total of 256,147 hotspots in 140 countries.
- Major hostspot/roaming operators are iPass, T-Mobile, WeRoam, Trustive, Swisscom, Boingo, BT Openzone, Orange, GoRemote (GRIC), GBIA and NTT.

- Community initiatives have sprung up in developed and developing countries. In the Netherlands, a small country, thirty networks are in operation or being constructed, the largest network being the neighbourhood area network of Wireless Leiden. In 2005 in the United States over 100 cities and counties were reported as having operational municipal networks, networks under deployment or tenders issued for Wi-Fi networks. In 2007 200 municipal networks were in operation or under construction and another 215 were being planned.

Reflecting on the innovation process, this is a case of innovation rather than invention. The spread-spectrum principle and two of its application variants, frequency hopping and direct sequence, had already been invented, and early applications existed in the military domain.

Initially, there is a clear case of product innovation, by firms applying a new technology to provide more flexible solutions to their clients; through the application of wireless data communication and data capture. This applies to the major firms that will start competing in this new market segment, such as NCR, Symbol Technologies, a leader in barcode-based data-capturing systems, and Proxim.

The developments within NCR are *grosso modo* in line with the sequential model of innovation: a firm perceives a customer need or market opportunity and directs resources in its R&D department towards the development of new solutions. The source of innovation was NCR, the manufacturer of transaction terminals seeking more flexible ways of connecting cash registers to the computer networks of its clients. The major challenge was the application of the technology in products that were affordable in a commercial rather than a military setting. NCR had no experience with military applications of spread spectrum nor had it applied radio frequency technology.

The development had a strong regional focus, as the FCC was the first national regulatory authority to allow civil spread-spectrum applications in the ISM bands. The firms involved in the initial stages were American and Canadian. The fact that the Netherlands played a role in the development is coincidental rather than structural. The only specific Dutch government programme in existence at the time that can be construed as having had an important role in the course of events was the WBSO tax facility. More generally, throughout the innovation journey of Wi-Fi, the interactions with the universities of technology played an important role.

What was important in the initial decision-making process was the comparative advantage of NCR's Systems Engineering Centre in Utrecht in terms of its knowledge base, which matched the opportunity that arose. One can argue that the RF expertise accumulated by Philips and its proximity facilitated the developments. It facilitated the acquisition of RF knowledge by NCR, in particular the acquisition of tacit knowledge through the hiring of staff. Moreover, the establishment of the NCR Systems Engineering Centre in the Netherlands can be construed as the result of a comparative analysis process looking into the conditions of alternative locations in Europe, in which the Netherlands topped the list. It was the quality of the knowledge infrastructure that was important.

12.3   Reflecting on the standardisation process

Following the success of the IEEE wired LAN standard, in particular the Ethernet (see von Burg, 2001), Wi-Fi represents the success of the wireless LAN standardisation process within the IEEE as a standard-developing organisation (for a comparison of the cellular standardisation with that of Wi-Fi, see Lemstra and Hayes, 2009a, and, for an expansion on the standardisation process, see Lemstra and Hayes, 2009b). Although conflict was rife during the wired LAN standardisation process – three versions were, ultimately, settled upon: Ethernet, token bus and token ring – Wi-Fi has not been without competition. In the standardisation arena it was challenged by HomeRF and HIPERLAN. After fierce battles it succeeded, however. Moreover, although the IEEE 802.11 standard includes multiple options, the market has decided for one variant, facilitated by the leading vendors collaborating in the Wi-Fi Alliance.

Issues over intellectual property in the IEEE 802.11 working group have remained relatively minor. The position of the IEEE vis-à-vis the use of patents in standards changed over the lifetime of the project. Until the end of 1995 the preferred policy was to avoid the use of patented material in the standard, and 'if the committee intends to use patented material it must explain the reasons why' (by-laws of the IEEE Standards Board). By the end of 1995 the by-laws were changed to read: 'IEEE standards may include the known use of patents, including patent applications, if there is compelling technical justification . . . and provided the IEEE receives assurance from the patent holder that it will license applicants under reasonable terms and conditions for the purpose of implementing the standard'.[4] In 1996 the IEEE 802.11 chair collected, out of the sixty-five firms actively participating in the standardisation process, sixteen FRAND usage statements (fair, reasonable and non-discriminatory), one firm listing an IP claim without a use statement and five firms stating that no IP was being claimed; forty-three firms did not respond to the query.[5]

The more contentious issues were related to the perceived advantages of one firm over others in the implementation of the standard in silicon.

12.4   Reflecting on radio spectrum management

The innovation journey of Wi-Fi was triggered by a formal change in the institutional environment, in the regulatory regime of radio frequency spectrum. As a resource in 'common use', the RF spectrum is managed by governments at the national level, and coordinated at the international level through the International Telecommunications Union, as a part of the UN.

The main goal of the frequency management paradigm is to avoid harmful interference and to provide a fair allocation of access to the radio spectrum to a variety of uses and users, such as radio and television broadcasting, terrestrial and satellite communications, emergency services (police, fire, ambulance), the military and astronomical research.

At first glance, the decision by the FCC to assign spectrum to applications for which no clear market demand had been demonstrated appears strange, given that radio frequency spectrum is a resource in limited supply. The motivation was one of regulatory reform, of reducing the rules and regulations set by government, with the aim of providing the industry with more freedom to innovate. The assignment of spread spectrum to the existing ISM bands made the decision far less controversial, however: it is one more application in an existing band and in shared mode – i.e. without exclusivity and with limited protection against interference. As Marcus has observed on the lack of strong opposition to the assignment: 'Microwave ovens don't protest.' Moreover, there was no strong perception of scarcity at that stage. The introduction of cellular systems in the United States was in its infancy; the FCC had started the acceptance of applications for cellular licences in 1982, and in 1983 the first cellular system had been introduced in Chicago. The boom in the mobile phone business would not get under way till the early 1990s.

12.5   Implications for government policy

For government policy, the Wi-Fi case is important, as it reflects the first large-scale deployment of radio communication on an unlicensed basis. The worldwide adoption of Wi-Fi demonstrates that RF spectrum can be used effectively using a licence-exempt regime. As the initial RF assignment was based on the use of the existing bands designated for the use of industrial, scientific and medical applications, the usage can be considered to be highly efficient, as no new spectrum had to be allocated.

The common understanding that open access regimes lead to a 'tragedy of the commons' is shown not to be applicable to this case. Although access is not restricted and no protection is offered under this unlicensed regime, the limitations set to the power levels used appear to be effective in creating a localised use that resembles the characteristics of a private property regime. The extent of the adoption and use appears not to be restrained by the lack of protection, although the regime does not provide for any indicators that signal whether congestion or a deterioration of service is leading to users abandoning the use of Wi-Fi. In other words, there may be an undisclosed albeit very localised 'tragedy of the commons'. Close monitoring of the usage by the national regulatory agencies will therefore be required.

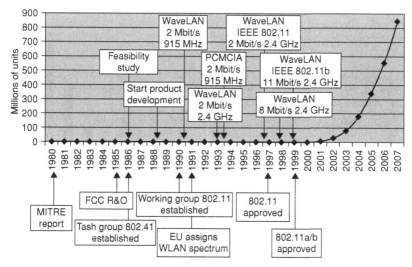

Figure 12.2 Wi-Fi standards and NCR products
Source: This figure appears in 'The shaping of the IEEE 802.11 standard',
in *Information Communication Technology Standardization for E-Business
Sectors* (ed. Jakobs); copyright © 2009, IGI Global; reprinted by permission
of the publisher.

The relatively low power levels represent a genuine limitation to the deployment of Wi-Fi, in particular in the case of community Wi-Fi networks or municipal Wi-Fi, as the signal does not penetrate deeply enough, without antenna
boosters, into homes and offices to provide an acceptable quality of service.

The lack of 'exclusivity' that is associated with open access regimes has been
shown to be less of an issue in this case. Multiple product vendors and, later,
service providers have been seen to be willing to invest in the development of
products and services to exploit the unlicensed part of the RF spectrum. One
could argue that this is the result of the return on investment largely being based
on the sale of the Wi-Fi equipment, and not on the exploitation of a service
requiring complementary and deep investment in the creation of a network
infrastructure, as is the case in mobile cellular communications.

For government policy, the case shows that innovation can be triggered by a
change in policy, by lowering the barriers to the use of radio frequency spectrum
as an input to the production function. The Wi-Fi case illustrates the innovation
potential of a licence-exempt RF spectrum regime. It also shows the constancy
of purpose required to be able ultimately to reap the economic and social
benefits: the original idea dates back to 1980, while the large scale-deployment
of Wi-Fi started only in 2000. See also Figure 12.2 for the development of
Wi-Fi-related standards and NCR products.

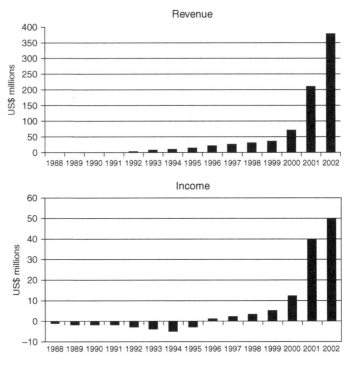

Figure 12.3 The Wi-Fi business case in hindsight
Source: Personal communication from Cees Links, 2007.

In terms of innovation policy, the case shows the global nature of today's ICT industry, in that the locus of invention (the United States) or of innovation (the Netherlands) is not necessarily the locus of manufacturing (Taiwan) or the locus where, ultimately, most of the value is being appropriated. Nonetheless, the case does illustrate the contribution by a Dutch entity to innovation in the field of ICT; moreover, it shows that this contribution was not incidental. Although the entity that is associated with the emergence of Wi-Fi may have been dissolved, the individuals involved continue to contribute to the process of innovation, by enhancing the Wi-Fi product and/or expanding in adjacent application areas, such as WiMAX, Zigbee and Bluetooth.

12.6   Implications for firm strategy

Considering the long lead times involved in the development of Wi-Fi, almost fifteen years from the start of the feasibility study to mass-market take-off, the most important strategic question is whether the Wi-Fi case has generated a positive return. This is indeed the case; as Figure 12.3 shows, the income stream turned positive in 1996 and break-even was achieved in 2000.

The case story of Wi-Fi is a good example of how the innovation process works in practice. It shows the linkage to corporate strategy; and it shows the role of individuals in various parts of the organisation in driving the course of events. It shows the importance of teamwork, of personal commitment and dedication. The extensive period required for the standardisation illustrates the commitment, the tenacity and the resources required from an emerging industry leader involved in 'rule breaking' (de Wit and Meyer, 2004). Moreover, it shows the importance of institutions in technology and product development, as with the FCC, in its role as national regulatory agency, providing the governance of the radio spectrum and the IEEE providing the ICT industry with a platform to develop standards.

The behaviour of NCR can be connected to the role of the entrepreneur, as in the view of Casson 'an entrepreneur is someone who specialises in taking judgmental decisions about the coordination of scarce resources' (Ricketts, 2002). A particular challenge for the entrepreneur is to move the business beyond the early adopter phase into the mass-market phase – i.e. from selling successfully to the technology enthusiasts and visionaries to selling to the pragmatists. To dramatise this difficulty, Moore (1991) uses the metaphor of 'crossing the chasm'. To cross the chasm successfully, he argues that it is important to target the right initial product segment. If properly selected and executed, the attack then moves to adjacent segments. Thereby the success in the first market segment will work like the head pin at a bowling alley, ultimately leading to mass-market success (Moore, 1995). In Moore's terms, the 'chasm' was crossed in 1999, through a strategic cooperation of Lucent Technologies with Apple and, subsequently, Microsoft.

While Wi-Fi started as a technological innovation, its development became characterised by subsequent releases of enhancements to the IEEE 802.11 standard, providing increasing data rates and functionality.

These standards were translated into chipsets, which became incorporated in products, which in turn became part of communications systems. This connects to the economic literature, as, for instance, Nelson and Winter argue that, once a dominant design has come into existence, radical product innovation slows down and product design improvements become incremental. Attention shifts to the improvement of the related process technology. The growth in the number of people who own and use a particular technology variant plays an increasing role, as skills develop that are particular to a certain variant, as are investments in complementary products designed to fit with a particular variant (Arthur, 1996; Katz and Shapiro, 1985, 1994; Nelson and Winter, 1977, 1982).

Aspects that have contributed significantly to the ultimate success of Wi-Fi are the following. (1) The involvement of the same 'cast of characters' over the full period of the innovation journey and corporate transitions. (2) The involvement of a relatively small and close-knit team in managing the innovation journey, allowing for a direct interplay between standards development, product development and the introduction of the product on the market. As an industry rather than a firm factor, we should note another success factor: (3) the concurrence in the developments in communications and computing technologies, in particular the laptop and the Internet.

In our case study, we have observed that these WLAN systems were first applied in the corporate domain, subsequently in the private domain, followed by the public domain. As a result, the industry's orientation evolved from a component and product focus to a product and service focus. An expanding value network has been the result. With the emphasis shifting from invention to mass production, the industrial activities within NCR/AT&T/Lucent Technologies shifted from the Netherlands and the United States to Taiwan and China. Lucent Technologies, severely affected by the downturn in telecommunication spending in the aftermath of the telecom bubble, divested its WLAN activities through the spin-off of Agere Systems in 2001. In 2004 Agere discontinued its WLAN development activities, and the team in Utrecht was dissolved.

Just as the original radio expertise moved with the people concerned from Philips to NCR, however, the success of Wi-Fi developments has triggered new start-ups by former staff of Lucent Technologies, continuing the innovation process. For instance, Airgo was established in the Netherlands in 2001; recently acquired by Qualcomm, it continues to lead developments in the Wi-Fi space, in particular with MIMO. Airgo-designed chips have resulted in the first ever MIMO consumer products being introduced into the market. Following in the footsteps of NCR, Airgo is contributing extensively to IEEE 802.11 task group 'n', aimed at achieving high throughput extension (van Nee, 2006).

In addition to knowledge diffusion through start-ups, former Agere staff have moved to other (leading) companies in the wireless industry, including Motorola, and they continue to 'push the envelope' in terms of innovation in wireless communications.

NCR survived the acquisition by AT&T, and continues to be a successful independent company in the field of transaction processing, with an increasing focus on services.

12.7   Concluding remarks

The case of Wi-Fi has shown that policy makers do not necessarily have to wait until industry representatives request the allocation and assignment of radio spectrum for a particular use. Proactive allocation can provide opportunities for innovation, and an unlicensed regime can result in highly successful products and services. The case illustrates the need for industry to provide leadership in the development of standards, in the harmonisation of spectrum use and in achieving product compatibility so as to facilitate the creation of a mass

~market. It shows that significant lead times are involved, and, hence, constancy of purpose is required by the governments and the firms involved. Ultimately, the end users extend the deployment of the product in unforeseen directions, in this case in providing voice and data services to areas that hitherto had remained unserved. In a variation on another Dutch theme: 'Wi-Fi reaches the parts that other networks cannot reach.'

Notes

1 See also the summaries and reflections on the innovation journey that are included in Chapters 2 to 6.
2 The IEEE, for instance, uses *Robert's Rules of Order* (Robert, 2000 [1876]).
3 The evolutionary metaphor has purposely been limited to the domain of wireless LANs, but it could have been extended to include a wider family of wireless systems, such as wireless local loop systems and cellular systems. For a comparison of the development of Wi-Fi and cellular systems, see Lemstra and Hayes (2009a).
4 Document: IEEE P802.11–96/14, V. Hayes, 'Changes in IEEE's patent policy rules', 9 January 1996.
5 It should be noted that copyrights automatically transfer to the IEEE when copyrighted material from submissions is added into the standard.

References

Abernathy, W. J., and J. M. Utterback (1978). 'Patterns of industrial innovation'. *Technology Review*. **80** (7), 40–7.
Arthur, W. B. (1996). 'Increasing returns and the new world of business'. *Harvard Business Review*. **74** (4), 100–9.
De Leeuw, G.-J. (2006). 'Wi-Fi in the Netherlands'. Paper presented at the ninth annual international 'Economics of infrastructures' conference. Delft, 16 June.
  (2007). *A Snapshot of the Wi-Fi World in 2007*. Delft: Delft University of Technology.
De Wit, B., and R. Meyer (2004). *Strategy: Process, Content, Context – An International Perspective*. London: Thomson.
Gawer, A., and M. A. Cusumano (2002). *Platform Leadership: How Intel, Microsoft and Cisco Drive Industry Innovation*. Boston: Harvard Business School Press.
Kamp, D. (2005). *Analysis of the Emergence of Wi-Fi*. Delft: Delft University of Technology.
Katz, M. L., and C. Shapiro (1985). 'Network externalities, competition, and compatibility'. *American Economic Review*. **75** (3), 424–40.
  (1994). 'Systems competition and network effects'. *Journal of Economic Perspectives*. **8 (2)**, 93–115.
Lemstra, W., and V. Hayes (2009a). 'License exempt: Wi-Fi complement to 3G'. *Telematics and Informatics*. **26** (3), 227–39.
  (2009b). 'The shaping of the IEEE 802.11 standard: the role of the innovating firm in the case of Wi-Fi'. In K. Jakobs (ed.). *Information Communication Technology Standardization for E-Business Sectors: Integrating Supply and Demand Factors*. Hershey, PA: IGI Global, 98–126.

Moore, G. A. (1991). *Crossing the Chasm: Marketing and Selling High-tech Products to Mainstream Customers*. New York: HarperCollins.
   (1995). *Inside the Tornado: Marketing Strategies from Silicon Valley's Cutting Edge*. New York: HarperCollins.
Nelson, R. R., and S. G. Winter (1977). 'In search of a useful theory of innovation'. *Research Policy*. **6 (1)**, 36–76.
   (1982). *An Evolutionary Theory of Economic Change*. Cambridge, MA: Belknap Press.
Ricketts, M. (2002). *The Economics of Business Enterprise: An Introduction to Economic Organisation and the Theory of the Firm*. Cheltenham: Edward Elgar.
Robert, H. M. (2000 [1876]). *Robert's Rules of Order: Newly Revised*. Cambridge, MA: DaCapo Press.
Sahal, D. (1981). *Patterns of Technological Innovation*. Reading, MA: Addison-Wesley.
   (1985). 'Technology guideposts and innovation avenues'. *Research Policy*. **14** (2), 61–82.
Van de Ven, A. H., D. E. Polley, R. Garud and S. Venkataraman (1999). *The Innovation Journey*. Oxford: Oxford University Press.
Van der Steen, M. (1999). *Evolutionary Systems of Innovation: A Veblian-oriented Study into the Role of the Government Factor*. Assen, Netherlands: van Gorcum.
Van Nee, R. (2006). 'Current status of Wi-Fi standardization'. Paper presented at the ninth annual international 'Economics of infrastructures' conference. Delft, 16 June.
Von Burg, U. (2001). *The Triumph of Ethernet: Technological Communities and the Battle for the LAN Standard*. Stanford, CA: Stanford University Press.
Von Hippel, E. (1988). *The Sources of Innovation*. Oxford: Oxford University Press.
   (2005). *Democratizing Innovation*. Cambridge, MA: MIT Press.

Part 3

Annexes

Annex 1: Glossary

Wolter Lemstra

Acronym	Meaning	Remarks
2G	second-generation cellular communications system	e.g. GSM and D-AMPS: provides voice and low-data-rate services, based on circuit switching
2.5G	intermediate generation between 2G and 3G	e.g. GPRS: provides packet data services
3G	third-generation cellular communications system	e.g. UMTS: provides voice and broadband data communication services
3GPP	3G Partnership Project	industry standards group
3GPP2	3G Partnership Project 2	specification-setting project
3.5G	intermediate generation between 3G and 4G	
4G	fourth-generation cellular communications systems	also denoted with LTE, to include: high-data-rate/broadband communication services, all-IP, end-to-end and adaptive QoS
16QAM	quadrature amplitude modulation, with sixteen states	
64QAM	quadrature amplitude modulation, with sixty-four states	
10BASE-T	adaptation of Ethernet standard (IEEE 802.3) operating at 10 Mbit/s using twisted pair cable	
100BASE-T	adaptation of Ethernet standard (IEEE 802.3) operating at 100 Mbit/s using two or four twisted pair cables	
AAA	authentication, authorisation and accounting	for gaining access to the Internet using 'hotspots'
AAA-H	AAA home (network provider)	
AAA-V	AAA visiting (network provider)	

Acronym	Meaning	Remarks
ACIF	Australian Communications Industry Forum	
ADPCM	adaptive differential pulse code modulation	
ADSL	asymmetrical digital subscriber line	
AES	advanced encryption security	
AM	amplitude modulation	
AMPS	Advanced Mobile Phone System	US standard
ANEC	European Association for the Co-ordination of Consumer Representation in Standardisation	
ANSI	American National Standards Institute	
AP	access point	as in a Wi-Fi system
ARP	Address Resolution Protocol	
ARPA	Advanced Research Projects Agency	also DARPA, Defense ARPA
ATIS	Alliance for Telecommunication Industry Solutions	US standards coordination organisation
ATM	asynchronous transfer mode	
B3G	broadband version of 3G	
BPSK	binary phase shift keying	modulation method
BRAN	Broadband Radio Access Networks	subgroup within ETSI
BSI	British Standards Institution	
CAC	channel access and control	related to HIPERLAN
CAP	competitive access provider	
CB	Civil Band	
CCITT	International Telegraph and Telephone Consultative Committee	the predecessor of the ITU-T
CCK	complementary code keying	modulation method
CCM	counter with CBC-MAC (cipher block chaining message authentication code)	
CCMP	CCM Protocol	
CDMA	code division multiple access	
CDPD	cellular digital packet data	

Acronym	Meaning	Remarks
CEN	Comité Européen de Normalisation	European standardisation organisation
CENELEC	Comité Européen de Normalisation Electrotechnique	European standardisation organisation
CEPT	Conférence des Administrations Européennes des Postes et Télécommunications	European Conference of Postal and Telecommunications Administrations (PTTs)
CERN	European Organization for Nuclear Research	
CeTIM	Centre for Technology and Innovation Management	
CF/SDIO	compact flash/secure digital input output	
CMOS	complementary metal oxide semiconductor	
CMU	Carnegie Mellon University	
Com. Comp.	commercial computer	
CPC	cognition-supporting pilot channel or cognitive pilot channel	as used in cognitive radio systems
CPR	common pool resource	
CSMA/CA	carrier sense multiple access with collision avoidance	
CSMA/CD	carrier sense multiple access with collision detection	
DAB	digital audio broadcasting	
DARPA	Defense Advanced Research Projects Agency	
Db	data base	
dBi	decibel isotropic	forward gain of an antenna compared with the hypothetical isotropic antenna
dBm	decibel, with 0 dB at 1 milliwatt	unit of measurement expressing gain or loss relative to the reference point
DCCP	Datagram Congestion Control Protocol	
DECT	Digital Enhanced Cordless Telecommunications	originally Digital European Cordless Telecommunications
DES	data encryption security	
DHCP	Dynamic Host Configuration Protocol	used within the Internet

Acronym	Meaning	Remarks
DiffServ	differentiated services	used within the Internet to support QoS
DIN	Deutsches Institut für Normung	German national standards body
DIX	Digital, Intel, Xerox	alliance in the context of Ethernet
DLL	data link layer	layer in OSI protocol stack
DNS	domain name system	used within the Internet
DoJ	Department of Justice	United States
DoS	Department of State	United States
DS	direct sequence	as in spread spectrum
DS	distribution system	
DSA	dynamic spectrum access	
DSCP	differentiated services code point	
DSL	digital subscriber line	
DSSS	direct sequence spread spectrum	
DVB	digital video broadcasting	
EAP	Extensible Authentication Protocol	as used in Wi-Fi
ECC	Electronic Communications Committee	European committee
ECMA	European Computer Manufacturers Association	since 1994, ECMA International
ECT	European Container Terminal	
EDGE	Enhanced Data rates for GSM Evolution	
EIA	Electronic Industries Alliance	standard for, e.g., serial binary data communication
ERC	European Radiocommunications Committee	
ERO	European Radiocommunications Office	
ESO	European Standards Organisation	
ETNO	European Telecommunications Network Operators Association	
ETSI	European Telecommunication Standards Institute	
FAA	Federal Aviation Administration	United States

Acronym	Meaning	Remarks
FCC	Federal Communications Commission	US national regulatory agency
FCFS	first come first served	
FDDI	fibre distributed data interface	
FDMA	frequency division multiple access	
FH	frequency hopping	as in spread spectrum
FHSS	frequency hopping spread spectrum	
FIPS	Federal Information Processing Standards	United States
FM	frequency modulation	
FNPRM	further notice of proposed rulemaking	part of FCC's rule-making procedure
FOSS	free and open source software	
FPLMTS	future public land mobile telecommunications service	
FRAND	fair, reasonable and non-discriminatory	as in the use of IPR in standards
FSK	frequency shift keying	modulation method
FSS	fixed satellite services	
FTP	File Transfer Protocol	as used in the Internet
FTTH/FttH	fibre to the home	
GAQSIQ	General Administration of Quality Supervision, Inspection and Quarantine	China
GFSK	Gaussian frequency shift keying	modulation method
GMSK	Gaussian minimum shift keying	modulation method
GP	general purpose	
GPL	General Public License	
GPRS	general packet radio service	as in mobile systems
GSC	Global Standards Collaboration	
GSM	Groupe Spéciale Mobile, later to be known as Global System for Mobile Communications	working party of CEPT
HC-SDMA	high capacity space division multiple access	also known as iBurst
HIPERLAN	high performance radio LAN	
HRFWG	HomeRF Working Group	
HS	harmonised standard	

Acronym	Meaning	Remarks
HSDMA	high-speed space division multiple access	
HSDPA	high speed downlink packet access	as in mobile systems
HSPA	high speed packet access	as in mobile systems
HSUPA	high speed uplink packet access	as in mobile systems
http	HyperText Transfer Protocol	used in the Internet
https	HyperText Transfer Protocol Secure	used in the Internet
IAB	Internet Architecture Board	
IC	industry consortium	operating within the IEEE
IC	integrated circuit	
ICA	Institute for Connectivity in the Americas	
ICMP	Internet Control Message Protocol	
ICT	information and communication technology	
ICTSB	ICT Standards Board	
IDM	infrastructure development model	
IDRC	International Development Research Centre	based in Canada
IEC	International Electrotechnical Commission	
IEE	Institution of Electrical Engineers	since 2006 the Institution of Engineering and Technology
IEEE	Institute of Electrical and Electronic Engineers	
IETF	Internet Engineering Task Force	
IGMP	Internet Group Management Protocol	
IMAP	Internet Message Access Protocol	
IMI	Instituut voor Maatschappelijke Innovatie	Institute for Social Innovation (the Netherlands)
INT	intermediary function or provider	
IP	intellectual property	
IP	Internet Protocol	
IPO	initial public offering	
IPR	intellectual property rights	
IRC	internet relay chat	

Acronym	Meaning	Remarks
ISDN	integrated services digital network	
ISM	industrial, scientific and medical	
ISO	International Organisation for Standardisation	not an acronym
ISOC	Internet Society	
ISP	internet service provider	
ISSS	Information Society Standardization System	ICT activities within CEN
ITU	International Telecommunications Union	part of the United Nations
ITU-R	ITU – Radiocommunication Sector	
ITU-T	ITU – Telecommunication Standardization Sector	
JPG	Joint Presidents' Group	standards coordination group
JTC 1	Joint Technical Committee 1	between ISO and IEC
kbit/s	kilobits per second	
LACNIC	Latin American and Caribbean Internet Addresses Registry	
LAN	local area network	
LBT	Listen Before Talk	protocol
LEC	local exchange carrier	United States
LTE	Long Term Evolution	as related to cellular communication, 4G
MAC	medium access control	layer in OSI protocol stack
Mbit/s	megabits per second	
MHz	megahertz	unit of frequency; 1 Hz is one cycle per second
MIC	Ministry of Internal Affairs and Communications	Japan
MII	Ministry of Information Industry	China
MIMO	multiple input/multiple output	
MIT	Massachusetts Institute of Technology	
MSS	mobile satellite services	
NA	network adapter	
NAN	neighbourhood area network	

Acronym	Meaning	Remarks
NAV	node adoption volunteer	related to Wireless Leiden NAN
NCSA	National Center for Supercomputing Applications	United States
NesCOM	New Standards Committee	within IEEE
NGO	non-governmental organisation	
NIC	network interface card	
NIS	national innovation system	
NIST	National Institute of Standards and Technology	United States
NMT	Nordic Mobile Telephone system	
NNI	Nederlands Normalisatie Instituut	Dutch standards body
NNTP	Network News Transfer Protocol	
NOI	notice of inquiry	part of FCC's rule-making procedure
NORMAPME	European Office of Crafts, Trades and SMEs for Standardisation	
NPRM	notice of proposed rulemaking	part of FCC's rule-making procedure
NRA	national regulatory agency	
NSA	National Security Agency	United States
NSF	Nederlandse Seintoestellen Fabriek	Dutch communications firm
NTIA	National Telecommunications and Information Administration	US governmental organisation
NWN	No Wires Needed	Dutch communications firm
OASIS	Organisation for the Advancement of Structured Information Standards	
ODM	offshore developer and manufacturer	
OECD	Organisation for Economic Co-operation and Development	
OEM	original equipment manufacturer	
OFDM	orthogonal frequency division multiplexing	
OMG	Object Management Group	
OSA	opportunistic spectrum access	
OSI	open system interconnection	
OSPF	Open Shortest Path First	routing protocol
OSS	open source software	
PAR	Project Authorization Request	as applied within IEEE

Acronym	Meaning	Remarks
PARC	Palo Alto Research Center	started as Xerox PARC
PatCOM	Patent Committee	within IEEE
PCI	peripheral component interconnect	
PCMCIA	Personal Computer Memory Card International Association	referring to the card or card slot for credit-card-sized peripheral devices such as modems
PCS	personal communication services	
PDA	personal digital assistant	
PHY	physical layer	layer in OSI protocol stack
PN	pseudo-noise (code)	spread spectrum technique
POP3	Post Office Protocol version 3	
PPP	Point-to-Point Protocol	
PSTN	public switched telephone network	
PTA	packet traffic arbitration	
PTI	Philips Telecommunicatie Industrie	Dutch communications firm
PTT	postal, telegraph and telephone	
QoS	quality of service	
QPSK	quadrature phase shift keying	modulation method
R&O	Report and Order	part of FCC's rule-making procedure
RAND	reasonable and non-discriminatory	as applied to IPR
RevCOM	Review Committee	within IEEE
RF	radio frequency	
RFC	request for comment	procedure applied within the IETF
RFID	radio frequency identification device	
RLAN	radio local area network	
RS	standard for serial binary data communication	
RSC	Radio Spectrum Committee	Europe
RTP	Real-time Transfer Protocol	
SA	Standards Association	part of the IEEE
SABRE	Semi-Automatic Business-Related Environment	United States
SAC	Standardization Administration of China	

Acronym	Meaning	Remarks
SAGE	Semi-Automatic Ground Environment	United States
SAW	surface acoustic wave	
SCTP	Stream Control Transmission Protocol	
SDM	space division multiplexing	
SDO	standard-developing organisation	
SIM	subscriber identity module	
SIP	Session Initiation Protocol	related to signalling
SME	small and medium-sized enterprise	
SMTP	Simple Mail Transfer Protocol	
SNMP	Simple Network Management Protocol	
SRD	short-range device	
SS	spread spectrum	
SSB	standard-setting body	
SSH	Secure SHell	routing protocol
SSID	service set identifier	
SSL	secure sockets layer	
STC	space-time coding	
STP	shielded twisted pair	
STS	science and technology studies	
SWA-CA	Shared Wireless Access – Cordless Access	protocol related to HomeRF
T1	Primary order multiplex, 1.5 Mbit/s consisting of 24 channels at 56 kbit/s each, including overhead	US standard; equivalent of the primary multiplex of 2Mbit/s and 32 channels used in, e.g., Europe
TAM	technology acceptance model	
TCB	telecommunication certification body	United States
TCO	total cost of ownership	
TCP	Transmission Control Protocol	as used in the Internet
TDD	time division duplex	
TDMA	time division multiple access	
TIA	Telecommunications Industry Association	US industry organisation

Acronym	Meaning	Remarks
TKIP	Temporary Key Integrity Protocol	
TOR	teletype over radio	
TTC	Teletype Corporation	
UAM	universal access method	
UDP	User Datagram Protocol	
UMA	unlicensed mobile access	
UMTS	Universal Mobile Telecommunications System	related to 3G
U-NII	unlicensed – national information infrastructure	United States
USB	universal serial bus	
USI	Universal Scientific Inc.	Taiwanese company
UUCP	Unix to Unix copy	
UWB	ultra-wideband	
VAR	value adding reseller	
VoIP	voice over IP	
VPN	virtual private network	
VSAT	very small aperture terminal	satellite ground station with dish antenna smaller than 3 m
W3C	World Wide Web Consortium	
WAN	wide area network	
WAPI	WLAN Authentication and Privacy Infrastructure	China
WAS	wireless access system	
WBN	wireless broadband network	
WBSO	Wet Bevordering Speur- en Ontwikkelingswerk	Dutch tax facility
W-CDMA	wideband code division multiple access	
WECA	Wireless Ethernet Compatibility Alliance	original name for the Wi-Fi Alliance
WEP	wired equivalent privacy	
WHQL	Windows Hardware Quality Labs	
WISP	wireless ISP	
WLAN	wireless local area network	
WLANA	Wireless LAN Association	

Acronym	Meaning	Remarks
WLL	wireless local loop	
WMAN	wireless metropolitan area network	
WMC	Wi-Fi–mobile convergence	
WMM	Wi-Fi multimedia	
WPA	Wi-Fi protected access	
WPAN	wireless personal area network	
WRAN	wireless regional area network	
X3	an accredited ANSI committee	since 1996 INCITS, the InterNational Committee for Information Technology Standards

Annex 2: Timeline of major events related to Wi-Fi

Wolter Lemstra and Vic Hayes

Year	Event	Remarks
Early technological developments		
1831	Faraday discovers electromagnetic induction	
1858	Feddersen demonstrates oscillating character of spark discharge	
1873	Maxwell posits the theoretical concept of electromagnetic (EM) waves	
1888	Hertz demonstrates the creation, detection and measurement of electromagnetic waves	
1894	Marconi invents the wireless telegraph, using Morse code	
1906	Fessenden transmits human voice by radio	
1910	De Forest files patent for electronic valve	
Early corporate history		
1884	National Cash Register Co. is founded by Patterson	
1885	American Telephone & Telegraph Co. is incorporated	
1891	Philips and Co. is founded	
The Wi-Fi journey		
1942	Invention of frequency-hopping spread spectrum by Lamarr and Antheil	
1960	Invention of packet switching independently at Rand Corporation by Baran and at National Physics Laboratory, UK, by Davies	
1970	Packet radio experiments by Abrahamson at University of Hawaii, leading to ALOHAnet	
1971	First LAN: University of California's Irvine Ring	
1973	Ethernet is invented by Metcalfe at Xerox PARC	
1974	PC is invented by Roberts, designer of Altair	

Year	Event	Remarks
	The Wi-Fi Journey	
1975	Ethernet is created by Metcalfe	
	Microsoft is founded by Gates and Allen	
1977	Apple II PC is launched by Jobs and Wozniak	
1979	**FCC initiates study by MITRE Corporation to assess need for civil use of spread spectrum**	
1980	First meeting of IEEE 802 on LAN standardisation is convened	
1981	IBM PC is launched	
1984	Internet is named, and 1,000 hosts convert en masse to using TCP/IP	
	AT&T introduces Starlan: first 1 Mbit/s Ethernet implementation on telephone wire	
1985	**FCC assigns spectrum for radio communication in three bands designated for ISM applications on a non-protective, non-interference basis, but without the need for an end user licence**	915 MHz, 2.4 GHz and 5.8 GHz
	Qualcomm is founded by Jacobs, Viterbi, etc.	
	IEEE 802.3 Ethernet standard is approved	
1986	NCR initiates feasibility study into use of spread spectrum	Includes two design cycles of nine months for a demonstration unit to prove the concept
	IEEE working group 802.4 forms task group 'l' to create wireless extension for token bus standard	
1988	NCR starts product development of WLAN based on direct sequence spread spectrum	
	NCR engages with IEEE 802.4l	
1989	IETF is established	
1990	IEEE 802.4 abandons wireless extension work on token bus	
	IEEE 802.3 passes motion of not being interested in a wireless extension of Ethernet	
	IEEE working group 802.11 is established	
	NCR releases first 915 MHz WLAN product	PC adapter for the US market: 2Mbit/s, 1 channel, external antenna
	10BASE-T Ethernet standard is approved	
	Development of HTML and creation of www application by Berners-Lee at CERN	

Year	Event	Remarks
	The Wi-Fi Journey	
1991	Requirements for WLAN standard are agreed in IEEE working group 802.11; MAC and PHY subgroups are established	
	AT&T acquires NCR for US$7.4 billion	
	ERC assigns 2.4 GHz ISM band for WLAN use; on a non-protective and non-interference basis, without the need for an end user licence	
1993	AT&T releases 2.4 GHz WaveLAN product	PC adapter for the global market: 2 Mbit/s, 13 channels, external antenna
	AT&T releases 915 MHZ WaveLAN product on PCMCIA card format	PC card for the US market: 2 Mbit/s, 1 channel, external antenna
	IEEE 802.11 selects the foundation for the MAC protocol from a proposal from NCR, Symbol Technologies and Xircom	
	First large-scale campus deployment at Carnegie Mellon University	Project Andrew, led by Hills
	NoWires Needed is established by Blum, Zwemmer, Blokker, Hoeben and Brockmann	
	Wayport is conceived by Stewart while at AMD to provide wireless internet access in public areas	
	100BASE-T Ethernet standard is approved	
	Mosaic browser is introduced by Andreesen at NCSA	
1994	NCR's name is changed to AT&T Global Information Solutions (GIS)	
1995	AT&T releases 2.4 GHz WaveLAN product	PC card for the global market: 2 Mbit/s, 13 channels, external antenna
	Plancom is founded to provide public WLAN access	Predecessor of Wayport and MobileStar
1996	Release of 5.15–5.35 GHz band in Europe	
	AT&T trivestiture: AT&T/NCR/Lucent Technologies separation	AT&T-GIS is divested as an independent company and changes name back to NCR; WLAN/Wi-Fi activities remain within Lucent Technologies
	Wayport is incorporated, and first deployment of 'hotspots'	
	MobileStar is founded by Goods and Jackson	

Year	Event	Remarks
The Wi-Fi Journey	
1997	HomeRF industry consortium is formed	
	IEEE 802.11 standard is approved	2.4 GHz, 1 Mbit/s FHSS and 1–2 Mbit/s DSSS
	Release of 5.15–5.35 GHz band and 5.725–5.825 GHz band in the United States	
	Lucent Technologies releases IEEE-802.11-compliant WaveLAN product at 2.4 GHz	PC card for the global market: 1 and 2 Mbit/s, 13 channels, integrated antenna
	HIPERLAN/1 specification is released by ETSI	
1998	Lucent Technologies releases 2.4 GHz 8 Mbit/s proprietary WaveLAN product	PC card for the global market: 1, 2, 4 and 8 Mbit/s, 13 channels
	Agreement between Lucent Technologies and Apple to supply WLAN chips for the Apple AirPort	WLAN functionality to become part of the new iBook laptop
1999	**IEEE 802.11b standard for 11 Mbit/s is approved**	2.4 GHz, 5.5 and 11 Mbit/s, CCK modulation, 1 and 2 Mbit/s DSSS mandatory
	Lucent Technologies releases 2.4 GHz 11 Mbit/s IEEE-802.11b-compliant WaveLAN product	PC card for the global market: 1, 2, 5.5 and 11 Mbit/s, 13 channels, integrated antenna
	Apple AirPort is launched	
	IEEE 802.11a standard for 54 Mbit/s is approved	5 GHz, 6, 12 and 24 Mbit/s, OFDM modulation, optionally 9, 18, 24, 36 or 54 Mbit/s
	ISO ratifies 802.11 standard	
	WECA is established; Wi-Fi certification logo is introduced	Non-profit organisation with the goal of driving the adoption of a single standard, accepted worldwide, for high-speed wireless local area networking
	IEEE publishes the *IEEE 802.11 Handbook: A Designer's Companion*, by O'Hara and Petrick	
	Xircom is acquired by Intel	

Year	Event	Remarks
	The Wi-Fi Journey	
2000	European Union assigns an additional 255 MHz of spectrum in the 5 GHz band for use by wireless access systems	
	FCC releases Report and Order changing the frequency hopping rules	
	At world radiocommunication conference an agenda item is raised for the 2003 conference to allocate 455 MHz of spectrum in the 5 GHz band for WASs in the MOBILE service	
	Agere Systems is established as a subsidiary of Lucent Technologies	
	Cisco acquires Aironet	
	First Bluetooth product is introduced	
2001	Starbucks selects MobileStar as wireless partner	Through its acquisition of VoiceStream, T-Mobile acquires MobileStar
	Microsoft releases XP operating system with built-in support for IEEE 802.11	
	The term 'wardriving' is introduced by Shipley and Poulson	
	Lucent Technologies spin-off of Agere Systems	WLAN/Wi-Fi activities remain with Agere Systems
	NoWires Needed is acquired by Intersil	
	VoiceStream is acquired by T-Mobile (Deutsche Telekom) for US$24 billion	Includes cellular assets
	Boingo Wireless is founded by Dayton	
	VoiceStream (part of Deutsche Telekom) acquires MobileStar	
	Merger of Breezecom and Floware	
	Enhancement IEEE 802.11d is approved	Support for specific country requirements
	Wireless Leiden NAN initiated	
2002	WECA changes name to Wi-Fi Alliance, to reflect its certification trademark	
	Proxim acquires WLAN infrastructure business of Agere Systems	This includes the ORiNOCO^{TM} trademark and the base station product line

Year	Event	Remarks
	The Wi-Fi Journey	
	Boingo launches software-based service providing aggregation of partner hotspots into a seamless, single sign-on network	
	Vivato demonstrates phased-array antenna in combination with Wi-Fi access point	
	Conexant acquires Intersil's WLAN technology	
2003	**IEEE 802.11g standard is approved**	2.4 GHz, 6, 12 and 24 Mbit/s, OFDM modulation, optionally 9, 18, 24, 36 or 54 Mbit/s OFDM, both 5.5 and 11 Mbit/s, CCK modulation, 1 and 2 Mbit/s DSSS mandatory
	World radiocommunication conference approves allocation of 455 MHz of radio spectrum in the 5 GHz band for wireless access, including RLANs at co-primary level	
	Intel launches Centrino chipset with built-in Wi-Fi for 2.4 and 5 GHz bands	The launch is supported with a US$300 million advertising campaign
	Conexant and GlobespanVirata merge	
	Enhancement IEEE 802.11h is approved	Extension to the MAC
	Recommended Practice IEEE 802.11f is approved for trial use	Inter-Access Point Protocol
	Wi-Fi Alliance introduces Wi-Fi ZONE for public access hotspots	
	HomeRF Industry Consortium is abandoned	
	Skype is founded by Friis and Zenström	
2004	**IEEE 802.11i standard is approved**	Dedicated to resolving security issues
	Agere Systems discontinues WLAN developments	The remaining WLAN expertise transitions 'in person' to Motorola and other companies
	HIPERLAN/2 specification is released by ETSI	
2005	**IEEE 802.11e standard is approved**	Extension of the MAC for full support of isochronous transfer
	FON is founded by Varsavsky	

Year	Event	Remarks
	The Wi-Fi Journey	
2006	For trial use Recommended Practice IEEE 802.11f is withdrawn	Inter-Access Point Protocol
2007	Revision of IEEE 802.11 is approved	Includes 11a, 11b, 11d, 11e, 11g, 11h, 11i and 11j
2008	Enhancement IEEE 802.11k is approved	Radio resource management (to reduce power consumption)
	Enhancement IEEE 802.11r is approved	Fast roaming
	Enhancement IEEE 802.11y is approved	Operation in 3.6 GHz band in the United States
2009	**Enhancement IEEE 802.11n is approved**	Throughput 100–600 Mbit/s with OFDM MIMO (20 and 40 MHz channel width) in 2.4 and 5 GHz bands, compatible with a, b and g
	Enhancement IEEE 802.11w is approved	Protects management frames
	Wi-Fi Direct is announced by the Wi-Fi Alliance	Also known as Wi-Fi peer-to-peer
2010	Apple iPad launched, including Wi-Fi functionality	

In addition to personal information provided on the development of Wi-Fi by Vic Hayes, the sources that have been used for the compilation of this timeline are Bar and Galperin (2004), Corver (1928) and Fleishman (2002) for the timeline maintained as an open source project, and von Burg (2001) on Ethernet.

References

Bar, F., and H. Galperin (2004). 'Building the wireless internet infrastructure: from cordless Ethernet archipelagos to wireless grids'. *Communications and Strategies.* **54** (2), 45–68.

Corver, J. (1928). 'Het draadloos amateurstation'. Rotterdam: luna.nl; http://home.luna. nl/-arjan-muil/radio/nederlands/corver1.html (accessed 8 August 2008).

Fleishman, G. (2002). 'Wi-Fi timeline'. Wi-Fi Net News; http://wifinetnews.com/ archives/001315.html (accessed 31 May 2006).

Von Burg, U. (2001). *The Triumph of Ethernet: Technological Communities and the Battle for the LAN Standard.* Stanford, CA: Stanford University Press.

Annex 3: Overview of IEEE 802.11 wireless LAN standards

Vic Hayes[1]

IEEE designation	ISO/IEC designation	Title	Includes
Main standard			
IEEE Std 802.11 – 2012		'IEEE standard for information technology – telecommunications and information exchange between systems – local and metropolitan area networks – specific requirements Part 11: wireless LAN medium access control (MAC) and physical layer (PHY) specifications'	Includes 802.11 – 2007 edition, 11k, 11r, 11y, 11w, 11n, 11p, 11z, 11v and 11s

Note: The full title has been given only for the basic standard.

IEEE designation	ISO/IEC designation	Title	Includes
Enhancement standard			
IEEE 802.11aa – 2012		'Video transport streams'	
IEEE 802.11ad – 2012		'Very high throughput, 60 GHz'	
IEEE 802.11ae – 2012		'QoS management'	
Active projects			
IEEE 802.11ac		'Very high throughput, <6 GHz'	
IEEE 802.11af		'TV whitespaces'	
IEEE 802.11ah		'Sub 1 GHz'	
IEEE 802.11aj		'China Millimeter Wave'	
IEEE 802.11ak		'General Link'	
IEEE 802.11aq		'Pre-association Discovery'	

IEEE designation	ISO/IEC designation	Title	Includes
Superseded standards			
IEEE 802.11 – 1997 (superseded)		'IEEE standard for wireless LAN medium access control (MAC) and physical layer (PHY) specifications'	Basic MAC with limited isochronous transfer support and WEP type of encryption and two radio PHYs, one for frequency hopping at 1 Mbit/s and direct sequence spread spectrum at 2 and 1 Mbit/s, and one Infrared for 1 Mbit/s
IEEE 802.11, 1999 edition (superseded)	ISO/IEC 8802 – 11: 1999 (superseded)	'IEEE standard for information technology – telecommunications and information exchange between systems – local and metropolitan area network – specific requirements – Part 11: wireless LAN medium access control (MAC) and physical layer (PHY) specifications'	Same as IEEE 802.11 – 1997
	ISO/IEC 8802 – 11: 2005 (superseded)	'Information technology – telecommunications and information exchange between systems – local and metropolitan area networks – specific requirements Part 11: wireless LAN medium access control (MAC) and physical layer (PHY) specifications'	Includes 802.11, 1999 edition; 11a, 11b, 11b / Cor. 1 and 11d
IEEE Std 802.11 – 2007		'IEEE standard for information technology – telecommunications and information exchange between systems – local and metropolitan area networks – specific requirements Part 11: wireless LAN medium access control (MAC) and physical layer (PHY) specifications'	Includes 802.11 – 2005 edition, 11g (Amd. 4), 11h (Amd. 5), 11i (Amd. 6), 11j (Amd. 7) and 11e (Amd. 8)

IEEE designation	ISO/IEC designation	Title	Includes
Superseded standards			
IEEE 802.11a – 1999 (superseded)	ISO/IEC 8802 – 11: 1999 / Amd. 1:2000 (superseded)	'Amendment 1: high-speed physical layer (PHY) in the 5 GHz band'	
IEEE 802.11b – 1999 / Cor. 1–2001 (superseded)	ISO/IEC 8802 – 11:1999 / Amd. 2:2000 (superseded)	'Amendment 2: higher-speed physical layer (PHY) extension in the 2.4 GHz band – Corrigendum 1'	
IEEE 802.11c (replaced)		'IEEE 802.11 frame definition for bridges'	
IEEE 802.11d – 2001 (replaced)	ISO/IEC 8802 – 11:1999 / Amd.:2001 (replaced)	'Specification for operation in additional regulatory domains'	
IEEE 802.11e – 2005 (replaced)	ISO/IEC 8802 – 11:1999 / Amd. 8 (replaced)	'Amendment 8: medium access control (MAC) quality of service enhancements'	
IEEE 802.11F – 2003 (withdrawn)		'IEEE trial use recommended practice for multi-vendor access point interoperability via an Inter-Access Point Protocol across distribution systems supporting IEEE 802.11 operation'	
IEEE 802.11g – 2003 (replaced)	ISO/IEC 8802 – 11:2005 / Amd. 4:2006	'Amendment 4: further higher-speed physical layer (PHY) extension in the 2.4 GHz band'	
IEEE 802.11h – 2003 (replaced)	ISO/IEC 8802 – 11:2005 / Amd. 5:2006	'Amendment 5: spectrum and transmit power management extensions in the 5 GHz band in Europe'	
IEEE 802.11i (replaced)	ISO/IEC 8802 – 11:2005 / Amd. 6:2006	'Amendment 6: medium access control (MAC) security eEnhancements'	
IEEE Std 802.11j – 2004 (replaced)	ISO/IEC 8802 –11:2005 / Amd. 7:2006	Amendment 7: 4.9–5 GHz; 'Operation in Japan'	
IEEE Std 802.11k – 2008 (replaced)		'Radio resource measurement'	

IEEE designation	ISO/IEC designation	Title	Includes
Superseded standards			
IEEE Std 802.11n – 2009 (replaced)		'Enhancements for higher throughput'	
IEEE 802.11p – 2010 (replaced)		'Wireless access vehicular environment (WAVE)'	
IEEE Std 802.11r – 2008 (replaced)		'Fast basic service set transition'	
IEEE 802.11s – 2011 (replaced)		'Mesh networking'	
IEEE 802.11u – 2011 (replaced)		'Interworking with external networks'	
IEEE 802.11v – 2011 (replaced)		'Wireless network management enhancements'	
IEEE Std 802.11w – 2009 (replaced)		'Protected management frames'	
IEEE Std 802.11y – 2008 (replaced)		3,650–3,700 MHz 'Operation in USA'	
IEEE 802.11z – 2010 (replaced)		'Extensions to direct link setup (DLS)'	

[1] This overview of standards and project situation report annex is as at 1 March 2013 and is based on material from the IEEE 802.11 'Working group timelines', which are available at http://grouper.ieee.org/groups/802/11/Reports/802.11_Timelines.htm.

Annex 4: The Wi-Fi ecosystem

Gerd-Jan de Leeuw

Wi-Fi chipsets and products

By 2000 the worldwide market for WLAN products had reached a level of US$785 million. Gartner/Dataquest estimated that worldwide shipments of WLAN adapters would reach 26.5 million units by the end of 2003, up from 15.5 million in 2002; the related revenues were expected to approach US$2.8 billion (Wi-Fi Alliance, 2004). This reflected the anticipated growth in chipset shipments, which has been realised if not exceeded when 2008 shipments of nearly 400 million units are considered, as reflected in Figure A4.1. In 2008, as a major growth component, shipments of (draft) IEEE 802.11n devices grew by 155 per cent over 2007. According to ABI Research, some 6 million draft 802.11n devices were shipped in 2008.

Figure A4.2 provides a breakdown of the shipments by device category in 2007 and 2008. Worldwide revenues in 2007 reached some US$1 billion per quarter, as shown in Figure A4.3. Revenues from (draft) IEEE 802.11n devices grew by 137 per cent in 2007.

The certification of Wi-Fi products by the Wi-Fi Alliance has grown significantly, from approximately fifty products in 2000 to a cumulative 4,300 products related to the IEEE 802.11a/b/g versions of the standard – plus another 600 related to the draft 802.11n version – by May 2009. See also Figure A4.4.

Of special significance is the convergence between Wi-Fi and cellular, which is reflected in the increasing number of mobile phones being certified. This is shown in Figure A4.5.

Wi-Fi hotspots

In May 2009 JiWire's Wi-Fi 'hotspot' directory showed a total of 266,813 hotspots in 140 countries, a 36 per cent growth rate compared with the number a year earlier. This growth trend is expected to continue. See also Figure A4.6. The number one position in the country league table, with approximately

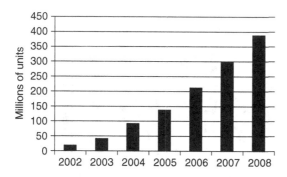

Figure A4.1 Wi-Fi chipset shipments, 2002–8
Sources: Wi-Fi Alliance (2009), based on In-Stat (2009).

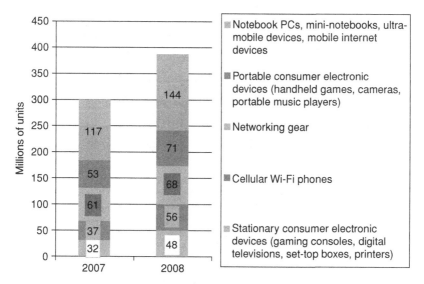

Figure A4.2 Wi-Fi chipset shipments by segment, 2007–8
Source: In-Stat (2009).

25 per cent of the hotspot total, is assumed by the United States, followed by France, the United Kingdom and China, the latter with some 18,000 hotspots.

In terms of addressable market, Boingo was quoted by the Wi-Fi Alliance as having identified in the United States nearly 2 million potential hotspot locations, consisting of 212 convention centres, 3,032 train stations, 5,352 airports, 53,500 hotels, 72,720 business centres, 202,600 petrol stations, 480,298 restaurants, bars and cafés and 1,111,300 retail stores. Gartner estimated that

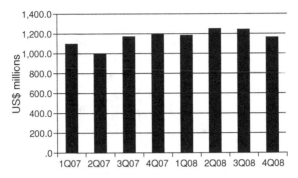

Figure A4.3 Wi-Fi shipment revenues, 1Q2007–4Q2008
Source: In-Stat (2009).

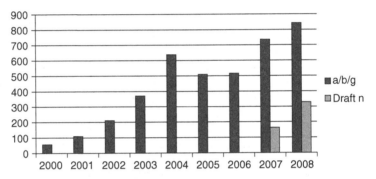

Figure A4.4 Number of certified products by the Wi-Fi Alliance, 2000–8
Source: Wi-Fi Alliance (2009).

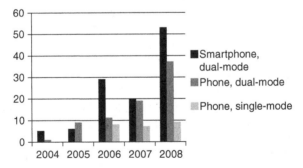

Figure A4.5 Wi-Fi-enabled cellular phones certified by the Wi-Fi Alliance,
2004–8
Source: Wi-Fi Alliance (2009).

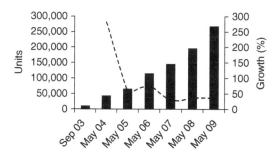

Figure A4.6 Wi-Fi hotspots, September 2003–May 2009
Source: JiWire (2009).

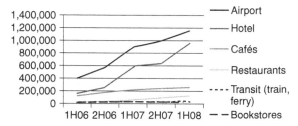

Figure A4.7 Hotspot communication sessions by venue type,
1H2006–1H2008
Source: iPass (2009).

in 2002 there were 59 million mobile workers in the United States who were potential clients of hotspot operators (Wi-Fi Alliance, 2004).

According to JiWire, the top five hotspot operators are T-Mobile, with 23,853 hotspots; France Télécom, with 18,648; Divine Management (United States), with 16,129; China Telecom, with 15,259; and Korea Telecom, with 12,803. There are three major roaming providers, each giving access to around 100,000 hotspots: iPass, Boingo and Trustive (JiWire, 2009). According to iPass, based on the number of communications sessions within a twenty-four-hour period, airports and hotels remain the most popular hotspots; see also Figure A4.7. With a duration of about 160 minutes, the session length in hotels topped the list, followed by bookstores with eighty minutes; airports accounted for forty minutes (iPass, 2009).

References

In-Stat (2009). *Wi-Fi Market Data*. London: Reed Business.
iPass (2009). 'Hotspot usage data'. Redwood Shores, CA: iPass. Available at www. ipass.com.au/pressroom/pressroom_wifi.html (accessed 13 August 2009).

JiWire (2009). 'Hospot directory'. San Francisco: JiWire. Available at www.jiwire.com/hotspots-hot-spot-directory-browse-by-country.htm (accessed 13 August 2009).

Wi-Fi Alliance (2004). 'Enabling the future of Wi-Fi public access'. Austin, TX: Wi-Fi Alliance.

(2009). 'Certified products'. Austin, TX: Wi-Fi Alliance.

Index